LLM Design Patterns

A Practical Guide to Building Robust and Efficient AI Systems

Ken Huang

‹packt›

Designing LLM Patterns

Copyright © 2025 Packt Publishing

The author acknowledges the use of cutting-edge AI, such as ChatGPT, with the sole aim of enhancing the language and clarity within the book, thereby ensuring a smooth reading experience for readers. It's important to note that the content itself has been crafted by the author and edited by a professional publishing team.

Portfolio Director: Gebin George
Relationship Lead: Vignesh Raju
Project Manager: Prajakta Naik
Content Engineer: Mark D'Souza
Technical Editor: Rahul Limbachiya
Copy Editor: Safis Editing
Indexer: Rekha Nair
Production Designers: Nilesh Mohite/Ponraj Dhandapani
Growth Lead: Nimisha Dua

First published: May 2025
Production reference: 1051125

Published by Packt Publishing Ltd.
Grosvenor House
11 St Paul's Square
Birmingham
B3 1RB, UK.

ISBN 978-1-83620-703-0
www.packtpub.com

Contributors

About the author

Ken Huang is a renowned AI expert, serving as co-chair of AI Safety Working Groups at Cloud Security Alliance and the AI STR Working Group at World Digital Technology Academy under the UN Framework. As CEO of DistributedApps.ai, he provides specialized GenAI consulting.

A key contributor to OWASP's Top 10 Risks for LLM Applications and NIST's Generative AI Working Group, Huang has authored influential books including *Beyond AI* (Springer, 2023), *Generative AI Security* (Springer, 2024), and *Agentic AI: Theories and Practice* (Springer, 2025)

He's a global speaker at prestigious events such as Davos WEF, ACM, IEEE, and RSAC. Huang is also a member of the OpenAI Forum and project leader for the OWASP AI Vulnerability Scoring System project.

About the reviewers

Varadharaj Krishnan, a seasoned leader in information security, currently oversees critical security functions at Tesla, including security engineering, infrastructure security, endpoint security, and vulnerability management. With over 18 years of experience in cybersecurity and cloud security, Varadharaj has played a pivotal role in driving cloud adoption and securing digital transformations at prominent companies. Previously at T-Mobile, he was instrumental in developing "PacBot," an open source cloud security posture management tool now widely adopted and commercialized. Varadharaj is recognized for his innovative contributions to the security field and his commitment to creating security tools that empower development teams.

Sai Kumar Arava leads GenAI implementations at Adobe, driving AI-powered task automation and intelligent workflows for hundreds of large enterprises. With over 12 years of experience in AI, machine learning, and large-scale software engineering, he has led multiple teams in developing GenAI products, intelligent assistants, and real-time ML systems at Adobe and PayPal. Sai is the author of the book *Building with LLM Agents: A Comprehensive Guide* and has published research at top machine learning conferences. He holds multiple patents in deep learning and AI applications and actively shares his expertise through teaching on platforms such as O'Reilly and Packt. Passionate about advancing AI, Sai brings deep insights from building intelligent automation solutions for Fortune 500 enterprises.

Meghana Puvvadi is an accomplished engineering leader specializing in artificial intelligence, machine learning systems, and platforms. Her expertise spans GenAI, large language models, and scalable distributed systems. As a technology leader with over a decade of software engineering and ML experience, Puvvadi has pioneered numerous innovations in AI-powered applications, inference platforms, and developer productivity tools. She has been awarded multiple patents for her contributions to natural language understanding and AI applications. She has served as a technical reviewer for prestigious conferences (NeurIPS, MATH-AI, ACL, IEEE), journals, and engineering books. Her work on inference engines, GenAI applications using agentic and RAG frameworks, and model hosting platforms has significantly advanced the field of GenAI, AI products, platforms, and ML infrastructure. Currently serving as director of engineering for AI products and platforms at NVIDIA, she manages comprehensive AI initiatives, including employee productivity tools, developer assistance systems, co-pilots to make employees, developers, and business processes efficient, and platforms for hosting AI assistants and RAG-based applications.

Prakash Reddy Putta is a tech lead manager and staff engineer at Instacart, focusing on improving search systems and personalization. He has led projects such as *Ask Instacart*, which uses LLMs to deliver real-time shopping recommendations, improving user experience and driving business growth. With 10+ patents, he has contributed to advancements in search relevance and efficiency. Previously, at Meta and Electronic Arts, Prakash worked on data integrity, content moderation, and analytics systems. His work centers on building reliable, scalable systems and applying AI to solve real-world problems.

Join our Discord and Reddit space

You're not the only one navigating fragmented tools, constant updates, and unclear best practices. Join a growing community of professionals exchanging insights that don't make it into documentation.

Stay informed with updates, discussions, and behind-the-scenes insights from our authors. Join our Discord space at `https://packt.link/z8ivB` or scan the QR code below:	Connect with peers, share ideas, and discuss real-world GenAI challenges. Follow us on Reddit at `https://packt.link/0rExL` or scan the QR code below:

Table of Contents

3

4

5

6

Dataset Annotation and Labeling   85

Part 2: Training and Optimization of Large Language Models   99

7

Training Pipeline   101

8

Hyperparameter Tuning   123

9

Regularization   149

10

Checkpointing and Recovery   161

11

Fine-Tuning   183

12

Model Pruning   197

13

Quantization   207

Part 3: Evaluation and Interpretation of Large Language Models   219

14

Evaluation Metrics   221

15

Cross-Validation   241

16

Interpretability   257

17

Fairness and Bias Detection   271

18

Adversarial Robustness   287

19

Reinforcement Learning from Human Feedback   297

Part 4: Advanced Prompt Engineering Techniques   309

20

Chain-of-Thought Prompting   311

21

Tree-of-Thoughts Prompting   321

22

Reasoning and Acting   337

23

Reasoning WithOut Observation   351

24

Reflection Techniques   361

25

Automatic Multi-Step Reasoning and Tool Use   373

Part 5: Retrieval and Knowledge Integration in Large Language Models   385

26

Retrieval-Augmented Generation   387

27

Graph-Based RAG   409

28

Advanced RAG   425

29

Evaluating RAG Systems   443

30

31

Preface

Imagine building a skyscraper without blueprints—every floor constructed on the fly, with no clear plan to ensure stability, efficiency, or even functionality. Developing **large language models** (**LLMs**) without a structured approach can feel much the same. These powerful models, capable of transforming industries and redefining human–computer interactions, are intricate structures that demand meticulous planning and execution. Without a framework to navigate their complexities, practitioners risk creating systems that are inefficient, unreliable, or unable to meet their potential.

This book, *LLM Design Patterns*, provides the blueprints you need. It is a practical guide for engineers, researchers, and innovators seeking to design, build, and implement LLMs effectively. It focuses on four critical pillars: preparing and preprocessing data, training and optimizing models, evaluating and interpreting their behavior, and integrating them seamlessly with advanced knowledge retrieval techniques. These domains are explored through the lens of design patterns, offering proven solutions to recurring challenges in LLM development.

The rapid evolution of LLMs brings both extraordinary opportunities and daunting challenges. Issues such as data quality, scalability, and interpretability demand adaptive methodologies and innovative strategies. This book equips practitioners at all levels with the design patterns to address these challenges head-on, providing actionable insights and frameworks to not only build models but excel in the rapidly advancing world of LLMs. Whether you're constructing your first model or refining a cutting-edge application, this book ensures that your approach is as robust as the technology you seek to harness.

Who this book is for

This book is for anyone involved in the development, deployment, or application of LLMs, including the following:

- **AI engineers and researchers**: Individuals implementing LLM techniques in their projects

- **Data scientists and machine learning practitioners**: Professionals seeking guidance on data preparation, model training, and optimization for LLMs

- **Software architects and project managers**: Those aiming to structure and manage LLM-based projects, ensuring alignment with business and technical objectives

What this book covers

Chapter 1, Introduction to LLM Design Patterns, provides a foundational understanding of LLMs and introduces the critical role of design patterns in their development.

Chapter 2, Data Cleaning for LLM Training, equips you with practical tools and techniques that allow you to effectively clean your data for LLM training.

Chapter 3, Data Augmentation, helps you understand the data augmentation pattern in depth, from increasing the diversity of your training dataset to maintaining its integrity.

Chapter 4, Handling Large Datasets for LLM Training, allows you to learn advanced techniques for managing and processing massive datasets essential for training state-of-the-art LLMs.

Chapter 5, Data Versioning, shows you how to implement effective data versioning strategies for LLM development.

Chapter 6, Dataset Annotation and Labeling, lets you explore advanced techniques for creating well-annotated datasets that can significantly impact your LLM's performance across various tasks.

Chapter 7, Training Pipeline, helps you understand the key components of an LLM training pipeline, from data ingestion and preprocessing to model architecture and optimization strategies.

Chapter 8, Hyperparameter Tuning, demonstrates what the hyperparameters in LLMs are and strategies for optimizing them efficiently.

Chapter 9, Regularization, shows you different regularization techniques that are specifically tailored to LLMs.

Chapter 10, Checkpointing and Recovery, outlines strategies for determining optimal checkpoint frequency, efficient storage formats for large models, and techniques for recovering from various types of failures.

Chapter 11, Fine-Tuning, teaches you effective strategies for fine-tuning pre-trained language models.

Chapter 12, Model Pruning, lets you explore model pruning techniques, designed to reduce model size while maintaining performance.

Chapter 13, Quantization, gives you a look into quantization methods that can optimize LLMs for deployment on resource-constrained devices.

Chapter 14, Evaluation Metrics, explores the most recent and commonly used benchmarks for evaluating LLMs across various domains.

Chapter 15, Cross-Validation, shows you how to explore cross-validation strategies specifically designed for LLMs.

Chapter 16, Interpretability, helps you understand how interpretability in LLMs refers to the model's ability to understand and explain how the model processes inputs and generates outputs.

Chapter 17, Fairness and Bias Detection, demonstrates that fairness in LLMs involves ensuring that the model's outputs and decisions do not discriminate against or unfairly treat individuals or groups based on protected attributes.

Chapter 18, Adversarial Robustness, helps you understand that adversarial attacks on LLMs are designed to manipulate the model's output by making small, often imperceptible changes to the input.

Chapter 19, Reinforcement Learning from Human Feedback, takes you through a powerful technique for aligning LLMs with human preferences.

Chapter 20, Chain-of-Thought Prompting, demonstrates how you can leverage chain-of-thought prompting to improve your LLM's performance on complex reasoning tasks.

Chapter 21, Tree-of-Thoughts Prompting, allows you to implement tree-of-thoughts prompting to tackle complex reasoning tasks with your LLMs.

Chapter 22, Reasoning and Acting, teaches you about the ReAct framework, a powerful technique for prompting your LLMs to not only reason through complex scenarios but also plan and simulate the execution of actions, similar to how humans operate in the real world.

Chapter 23, Reasoning WithOut Observation, teaches you the framework for providing LLMs with the ability to reason about hypothetical situations and leverage external tools effectively.

Chapter 24, Reflection Techniques, demonstrates reflection in LLMs, which refers to a model's ability to analyze, evaluate, and improve its own outputs.

Chapter 25, Automatic Multi-Step Reasoning and Tool Use, helps you understand how automatic multi-step reasoning and tool use significantly expand the problem-solving capabilities of LLMs, enabling them to tackle complex, real-world tasks.

Chapter 26, Retrieval-Augmented Generation, takes you through a technique that enhances the performance of AI models, particularly in tasks that require knowledge or data not contained within the model's pre-trained parameters.

Chapter 27, Graph-Based RAG, shows how to leverage graph-structured knowledge in RAG for LLMs.

Chapter 28, Advanced RAG, demonstrates how you can move beyond these basic RAG methods and explore more sophisticated techniques designed to enhance LLM performance across a wide range of tasks.

Chapter 29, Evaluating RAG Systems, equips you with the knowledge necessary to assess the ability of RAG systems to produce accurate, relevant, and factually grounded responses.

Chapter 30, Agentic Patterns, shows you how agentic AI systems using LLMs can be designed to operate autonomously, make decisions, and take actions to achieve specified goals.

To get the most out of this book

To get the most out of this book, you should ideally have a foundational understanding of machine learning concepts and basic proficiency in Python programming. These prerequisites will help in grasping the technical methodologies and implementation strategies discussed throughout the chapters. Machine learning knowledge is essential for understanding key aspects of LLM development, such as model training, hyperparameter tuning, regularization techniques, and optimization processes. Python programming skills are particularly valuable as they enable you to implement and experiment with the design patterns, workflows, and algorithms presented in the book.

Familiarity with natural language processing (NLP) frameworks and tools, such as Hugging Face Transformers, spaCy, or NLTK, will further enhance the learning experience. These frameworks are commonly used in LLM development and provide a practical means to work with pre-trained models, tokenize text, and process linguistic data. Understanding how these tools function will enable you to focus on the higher-level concepts and design patterns without being bogged down by foundational programming or NLP operations.

For those less familiar with these areas, supplementary resources on machine learning basics, Python programming, and NLP tools are recommended. This book's approach ensures that with some effort to bridge knowledge gaps, you can successfully navigate its concepts and apply them effectively in real-world projects.

> **Note**
>
> This book provides code snippets to illustrate LLM design patterns and implementation concepts. The code is intentionally focused on demonstrating ideas in a concise and readable way, rather than offering complete, executable programs. It is not intended for direct deployment or integration into production environments. You are encouraged to study and adapt the code to your own context, rather than copying and pasting it as is. For this reason, there is no accompanying GitHub repository; the examples presented are self-contained within the book and sufficient for understanding the intended concepts without requiring external code bases.

Download the color images

We also provide a PDF file that has color images of the diagrams used in this book. You can download it here: `https://packt.link/gbp/9781836207030`.

Conventions used

There are a number of text conventions used throughout this book.

Code in text: Indicates code words in text, database table names, folder names, filenames, file extensions, pathnames, dummy URLs, user input, and Twitter handles/X usernames. Here is an example: "Mount the downloaded WebStorm-10*.dmg disk image file as another disk in your system."

A block of code is set as follows:

```
# Model Architecture
model = AutoModelForCausalLM.from_pretrained("gpt2")
# Optimization
optimizer = AdamW(model.parameters(), lr=5e-5)
```

Any command-line input or output is written as follows:

```
pip install faiss-cpu sentence-transformers
```

Bold: Indicates a new term, an important word, or words that you see onscreen.

Tips or important notes

Appear like this.

Get in touch

Feedback from our readers is always welcome.

General feedback: If you have questions about any aspect of this book, email us at customercare@ packtpub.com and mention the book title in the subject of your message.

Errata: Although we have taken every care to ensure the accuracy of our content, mistakes do happen. If you have found a mistake in this book, we would be grateful if you would report this to us. Please visit www.packtpub.com/support/errata and fill in the form.

Piracy: If you come across any illegal copies of our works in any form on the internet, we would be grateful if you would provide us with the location address or website name. Please contact us at copyright@packt.com with a link to the material.

If you are interested in becoming an author: If there is a topic that you have expertise in and you are interested in either writing or contributing to a book, please visit authors.packtpub.com.

Share Your Thoughts

Once you've read LLM Design Patterns, we'd love to hear your thoughts! Scan the QR code below to go straight to the Amazon review page for this book and share your feedback.

https://packt.link/r/1-836-20703-4

Your review is important to us and the tech community and will help us make sure we're delivering excellent quality content.

Free Benefits with Your Book

This book comes with free benefits to support your learning. Activate them now for instant access (see the "*How to Unlock*" section for instructions).

Here's a quick overview of what you can instantly unlock with your purchase:

PDF and ePub Copies

Next-Gen Web-Based Reader

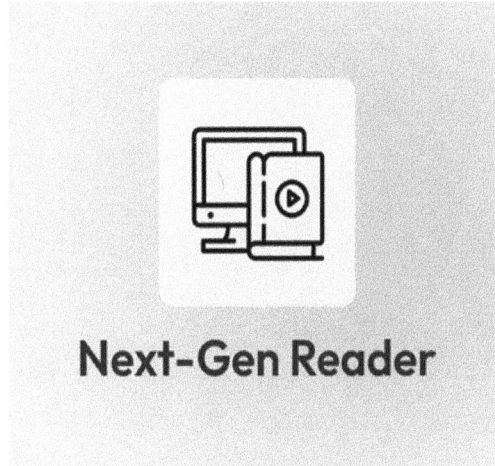

Access a DRM-free PDF copy of this book to read anywhere, on any device.

Use a DRM-free ePub version with your favorite e-reader.

Multi-device progress sync: Pick up where you left off, on any device.

Highlighting and notetaking: Capture ideas and turn reading into lasting knowledge.

Bookmarking: Save and revisit key sections whenever you need them.

Dark mode: Reduce eye strain by switching to dark or sepia themes

How to Unlock

UNLOCK NOW

Scan the QR code (or go to `packtpub.com/unlock`). Search for this book by name, confirm the edition, and then follow the steps on the page.

Note: Keep your invoice handly. Purchase made directly from packt don't require one.

Part 1:
Introduction and
Data Preparation

We begin this book by introducing the foundational concepts necessary to understand and work with large language models (LLMs). In this part, you will explore the critical role of data preparation in building high-quality LLMs. From understanding the significance of design patterns in model development to handling the immense datasets required for training, we guide you through the initial steps of the LLM pipeline. The chapters in this part will help you master data cleaning techniques to improve data quality, data augmentation methods to enhance dataset diversity, and dataset versioning strategies to ensure reproducibility. You will also learn how to efficiently handle large datasets and create well-annotated corpora for specific tasks. By the end of this part, you will have the skills to prepare robust and scalable datasets, providing a solid foundation for advanced LLM development.

This part has the following chapters:

- *Chapter 1, Introduction to LLM Design Patterns*
- *Chapter 2, Data Cleaning for LLM Training*
- *Chapter 3, Data Augmentation*
- *Chapter 4, Handling Large Datasets for LLM Training*
- *Chapter 5, Data Versioning*
- *Chapter 6, Dataset Annotation and Labeling*

1

Introduction to
LLM Design Patterns

Large language models (**LLMs**) are machine learning models capable of understanding and producing human-like text across diverse domains. They have opened up unprecedented possibilities while also presenting unique challenges.

In this chapter, we will introduce the world of LLMs and the critical role of **design patterns** in their development. You will learn about the evolution of language models, explore the core principles that power modern LLMs, and examine their impressive capabilities, as well as their limitations. We'll uncover the importance of design patterns – time-tested solutions to recurring problems in software development – and how they are being adapted and applied to address the specific challenges of LLM projects.

In this chapter, we'll be covering the following topics:

- Understanding LLMs
- Understanding design patterns
- Design patterns for LLM development
- Future directions in LLM patterns and their development

> **Free Benefits with Your Book**
>
> Your purchase includes a free PDF copy of this book along with other exclusive benefits. Check the *Free Benefits with Your Book* section in the Preface to unlock them instantly and maximize your learning experience.

Understanding LLMs

In this section, we will highlight the core concepts of LLMs, exploring their evolution, underlying principles, and the transformative impact they have had on the AI landscape. We will examine the key components that make LLMs so powerful, the challenges they present, and the ongoing developments shaping their future.

The evolution of language models

The journey toward modern LLMs has been marked by significant paradigm shifts in natural language processing, as illustrated in the timeline shown in *Figure 1.1*:

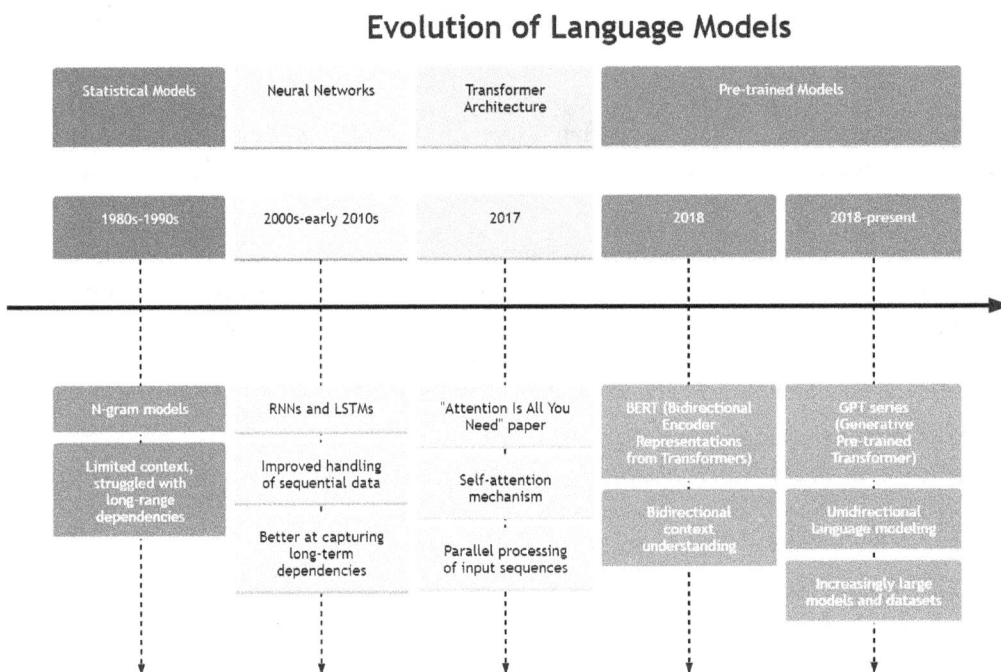

Evolution of Language Models

Statistical Models	Neural Networks	Transformer Architecture	Pre-trained Models	
1980s-1990s	2000s-early 2010s	2017	2018	2018-present
N-gram models	RNNs and LSTMs	"Attention Is All You Need" paper	BERT (Bidirectional Encoder Representations from Transformers)	GPT series (Generative Pre-trained Transformer)
Limited context, struggled with long-range dependencies	Improved handling of sequential data	Self-attention mechanism	Bidirectional context understanding	Unidirectional language modeling
	Better at capturing long-term dependencies	Parallel processing of input sequences		Increasingly large models and datasets

Figure 1.1 – Evolution of language models

Early statistical approaches, while groundbreaking, were limited in capturing the nuances of human language. The advent of **neural networks**, particularly **recurrent neural networks** (**RNNs**) and **long short-term memory** (**LSTM**) networks, allowed for better handling of sequential data and improved the ability to capture longer-term dependencies in text. Capturing longer-term dependencies in text is crucial for understanding the broader context and maintaining coherence over extended passages. Early statistical approaches struggled with this due to their inability to account for the relationships between words or concepts spread across long sequences. The development of neural networks, particularly RNNs and LSTM networks, significantly improved the ability to capture these dependencies. However, even with these advancements, capturing long-term dependencies alone is not sufficient; these models still face challenges in managing complex contexts and ensuring consistency across larger text sequences.

In 2017, the introduction of the **transformer architecture** revolutionized the field, paving the way for larger, more powerful language models. (For more on the transformer architecture, see the next section.) This breakthrough ushered in the era of pre-trained models such as **BERT** and the **GPT** series, which leveraged vast amounts of unlabeled text data to achieve unprecedented performance across various NLP tasks.

> **Note**
>
> For a comprehensive overview of the evolution of language models, including detailed discussions of statistical models, neural networks, and transformer-based approaches, see the book *Speech and Language Processing* by Dan Jurafsky and James H. Martin. The online manuscript is updated frequently and can be found at `https://web.stanford.edu/~jurafsky/slp3`.

Core features of LLMs

This section introduces the core features of LLMs, focusing on their transformer architecture, scale, few-shot learning, language understanding and generation, and multilingual capabilities.

The transformer architecture

The key component of any LLM is its **transformer architecture**. The transformer architecture leverages a **self-attention mechanism**, which allows the model to weigh the importance of different parts of the input when processing each element. In a transformer-based LLM, the input text is first tokenized into smaller units, typically words or subwords. These tokens are then embedded into a high-dimensional vector space, where each token is represented as a dense vector.

A dense vector is a mathematical object that's used in various fields, including AI, to represent data in a compact, high-dimensional space. In simple terms, it's a list of numbers (or values) that, when combined, form a representation of something, such as a word, an image, or any other type of data. These numbers in the vector can be thought of as the coordinates in a multidimensional space, where each number contributes to the description of the data point.

The self-attention mechanism operates on these vector representations, allowing the model to capture complex relationships between different parts of the input sequence. This is achieved through the process of computing attention scores between each pair of tokens in the sequence. These scores determine how much each token should attend to every other token when computing its contextual representation. This allows the model to capture long-range dependencies and complex relationships within the text, overcoming the limitations of previous sequential models (*Attention Is All You Need*, `https://arxiv.org/abs/1706.03762`).

The transformer architecture consists of multiple layers of self-attention and feedforward neural networks. Each layer refines the representations of the input tokens, capturing increasingly abstract and contextual information. The **multi-head attention mechanism**, another key component of transformers, allows the model to attend to different aspects of the input simultaneously, further enhancing its ability to capture complex patterns in the data.

Multi-head attention in transformers is a mechanism that allows the model to focus on different positions of the input sequence simultaneously for better representation learning. Instead of performing a single attention function, the model projects the queries, keys, and values into multiple lower-dimensional spaces (heads), performs attention in each of these spaces independently, and then concatenates the results before performing a final linear transformation. This approach enables the model to jointly attend to information from different representation subspaces and positions, capturing various aspects of the relationships between sequence elements – such as syntactic dependencies, semantic similarities, or contextual relevance – which significantly enhances the model's ability to understand complex patterns and relationships in the data.

Scale and computational resources

A defining characteristic of LLMs is their unprecedented scale, both in terms of model size and the amount of data they are trained on. The *large* in LLMs refers not just to the complexity of these models but also to the vast computational resources required to train and run them. Modern LLMs can have hundreds of billions of parameters, which require enormous amounts of memory and processing power.

This scaling up of model size and training data has been driven by empirical observations of consistent improvements in performance across various tasks as models become larger. These improvements often follow predictable scaling laws, where performance metrics such as perplexity or accuracy improve as a **power-law** function of model size and compute budget (*Scaling Laws for Neural Language Models*, `https://arxiv.org/pdf/2001.08361`). This phenomenon has led to a race to build ever-larger models, with some recent LLMs boasting trillions of parameters.

Few-shot capabilities

The **few-shot learning** capabilities of LLMs represent an advancement in the field of NLP. Traditional machine learning approaches typically require large amounts of labeled data for each specific task. In contrast, LLMs can often perform new tasks with just a few examples or even with just a natural language description of the task (**zero-shot learning**). This flexibility stems from the models' broad understanding of language and their ability to generalize patterns across different contexts.

For example, a pre-trained LLM might be able to perform a sentiment analysis task on product reviews without ever being explicitly trained on sentiment analysis, simply by being provided with a few examples of positive and negative reviews. This capability has opened up new possibilities for applying AI to a wide range of language tasks, particularly in domains where large amounts of task-specific labeled data are not available.

Language understanding and generation

One of the most striking capabilities of LLMs is their ability to understand and generate human-like text across a wide range of styles, topics, and formats. In terms of understanding, these models can process and interpret complex textual inputs, extracting meaning and context with a level of sophistication that mimics human-like comprehension in many scenarios. This ability extends to various subtasks, such as sentiment analysis, named entity recognition, and topic classification. LLMs can often discern nuanced differences in tone, identify implicit information, and recognize complex linguistic patterns.

On the generation side, LLMs have shown an unprecedented ability to produce coherent, contextually appropriate text. They can generate everything from creative fiction and poetry to technical documentation and code. The quality of this generated text often exhibits a high degree of fluency, grammatical correctness, and contextual relevance. This generative capability has opened up new possibilities in areas such as content creation, automated writing assistance, and conversational AI.

Multilingual and cross-lingual abilities

Many modern LLMs exhibit strong multilingual and cross-lingual abilities. When trained on diverse multilingual corpora, these models can understand and generate text in multiple languages. Some models have demonstrated the ability to perform cross-lingual tasks, such as translating between language pairs they were not explicitly trained on, or answering questions in one language based on context provided in another.

These capabilities open up possibilities for breaking down language barriers and enabling more inclusive global communication. However, it's important to note that the performance of LLMs can vary significantly across different languages. Models tend to perform best in languages that are well-represented in their training data, which often favors widely spoken languages such as English. Efforts are ongoing to develop more equitable multilingual models and to improve performance in low-resource languages.

Having examined the core features of LLMs, the next section turns to the role of design patterns in structuring and guiding LLM projects. Drawing from their origins in software engineering, design patterns offer reusable solutions that help manage complexity, improve collaboration, and support scalable, maintainable architectures. Understanding their evolution and principles sets the foundation for applying them effectively in the context of LLM development.

Understanding design patterns

Design patterns originated as a way to capture and share solutions to recurring design problems. Initially rooted in object-oriented programming, they offered a structured approach to building software by identifying repeatable strategies that enhance code clarity, reusability, and maintainability. Over time, design patterns have evolved beyond their original context, influencing a wide range of development practices and system architectures, including LLM development. The following discussion traces the origins of design patterns and outlines the principles that have shaped their continued relevance across different programming paradigms and application domains.

Origins and evolution

The concept of design patterns in software engineering gained prominence in the 1990s, largely popularized by the book *Design Patterns: Elements of Reusable Object-Oriented Software* by Erich Gamma, Richard Helm, Ralph Johnson, and John Vlissides, often referred to as the **Gang of Four**. This seminal work identified and cataloged common patterns in object-oriented software design, providing a vocabulary and set of best practices that quickly became foundational in the field (`https://books.google.com/books/about/Design_Patterns.html?id=6oHuKQe3TjQC`).

These patterns emerged from the collective experience of software developers, representing solutions that had proven effective across various projects and contexts. They offered a way to capture and communicate complex design ideas efficiently, enabling developers to build on the wisdom of their predecessors rather than reinventing solutions to recurring problems.

Initially focused on object-oriented programming, the concept of design patterns has since expanded to encompass a wide range of software development paradigms and domains. As software systems have grown in complexity and scale, the importance of design patterns has only increased, providing a means to manage this complexity and promote more maintainable, scalable, and robust software architectures.

Core principles of design patterns

At their core, design patterns embody several key principles that make them valuable in software development. First, they promote code reuse and modularity. By encapsulating solutions to common problems, patterns allow developers to apply proven approaches without having to duplicate code or reinvent solutions. This modularity also enhances the maintainability of software systems as changes can often be localized to specific components implementing a pattern.

Second, design patterns provide a shared vocabulary among developers. This common language facilitates communication within development teams and across projects. When a developer describes a solution using a well-known pattern, it immediately conveys a wealth of information about the structure and behavior of that solution to other developers familiar with the pattern.

Third, patterns often embody principles of good software design, such as loose coupling and high cohesion. They encourage developers to think about the relationships between components and the overall structure of their systems, leading to more thoughtful and well-architected solutions.

Lastly, design patterns are typically flexible and adaptable. While they provide a general structure for solving a problem, they are not rigid prescriptions. Developers can – and should – adapt patterns so that they fit the specific context and requirements of their projects, allowing for creativity within a proven framework.

Design patterns for LLM development

As the need to develop intelligent LLM-based applications grows, we see the emergence of specific design patterns tailored to address the unique challenges posed by these complex systems. These patterns differ significantly from traditional software design patterns, focusing on aspects inherent to the entire life cycle of LLMs – from data preparation and model training to evaluation, deployment, and sophisticated application design.

This book delves into **29 practical LLM design patterns**, explored in detail across *Chapters 2* through *30*. Developers and researchers can navigate the complexities of building LLM systems using these design patterns:

- **Establishing a solid data foundation (Chapters 2–6)**: Lay the groundwork for high-quality models by mastering patterns for **data cleaning** (*Chapter 2*), **data augmentation** (*Chapter 3*), **handling large datasets** (*Chapter 4*), implementing **data versioning** (*Chapter 5*), and ensuring effective **dataset annotation** (*Chapter 6*). These practices enhance input quality and manageability, thereby directly impacting model performance.

- **Optimizing training and model efficiency (Chapters 7–13)**: Streamline the core model-building process with patterns for robust **training pipelines** (*Chapter 7*), effective **hyperparameter tuning** (*Chapter 8*), **regularization** techniques (*Chapter 9*), reliable **checkpointing** (*Chapter 10*), task-specific **fine-tuning** (*Chapter 11*), and efficiency gains through **model pruning** (*Chapter 12*) and **quantization** (*Chapter 13*).

- **Addressing model quality and alignment (Chapters 14–19)**: Build confidence in your models by applying rigorous **evaluation metrics** (*Chapter 14*) and **cross-validation** (*Chapter 15*), enhancing **interpretability** (*Chapter 16*), proactively addressing **fairness and bias** (*Chapter 17*), improving **adversarial robustness** (*Chapter 18*), and aligning models with human preferences using **Reinforcement Learning from Human Feedback (RLHF)** (*Chapter 19*).

- **Enhancing reasoning and problem-solving capabilities (Chapters 20–25)**: Unlock more sophisticated model behaviors with advanced prompting and reasoning strategies such as **chain-of-thought** (*Chapter 20*), **tree-of-thoughts** (*Chapter 21*), **Reason and Act (ReAct) patterns** (*Chapter 22*), **Reasoning WithOut Observation** (*Chapter 23*), **reflection** techniques (*Chapter 24*), and enabling **automatic multi-step reasoning and tool use** (*Chapter 25*).

- **Integrating external knowledge with RAG (Chapters 26–29)**: Ground model responses in factual, up-to-date information by using **retrieval-augmented generation (RAG)** (*Chapter 26*), exploring variations such as **graph-based RAG** (*Chapter 27*) and **advanced RAG techniques** (*Chapter 28*), and learning how to **evaluate RAG systems** (*Chapter 29*) effectively.

- **Developing agentic AI applications (Chapter 30)**: Move toward creating more independent applications by understanding and implementing **agentic patterns** (*Chapter 30*), enabling LLMs to plan, use tools, and execute tasks autonomously.

Benefits of LLM design patterns

The design patterns for LLM development offer significant benefits, starting with the establishment of a robust data foundation. Data cleaning ensures improved data quality, resulting in increased model accuracy, reduced training time, and mitigation of biases. Data augmentation enhances model robustness and generalization, leading to better performance on unseen data, while handling large datasets unlocks the potential for capturing complex patterns and improved model capabilities. Data versioning enables reproducibility of experiments and model training runs, while dataset annotation provides high-quality labels for supervised learning tasks, improving model accuracy and efficiency.

Furthermore, optimizing training and model efficiency offers substantial advantages. Robust training pipelines automate the training process, leading to faster development cycles and consistent performance. Hyperparameter tuning optimizes model performance, improving accuracy and generalization, while regularization techniques prevent overfitting and improve robustness. Reliable checkpointing allows for the saving of model weights, facilitating experimentation and debugging. Task-specific fine-tuning optimizes a pre-trained LLM for a specific task, improving performance with few resources. Model pruning reduces the size and complexity of the LLM, leading to faster inference and improved deployment efficiency, and quantization further reduces model size and speeds up inference, enabling deployment on edge devices.

Addressing model quality and alignment is crucial for building trustworthy LLMs. Rigorous evaluation metrics provide a comprehensive assessment of model performance, enabling informed decision-making. Cross-validation improves the reliability of model evaluation and provides a more accurate estimate of generalization performance. Interpretability makes the model's decision-making process more transparent and understandable, while fairness and bias mitigation reduces bias in the model's predictions. Adversarial robustness makes the model more resistant to adversarial attacks, improving security, and RLHF aligns the model's behavior with human preferences, improving user satisfaction and trust.

Enhancing reasoning and problem-solving capabilities unlocks more sophisticated model behaviors. Chain-of-thought enables the model to break down complex problems, improving reasoning and accuracy. Tree-of-thoughts extends chain-of-thought by allowing the model to explore multiple reasoning paths, enhancing problem-solving capabilities for more complex tasks. ReAct integrates reasoning and action capabilities, enabling the model to interact with its environment and solve real-world problems. Reasoning WithOut Observation allows the model to apply reasoning skills even in the absence of explicit data, while reflection techniques empower the model to evaluate its own reasoning process and improve. Automatic multi-step reasoning and tool use automates the process of reasoning and tool usage, enabling the model to solve complex tasks.

Finally, integrating external knowledge with RAG enhances the model's knowledge and accuracy. RAG retrieves relevant information from external sources, overcoming the limitations of the model's pre-trained knowledge. Graph-based RAG uses knowledge graphs to represent and retrieve information, enabling more sophisticated reasoning. Advanced RAG techniques further refine RAG systems and improve the quality, relevance, and accuracy of the retrieved information. Evaluating RAG systems involves methods for assessing the performance of RAG systems, enabling optimization and improvement. The use of agentic patterns enables the creation of autonomous AI agents that can plan, use tools, and execute tasks independently, leading to more powerful and versatile applications.

Table 1.1 summarizes the benefits of the LLM design patterns, organized by category.

Category	Design pattern	Key benefits
Data Foundation	Data cleaning	Higher quality insights; more accurate predictions; faster model iteration; reduced bias in outcomes.
	Data augmentation	More reliable and generalizable models; improved performance in diverse situations; greater resilience to noisy data.
	Handling large datasets	Ability to extract deeper insights; higher performance potential; broader range of applications; more robust models.
	Data versioning	Increased confidence in results; easier debugging and auditing; reduced risk of data corruption; faster recovery from errors; improved data-driven decision making.
	Dataset annotation	More precise and effective models; faster learning rates; better alignment with desired outcomes.
Training and Efficiency	Robust training pipelines	Faster model development; more consistent results; reduced manual effort; higher productivity.
	Hyperparameter tuning	Optimized model performance; higher accuracy; faster training convergence; more efficient resource utilization.
	Regularization techniques	More stable and generalizable models; reduced risk of overfitting; improved performance on unseen data.
	Reliable checkpointing	Reduced risk of losing progress; faster experimentation; improved model development workflows.
	Task-specific fine-tuning	Significantly improved performance on target tasks; faster time to market; more efficient use of resources.
	Model pruning	Faster inference speeds; reduced storage requirements; lower computational costs; enabling deployment on resource-constrained devices.

Category	Design pattern	Key benefits
	Quantization	Reduced model size; accelerated inference; lower memory footprint; improved energy efficiency; wider deployment possibilities.
Quality and Alignment	Rigorous evaluation metrics	Data-driven decision making; improved model selection; better understanding of model strengths and weaknesses.
	Cross-validation	More reliable performance estimates; reduced risk of overfitting; improved model generalization.
	Interpretability	Increased trust in model predictions; easier identification of errors; improved model understanding; facilitates debugging and refinement.
	Fairness and bias mitigation	More equitable and ethical outcomes; reduced risk of discrimination; increased user trust.
	Adversarial robustness	Enhanced security; improved reliability in unpredictable environments; protection against malicious attacks.
	Reinforcement Learning from Human Feedback	Models aligned with human values; improved user experience; increased safety and trustworthiness.
Reasoning and Problem Solving	Chain-of-thought	Enhanced problem-solving abilities; improved accuracy; increased transparency in decision-making.
	Tree-of-thoughts	Improved ability to handle complex and ambiguous problems; more robust solutions.
	ReAct	Ability to solve real-world problems effectively; improved adaptability; enhanced learning and reasoning.
	Reasoning WithOut Observation	Enhanced problem-solving in data-scarce environments; improved decision-making with incomplete information.
	Reflection techniques	More self-aware and reliable models; improved accuracy; enhanced learning and adaptation.
	Automatic multi-step reasoning	Ability to solve complex tasks autonomously; increased efficiency; reduced need for human intervention.
Knowledge Integration (RAG)	Retrieval-augmented generation	Access to up-to-date information; reduced reliance on pre-trained knowledge; improved accuracy and relevance.
	Graph-based RAG	More sophisticated reasoning; improved accuracy in complex knowledge domains; enhanced understanding of relationships.

Category	Design pattern	Key benefits
	Advanced RAG techniques	Higher quality and more relevant information; improved accuracy and reliability of results.
	Evaluating RAG systems	Optimized RAG systems; greater user satisfaction; higher quality outcomes.
Agentic AI	Agentic patterns	Ability to create autonomous systems; increased efficiency; reduced human intervention; enabling new applications.

Table 1.1 – Benefits of LLM design patterns

Challenges in applying design patterns to LLMs

While the benefits of design patterns in LLM development are clear, their application is not without significant challenges. The unique nature of LLM systems, their rapid evolution, and the breadth of areas these patterns cover – from foundational data handling to complex agentic systems – present several obstacles:

- **Rapid technological evolution**: One of the primary challenges that remains is the breakneck speed of advancement in the LLM field. New model architectures, training methodologies, sophisticated prompting strategies, knowledge retrieval techniques, and agentic frameworks emerge constantly. This rapid flux means that patterns, even recently established ones for optimizing training or enhancing reasoning, may require frequent adaptation; otherwise, they can become less optimal quickly. Developers need a flexible mindset, balancing the need for stable practices such as disciplined data management with the agility to integrate breakthroughs.

- **Complexity, scale, and unpredictability**: LLMs are inherently complex, operate at a massive scale, and often exhibit non-deterministic behavior. This poses challenges across the pattern spectrum:

  - **Data and training**: Applying patterns for managing large datasets, structuring training pipelines, or tuning hyperparameters effectively requires managing immense computational resources and data volumes.

  - **Behavioral control**: The stochastic nature of LLMs complicates the process of applying patterns that aim to ensure desired outcomes, such as those addressing fairness, bias, adversarial robustness, or even advanced techniques for step-by-step reasoning and action. Achieving consistent, predictable behavior is harder than in traditional software.

  - **Error handling and debugging**: Pinpointing failures when using complex patterns, such as those involving multi-step reasoning chains or autonomous agent behaviors, can be incredibly difficult due to the opaque nature of the models.

- **Evaluation difficulties**: Measuring the effectiveness of applying many LLM design patterns is a major challenge. While patterns exist for defining evaluation metrics and validation processes, assessing nuanced aspects such as the quality of generated reasoning paths, the true helpfulness of retrieved context in RAG systems, or the overall robustness and task success of an agent often requires more than standard benchmarks. Developing reliable and comprehensive evaluation strategies for these advanced patterns is an ongoing research area.

- **Cost and resource constraints**: Implementing many LLM patterns can be resource-intensive in various ways:

  - **Data costs**: Thorough data annotation and preparation can be expensive and time-consuming.

  - **Compute costs**: Core model training, extensive fine-tuning, large-scale hyperparameter searches, or running inference for complex retrieval-augmented or agentic systems requires significant computational power.

  - **Optimization trade-offs**: Patterns aimed at model optimization, such as pruning or quantization, seek to reduce costs but involve their own complexities and potential performance trade-offs. The cost factor can limit the practical applicability of certain patterns for teams with constrained budgets.

- **The interdisciplinary nature of LLM development**: Building effective LLM systems requires collaboration between diverse roles – software engineers, ML researchers, data scientists, prompt engineers, domain experts, ethicists, and more. Establishing a shared understanding and consistent application of patterns across these disciplines is crucial but challenging. For instance, ensuring everyone aligns on data management practices, interprets evaluation results similarly, or understands the implications of patterns designed to ensure fairness requires deliberate effort and clear communication.

Summary

This chapter provided a foundational understanding of LLMs and introduced the role of design patterns in their development. It traced the evolution of language models from early statistical approaches to the transformer architecture-based LLMs of today, emphasizing key features such as the self-attention mechanism, the significance of scale and computational resources, few-shot learning, language understanding and generation capabilities, and multilingual abilities.

Then, this chapter transitioned to the importance of design patterns, drawing parallels with their established role in software engineering. This highlighted the benefits of applying design patterns to LLM development, outlining a structured approach for improving data quality, optimizing training, addressing model quality and alignment, enhancing reasoning capabilities, integrating external knowledge through RAG, and developing agentic applications. Then, the 29 patterns that will be explored throughout this book were outlined, as well as what stage of the LLM life cycle they focus on.

Finally, this chapter acknowledged the challenges in applying design patterns to LLMs, all of which stem from rapid technological evolution, complexity and scale, evaluation difficulties, cost constraints, and the interdisciplinary nature of LLM development.

In the rest of this book, we will guide you through the LLM development life cycle using design patterns, starting with building a solid data foundation (*Chapters 2 to 6*) and optimizing model training (*Chapters 7 to 13*). Then, we'll focus on ensuring model quality, alignment, and robustness (*Chapters 14 to 19*) before exploring advanced reasoning and problem-solving capabilities (*Chapters 20 to 25*). Finally, we'll cover integrating external knowledge with RAG (*Chapters 26 to 29*) and delve into the future of LLMs with agentic AI (*Chapter 30*), thus providing a comprehensive toolkit for building intelligent applications.

## 2

Data Cleaning for LLM Training

In this chapter, we'll dive into the **data cleaning** pattern for LLM training.

Clean, high-quality data is the foundation of robust and reliable language models. We'll explore common data quality issues, preprocessing techniques, and strategies for handling diverse data types. *Figure 2.1* depicts a data cleaning pipeline specifically designed for processing raw text data before it's used to train language models.

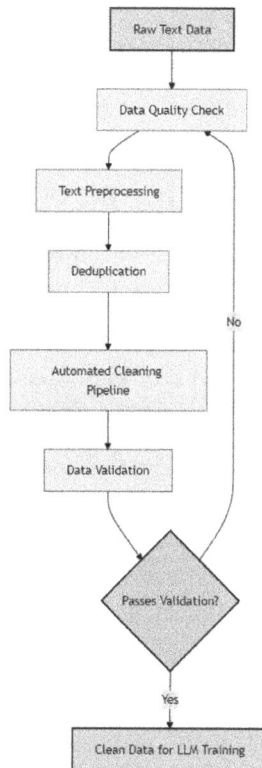

Figure 2.1 – Data cleaning pipeline

The process begins with an initial data quality check to assess the raw data's suitability. Following this, text preprocessing and deduplication steps are applied to refine and streamline the dataset. If the data fails to meet the required standards at any point, it is rerouted through an automated cleaning pipeline for additional processing. Successful completion of this stage leads to data validation to ensure the dataset's integrity and compliance with training standards. If the data passes validation, it is marked as clean and ready for use in language model training, ensuring high-quality input for effective model development.

By the end of this chapter, you'll be equipped with practical tools and techniques to clean your data for LLM training.

In this chapter, we'll be covering the following topics:

- Understanding the importance of clean data
- Common data quality issues in language datasets
- Text preprocessing techniques for LLMs
- Handling multilingual and code-mixed data
- Deduplication strategies for large text corpora
- Automated data cleaning pipelines
- Data validation and quality assurance

Understanding the importance of clean data

The quality of data used in training LLMs directly impacts their performance and reliability. When we train LLMs on noisy or inconsistent data, we risk introducing bias, errors, and inconsistency into the model's learned representations and outputs.

To illustrate the impact of data quality on LLM performance, we can use a simple Python script to compare the perplexity scores of models trained on clean and noisy data.

1. First, install the necessary packages and import them:

```
pip install torch
pip install transformers
import torch
from transformers import GPT2LMHeadModel, GPT2Tokenizer
```

PyTorch (`torch`) is a powerful deep learning framework that provides dynamic computational graphs, GPU acceleration, and extensive neural network building blocks, making it popular for machine learning research and development. The `transformers` package, developed by Hugging Face, complements PyTorch by providing a comprehensive library of pre-trained transformer models (such as BER, GPT, and T5) and tools for natural language processing tasks. Together, these packages offer a robust ecosystem in which `torch` provides the foundational deep learning operations, tensor computations, and automatic differentiation capabilities, while `transformers` provides high-level abstractions for working with state-of-the-art language models, including functions for tokenization, model fine-tuning, and inference.

2. Then, define the initial part of the function:

```
def calculate_perplexity(model, tokenizer, text):
    inputs = tokenizer(text, return_tensors="pt")
    with torch.no_grad():
    outputs = model(inputs, labels=inputs["input_ids"])
    return torch.exp(outputs.loss).item()



model = GPT4LMHeadModel.from_pretrained("GPT4")
tokenizer = GPT4Tokenizer.from_pretrained("GPT4")
```

The `calculate_perplexity` function tokenizes the input text into PyTorch tensors using the provided tokenizer. It then passes the tokenized input to the model with `input_ids` also used as labels, allowing the model to compute a loss representing prediction error. This loss is exponentiated to derive a scalar perplexity score and returned as a Python float.

The second part of the code initializes a language model and tokenizer using `GPT4LMHeadModel`. `from_pretrained("GPT4")` and `GPT4Tokenizer.from_pretrained("GPT4")`, which load the model and tokenizer weights from a pre-trained source identified as `"GPT4"`.

Perplexity

Perplexity is a measure used to evaluate language models. It quantifies how well a probability model predicts a sample.

Lower perplexity indicates that the model is more confident in its predictions and considers the text more likely or "normal". Higher perplexity suggests that the model finds the text more surprising or unusual.

---

3. Here are example texts:

```
clean_text = "The quick brown fox jumps over the lazy dog."
noisy_text = "Th3 qu1ck br0wn f0x jumps 0ver th3 l@zy d0g."
```

The code snippet defines two string variables: `clean_text` and `noisy_text`. `clean_text` holds a standard English sentence, while `noisy_text` contains the same sentence with deliberate character substitutions, making it "noisy" or corrupted. The `clean_text` and `noisy_text` examples are used to evaluate a language model's perplexity, where `clean_text` provides a baseline for ideal text prediction and `noisy_text` assesses the model's robustness to real-world data corruption; by comparing the perplexity scores, we determine how well the model handles noisy input and its suitability for applications where text data is not always perfectly formatted.

4.   Finally, calculate perplexity and print the results:

```
clean_perplexity = calculate_perplexity(model, tokenizer,
    clean_text)
noisy_perplexity = calculate_perplexity(model, tokenizer,
    noisy_text)

print(f"Clean text perplexity: {clean_perplexity:.2f}")
print(f"Noisy text perplexity: {noisy_perplexity:.2f}")
```

This script demonstrates how even small amounts of noise in the input data can significantly impact the model's perplexity.

The perplexity score is calculated as the exponential of the cross-entropy loss. In this code, it's computed using `torch.exp(outputs.loss).item()`.

Here are our possible outcomes:

- **Clean text perplexity**: The clean text `The quick brown fox jumps over the lazy dog` is a common, grammatically correct English sentence. The clean text perplexity might be something like `10.25`.

- **Noisy text perplexity**: The noisy text `Th3 qu1ck br0wn f0x jumps 0ver th3 l@zy d0g` contains numbers and symbols in place of letters, making it less common and more difficult for the model to predict. The noisy text perplexity might be something like `52.87`.

The exact numbers will depend on the specific model and tokenizer used, but the noisy text should consistently have a higher perplexity score than the clean text.

This difference in scores demonstrates the model's ability to distinguish between standard, easily predictable text and unusual, harder-to-predict text. It's a useful metric for tasks such as detecting machine-generated or tampered text, as such text often has higher perplexity scores compared to human-written text.

Common data quality issues in language datasets

Language datasets often contain various quality issues that can negatively impact LLM training:

- Spelling and grammatical errors can introduce noise and inconsistencies in the learned representations.
- Inconsistent formatting can lead to unnecessary complexity in the model's learned patterns.
- Redundant data can cause models to overfit to specific patterns or bias present in the duplicates.
- Irrelevant or low-quality content can dilute the useful information in the dataset.
- Incomplete or truncated sentences can lead to models learning incomplete language structures.
- Code-switching and mixed languages can confuse models trained for specific languages.
- **Personally identifiable information** (**PII**) raises privacy concerns and can lead to the memorization of sensitive data.

To detect these issues, we can use various Python libraries and techniques. Here's an example using spaCy for basic text quality checks:

1. Provide the imports and an overall function definition:

```
import spacy
from collections import Counter

# Load spaCy model
nlp = spacy.load("en_core_web_sm")

def analyze_text_quality(text):
    doc = nlp(text)
```

2. Check for spelling errors (using spaCy's built-in spell checker):

```
misspelled = [
    token.text for token in doc if token._.is_misspelled
]
```

3. Check for grammatical issues (a simplistic approach using parts of speech (pos) tags):

```
pos_counts = Counter(token.pos_ for token in doc)
grammar_score = pos_counts['NOUN'] + pos_counts['VERB']
    + pos_counts['ADJ'] + pos_counts['ADV']
```

Parts of speech (**POS**) tags are labels assigned to each word in a sentence to indicate its grammatical role. These tags help systems to understand the syntactic structure of sentences and are used in tasks such as parsing, machine translation, sentiment analysis, and information extraction. Each tag corresponds to a POS such as a noun, verb, or adjective, often with finer-grained distinctions to capture tense, number, or function.

4. Check for sentence completeness:

```
incomplete_sentences = [
    sent.text for sent in doc.sents if len(sent) < 3
]


return {
    "misspelled_words": misspelled,
    "grammar_score": grammar_score,
    "incomplete_sentences": incomplete_sentences
}
```

5. Here's an example usage of the code:

```
text = "This iz a smple txt with sum issues. Incomplet"
quality_report = analyze_text_quality(text)
print(quality_report)
```

The script provided in *steps 1 to 5* illustrates a basic framework for identifying some common text quality issues. We will address other quality issues in the following sections.

Text preprocessing techniques for LLMs

Effective text preprocessing is crucial for preparing data for LLM training. We employ various techniques, including lowercasing, punctuation handling, whitespace normalization, special character handling, **tokenization**, number normalization, and contraction expansion. Tokenization is the process of breaking text into smaller units for further analysis or processing. Tokens are the smallest meaningful units of text in natural language processing. They can be words, but they could also include punctuation, numbers, or other elements depending on the tokenization strategy.

In addition, **subword tokenization** is an advanced text processing technique that breaks words into smaller meaningful units (subwords), enabling more efficient handling of rare words, compound words, and morphological variations in natural language processing tasks. Unlike traditional word-level tokenization, subword tokenization can identify common prefixes, suffixes, and root words, allowing models to understand and process previously unseen words by recognizing their familiar components.

As an example, consider the word "unbelievably". Traditional word-level tokenization would treat this as a single token. If the model has never seen this word before, it may struggle to interpret it correctly. In contrast, subword tokenization would break it down into smaller components such as "un", "believ", and "ably". These subwords are more likely to appear across different contexts—"un-" in "unlikely", "believ" in "believe", "ably" in "capably"—allowing the model to derive meaning even if it encounters "unbelievably" for the first time. This decomposition enhances generalization, reduces vocabulary size, and improves the model's ability to handle rare or morphologically complex words.

Popular subword tokenization algorithms include **byte pair encoding** (**BPE**), WordPiece, and SentencePiece, which learn to identify frequently occurring character sequences in a training corpus and create a vocabulary of subword tokens. This approach is particularly valuable for handling morphologically rich languages, reducing vocabulary size while maintaining semantic meaning, and has become fundamental in modern language models such as Gemini, Claude, GPT, and other transformer-based architectures.

These methods help clean and standardize the text data, reducing noise and improving the model's ability to generalize. Here's a Python script demonstrating these preprocessing techniques:

1. First, import the necessary Python packages:

```
import unicodedata
import re
from nltk.tokenize import word_tokenize
from nltk.corpus import stopwords
import nltk

# Download required NLTK data
nltk.download('punkt')
nltk.download('stopwords')
```

2. Then, define the overall preprocessing function:

```
def preprocess_text(text):
    # Lowercase the text
    text = text.lower()

    # Normalize unicode characters
    text = unicodedata.normalize(
        'NFKD', text
    ).encode(
        'ascii', 'ignore'
    ).decode('utf-8')

    # Remove punctuation
```

```
text = re.sub(r'[^\w\s]', '', text)

# Normalize whitespace
text = ' '.join(text.split())

# Tokenize :
tokens = word_tokenize(text)
```

3. Remove stopwords (stopwords are common words such as "the", "is", and "at") that are often removed in text processing as they carry little semantic meaning):

```
stop_words = set(stopwords.words('english'))
tokens = [
    token for token in tokens if token not in stop_words
]

# Join tokens back into text
preprocessed_text = ' '.join(tokens)

return preprocessed_text
```

4. Here's an example usage of the code:

```
raw_text = "This is an EXAMPLE of text preprocessing... It's
quite useful!"
cleaned_text = preprocess_text(raw_text)
print(f"Original: {raw_text}")
print(f"Preprocessed: {cleaned_text}")
```

This script demonstrates basic text preprocessing techniques. For LLM training, we might need to adapt these techniques based on the specific requirements of the model and the dataset.

Handling multilingual and code-mixed data

LLMs often encounter multilingual and code-mixed data, which is text that blends two or more languages within a single sentence or conversation. This presents a challenge as LLMs must interpret linguistic nuances, grammar, and semantic connections across multiple languages. To handle code-mixed data, LLMs need to learn language switching, vocabulary and syntax variations, and maintain coherent responses, which demands strong language modeling and multilingual training data.

We need to implement strategies to handle these scenarios effectively. The following steps are needed because they create cleaner, more consistent training data that helps LLMs better understand and process text across different languages and mixed-language scenarios, ultimately improving their performance in real-world applications where language mixing is common.

For multilingual data, certain tasks are crucial:

- **Language identification**: Detects the primary language of each text sample
- **Script normalization**: Converts text to a consistent script (e.g., transliteration)
- **Language-specific preprocessing**: Applies language-specific tokenization and normalization

Meanwhile, you should carry out the following steps for code-mixed data:

- **Token-level language identification**: Identifies the language of individual tokens
- **Consistency enforcement**: Ensures consistent handling of code-switching patterns

Here's a Python script demonstrating language detection and script normalization.

1. Let's provide the imports and the overall function definition:

```
from langdetect import detect
from unidecode import unidecode
from nltk import word_tokenize
import nltk

# Download required NLTK data
nltk.download('punkt')

def handle_multilingual_text(text):
    # Detect language
    try:
        lang = detect(text)
    except:
        lang = 'unknown'

    # Transliterate non-ASCII characters
    transliterated_text = unidecode(text)
```

2. Tokenize (using NLTK for simplicity, but consider language-specific tokenizers):

```
    tokens = word_tokenize(transliterated_text)

    return {
        'original': text,
        'language': lang,
        'transliterated': transliterated_text,
        'tokens': tokens
    }
```

3. Here's the example usage:

```
texts = [
    "This is English text.",
    "Dies ist deutscher Text.",
    "これは日本語のテキストです。",
    "This is mixed language text avec un peu de français."
]

for text in texts:
    result = handle_multilingual_text(text)
    print(f"Original: {result['original']}")
    print(f"Detected Language: {result['language']}")
    print(f"Transliterated: {result['transliterated']}")
    print(f"Tokens: {result['tokens']}\n")
```

This code iterates through a list of multilingual text strings, including English, German, Japanese, and a code-mixed example, and for each string, it calls a `handle_multilingual_text` function (presumably defined elsewhere) to process the text, returning a dictionary containing the original text, detected language, transliterated text (if applicable), and tokenized words, which are then printed to the console.

Putting the preceding three code blocks together, we provide a basic framework for handling multilingual text. For more advanced scenarios, we would use specialized libraries such as Polyglot for language-specific processing and code-mixing analysis when multiple languages are used in the same conversation (`https://dl.acm.org/doi/10.1145/3544548.3581445`).

For example, Polyglot includes built-in language detection, named entity recognition, sentiment analysis, and transliteration capabilities across multiple languages, all while maintaining a relatively lightweight footprint compared to larger multilingual frameworks. The library is particularly valuable for projects dealing with international text data, as it provides consistent APIs across languages and comes with pre-trained models, making it an efficient choice for multilingual text analysis tasks without the complexity of managing multiple language-specific tools.

Deduplication strategies for large text corpora

Deduplication is a critical step in preparing large text corpora for LLM training. Duplicate content can lead to biased models and wasted computational resources. We employ various strategies to identify and remove duplicates efficiently:

- **Exact match deduplication**: Remove identical text samples.
- **Near-duplicate detection**: Identify and remove highly similar text samples.
- **Shingling**: Create small overlapping sequences of words for comparison.
- **Locality sensitive hashing**: Efficiently find similar items in large datasets.

The following sections show examples of each strategy.

Exact match deduplication

Scenario: You have a list of customer addresses:

- **Data**:

    - "123 Main St, Anytown, CA 91234"

    - "456 Oak Ave, Somecity, NY 56789"

    - "123 Main St, Anytown, CA 91234"

- **Result**: The third entry, "123 Main St, Anytown, CA 91234", is removed because it is an exact duplicate of the first entry.

- **Remaining data**:

    - "123 Main St, Anytown, CA 91234"

    - "456 Oak Ave, Somecity, NY 56789"

Near-duplicate detection

Scenario: You have a collection of news articles:

- **Data**:

    - Article 1: "The company reported a significant increase in quarterly profits."

    - Article 2: "Quarterly profits saw a large increase, the company reports."

- **Result**: A near-duplicate detection algorithm determines that these articles are highly similar in content, even though the wording is slightly different. One of the articles is removed, based on a similarity threshold.

- **Remaining data**: "The company reported a significant increase in quarterly profits."

Shingling

Scenario: You want to compare the similarity of text documents:

- **Data**:

    - Document 1: "The quick brown fox jumps over the lazy dog."

    - k=3 word shingle.

- **Result**: The shingles generated are as follows:

  - "The quick brown"
  - "quick brown fox"
  - "brown fox jumps"
  - "fox jumps over"
  - "jumps over the"
  - "over the lazy"
  - "the lazy dog"

The document is then represented by the set of those shingles. Then another document could be turned into shingles, and the sets of shingles can be compared.

Locality Sensitive Hashing (LSH)

Scenario: You have a very large database of online product descriptions:

- **Process**:

  - LSH is used to hash the product descriptions.
  - Similar product descriptions are more likely to be hashed into the same "buckets."
  - Only the descriptions within the same buckets are then compared in detail to find near duplicates.

- **Result**: Instead of comparing every product description to every other description, LSH narrows down the comparisons to only those descriptions within the same buckets, greatly increasing the efficiency of finding near duplicates.

> **Note**
>
> Deduplicating is computationally very expensive, so techniques such as minhashing or parallel processing can be used to scale the deduplicating with the increase in corpus data.
>
> Minhashing efficiently approximates the similarity between documents using smaller, more manageable representations, reducing the computational load. Parallel processing further distributes the deduplication task across multiple processors or machines, allowing for simultaneous comparisons and significantly speeding up the overall process, thus enabling effective deduplication of massive corpora.

Here's a Python script demonstrating basic deduplication techniques:

1. First, define the overall function:

```
from sklearn.feature_extraction.text import TfidfVectorizer
from sklearn.metrics.pairwise import cosine_similarity
def deduplicate_corpus(corpus, similarity_threshold=0.9):
    # Create TF-IDF vectorizer
    vectorizer = TfidfVectorizer()
    tfidf_matrix = vectorizer.fit_transform(corpus)


    # Compute pairwise similarities
    similarity_matrix = cosine_similarity(tfidf_matrix)
```

This code snippet utilizes scikit-learn's `TfidfVectorizer` to convert a text corpus into a numerical **term frequency-inverse document frequency (TF-IDF)** matrix representing the importance of words in each document and then employs `cosine_similarity` to calculate the pairwise similarity between all documents in the corpus, providing a matrix of similarity scores that can be used to identify near-duplicate texts based on a specified threshold.

2. Then, find duplicates:

```
duplicates = set()
for i in range(len(corpus)):
    for j in range(i + 1, len(corpus)):
        if similarity_matrix[i, j] > similarity_threshold:
            duplicates.add(j)
```

3. Create a deduplicated corpus:

```
deduplicated_corpus = [
    doc for i, doc in enumerate(corpus)
    if i not in duplicates
]


return deduplicated_corpus
```

4. Here's an example:

```
corpus = [
    "The quick brown fox jumps over the lazy dog.",
    "A fast auburn fox leaps above the sleepy canine.",
    "The quick brown fox jumps over the lazy dog.",
    "An entirely different sentence about cats.",
]
```

```
deduplicated = deduplicate_corpus(corpus)
print(f"Original corpus size: {len(corpus)}")
print(f"Deduplicated corpus size: {len(deduplicated)}")
print("Deduplicated corpus:")
for doc in deduplicated:
    print(f"- {doc}")
```

This script demonstrates a basic near-duplicate detection approach using TF-IDF and **cosine similarity**. TF-IDF is a numerical statistic used to reflect the importance of words in documents within a collection. It combines how often a word appears in a document (TF) with how unique it is across all documents (IDF). TF-IDF converts text into numerical vectors, enabling mathematical comparisons between documents, which is crucial for the similarity calculations used in the deduplication process. For large-scale deduplication, we would use more efficient algorithms and distributed computing techniques.

Here, the similarity threshold of 0.9 used in the deduplication function code determines how similar documents must be to be considered duplicates, with 90% similarity required by default. This value can be adjusted based on specific use cases—a higher threshold (e.g., 0.95 or 1, which is maximum) is stricter and reduces false positives, while a lower threshold (e.g., 0 which is minimum or 0.8) is more lenient and catches more potential duplicates.

Next, let's discuss automated data cleaning pipelines.

Automated data cleaning pipelines

To handle the massive datasets required for LLM training, we need to implement automated data cleaning pipelines. These pipelines should be scalable, efficient, and capable of handling various data quality issues.

The key components of an automated data cleaning pipeline are as follows:

- **Data ingestion**: Efficiently load and parse large text corpora.
- **Quality assessment**: Automatically detect and flag data quality issues.
- **Preprocessing**: Apply text cleaning and normalization techniques.
- **Deduplication**: Remove exact and near-duplicate content.
- **Filtering**: Remove low-quality or irrelevant samples based on predefined criteria.
- **Validation**: Ensure the cleaned data meets quality standards.
- **Output**: Save the cleaned data in an appropriate format for LLM training.

Here's a Python script outlining a basic automated data cleaning pipeline:

1. We will start by defining the overall class structure:

```
import pandas as pd
import re
from nltk.corpus import stopwords
from sklearn.feature_extraction.text import TfidfVectorizer
from sklearn.metrics.pairwise import cosine_similarity
import nltk
# Download required NLTK data
nltk.download('stopwords')
stop_words = set(stopwords.words('english'))

class DataCleaningPipeline:
    def __init__(
        self, similarity_threshold=0.9, min_length=10,
        max_length=1000
    ):
        self.similarity_threshold = similarity_threshold
        self.min_length = min_length
        self.max_length = max_length
        self.vectorizer = TfidfVectorizer(stop_words='english')
```

This code snippet defines a `DataCleaningPipeline` class that encapsulates text preprocessing, length filtering, and near-duplicate removal functionalities. It initializes with configurable parameters such as similarity threshold and text length constraints, leverages NLTK for stop word removal, and employs scikit-learn's `TfidfVectorizer` and `cosine_similarity` to identify and eliminate similar text entries from a pandas DataFrame.

2. Then, we will define a preprocess function:

```
def preprocess(self, text):
    # Basic preprocessing
    text = text.lower()
    text = re.sub(r'[^\w\s]', '', text)
    tokens = [
        word for word in text.split()
        if word not in stop_words
    ]
    return ' '.join(tokens)

def filter_by_length(self, df):
    return df[
        (df['text'].str.len() >= self.min_length) &
        (df['text'].str.len() <= self.max_length)
    ]
```

This code snippet defines two methods within a class for text processing.

- `preprocess`: This method takes a text string as input, converts it to lowercase, removes punctuation, splits it into words, filters out common stop words, and then joins the remaining words into a string, effectively cleaning and normalizing the text.

- `filter_by_length`: This method takes a pandas DataFrame containing a `text` column and filters the DataFrame to include only rows where the length of the `text` column falls within a specified minimum and maximum length, allowing the selection of text samples within a desired character range.

3. We then define the deduplication function:

```
def deduplicate(self, df):
    tfidf_matrix = self.vectorizer.fit_transform(df['text'])
    similarity_matrix = cosine_similarity(tfidf_matrix)

    duplicates = set()
    for i in range(len(df)):
        for j in range(i + 1, len(df)):
            if similarity_matrix[i, j] > \
                    self.similarity_threshold:
                duplicates.add(j)

    return df.drop(df.index[list(duplicates)])
```

This `deduplicate` method takes a pandas DataFrame as input and removes near-duplicate text entries based on their similarity. It first transforms the `text` column of the DataFrame into a TF-IDF matrix using a vectorizer, representing each text sample as a numerical vector. Then, it calculates the cosine similarity between all pairs of text samples using the TF-IDF matrix, resulting in a similarity matrix. The code iterates through the similarity matrix, and if the similarity between two text samples exceeds a defined `similarity_threshold`, the index of the second sample is added to a set of duplicates. Finally, it removes the rows corresponding to the identified duplicate indices from the DataFrame and returns the deduplicated DataFrame.

4. Putting all the functions together, we can now define a `clean` function:

```
def clean(self, input_file, output_file):
    # Read data
    df = pd.read_csv(input_file)

    # Preprocess
    df['text'] = df['text'].apply(self.preprocess)

    # Filter by length
```

```
            df = self.filter_by_length(df)

            # Deduplicate
            df = self.deduplicate(df)

            # Save cleaned data
            df.to_csv(output_file, index=False)

            print(f"Cleaned data saved to {output_file}")
```

This `clean` method orchestrates a series of data cleaning steps on a CSV file. It begins by reading the input CSV file into a pandas DataFrame. Then, the `preprocess` method is applied to each text entry in the `text` column, normalizing and cleaning the text. Subsequently, it filters the DataFrame using the `filter_by_length` method to retain only text entries within a specified length range. After length filtering, near-duplicate entries are removed using the `deduplicate` method. Finally, it saves the cleaned DataFrame to a new CSV file specified by `output_file`, excluding the index, and prints a confirmation message indicating the output file's location. Essentially, this method performs a complete text cleaning pipeline, encompassing preprocessing, length filtering, and deduplication.

5. The following is an example usage:

```
pipeline = DataCleaningPipeline()
pipeline.clean('input_data.csv', 'cleaned_data.csv')
```

Overall, this script provides a basic framework for an automated data cleaning pipeline. In practice, we would extend this pipeline with more sophisticated cleaning techniques, error handling, and parallel processing capabilities to handle large-scale datasets efficiently.

The values `10` and `1000` in the code represent the minimum and maximum allowed lengths for text documents in the data cleaning pipeline:

- `min_length=10`: This sets the minimum number of characters a document must have to be included in the cleaned dataset. It helps to filter out very short texts that might not contain meaningful information, such as single words or brief phrases.

- `max_length=1000`: This establishes the maximum number of characters allowed for a document. It excludes extremely long texts that might be atypical or potentially problematic for processing, such as entire books or very large documents that could skew the analysis.

These length constraints help ensure that the cleaned dataset contains documents of a reasonable and consistent size range, which can improve the quality and efficiency of subsequent text analysis or machine learning tasks. You can adjust the length based on your use cases.

Data validation and quality assurance

After cleaning the data, you need to validate the results and ensure that the cleaned dataset meets the required quality standards for LLM training. We implement various validation checks and quality assurance measures to verify the effectiveness of our cleaning process.

Key aspects include performing statistical analyses, sampling and manual reviews, automated tests, consistency verifications, and performance impact assessments.

Here's a Python script demonstrating basic data validation techniques:

1. First, define the basic function:

```python
def validate_cleaned_data(file_path, sample_size=100):
    df = pd.read_csv(file_path)

    # Basic statistics
    print(f"Total samples: {len(df)}")
    print(
        f"Average text length: "
        f"{df['text'].str.len().mean():.2f}"
    )

    print(f"Unique samples: {df['text'].nunique()}")
```

2. Then, check for empty or very short texts:

```python
short_texts = df[df['text'].str.len() < 10]
print(
    f"Texts shorter than 10 characters: "
    f"{len(short_texts)}"
)
```

3. Sample for a manual review:

```python
    sample = df.sample(n=min(sample_size, len(df)))
    print("\nSample for manual review:")
    print(sample['text'].head())

    # Check for common issues
common_issues = {
        'special_chars': df['text'].str.contains(
            r'[^a-zA-Z0-9\s]'
        ),
        'numbers': df['text'].str.contains(r'\d'),
        'all_caps': df['text'].str.isupper()
}
```

```
        for issue, mask in common_issues.items():
            print(f"Samples with {issue}: {mask.sum()}")
```

4. Evaluate the impact on the model's perplexity:

```
        model = GPT4LMHeadModel.from_pretrained('GPT4')
        tokenizer = GPT4Tokenizer.from_pretrained('GPT4')

        def calculate_perplexity(text):
            inputs = tokenizer(
                text, return_tensors='pt', truncation=True,
                    max_length=1024
            )
            with torch.no_grad():
                outputs = model(inputs, labels=inputs['input_ids'])
            return torch.exp(outputs.loss).item()

        sample_perplexities = sample['text'].apply(
            calculate_perplexity)
        print(
            f"\nAverage perplexity on sample: "
            f"{sample_perplexities.mean():.2f}"
        )
```

5. Let's see an example:

```
        validate_cleaned_data('cleaned_data.csv')
```

The script defines a function called `validate_cleaned_data` that's designed to perform a basic quality assessment on a text dataset stored in a CSV file (presumably after some initial cleaning steps). It loads the data, calculates some basic statistics, checks for specific potential issues in the text content, provides a sample for manual inspection, and uses a pre-trained language model (hypothetically GPT-4) to evaluate the naturalness or quality of a sample of the text via perplexity.

The following issues are being checked for:

- Dataset size and basic properties:

    - **Issue**: Understanding the overall scale and basic characteristics of the dataset

    - **How the issue is checked**:

        - `len(df)`: Checks the total number of samples (rows) in the CSV.

        - `df['text'].str.len().mean()`: Calculates the average length of the text entries, which is useful to see if texts are generally long or short.

        - `df['text'].nunique()`: Counts the number of unique text entries. A low number compared to the total number of samples might indicate many duplicates.

- **Very short texts:**

  - **Issue**: Identifying text entries that might be too short to be meaningful or could represent errors/placeholders (e.g., empty strings mistakenly kept, such as *N/A*)

  - **How the issue is checked:**

    - `df[df['text'].str.len() < 10]`: Filters the DataFrame to find rows where the length of the string in the `text` column is less than 10 characters

    - `len(short_texts)`: Counts how many such short texts were found

- **Presence of special characters (non-alphanumeric, non-whitespace):**

  - **Issue**: Detecting text that contains characters other than letters, numbers, and standard whitespace. This could indicate leftover HTML tags, uncleaned punctuation, encoding issues, or other artifacts.

  - **How the issue is checked:**

    - `df['text'].str.contains(r'[^a-zA-Z0-9\s]')`: Uses a regular expression (`r'[^a-zA-Z0-9\s]'`) with pandas' `.str.contains()` method. The regex pattern `[^...]` matches any character *not* in the specified set (a-z, A-Z, 0-9, whitespace \s).

    - `mask.sum()`: Sums the resulting Boolean series (true=1, false=0) to count how many texts contain at least one such special character.

- **Presence of numbers:**

  - **Issue**: Identifying text entries that contain digits. Depending on the downstream task, numbers might be undesirable or require special handling.

  - **How the issue is checked:**

    - `df['text'].str.contains(r'\d')`: Uses the regular expression `\d` (which matches any digit) with `.str.contains()`

    - `mask.sum()`: Counts how many texts contain at least one digit

- **All caps text:**

  - **Issue**: Finding text written entirely in uppercase. This can sometimes indicate shouting, headings, or specific types of formatting that might affect model performance or analysis.

  - **How the issue is checked:**

    - `df['text'].str.isupper()`: Uses the pandas `.str.isupper()` string method, which returns `True` if all cased characters in the string are uppercase and there is at least one alphabetic character (i.e., a letter) that is uppercase and not just symbols or digits. If the string is all non-alphabetic (like numbers or punctuation), it will return `False`—even though those characters aren't lowercase either.

* `mask.sum()`: Counts how many texts are entirely in uppercase

- **General text quality/naturalness (via perplexity)**:

  - **Issue**: Assessing how typical or well-formed the text looks from the perspective of an LLM. Very high perplexity can indicate unnatural language, repetitive sequences, code snippets mixed with text, or data that is very different from the model's training data.

  - **How the issue is checked**:

    - **Sampling**: First, a random sample is taken from the dataset (`df.sample(...)`). Perplexity calculations can be computationally expensive, so they are often done on a representative sample rather than the whole dataset.

    - **Model loading**: A pre-trained language model (`GPT4LMHeadModel`) and its corresponding tokenizer (`GPT4Tokenizer`) are loaded. (Note: `'GPT4'` here is illustrative; you'd use actual model identifiers such as `'gpt2'` or `'bert-base-uncased'` from libraries such as Hugging Face Transformers).

    - **Perplexity calculation**: For each text in the sample, the `calculate_perplexity` function tokenizes the text, feeds it to the model, obtains the loss (a measure of how surprised the model was by the text), and calculates perplexity using `torch.exp(outputs.loss)`.

    - **Averaging**: The perplexities of all texts in the sample are averaged (`sample_perplexities.mean()`) to get a single score representing the sample's average quality according to the model.

- **Manual review facilitation**:

  - **Issue**: Catching unexpected or subtle issues not covered by automated checks. Human intuition is valuable.

  - **How the issue is checked**:

    - `sample = df.sample(...)`: Takes a random sample of the data

    - `print(sample['text'].head())`: Prints the first few text entries from that random sample, making it easy for a user running the script to quickly eyeball some examples

To ensure comprehensive quality assurance, you can do the following:

- Implement more sophisticated automated tests tailored to your specific data characteristics and cleaning rules.

- Develop a systematic process for manual review, including guidelines for human annotators to assess data quality consistently.

- Use a known synthetic dataset with known issues to benchmark and assess the performance of the pipeline.

- Compare the cleaned dataset against the original dataset to verify that no unintended data loss or alteration occurred during the cleaning process.

- Conduct regular audits of your data cleaning pipeline to identify any emerging issues or bias introduced during cleaning.

- Maintain detailed logs of the cleaning process, including any decisions made and their rationale, to ensure reproducibility and facilitate future improvements.

By implementing these measures, you can ensure that your cleaned dataset is of high quality and suitable for training robust LLMs.

Summary

In this chapter, we explored the critical process of data cleaning for LLM training. We discussed the importance of clean data in developing robust and reliable language models and covered common data quality issues specific to language datasets. We provided techniques to address these issues, including text preprocessing, handling multilingual and code-mixed data, and deduplication strategies for large text corpora.

We also delved into the implementation of automated data cleaning pipelines, which are essential for handling the massive datasets used in LLM training. Finally, we discussed data validation and quality assurance measures to ensure the effectiveness of the cleaning process.

In the next chapter, we will focus on the data augmentation pattern for LLMs.

Subscribe for a free eBook

New frameworks, evolving architectures, research drops, production breakdowns—AI_Distilled filters the noise into a weekly briefing for engineers and researchers working hands-on with LLMs and GenAI systems. Subscribe now and receive a free eBook, along with weekly insights that help you stay focused and informed. Subscribe at `https://packt.link/8Oz6Y` or scan the QR code below.

3

Data Augmentation

Data augmentation plays a pivotal role in enhancing the performance and generalization capabilities of LLMs. By artificially expanding the training dataset, we can expose our models to a wider range of linguistic variations and contexts, improving their ability to handle diverse inputs and generate more coherent and contextually appropriate outputs.

In the context of LLMs, data augmentation takes on unique challenges and opportunities. Unlike **image data**, where simple transformations such as rotation or flipping can create valid new samples, **text data** requires more nuanced approaches to maintain semantic integrity and linguistic coherence. The main goals of data augmentation for LLMs include increasing dataset size and diversity, addressing data imbalance and bias, improving model robustness to variations in input, and enhancing generalization to unseen data.

In *Figure 3.1*, I illustrate the key aspects of data augmentation.

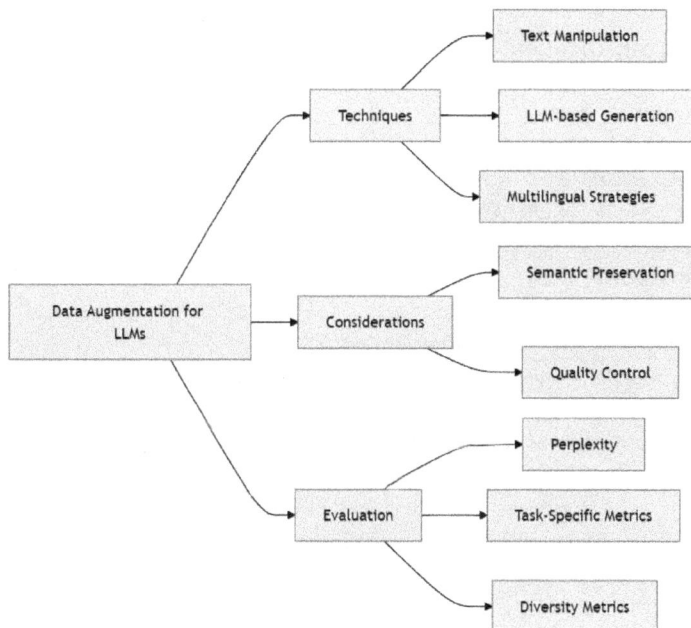

Figure 3.1 – Key elements of data augmentation

There are three main components, namely **Techniques**, **Considerations**, and **Evaluation**. Each has specific sub-components, which we'll cover in detail in this chapter.

By the end of this chapter, you'll have learned about the **data augmentation** pattern in depth, from increasing the diversity of your training dataset to maintaining its integrity:

- Text data augmentation techniques
- Leveraging existing LLMs for data generation
- Multilingual data augmentation strategies
- Semantic preservation in text augmentation
- Balancing augmentation and data quality
- Evaluating the impact of data augmentation

Text data augmentation techniques

Text data augmentation encompasses a wide range of techniques, from simple word-level manipulations to more complex semantic transformations.

Synonym replacement

This technique involves replacing words in the original text with their synonyms. We can use **WordNet**, a lexical database for the English language, to find synonyms:

```
def synonym_replacement(text, n=1):
    words = text.split()
    new_words = words.copy()
    random_word_list = list(
        set([word for word in words if word.isalnum()])
    )
    random.shuffle(random_word_list)
    num_replaced = 0

    for random_word in random_word_list:
        synonyms = get_synonyms(random_word)
        if len(synonyms) >= 1:
            synonym = random.choice(list(synonyms))
            new_words = [
                synonym if word == random_word else word
                for word in new_words
            ]
```

```
            num_replaced += 1
      if num_replaced >= n:
          break

   return ' '.join(new_words)
```

The `synonym_replacement` function takes a text input and replaces a specified number (the default is 1) of words with their synonyms. The default value of 1 is chosen to minimize text alteration, preserving meaning and readability while allowing easy experimentation. You can increase this number if you want more replacements.

The function splits the text into words, creates a list of unique alphanumeric words, shuffles this list, and then iterates through it. For each word, it attempts to find synonyms using an undefined `get_synonyms` function. If synonyms are found, it randomly selects one and replaces all occurrences of the original word in the text. The function keeps track of how many words have been replaced and stops when it reaches the specified number. Finally, it rejoins the modified words into a single string and returns it.

Back-translation

This method involves translating the text to another language and then back to the original language. It's particularly effective for introducing natural variations in sentence structure and word choice:

```
def back_translation(text, target_lang='fr'):
    translator = Translator()
    translated = translator.translate(text, dest=target_lang)
    back_translated = translator.translate(translated.text, dest='en')
    return back_translated.text
```

Text generation with T5

The **Text-To-Text Transfer Transformer** (**T5**) model, developed by Google Research, is a versatile **natural language processing** (**NLP**) model based on the transformer architecture. Its key innovation is framing all NLP tasks as text-to-text problems, allowing it to handle multiple tasks without task-specific architectures. Pre-trained on a large web text corpus using a "span corruption" objective, T5 is available in various sizes and has demonstrated powerful performance across a wide range of NLP tasks.

T5 handles a wide range of text-based tasks by framing them all as text-to-text problems. This means that irrespective of the task, whether it's summarization, translation, question answering, or classification, both the input and output are treated as text. This unified approach allows T5 to perform various tasks without needing task-specific modifications, making it highly adaptable for different use cases.

When it comes to data augmentation, T5 plays a key role by generating variations of existing text data, which is essential for expanding and diversifying datasets. Data augmentation is especially valuable when training machine learning models, as it helps them generalize better by exposing them to a wider variety of examples, reducing overfitting and improving robustness. Here's how T5 aids in data augmentation:

- **Paraphrasing**: T5 can rephrase sentences while maintaining their original meaning. For example, if the input is "The movie was boring," T5 could generate a paraphrased version such as "The film was dull." This variety in expression provides additional examples for a model to learn from, helping it generalize better to different ways of phrasing the same idea.

- **Synonym replacement**: T5 can replace words with their synonyms, creating slight variations in meaning while retaining the overall sentiment or context. For instance, from "The movie was long and tedious," T5 might generate "The film was lengthy and boring." This simple modification increases the diversity of the dataset, offering more training examples for models that rely on understanding slight variations in language.

- **Sentiment-based transformation**: T5 can also transform the sentiment of a sentence. For example, given a negative sentence such as "The movie was very disappointing," T5 can generate a neutral or positive version, such as "The movie had a slow start but improved later." This capability allows for the creation of multiple examples across different sentiment categories, which is particularly useful in tasks such as sentiment analysis, where a model needs to distinguish between positive, neutral, and negative sentiments.

- **Text expansion**: T5 can take a short sentence and expand it by adding more context, details, or descriptions. For instance, from the sentence "The event was great," T5 could generate a more detailed version such as "The event was great, with excellent speakers and engaging discussions." By adding more context, T5 provides additional variations of the sentence that help in training models to handle more complex inputs.

We can use a pre-trained T5 model to generate variations of input text. This method is particularly powerful as it can produce more diverse and contextually rich augmentations. Let's see this:

```
def t5_augmentation(text, model, tokenizer, num_return_sequences=1):
    input_ids = tokenizer.encode(
        f"paraphrase: {text}",
        return_tensors="pt",
        max_length=512,
        truncation=True
    )
    outputs = model.generate(
        input_ids=input_ids,
        max_length=150,
        num_return_sequences=num_return_sequences,
        num_beams=5,
```

```
        no_repeat_ngram_size=2,
        top_k=50,
        top_p=0.95,
    )
    return [
        tokenizer.decode(
            output, skip_special_tokens=True
        ) for output in outputs
    ]
```

This function takes a text input, a pre-trained T5 model, its tokenizer, and the number of paraphrases to generate (the default is 1). The default of 1 return sequence is chosen for simplicity, but you can request multiple paraphrases by increasing this value.

The function encodes the input text with a `"paraphrase:"` prefix, limiting it to `512` tokens. It then uses the model to generate paraphrases with a maximum length of `150` tokens. The generation process uses beam search with 5 beams, prevents repetition of 2-grams, and applies **top-k** (`50`) and **top-p** (`0.95`) **sampling** for diversity. The numerical parameters (`512, 150, 5, 2, 50, 0.95`) can also be adjusted based on specific use cases to control the length, diversity, and quality of the generated paraphrases.

The function decodes and returns the generated paraphrases, skipping any special tokens added during the process.

Using temperature control as an additional parameter in language generation systems allows fine-tuning the balance between creativity and coherence. Temperature is a scalar value, typically ranging from 0 to 1, that influences the probability distribution over the next token during generation. Low values (close to 0) concentrate the distribution, making the model more deterministic and coherent but potentially repetitive or conservative. High values (close to 1) flatten the distribution, increasing randomness and diversity at the cost of coherence.

Leveraging existing LLMs for data generation

One of the most powerful approaches to data augmentation for LLMs is to use existing models to generate new training examples. This technique, often referred to as **self-supervised learning** or **model-based data augmentation**, allows us to create vast amounts of diverse, high-quality training data.

We'll explore how to use **GPT-4o** and the **OpenAI API** for data generation:

```
def gpt4o_data_generation(prompt, num_samples=5):
    response = openai.ChatCompletion.create(
        model="gpt-4o",
        messages=[{"role": "user", "content": prompt}],
        max_tokens=150,
```

```
        n=num_samples,
        temperature=0.7,
    )
    return [choice.message.content.strip()
        for choice in response.choices
    ]
```

This function sends a single user message containing the provided prompt for a chat completion request. It limits the response to a maximum of 150 tokens, which balances between getting a substantive response and controlling the output length. The n parameter, set to num_samples, determines the number of alternative completions to generate. A temperature of 0.7 is used, which provides a balance between creativity and coherence in the generated text: high values increase randomness, while low values would make the output more deterministic. The function then extracts and returns the content of each generated completion, stripping any leading or trailing whitespace. These parameters (150 tokens, 0.7 temperature) can be adjusted based on specific needs for output length and creativity.

When using this approach, we need to consider the following:

- **Prompt engineering**: Crafting effective prompts is needed for generating relevant and diverse samples.

- **Quality control**: Implement filtering mechanisms to ensure the generated data meets your quality standards.

- **Diversity**: Use temperature and top-p sampling to control the randomness and diversity of generated samples.

We've explored data augmentation techniques using GPT-4o and examined essential considerations. Now, let's turn our attention to strategies for multilingual data augmentation.

Multilingual data augmentation strategies

For LLMs designed to handle multiple languages, multilingual data augmentation is essential. We can adapt our previous techniques to work across languages.

Cross-lingual back-translation

Translate the text into multiple languages before translating it back to the original language:

```
def cross_lingual_back_translation(text,
    target_langs=['fr', 'de', 'es']
):
    translator = Translator()
    augmented_texts = []
```

```
    for lang in target_langs:
        translated = translator.translate(text, dest=lang)
        back_translated = translator.translate(
            translated.text, dest='en'
        )
        augmented_texts.append(back_translated.text)
    return augmented_texts
```

The cross_lingual_back_translation function takes a text input and generates augmented versions of it by first translating it into multiple target languages (defaulting to French, German, and Spanish) and then back to English. The function uses the Translator object to perform these translations, storing each back-translated version in a list, which is returned as the output.

Multilingual T5 augmentation

You can use a multilingual T5 model to generate paraphrases in different languages:

```
def multilingual_t5_augmentation(
    text, model, tokenizer, target_langs=['fr', 'de', 'es']
):
    augmented_texts = []
    for lang in target_langs:
        input_ids = tokenizer.encode(
            f"translate English to {lang}: {text}",
            return_tensors="pt", max_length=512,
            truncation=True
        )
        outputs = model.generate(input_ids=input_ids, max_length=150)
        translated = tokenizer.decode(outputs[0],
            skip_special_tokens=True)
        augmented_texts.append(translated)
    return augmented_texts
```

The multilingual_t5_augmentation function uses a T5 model to augment a given text by translating it into multiple target languages (defaulting to French, German, and Spanish). For each target language, it encodes the text with a prompt for translation, generates the translated output using the model, and decodes the result. The translated texts are collected in a list and returned as the augmented versions of the original text.

Semantic preservation in text augmentation

Maintaining semantic integrity is crucial when augmenting data for LLMs. We must ensure that our techniques don't alter the original meaning of the text.

Use of sentence embeddings

By comparing the **sentence embeddings** of the original and augmented texts, you can ensure **semantic similarity**:

```
def semantic_similarity(original, augmented, model):
    original_embedding = model.encode(original)
    augmented_embedding = model.encode(augmented)
    similarity = cosine_similarity(
        [original_embedding], [augmented_embedding]
    )[0][0]
    return similarity

def filter_by_semantic_similarity(
    original, augmented_list, model, threshold=0.8
):
    return [
        aug for aug in augmented_list
        if semantic_similarity(original, aug, model) >= threshold
    ]
```

We define two functions for measuring and filtering text based on semantic similarity:

- `semantic_similarity(original, augmented, model)` calculates the semantic similarity between two texts using the cosine similarity of their embeddings. It uses a provided model (probably a sentence embedding model) to encode the original and augmented texts into vector representations. The cosine similarity between these vectors is then computed, resulting in a value between -1 and 1, where 1 indicates perfect similarity.

- `filter_by_semantic_similarity(original, augmented_list, model, threshold=0.8)` filters a list of augmented texts based on their semantic similarity to the original. The `semantic_similarity` function compares each augmented text with the original. The default threshold is set to 0.8: by default, it will keep only the augmented texts that have a similarity of 0.8 or higher to the original. This threshold is commonly used in NLP tasks, as it typically indicates a strong semantic similarity while allowing some variation. It can be adjusted based on how strict or lenient you want the filtering to be: a higher threshold will result in more similar (but possibly fewer) augmentations; a lower threshold will allow more diverse (but potentially less relevant) augmentations.

Contextual word embeddings for synonym replacement

You can use **contextual word embeddings** to find more appropriate synonyms based on the context. Contextual word embeddings refer to the use of word representations generated by language models that capture the meaning of a word within its specific sentence or passage, rather than treating the word as having a fixed meaning. Unlike traditional static embeddings where a word has the same vector regardless of context, contextual embeddings assign different vectors to the same word depending on its surrounding words. This allows for more accurate synonym replacement as the chosen synonym aligns not only with the dictionary meaning but also with how the word is used in a particular context. For example, the word "bank" in "river bank" versus "savings bank" would be represented differently, leading to contextually appropriate synonym suggestions such as "shore" or "financial institution," respectively. The following code snippet shows how it works:

```
def contextual_synonym_replacement(text, model, tokenizer, n=1):
    words = text.split()
    new_words = words.copy()

    for i in range(n):
        word_index = random.randint(0, len(words) - 1)
        original_word = words[word_index]

        inputs = tokenizer(text, return_tensors="pt")
        with torch.no_grad():
            outputs = model(inputs)

        word_embedding = outputs.last_hidden_state[0, word_index]
        similar_words = find_similar_words(
            word_embedding, model, tokenizer
        )

        if similar_words:
            new_words[word_index] = random.choice(similar_words)

    return ' '.join(new_words)
```

This function performs context-aware word replacement using a language model:

1. It takes a text input, a pre-trained language model, its tokenizer, and the number of words to replace (the default is 1).

2. The text is split into words, and a copy is made for modification.

3.   The function iterates n times (the default is 1). It does the following each time:

   I.   Randomly selects a word index

   II.   Tokenizes the entire text

   III.   Runs it through the model to get contextualized embeddings

   IV.   Extracts the embedding of the chosen word

   V.   Finds similar words based on this embedding (using an undefined `find_similar_words` function)

   VI.   If similar words are found, it randomly chooses one to replace the original

4.   Finally, it joins the modified words back into a string and returns it.

The default n=1 is chosen to make minimal changes while still introducing variation. This preserves most of the original meaning and structure. You can increase n to get more replacements, but higher values might alter the text's meaning more significantly.

This method is more context-aware than simple synonym replacement as it considers the word's usage in the full text when finding replacements. The exact behavior will depend on the model and tokenizer used, as well as the implementation of the `find_similar_words` function.

Balancing augmentation and data quality

While data augmentation can significantly improve LLM performance, we need to strike a balance between quantity and quality.

You should limit the proportion of augmented data in your training set. A common practice is to start with a 1:1 ratio of original to augmented data and adjust based on model performance.

Quality filtering

You can implement quality checks to filter out low-quality augmented samples:

```
def quality_filter(
    augmented_texts, original_text,
    similarity_threshold=0.8, perplexity_threshold=100
):
    filtered_texts = []
    for aug_text in augmented_texts:
        if (
            semantic_similarity(
                original_text, aug_text, similarity_model
            ) >= similarity_threshold and
```

```
        calculate_perplexity(
            aug_text, perplexity_model
        ) <= perplexity_threshold
    ):
        filtered_texts.append(aug_text)
    return filtered_texts
```

Human-in-the-loop validation

For critical applications, incorporate human validation into your augmentation pipeline.

Human-in-the-loop (**HITL**) validation is a control mechanism used in AI pipelines where humans are deliberately inserted into automated workflows to ensure correctness, especially in tasks involving subjective judgment, sensitive content, or critical decision-making. This is particularly important in applications where data quality directly affects safety, fairness, or compliance—for example, healthcare diagnostics, legal document analysis, or autonomous systems. In the context of data augmentation, where the goal is to expand the training dataset by generating variations of existing samples, HITL is used to validate whether the generated samples are coherent, accurate, and aligned with the intended label or task:

```
def human_validation(augmented_texts):
    validated_texts = []
    for text in augmented_texts:
        if input(
            f"Is this text valid? (y/n)\n{text}\n"
        ).lower() == 'y':
            validated_texts.append(text)
    return validated_texts
```

This function is designed to manually validate a list of augmented text samples by soliciting binary feedback—yes or no—from a human operator. Its presence within an augmentation pipeline acknowledges that not all automatically generated data can be trusted at face value. The decision to retain or discard a given sample is made interactively, reinforcing human oversight in tasks where semantic integrity is non-negotiable.

Each iteration of the function's loop represents a decision point. The human validator is shown the generated text and asked to assess whether it meets the expected criteria. These criteria are typically based on task-specific requirements such as grammaticality, semantic equivalence to the original data, tone appropriateness, or domain alignment. For example, in a medical text classification task, a paraphrased sentence must preserve all critical clinical entities. A slight shift in terminology introduced by an augmentation technique could mislead the model if not caught during validation. This is where human evaluation becomes indispensable.

The logic behind converting the input to lowercase is to handle inconsistent user input. Whether the user types Y, y, or any other casing, the comparison becomes case-agnostic. Only if the input is equivalent to y does the function accept the sample. This binary check is deliberately strict to prevent ambiguous approvals. The rejected samples are silently discarded and not logged or returned, implying that any further inspection or correction of rejected samples would need to be implemented separately.

The function concludes by returning a list of only those samples that have been explicitly validated. This output can then be used to expand the training dataset with higher confidence in the integrity of the new data points. Importantly, this approach does not replace automated quality checks but supplements them in high-stakes applications. HITL validation is particularly useful when deploying models in environments where false positives or negatives carry high costs, such as legal recommendation systems, fraud detection, or autonomous navigation. The manual validation process helps to mitigate risks that stem from over-reliance on generative augmentation methods that lack explicit semantic guarantees.

In a larger system, this kind of function would usually be embedded in a broader workflow where automated filters screen out obviously low-quality or irrelevant augmentations first. The human validator would only evaluate the borderline or high-impact cases. For operational efficiency, the interaction would typically be handled via a web interface or integrated annotation tool rather than a command-line prompt. However, the function demonstrates the principle in its simplest form: human judgment is used as the final arbiter of quality before incorporating augmented data into model training.

Evaluating the impact of data augmentation

To assess the effectiveness of our data augmentation techniques, we need to assess their impact on LLM performance.

Perplexity

You can measure a model's perplexity (see *Chapter 2*) on a held-out test set before and after data augmentation to assess whether it has improved the model's ability to predict unseen text:

```
def evaluate_perplexity(model, tokenizer, test_data):
    model.eval()
    total_loss = 0
    total_tokens = 0

    with torch.no_grad():
        for text in test_data:
            inputs = tokenizer(
                text, return_tensors="pt"
            ).to(model.device)
            outputs = model(inputs, labels=inputs["input_ids"])
            total_loss += (
                outputs.loss.item() * inputs["input_ids"].size(1)
```

```
        )
            total_tokens += inputs["input_ids"].size(1)

    perplexity = math.exp(total_loss / total_tokens)
    return perplexity
```

This function, `evaluate_perplexity`, calculates the perplexity of a language model on a given test dataset. Here's a breakdown:

1. It takes a pre-trained language model, its tokenizer, and a test dataset as input.
2. The model is set to evaluation mode to disable dropout and other training-specific behavior.
3. It initializes variables to track the total loss and total number of tokens processed.
4. For each text in the test data, the following is carried out:

    I.   The text is tokenized and converted to tensors.
    II. The model processes the input, calculating the loss.
    III. The loss is accumulated, weighted by the number of tokens in the input.

5. After processing all texts, it calculates the perplexity using the following formula: `exp(total_loss / total_tokens)`.

This implementation uses the model in a zero-shot manner, treating each input as both the context and the target to predict. The use of `torch.no_grad()` ensures that no gradients are computed, making the evaluation more efficient.

This function assumes the model and data are compatible (i.e., the model can handle the maximum sequence length of the data). In practice, you might need to add checks or truncation to handle very long sequences.

Task-specific metrics

You can evaluate the model on downstream tasks relevant to your use case, such as text classification or question answering:

```
def evaluate_classification(
    model, tokenizer, test_data, test_labels
):
    model.eval()
    predictions = []

    with torch.no_grad():
        for text in test_data:
            inputs = tokenizer(
```

```
                    text, return_tensors="pt"
                ).to(model.device)
                outputs = model(inputs)
                predictions.append(torch.argmax(outputs.logits).item())

        accuracy = accuracy_score(test_labels, predictions)
        f1 = f1_score(test_labels, predictions, average='weighted')
        return accuracy, f1
```

This function assesses the performance of a classification model on a test dataset:

1. It takes a pre-trained classification model, its tokenizer, test data (text), and corresponding test labels as inputs.

2. The model is set to evaluation mode to disable dropout and other training-specific behavior.

3. It processes each text in the test data, tokenizing it and using the model to make predictions.

4. After processing all texts, it calculates two evaluation metrics:

   - **Accuracy**: The proportion of correct predictions out of all predictions made.

   - **F1 score**: A balanced measure of the model's precision and recall. The F1 score is the harmonic mean of **precision** (the ratio of true positive predictions to all positive predictions) and **recall** (the ratio of true positive predictions to all actual positive instances).

   The F1 score formula is *F1 = 2 * (precision * recall) / (precision + recall)*.

   The F1 score ranges from 0 to 1, where 1 indicates perfect precision and recall. It's particularly useful for imbalanced datasets where accuracy alone might be misleading. The weighted average calculates F1 for each class and averages them, weighted by the number of instances in each class.

5. The function returns both the accuracy and F1 score, providing a more comprehensive evaluation of the model's performance across potentially imbalanced classes.

This implementation also uses `torch.no_grad()` for efficiency and assumes that the necessary scikit-learn metrics are imported. In practice, you might want to add error handling for unexpected model outputs or mismatched prediction/label counts.

Diversity metrics

It's important to assess the diversity of your augmented dataset:

```
def calculate_diversity_metrics(texts):
    all_words = [word for text in texts for word in text.split()]
    vocab_size = len(set(all_words))
```

```
all_trigrams = [text[i:i+3] for text in texts
    for i in range(len(text)-2)]
unique_trigrams = len(set(all_trigrams))

return {
    "vocabulary_size": vocab_size,
    "unique_trigrams": unique_trigrams
}
```

This function takes a collection of texts as input and computes **diversity metrics**. Once this has been done, this function returns a dictionary with these two metrics:

- **Vocabulary size** (ranging from 1 to the total number of words): This gives an idea of lexical diversity. A high number suggests diverse word usage across the texts. This metric splits each text into words, combines all words from all texts, and then counts the number of unique words using a **set**. In this context, a set refers to a data structure that automatically removes duplicate elements.

- **Unique trigrams** (ranging from 1 to the total number of trigrams): These indicate character-level diversity. A high number suggests varied character sequences, potentially indicating diverse sentence structures or word choices. This metric creates trigrams (sequences of three characters) from each text and counts the number of unique trigrams using a set that only contains unique elements.

These metrics are useful for comparing the diversity of original texts versus augmented texts or for assessing the variety in a dataset. However, the results should be interpreted in context, as high diversity might indicate incoherence or noise in the data.

By systematically applying these techniques, we can quantify the impact of our data augmentation strategies on LLM performance and make informed decisions about which techniques to use and how to fine-tune our augmentation pipeline.

Summary

In this chapter, we explored advanced data augmentation techniques for LLMs, covering text manipulation methods, leveraging existing models for data generation, multilingual strategies, semantic preservation, quality control, and several metrics. We also discussed the importance of balancing augmentation with data quality and provided practical Python implementations for various techniques.

In the next chapter, we'll focus on handling large datasets for LLM training.

Get This Book's PDF Version and Exclusive Extras

UNLOCK NOW

Scan the QR code (or go to `packtpub.com/unlock`). Search for this book by name, confirm the edition, and then follow the steps on the page.

Note: Keep your invoice handly. Purchase made directly from packt don't require one.

4

Handling Large Datasets for LLM Training

In this chapter, you'll learn advanced techniques for managing and processing massive datasets essential for training state-of-the-art LLMs. We'll explore the unique challenges posed by large-scale language datasets and provide you with practical solutions to overcome them.

The aim of this chapter is to equip you with the knowledge and tools to efficiently handle data at scale, enabling you to train more powerful and effective LLMs.

In this chapter, we'll be covering the following topics:

- Challenges of large datasets
- Data sampling techniques
- Distributed data processing
- Data sharding and parallelization strategies
- Efficient data storage formats
- Streaming data processing for continuous LLM training
- Memory-efficient data loading techniques

Challenges of large datasets

Training LLMs requires enormous datasets, often in the terabytes or even petabytes range. This scale introduces several challenges:

- **Storage requirements**: Datasets can exceed the capacity of single machines, necessitating distributed storage solutions.

- **Input/output (I/O) bottlenecks**: Reading large volumes of data can become a significant bottleneck, limiting training speed.

- **Preprocessing overhead**: Tokenization and other preprocessing steps can be time-consuming at scale due to the computational overhead of processing large volumes of text data through multiple sequential operations. The challenge arises from having to perform multiple steps on each piece of text – tokenization, normalization, cleaning, language detection, and other transformations – multiplied across millions or billions of text samples. This process is inherently sequential (each step depends on the previous one), requires CPU/memory resources, and can involve complex operations such as **regular expressions (regexes)**, dictionary lookups, and language-specific rules. When dealing with multilingual or code-mixed data, the complexity increases further as different language rules need to be applied, and additional steps such as script normalization or language detection are required for each text segment, making the preprocessing pipeline a significant bottleneck in large-scale **natural language processing (NLP)** systems.

- **Memory constraints**: Loading entire datasets into memory is often infeasible, requiring streaming or batching approaches.

- **Data quality and diversity**: Ensuring dataset quality and representativeness becomes more challenging as size increases.

To address these challenges, we need to employ sophisticated data-handling techniques. Let's explore a Python implementation using the **Datasets** library from Hugging Face, which is designed to handle large-scale datasets efficiently:

```python
from datasets import load_dataset, Dataset
import psutil

def load_and_process_large_dataset(dataset_name, num_proc):
    # Load the dataset
    dataset = load_dataset(dataset_name, streaming=True)

    # Define a preprocessing function
    def preprocess_function(examples):
        # Implement your preprocessing logic here
        return examples

    # Apply preprocessing in parallel
    processed_dataset = dataset.map(
        preprocess_function,
        batched=True,
        num_proc=num_proc,
```

```
        remove_columns=dataset["train"].column_names
    )

    return processed_dataset
#Determine the number of CPU cores for parallel processing
num_cores = psutil.cpu_count(logical=False)

#Load and process a large dataset (e.g., C4 dataset)
large_dataset = load_and_process_large_dataset("c4",
    num_proc=num_cores)

#Print the first few examples
for example in large_dataset["train"].take(5):
    print(example)
```

In this code, we use the Datasets library to efficiently load and process a large dataset (in this case, the C4 dataset). The num_proc parameter specifies the number of processor cores to use for parallel processing in the dataset mapping operation. When preprocessing large datasets, using multiple CPU cores through parallel processing can significantly speed up the operation. For example, if num_proc=4, the preprocessing function will be executed on four processor cores simultaneously, processing different batches of data in parallel rather than sequentially.

To better understand the context in which large datasets are used, it is helpful to explore a specific example. One such dataset used in the preceding code snippet is the **Colossal Clean Crawled Corpus (C4)** dataset, which plays a significant role in training modern LLMs.

The **C4** dataset is a massive, cleaned web-crawled text corpus created by Google for training LLMs. Containing approximately 750 GB of English-language text, C4 is derived from Common Crawl data and has undergone extensive filtering to remove duplicates, non-English content, and offensive material. It comes in several variants, including a standard cleaned version, an unfiltered version, and a subset focused on news-like content. While publicly available, accessing C4 requires some effort, typically through Google Cloud Storage or libraries such as Hugging Face datasets. Despite its cleaning process, C4 still has some limitations regarding content quality and potential biases, which researchers should consider when using it for model training. Nevertheless, it remains a valuable resource for NLP tasks and has been instrumental in training prominent models such as **Text-to-Text Transfer Transformer (T5)** and **Language Model for Dialogue Applications (LaMDA)**.

We employ streaming to avoid loading the entire dataset into memory at once. The num_proc parameter is set to the number of physical CPU cores to maximize parallel processing efficiency.

The preprocess_function function is where you implement dataset-specific preprocessing logic. This function is applied in parallel across the dataset, significantly speeding up preprocessing for large datasets.

You can also use a GPU for the task. See the following code example (keep in mind that while GPU-based preprocessing is particularly beneficial for operations such as tokenization and embedding generation, it may not significantly accelerate simpler text manipulations):

```python
import torch
from datasets import load_dataset
from torch.utils.data import DataLoader
from transformers import AutoTokenizer

def load_and_process_dataset(dataset_name, batch_size):
    dataset = load_dataset(dataset_name, streaming=True)
    tokenizer = AutoTokenizer.from_pretrained("bert-base-uncased")

    def preprocess(examples):
        return tokenizer(
            examples["text"], padding="max_length",
            truncation=True, return_tensors="pt"
        )

    def process_batch(batch):
        return {k: v.to(device) for k, v in preprocess(batch).items()}

    return DataLoader(
        dataset["train"].map(process_batch),
        batch_size=batch_size, num_workers=2,
        pin_memory=True
    )

device = torch.device("cuda" if torch.cuda.is_available() else "cpu")
dataloader = load_and_process_dataset("c4", batch_size=32)

for i, batch in enumerate(dataloader):
    if i >= 5: break
    print(f"Batch {i}:", {k: v.shape for k, v in batch.items()})
```

This code uses the PyTorch and Hugging Face libraries to process a dataset (for example, C4) with GPU acceleration. It employs a data loader for efficient batch processing, moves data to GPU memory, and uses a pre-trained tokenizer. The main GPU benefits come from parallel batch processing and GPU-accelerated tokenization. While this setup enables GPU usage, the most significant GPU advantages typically occur during model training or inference rather than preprocessing.

Data sampling techniques

Data sampling is a practical approach to reducing the size of large datasets without sacrificing representativeness. Several techniques exist, each with specific use cases and trade-offs. **Random sampling** selects data points uniformly at random from the dataset. It is simple and effective when the data is independently and identically distributed, but it may miss important subgroups if the data is imbalanced. **Systematic sampling** selects every kth item from a list after a random starting point. It is more structured than random sampling and can be useful when the data is ordered in a meaningful way, though it risks introducing bias if the ordering aligns with hidden periodic patterns. **Reservoir sampling** is designed for streaming of unknown-size datasets. It maintains a fixed-size sample while iterating through the data sequentially and ensures that every item has an equal probability of being included. This is particularly useful in online or incremental learning scenarios where data arrives in continuous flows.

Due to the length constraints of this chapter, we focus only on **stratified sampling**, a technique that preserves the proportional representation of subgroups within a dataset. It is especially suitable when certain attributes—such as label classes, sentence lengths, or metadata categories—are known to affect model performance and need to be maintained in the sampled subset. In NLP, text length is a common stratification variable, given its impact on model input dynamics.

The following implementation demonstrates how to apply stratified sampling based on text length. It divides the dataset into percentile-based strata and samples proportionally from each stratum to create a subset that retains the length distribution of the full dataset:

```python
import numpy as np
from datasets import Dataset

def stratified_length_sampling(
    dataset, num_samples, num_strata=10
):
    # Calculate text lengths
    lengths = [len(example['text']) for example in dataset]

    # Create strata based on text length
    strata_bounds = np.percentile(
        lengths, np.linspace(0, 100, num_strata + 1)
    )

    sampled_data = []
    for i in range(num_strata):
        stratum = [
            example for example in dataset
            if strata_bounds[i] <= len(example['text']) < \
                strata_bounds[i+1]
```

```
        ]
        stratum_samples = np.random.choice(
            stratum,
            size=num_samples // num_strata,
            replace=False
        )
        sampled_data.extend(stratum_samples)

    return Dataset.from_dict({
        key: [example[key] for example in sampled_data]
        for key in dataset[0].keys()
    })
#Usage
sampled_dataset = stratified_length_sampling(large_dataset,
    num_samples=100000)
```

This stratified sampling technique ensures that we maintain a representative distribution of text lengths in our sampled dataset. We use 10 strata (`num_strata=10`) to balance granularity and computational efficiency. Adjust this value based on your specific dataset characteristics and sampling requirements.

As datasets grow in size and complexity, single-machine processing becomes a bottleneck in both speed and scalability. Techniques such as data sampling offer partial relief, but they do not resolve the computational limitations inherent in centralized architectures. To address these constraints, the next section introduces distributed data processing, where computation is spread across multiple machines or nodes to improve throughput, reduce latency, and support parallel workflows required for large-scale LLM training pipelines.

Distributed data processing

For truly massive datasets, distributed processing becomes necessary. Here's an example using **Dask**, a flexible library for parallel computing in Python (https://www.dask.org/).

Dask and Apache Spark are both distributed computing frameworks, but their main differences lie in their architecture and use cases. Spark is built around the concept of **resilient distributed datasets (RDDs)** and requires a cluster setup, making it ideal for large-scale production data processing. Dask, on the other hand, is designed to integrate seamlessly with the Python ecosystem and can scale from a single laptop to a cluster, using familiar APIs that mirror NumPy, pandas, and scikit-learn. While Spark excels at batch processing of massive datasets, Dask is more flexible for interactive computing and scientific workflows, particularly when working with Python-native libraries and when you need to scale up existing Python code with minimal modifications.

Let's get back to our code:

```python
import dask.dataframe as dd
from dask.distributed import Client

def distributed_preprocessing(data_path, num_partitions):
    # Initialize Dask client
    client = Client()

    # Read the dataset into a Dask DataFrame
    df = dd.read_csv(data_path, blocksize="64MB")

    # Repartition the data for better distribution
    df = df.repartition(npartitions=num_partitions)

    # Define preprocessing function
    def preprocess(text):
        # Implement your preprocessing logic here
        return processed_text

    # Apply preprocessing in parallel
    df['processed_text'] = df['text'].map(preprocess)

    # Trigger computation and return results
    result = df.compute()

    client.close()
    return result

#Usage
processed_data = distributed_preprocessing(
    "path/to/large/dataset.csv", num_partitions=100
)
```

In this example, we use Dask to distribute the preprocessing workload across multiple machines or cores. The num_partitions parameter (set to 100) determines the level of parallelism and should be adjusted based on your available computational resources and dataset size.

Data sharding and parallelization strategies

Data sharding refers to the technique of breaking up a large dataset into smaller, more manageable pieces, known as "shards," which are then distributed across multiple machines or storage systems. Each shard can be processed independently, making it easier to handle large datasets, especially those that don't fit into the memory of a single machine. This approach is widely used in machine learning to distribute the processing of large datasets, thereby allowing for the training of larger models or faster computation.

Data sharding enables more efficient use of computational resources as each shard can be processed independently, and the results can be aggregated later.

However, careful consideration must be given to ensuring that the sharding strategy maintains the integrity and representativeness of the data distribution across all shards to avoid biases or inconsistencies in the trained model.

Here's an example of a sharding strategy:

```python
import hashlib

def shard_data(dataset, num_shards):
    shards = [[] for _ in range(num_shards)]

    for item in dataset:
        # Use a hash function to determine the shard
        shard_index = int(
            hashlib.md5(
                item['id'].encode()
            ).hexdigest(), 16
        ) % num_shards
        shards[shard_index].append(item)

    return shards

#Usage
sharded_data = shard_data(large_dataset, num_shards=10)
```

This sharding strategy uses a hash function to distribute data items across shards. The num_shards parameter (set to 10) should be adjusted based on your infrastructure and parallelization needs.

The `shard_data` function distributes items from a dataset into a specified number of shards by applying a consistent hashing scheme based on each item's unique identifier. It initializes a list of empty lists, each representing a shard, and for every item in the input dataset, it calculates a shard index using the **Message Digest Algorithm 5 (MD5)** hash of the item's `'id'` field. The hash output is converted to an integer and taken modulo the number of shards to ensure uniform distribution across shards. This method guarantees that items with the same ID are consistently mapped to the same shard across executions, which is useful for tasks such as distributed storage or parallel processing where determinism and balance are important.

Sharding strategies are chosen based on the nature of the data and expected query patterns, with each approach offering distinct trade-offs in scalability, performance, and complexity:

- **Hash sharding**: Suitable for uniformly distributed data by mapping keys through a hash function to distribute load evenly across shards

- **Range sharding**: Effective for ordered datasets such as time-series logs, where each shard holds a contiguous range of data values

- **Geographic sharding**: Designed to optimize location-based queries by partitioning data according to geographical regions

- **Key-value sharding**: Enables manual control of hotspots by assigning specific key ranges or values to defined shards

- **Directory-based sharding**: Supports dynamic shard allocation using a lookup service to determine data placement, adapting to changes in data distribution

- **Consistent hashing**: Minimizes data movement when the number of shards changes, maintaining stability and reducing rebalancing overhead

- **Round-robin sharding**: Distributes data sequentially across shards, providing simplicity but poor performance for range-based queries

- **Workload-based sharding**: Balances access load by assigning high-traffic data to separate shards based on observed query patterns

- **Composite sharding**: Combines multiple strategies to support complex systems with diverse data types and query needs

- **Tag-based sharding**: Categorizes data based on labels such as user roles or data categories, supporting domain-specific partitioning strategies

For the preceding code block, we can also define the following function as the main orchestrator to process and aggregate shards:

```
def process_with_sharding(
    dataset: List[Dict], num_shards: int
) -> List[Dict]:
    # Step 1: Shard the data
    shards = shard_data(dataset, num_shards)

    # Step 2: Process shards in parallel
    with ProcessPoolExecutor(max_workers=num_shards) as executor:
        processed_shards = list(executor.map(process_shard, shards))

    # Step 3: Aggregate results
    aggregated_results = []
    for shard_results in processed_shards:
        aggregated_results.extend(shard_results)
```

The `process_with_sharding` function takes a dataset represented as a list of dictionaries and divides it into a specified number of shards using the `shard_data` function. It then uses `ProcessPoolExecutor` with as many workers as shards to process each shard concurrently by applying the `process_shard` function in parallel. After all shards have been processed, it aggregates the individual results from each shard into a single list by iterating over the processed shards and extending the final result list with their contents.

Once data has been effectively partitioned and distributed for parallel processing, attention must then turn to how it is physically stored and accessed—bringing us to the choice of efficient storage formats.

Efficient data storage formats

Choosing the right storage format can significantly impact data loading and processing speed.

As an example, we can use **Apache Parquet** (`https://parquet.apache.org/`), a columnar storage format that's particularly efficient for large datasets.

Here's a table comparing different column formats and their characteristics for storing large language datasets:

Feature	CSV	JSON	Apache Parquet	Apache Arrow
Storage type	Row-based	Row-based	Columnar	Columnar
Compression	Basic	Poor	Excellent	Excellent
Query speed	Slow	Slow	Fast	Very fast
Nested structures	No	Yes	Yes	Yes

Feature	CSV	JSON	Apache Parquet	Apache Arrow
Schema support	No	Limited	Yes	Yes
Random access	Poor	Poor	Good	Excellent
Memory efficiency	Poor	Poor	Good	Excellent
Python integration	Simple	Simple	Good (via PyArrow)	Native
Typical use case	Small datasets	API responses	Large analytics	In-memory processing
Loading speed	Slow	Medium	Fast	Very fast
NLP feature support	Basic	Good	Excellent	Excellent
Cross-platform	Yes	Yes	Yes	Yes
Metadata support	No	Limited	Yes	Yes

Table 4.1 – Characteristics of different column formats

This table highlights why Parquet is often preferred for LLM datasets due to its columnar storage format, efficient compression, and strong support for complex data structures commonly found in NLP tasks.

Here's an example of how data is typically structured in Apache Parquet columns for an NLP dataset:

Column Name	Data Type	Example Values
`text_id`	Integer	`1, 2, 3, 4`
`Text`	String	`"This is sample text", "Another example"`
`Tokens`	List[String]	`["This", "is", "sample", "text"],` `["Another", "example"]`
`Embeddings`	List[Float]	`[0.1, 0.2, 0.3], [0.4, 0.5, 0.6]`
`Metadata`	Struct	`{"lang": "en", "source": "web"}, {"lang":` `"fr", "source": "news"}`
`Labels`	Integer	`1, 0, 1, 0`
`Timestamp`	Timestamp	`2024-01-01 10:30:00, 2024-01-01 10:31:00`
`language_score`	Float	`0.95, 0.87, 0.92`
`Entities`	List[Struct]	`[{"text": "Google", "type": "ORG"},` `{"text": "New York", "type": "LOC"}]`
`doc_stats`	Struct	`{"word_count": 150, "char_count": 750,` `"sentence_count": 8}`

Table 4.2 – Structure of data in Apache Parquet columns

Each column is stored separately and can be efficiently compressed and accessed independently, which is particularly useful for large-scale NLP processing.

The following code snippet uses the PyArrow library to convert a dataset represented as a list of Python dictionaries into a Parquet file and read it back:

```python
import pyarrow as pa
import pyarrow.parquet as pq

def convert_to_parquet(dataset, output_path):
    # Convert dataset to Arrow Table
    table = pa.Table.from_pydict(dataset[0])

    # Write to Parquet file
    pq.write_table(table, output_path)

def read_from_parquet(file_path):
    # Read Parquet file
    table = pq.read_table(file_path)

    # Convert back to dictionary
    return table.to_pydict()

#Usage
convert_to_parquet(large_dataset, "large_dataset.parquet")
loaded_dataset = read_from_parquet("large_dataset.parquet")
```

In the preceding snippet, the `convert_to_parquet` function takes a dataset and an output file path, converts the first dictionary in the dataset to a PyArrow Table using `pa.Table.from_pydict`, and writes it to a Parquet file with `pq.write_table`. The `read_from_parquet` function reads a Parquet file from the specified path into a PyArrow Table using `pq.read_table` and then converts it back into a Python dictionary using `table.to_pydict`. In the usage example, a variable `large_dataset` is serialized to `"large_dataset.parquet"` and then deserialized back into `loaded_dataset`.

Parquet offers several advantages for LLM datasets:

- Columnar storage for efficient querying
- Compression to reduce storage requirements
- Support for complex nested structures common in NLP data

While previous sections have addressed methods for managing large-scale static datasets through sampling, distributed computation, and optimized storage strategies, these approaches assume a finite and well-defined corpus. However, training scenarios increasingly involve continuous inflow of data, such as user interactions, real-time telemetry, or evolving content streams. These dynamic contexts require a shift from traditional data pipelines to architectures capable of handling real-time ingestion and processing. The following section introduces streaming data processing as a necessary evolution for sustaining long-context, adaptive training regimes in LLMs.

Streaming data processing for continuous LLM training

For scenarios where new data is constantly being generated, streaming processing allows for continuous model updates. Here's an example using **Apache Kafka** (`https://kafka.apache.org/`) and **Faust** (`https://faust.readthedocs.io/en/latest/`).

Apache Kafka is a distributed streaming platform that serves as the backbone for building real-time data pipelines and streaming applications. It uses a **publish-subscribe** (**pub-sub**) model where data producers send messages to topics and consumers read from these topics, allowing for scalable, fault-tolerant data distribution across multiple brokers. When combined with async processing, these technologies enable systems to handle massive amounts of data in real time without blocking operations. Multiple brokers in Kafka provide redundancy and load balancing, ensuring high availability and throughput. This architecture is particularly useful in scenarios requiring real-time data processing, such as log aggregation, metrics collection, stream processing, and event sourcing.

Faust, on the other hand, is a Python-based stream processing library designed to handle real-time data processing tasks by treating data as continuous streams of events. Similar to Kafka Streams but written in Python, Faust enables developers to build streaming applications that can process, transform, and analyze data in real time. It provides high-level abstractions for working with streams, making it easier to implement complex streaming workflows while maintaining the simplicity and expressiveness of Python. Faust internally uses modern Python features such as `async/await` and leverages the power of Python's asyncio library for handling concurrent operations efficiently.

The following code defines a simple real-time data processing application using Faust, a Python stream processing library built on top of Kafka. It demonstrates how to consume messages from a Kafka topic, apply preprocessing logic, and prepare data for downstream tasks such as training an LM:

```python
import faust

class Text(faust.Record):
    content: str

app = faust.App('llm-training', broker='kafka://localhost:9092')
topic = app.topic('raw-text', value_type=Text)
```

```
@app.agent(topic)
async def process(stream):
    async for text in stream:
        processed_text = preprocess(text.content)
        # Here you would typically send the processed text to your LLM
training pipeline
        print(f"Processed: {processed_text}")

if __name__ == '__main__':
    app.main()
```

First, the code defines a `Text` class using `faust.Record` to represent incoming Kafka messages, which are expected to contain a single string field called `content`. The Faust application is then created with the `'llm-training'` identifier, and it connects to a local Kafka broker running at `kafka://localhost:9092`. The application subscribes to a topic named `'raw-text'`, with incoming messages deserialized into `Text` objects.

The core processing logic is implemented in the `process` function, which is decorated with `@app.agent(topic)`, making it a Faust agent that processes events from the `raw-text` topic. The function asynchronously iterates over each message in the stream, applies a `preprocess` function to the `content` field, and prints the result. Although the code currently prints the processed text, in a real-world setup, this is where one would typically pass the output to a language model training pipeline or to further processing stages.

Finally, the script includes a standard Python entry point to start the Faust application when the script is run directly. Note that the `preprocess` function is assumed to be defined elsewhere in the full implementation, as it is not included in the provided snippet.

This setup allows you to continuously process incoming text data, which can then be used to update your LLM in real time or near real time. The `preprocess` function would contain your specific preprocessing logic.

Memory-efficient data loading techniques

For datasets too large to fit in memory, we can use **memory mapping** or **chunking** techniques.

Memory mapping leverages OS-level functionality to map large files directly into memory without loading the entire file. This enables random access to portions of the file, making it suitable for scenarios requiring frequent but non-sequential access. It is fast for large, structured datasets such as embeddings or tokenized text files but may have higher overhead for small, scattered reads.

Chunking, on the other hand, divides data into smaller, sequentially processed chunks. This is effective for streaming large, sequentially accessed datasets (for example, text or logs) into memory-limited environments. While simpler and more portable, chunking may be slower for random access patterns compared to memory mapping.

Here's an example using NumPy's memmap feature, which creates array-like objects that map to files on disk, permitting efficient read and write operations without loading the entire array into memory. The memmap feature leverages the operating system's virtual memory capabilities to provide seamless array operations while minimizing memory usage:

```python
import numpy as np

def create_memmap_dataset(dataset, output_file):
    # Determine the shape of the dataset
    num_samples = len(dataset)
    sample_shape = dataset[0]['input'].shape

    # Create a memory-mapped array
    mmap = np.memmap(
        output_file, dtype='float32', mode='w+',
        shape=(num_samples, *sample_shape)
    )

    # Write data to the memory-mapped array
    for i, sample in enumerate(dataset):
        mmap[i] = sample['input']

    # Flush to disk
    mmap.flush()

def load_memmap_dataset(file_path, shape):
    # Load the memory-mapped array
    return np.memmap(file_path, dtype='float32',
        mode='r', shape=shape)

#Usage
create_memmap_dataset(large_dataset, "large_dataset.mmap")
mmap_dataset = load_memmap_dataset(
    "large_dataset.mmap", shape=(len(large_dataset),
    *large_dataset[0]['input'].shape)
)
```

This technique allows you to work with datasets larger than available RAM by keeping most of the data on disk and only loading the necessary portions into memory as needed.

Here is an example of the chunking technique, which is particularly useful when working with large datasets that must be processed sequentially but do not fit into memory all at once. Unlike memory mapping, which allows random access, chunking explicitly loads and processes fixed-size blocks of data in sequence. This is a common pattern when dealing with large CSV files, text corpora, or streaming logs. In the following example, a large CSV file is processed in chunks using pandas, which internally reads blocks of rows into memory, minimizing the peak memory footprint:

```python
import pandas as pd

def process_chunk(chunk):
    # Placeholder: process or transform the chunk here
    # For example, compute the mean of a column
    return chunk['value'].mean()

def process_large_csv(file_path, chunk_size=10000):
    results = []

    for chunk in pd.read_csv(file_path, chunksize=chunk_size):
        result = process_chunk(chunk)
        results.append(result)

    return results

# Usage
file_path = 'large_dataset.csv'
aggregated_results = process_large_csv(file_path)
print("Processed chunk-level results:", aggregated_results)
```

In this example, the CSV file is read in blocks of 10,000 rows at a time. Each chunk is passed to a processing function, and intermediate results (in this case, the mean of a column named 'value') are stored for further aggregation or analysis. This approach is flexible and easily extended to tasks such as filtering, transformation, or writing chunked outputs to new files.

Chunking is especially appropriate when data is accessed linearly and each chunk is independent. However, if random access to individual records or records across chunks is required, memory-mapping or indexed database solutions may be more efficient.

Summary

In this section, we explored advanced techniques for managing and processing large datasets for LLM training. You learned about the challenges of large datasets, data sampling techniques, distributed processing, efficient storage formats, streaming processing, data sharding, and memory-efficient loading.

These techniques are essential for scaling up LLM training to massive datasets while maintaining efficiency and data quality, each with its own contribution to processing large datasets for LLMs:

- **Data sampling techniques**: They reduce the computational load by focusing on high-impact or representative data, enhancing efficiency and ensuring quality without processing the entire dataset
- **Distributed processing**: Speeds up data preparation and training by parallelizing tasks across machines, enabling scalability for massive datasets
- **Efficient storage formats**: They improve data retrieval speed and reduce storage size, streamlining access to large datasets and boosting I/O efficiency
- **Streaming processing**: Minimizes memory usage by handling data incrementally, supporting real-time updates and efficient processing of continuous data streams
- **Data sharding**: Balances workloads and reduces latency by splitting data into smaller chunks, enabling parallelism and seamless scaling
- **Memory-efficient loading**: Limits memory usage by loading data in manageable portions, ensuring efficient processing of datasets that exceed memory capacity

In the next chapter, we will introduce another pattern: data versioning for LLM development.

Subscribe for a free eBook

New frameworks, evolving architectures, research drops, production breakdowns—AI_Distilled filters the noise into a weekly briefing for engineers and researchers working hands-on with LLMs and GenAI systems. Subscribe now and receive a free eBook, along with weekly insights that help you stay focused and informed. Subscribe at `https://packt.link/8Oz6Y` or scan the QR code below.

5
Data Versioning

Data versioning refers to the systematic tracking and management of different iterations of datasets used throughout the life cycle of model development, including pre-training, fine-tuning, evaluation, and deployment. It involves assigning unique identifiers to datasets or subsets thereof, capturing changes over time, and enabling reproducibility by ensuring that any specific model version can be linked back to the exact data version used.

In this chapter, you'll learn how to implement effective data versioning strategies for LLM development. For instance, when we want to add 10,000 new oncology research papers to a dataset, the system automatically creates a new dataset version. If the model performance then degrades, the dataset can instantly roll back to the previous verified dataset version, ensuring reproducibility and maintaining the integrity of the research process.

This design pattern transforms dataset management from a chaotic, manual process into a structured, trackable workflow in LLM model development.

In this chapter, we'll be covering the following topics:

- Understanding the need for data versioning
- Data versioning strategies for large language datasets
- Tools for data versioning
- Integrating data versioning in training workflows
- Version control for text corpora
- Managing dataset variants and experiments
- Best practices for data versioning

Understanding the need for data versioning

Data versioning is particularly important in LLM projects due to the massive scale and complexity of language datasets. As an LLM engineer, you need to track changes in your datasets to ensure the reproducibility of your models and maintain a clear history of data modifications.

Let's start by implementing a basic data versioning system using Python:

```python
from datetime import datetime
import hashlib
import json

class DatasetVersion:
    def __init__(self, data, metadata=None):
        self.data = data
        self.metadata = metadata or {}
        self.timestamp = datetime.now().isoformat()
    //creation timestamp for each version
        self.version_hash = self._generate_hash()

    def _generate_hash(self):
        data_str = json.dumps(self.data, sort_keys=True).encode()
        return hashlib.sha256(data_str).hexdigest()
```

This part of the `DatasetVersion` class initializes the basic structure for versioning your LLM datasets. It generates a unique hash for each version of the data and timestamps the version. The `_generate_hash` method creates a deterministic hash based on the sorted JSON representation of the data, ensuring that identical data always produces the same hash.

Now, let's add the `save` and `load` methods for dataset versions:

```python
class DatasetVersion:
    # ... (previous methods)

    def save(self, filename):
        with open(filename, 'w') as f:
            json.dump({
                'data': self.data,
                'metadata': self.metadata,
                'timestamp': self.timestamp,
                'version_hash': self.version_hash
            }, f, indent=2)

    @classmethod
```

```
def load(cls, filename):
    with open(filename, 'r') as f:
        data = json.load(f)
    instance = cls(data['data'], data['metadata'])
    instance.timestamp = data['timestamp']
    instance.version_hash = data['version_hash']
    return instance
```

The `save` method serializes the dataset version to a JSON file, including all relevant information. The `load` method is a class method that reconstructs a `DatasetVersion` instance from a saved file. This allows you to easily store and retrieve different versions of your dataset.

Having discussed the need for data versioning, now let us outline key strategies for managing versioning in large language datasets to support traceability, reproducibility, and efficient storage.

Data versioning strategies for large language datasets

Among the various strategies available for handling data versioning—such as snapshotting, content-addressable storage, and checksum-based tracking—this section focuses on the **delta-based system** due to its potential for minimizing storage costs when dealing with iterative updates in large language datasets. Delta-based versioning stores only the differences between dataset versions rather than duplicating entire files, making it particularly effective in scenarios involving frequent but minor changes. However, its effectiveness decreases when the dataset structure undergoes significant reformatting or involves binary files. Schema changes, column reordering, or file splitting can disrupt the delta mechanism, often necessitating a full dataset rewrite. Similarly, binary files, due to their opaque structure and compression, tend to change globally with even minor edits, limiting the advantage of delta-based storage. This approach is discussed here for its relevance in typical LLM workflows where data evolves gradually but remains largely text-based and structured.

Here's an example of how you might implement a delta-based versioning system:

```
import difflib

class DeltaDatasetVersion(DatasetVersion):
    def __init__(
        self, data, base_version=None, metadata=None
    ):
        super().__init__(data, metadata)
        self.base_version = base_version
        self.delta = self._compute_delta() if base_version else None

    def _compute_delta(self):
        base_data = json.dumps(
            self.base_version.data, sort_keys=True).splitlines()
```

```
        current_data = json.dumps(
            self.data, sort_keys=True).splitlines()
        diff = list(
            difflib.unified_diff(
                base_data, current_data, lineterm='')
        )
        return '\n'.join(diff)
```

This part of the `DeltaDatasetVersion` class extends our previous `DatasetVersion` class to implement delta-based versioning. The `_compute_delta` method calculates the differences between the current version and a base version using Python's `difflib`. This approach can significantly reduce storage requirements for large datasets by only storing the changes.

Now, let's add methods to save and load these delta-based versions:

```
class DeltaDatasetVersion(DatasetVersion):
    # ... (previous methods)

    def save(self, filename):
        with open(filename, 'w') as f:
            json.dump({
                'metadata': self.metadata,
                'timestamp': self.timestamp,
                'version_hash': self.version_hash,
                'base_version_hash': (
                    self.base_version.version_hash
                    if self.base_version else None
                ),
                'delta': self.delta
            }, f, indent=2)

    @classmethod
    def load(cls, filename, base_version):
        with open(filename, 'r') as f:
            data = json.load(f)

        # Apply delta to base version
        base_data = json.dumps(
            base_version.data, sort_keys=True
        ).splitlines()
        patched_data = difflib.restore(
            base_data, data['delta'].splitlines(), 1
        )
        current_data = json.loads('\n'.join(patched_data))
```

```
    instance = cls(current_data, base_version, data['metadata'])
    instance.timestamp = data['timestamp']
    instance.version_hash = data['version_hash']
    instance.delta = data['delta']
    return instance
```

The `save` method now stores only the delta and metadata, significantly reducing the file size of large datasets. The `load` method reconstructs the full dataset by applying the delta to the base version. This approach allows for the efficient storage and retrieval of multiple versions of large language datasets.

Tools for data versioning

While custom solutions can be effective, there are also specialized tools designed for data versioning in machine learning projects. One such tool is **Data Version Control** (**DVC**), which integrates with Git and provides powerful features for managing large datasets and is widely used. DVC is an open-source tool that extends Git to manage large datasets and machine learning artifacts by storing data in external storage while tracking metadata in the Git repository. It enables reproducible pipelines, efficient data sharing, and experiment tracking, making it a popular choice for managing LLM datasets and training workflows.

Given the scale of LLM models, DVC's versioning approach must carefully balance comprehensive tracking with computational efficiency, requiring intelligent checksum and metadata calculation strategies that minimize latency and processing overhead to prevent versioning from becoming a bottleneck in the model development workflow.

Here's an example of how you might use DVC in your LLM project:

```
import subprocess

def initialize_dvc():
    subprocess.run(["dvc", "init"])
    print("DVC initialized in the current directory.")

def add_dataset_to_dvc(dataset_path):
    subprocess.run(["dvc", "add", dataset_path])
    print(f"Dataset {dataset_path} added to DVC.")

def commit_dataset_version(message):
    subprocess.run(["git", "add", ".dvc"])
    subprocess.run(["git", "commit", "-m", message])
    print(f"Dataset version committed with message: {message}")
```

This part of the script demonstrates how to initialize DVC, add a dataset to DVC tracking, and commit a new version of the dataset. DVC works alongside Git, allowing you to version your data in a similar way to how you version your code.

Similar to Git, DVC uses `init`, `add`, `commit`, and `push` commands. The following list briefly describes each command:

- `dvc init`: Initializes a new DVC project by creating a `.dvc` directory in your project and setting up the necessary metadata tracking infrastructure. This is analogous to `git init`, but specifically for data version control, preparing your project to track large datasets and model files.

- `dvc add`: Adds large data files to DVC tracking, creating a lightweight `.dvc` metadata file that contains a hash of the file. This command moves the actual data to a separate storage location while maintaining a reference in your Git repository, allowing you to version large files without bloating your Git repository.

- `dvc commit`: Creates a snapshot of the current state of your tracked data files, similar to a Git commit but specifically for data files. This command helps you mark significant points in your data's history and creates a clear record of when and how your datasets changed.

- `dvc push`: Uploads your tracked data files to a remote storage location (such as cloud storage, network drive, or local external storage). This command ensures that your data versions are safely backed up and can be retrieved by other team members or across different development environments.

Now, let's add a function to push the dataset to remote storage:

```
def push_dataset_to_remote():
    subprocess.run(["dvc", "push"])
    subprocess.run(["git", "push"])
    print("Dataset pushed to remote storage.")

# Usage example
if __name__ == "__main__":
    initialize_dvc()
    add_dataset_to_dvc("path/to/your/large_language_dataset.txt")
    commit_dataset_version("Add initial version of language dataset")
    push_dataset_to_remote()
```

The `push_dataset_to_remote` function pushes both the DVC-tracked data and the Git repository to their respective remote storage locations. This allows you to store your large datasets separately from your code repository while maintaining version control for both.

Next, we will focus on integrating data versioning within the training workflow.

Integrating data versioning in training workflows

To make data versioning an integral part of your LLM training workflow, you need to incorporate version checking and logging into your training scripts. Here's an example of how you might do this:

```
import json
from dataclasses import dataclass
from typing import Dict, Any


@dataclass
class DatasetInfo:
    version_hash: str
    metadata: Dict[str, Any]

def load_dataset_info(filename: str) -> DatasetInfo:
    with open(filename, 'r') as f:
        data = json.load(f)
    return DatasetInfo(data['version_hash'], data['metadata'])

def train_llm(model, dataset, dataset_info: DatasetInfo):
    # Log dataset version information
    print(
        f"Training model with dataset version: "
        f"{dataset_info.version_hash}"
    )
    print(f"Dataset metadata: {dataset_info.metadata}")

    # Actual training code would go here
    # ...

    # Save model with dataset version information
    model.save(f"model_trained_on_{dataset_info.version_hash[:8]}.pt")
```

This code snippet shows how to incorporate dataset version information into your LLM training workflow. The `DatasetInfo` class encapsulates the essential version information, while the `load_dataset_info` function retrieves this information from a JSON file. The `train_llm` function demonstrates how to log the dataset version and metadata during training, ensuring that each trained model is associated with a specific version of the data.

Here's how you might use this in a training script:

```
# Usage in training script
dataset_info = load_dataset_info("dataset_info.json")
dataset = load_dataset()  # Your dataset loading function
model = initialize_model()  # Your model initialization function

train_llm(model, dataset, dataset_info)
```

By integrating dataset version information into your training process, you enhance reproducibility and make it easier to track which version of the data was used for each trained model.

Version control for text corpora

When dealing with text corpora for LLM training, you often need to handle large collections of documents. Here's an approach to version control for text corpora using a combination of file hashing and metadata tracking:

```python
import os
import hashlib
from typing import Dict, List

def hash_file(filepath: str) -> str:
    with open(filepath, 'rb') as f:
        return hashlib.sha256(f.read()).hexdigest()

def generate_corpus_manifest(corpus_dir: str) -> Dict[str, str]:
    manifest = {}
    for root, _, files in os.walk(corpus_dir):
        for file in files:
            filepath = os.path.join(root, file)
            manifest[os.path.relpath(filepath, corpus_dir)] = \
                hash_file(filepath)
    return manifest
```

This part of the code defines functions to hash individual files and generate a manifest of all files in a corpus directory. The manifest is a dictionary mapping relative file paths to their corresponding hash values, providing a snapshot of the entire corpus. The manifest file is important because it serves as a compact, reproducible fingerprint of the entire dataset, enabling quick integrity checks, facilitating version tracking, and allowing researchers to verify the exact state of their corpus across different environments or points in time without needing to store or transfer the entire large dataset.

Now, let's add a function to compare two manifests and identify changes:

```python
def compare_manifests(
    old_manifest: Dict[str, str], new_manifest: Dict[str, str]
) -> Dict[str, List[str]]:
    changes = {
        "added": [],
        "removed": [],
        "modified": []
    }

    for file, hash in new_manifest.items():
        if file not in old_manifest:
            changes["added"].append(file)
```

```
        elif old_manifest[file] != hash:
            changes["modified"].append(file)

    for file in old_manifest:
        if file not in new_manifest:
            changes["removed"].append(file)

    return changes

# Usage example
old_manifest = generate_corpus_manifest("path/to/old_corpus")
new_manifest = generate_corpus_manifest("path/to/new_corpus")
changes = compare_manifests(old_manifest, new_manifest)

print("Corpus changes:")
for change_type, files in changes.items():
    print(f"{change_type.capitalize()}:")
    for file in files:
        print(f"  - {file}")
```

The compare_manifests function identifies added, removed, and modified files between two versions of the corpus. This approach allows you to track changes in your text corpus efficiently, even when dealing with large numbers of files.

Managing dataset variants and experiments

In LLM development, you often need to manage multiple variants of your dataset for different experiments. Here's a simple system for managing dataset variants:

```
from typing import Dict, Any
import json
import os

class DatasetVariantManager:
    def __init__(self, base_path: str):
        self.base_path = base_path
        self.variants: Dict[str, Dict[str, Any]] = {}
        self._load_variants()

    def _load_variants(self):
        if os.path.exists(
            os.path.join(self.base_path, "variants.json")
        ):
```

```
        with open(
            os.path.join(self.base_path, "variants.json"), 'r'
        ) as f:
            self.variants = json.load(f)

    def save_variants(self):
        with open(
            os.path.join(self.base_path, "variants.json"), 'w'
        ) as f:
            json.dump(self.variants, f, indent=2)
```

This part of the `DatasetVariantManager` class sets up the basic structure for managing dataset variants. It initializes the manager with a base path and loads existing variants from a JSON file, if available.

Now, let's add methods to create and retrieve variants:

```
class DatasetVariantManager:
    # ... (previous methods)

    def create_variant(
        self, name: str, base_variant: str, changes: Dict[str, Any]
    ):
        if name in self.variants:
            raise ValueError(f"Variant {name} already exists")

        self.variants[name] = {
            "base": base_variant,
            "changes": changes
        }
        self.save_variants()

    def get_variant(self, name: str) -> Dict[str, Any]:
        if name not in self.variants:
            raise ValueError(f"Variant {name} does not exist")

        variant = self.variants[name]
        base_data = self.get_variant(variant["base"])
            if variant["base"] else {}
        return {base_data, variant["changes"]}

# Usage example
manager = DatasetVariantManager("path/to/dataset/variants")
```

```
manager.create_variant(
    "base", None, {"size": 1000000, "language": "en"})
manager.create_variant("large", "base", {"size": 5000000})
manager.create_variant(
    "multilingual", "large", {"language": ["en", "es", "fr"]})

print(manager.get_variant("multilingual"))
```

The `create_variant` method allows you to create new dataset variants based on existing ones, specifying only the changes. The `get_variant` method retrieves a variant, applying all changes from its base variants recursively. This system allows you to efficiently manage and track different configurations of your dataset for various experiments.

A clear and consistent naming convention is recommended for managing dataset variants in LLM development to ensure traceability, reproducibility, and clarity. Here is a suggested naming convention that balances readability and scalability for managing dataset variants:

`<base>_<modifier1>_<modifier2>_..._<description>`

This format uses a **base name** to indicate the root dataset, followed by **modifiers** and optional descriptions to specify what changes or attributes differentiate the variant. Modifiers are concise and ordered hierarchically to reflect the transformation process.

Let's look at the key components closely:

- **Base name**: Represents the initial dataset, such as `base` or a descriptive name (e.g., `clean` or `raw`).

- **Modifiers**: Sequential changes or transformations applied to the base. Each modifier reflects an aspect of the dataset such as size, language, or preprocessing applied.

- **Description**: An optional part that provides extra context or details about the changes, typically used for experiments.

Best practices for data versioning

Over the years, I have gathered the following best practices:

- Use a dedicated data versioning tool such as DVC for large-scale projects.

- Include dataset version information in your model metadata.

- Use delta-based versioning for large datasets to save storage space.

- Implement regular backups of your versioned datasets.

- Use consistent naming conventions for dataset versions and variants.

- Integrate data versioning checks into your **continuous integration and continuous delivery (CI/CD)** pipeline for LLM training. This can be achieved by adding DVC-specific validation steps in your CI/CD workflow, such as running `dvc status` to verify no unexpected modifications have occurred, automatically comparing dataset checksums against approved versions, and blocking model training if any data discrepancies are detected. Key steps include creating a pre-training validation stage that compares current dataset versions with expected reference versions, automatically triggering alerts or stopping the pipeline if unverified data modifications are detected, and maintaining a comprehensive audit trail of dataset changes throughout the machine learning development process.

Summary

In this chapter, we explored various aspects of data versioning for LLM development. We implemented basic versioning systems and delta-based versioning for large datasets. We examined tools such as DVC for more advanced versioning needs. We also looked at integrating data versioning into LLM training workflows, managing text corpora versions, and handling dataset variants for experiments.

Data versioning is a critical practice in LLM development, ensuring reproducibility, facilitating collaboration, and enabling robust model governance. By implementing these techniques and best practices, you can significantly improve the manageability and reliability of your LLM projects.

In the upcoming chapter, we'll explore dataset annotation and labeling techniques specifically tailored for LLMs. In particular, we'll cover strategies for efficient annotation, quality control measures, and methods for scaling annotation processes to meet the demands of large language datasets.

6

Dataset Annotation and Labeling

Dataset annotation is the process of enriching raw data within a dataset with informative metadata or tags, making it understandable and usable for supervised machine learning models. This metadata varies depending on the data type and the intended task. For text data, annotation can involve assigning labels or categories to entire documents or specific text spans, identifying and marking entities, establishing relationships between entities, highlighting key information, and adding semantic interpretations. The goal of annotation is to provide structured information that enables the model to learn patterns and make accurate predictions or generate relevant outputs.

Dataset labeling is a specific type of dataset annotation focused on assigning predefined categorical tags or class labels to individual data points. This is commonly used for classification tasks, where the goal is to categorize data into distinct groups. In the context of text data, labeling might involve categorizing documents by sentiment, topic, or genre.

While labeling provides crucial supervisory signals for classification models, annotation is a broader term encompassing more complex forms of data enrichment beyond simple categorization. Effective dataset annotation, including appropriate labeling strategies, is fundamental for developing high-performing language models capable of tackling diverse and sophisticated language-based tasks.

Dataset annotation and labeling are the processes for developing high-performing models. In this chapter, we'll explore advanced techniques for creating well-annotated datasets that can significantly impact your LLM's performance across various tasks.

In this chapter, we'll be covering the following topics:

- The importance of quality annotations
- Annotation strategies for different tasks
- Tools and platforms for large-scale text annotation
- Managing annotation quality
- Crowdsourcing annotations – benefits and challenges
- Semi-automated annotation techniques
- Scaling annotation processes for massive language datasets

The importance of quality annotations

High-quality annotations are fundamental to the success of LLM training. They provide the ground truth that guides the model's learning process, enabling it to understand the nuances of language and perform specific tasks accurately. Poor annotations can lead to biased or inaccurate models, while high-quality annotations can significantly enhance an LLM's performance and generalization capabilities.

So, what are high-quality annotations?

High-quality annotations are characterized by consistent labeling across similar instances, complete coverage of all relevant elements within the dataset without omissions, and accurate alignment with ground truth or established standards – this means labels must precisely reflect the true nature of the data, follow predetermined annotation guidelines rigorously, and maintain reliability even in edge cases or ambiguous situations.

Let's illustrate the impact of annotation quality with a **named-entity recognition** (**NER**) task using the spaCy library. NER is a **natural language processing** (**NLP**) technique that identifies and classifies key information (entities) in text into predefined categories such as names of people, organizations, locations, expressions of times, quantities, monetary values, and more. SpaCy is a popular open source library for advanced NLP in Python, known for its efficiency and accuracy. It provides pre-trained models that can perform various NLP tasks, including NER, part-of-speech tagging, dependency parsing, and more, making it easier for developers to integrate sophisticated language processing capabilities into their applications.

The following Python code snippet demonstrates how to programmatically create training data in the spaCy format for NER tasks:

```
import spacy
from spacy.tokens import DocBin
from spacy.training import Example
```

```
def create_training_data(texts, annotations):
    nlp = spacy.blank("en")
    db = DocBin()

    for text, annot in zip(texts, annotations):
        doc = nlp.make_doc(text)
        ents = []
        for start, end, label in annot:
            span = doc.char_span(start, end, label=label)
            if span:
                ents.append(span)
        doc.ents = ents
        db.add(doc)

    return db

texts = [
    "Apple Inc. is planning to open a new store in New York.",
    "Microsoft CEO Satya Nadella announced new AI features."
]
annotations = [
    [(0, 9, "ORG"), (41, 49, "GPE")],
    [(0, 9, "ORG"), (14, 27, "PERSON")]
]

training_data = create_training_data(texts, annotations)
training_data.to_disk("./train.spacy")
```

This code creates a training dataset for NER using spaCy. Let's break it down:

1. We import necessary modules from spaCy, including DocBin for the efficient storage of training data.

2. The create_training_data function converts raw text and annotations into spaCy's training format:

    I.   It creates a blank English language model as a starting point.

    II. A DocBin object is initialized to store the processed documents efficiently.

    III. For each text and its annotations, we create a spaCy Doc object and add entity spans based on the provided annotations.

3. We provide two example sentences with their corresponding NER annotations.

4. In this code, `doc.char_span()` creates entity spans by mapping character-level `start` and end positions from the annotations to the actual token boundaries in the spaCy `Doc` object. It converts raw character indices (such as 0 to 9 for `Apple Inc.`) into proper spaCy `Span` objects that align with token boundaries, ensuring the entity labels are correctly attached to the exact text sequences they represent within the document.

5. The training data is saved to disk in spaCy's binary format.

The quality of these annotations directly impacts the model's ability to identify and classify entities correctly. For instance, if `Apple Inc.` were incorrectly labeled as a person instead of an organization, the model would learn to misclassify company names as people.

Annotation strategies for different tasks

Different LLM tasks require specific annotation strategies. Let's explore a few common tasks and their annotation approaches:

- **Text classification**: For tasks such as sentiment analysis or topic classification, we assign labels to entire text segments. Here's an example using the `datasets` library:

```
from datasets import Dataset

texts = [
    "This movie was fantastic!",
    "The service was terrible.",
    "The weather is nice today."
]
labels = [1, 0, 2]  # 1: positive, 0: negative, 2: neutral

dataset = Dataset.from_dict({"text": texts, "label": labels})
print(dataset[0])
# Output: {'text': 'This movie was fantastic!', 'label': 1}
```

  This code creates a simple dataset for sentiment analysis. Each text is associated with a label representing its sentiment.

- **NER**: For NER, we annotate specific spans of text with entity labels. Here's an approach using the **BIO tagging scheme**.

BIO tagging scheme

The **Beginning, Inside, Outside** (BIO) tagging scheme is a fundamental method for marking entity boundaries in text by labeling each word with a specific tag that indicates its role in named entities. This scheme uses `"B-"` to mark the beginning word of an entity, `"I-"` to mark any subsequent words that are part of the same entity, and `"O"` to mark words that aren't part of any entity. This approach solves the problem of distinguishing between adjacent entities and handling multi-word entities – for instance, helping models understand that `New York Times` is a single organization entity, or that in a sentence with `Steve Jobs met Steve Wozniak`, there are two distinct person entities rather than one or four separate entities. The simplicity and effectiveness of this labeling system make it a standard choice for teaching machines to recognize and classify named entities in text.

The following code demonstrates how to directly encode the text into a format suitable for the transformer model using the tokenizer:

```
from transformers import AutoTokenizer

tokenizer = AutoTokenizer.from_pretrained("bert-base-uncased")

text = "Apple Inc. was founded by Steve Jobs"
labels = ["B-ORG", "I-ORG", "O", "O", "O", "B-PER", "I-PER"]

tokens = tokenizer.tokenize(text)
inputs = tokenizer(text, return_tensors="pt")
print(list(zip(tokens, labels)))
```

This example demonstrates how to create BIO tags for NER tasks. The B- prefix indicates the beginning of an entity, I- indicates the continuation of an entity, and O represents tokens outside any entity.

* **Question answering**: For question-answering tasks, we annotate the start and end positions of the answer in the context:

```
context = "The capital of France is Paris. It is known for its
iconic Eiffel Tower."
question = "What is the capital of France?"
answer = "Paris"

start_idx = context.index(answer)
end_idx = start_idx + len(answer)

print(f"Answer: {context[start_idx:end_idx]}")
print(f"Start index: {start_idx}, End index: {end_idx}")
```

This code demonstrates how to annotate the answer span for a question-answering task.

Now, let's visit some tools and platforms for performing large-scale text annotation.

Tools and platforms for large-scale text annotation

Data annotation is the backbone of many machine learning projects, providing the labeled data needed to train and evaluate models. However, manual annotation, especially at scale, is time-consuming, error-prone, and difficult to manage. This is where specialized annotation tools become essential. They streamline the process, improve data quality, and offer features such as automation, collaboration, and integration with machine learning workflows, ultimately making large-scale annotation projects feasible and efficient.

Prodigy, a powerful commercial tool from the creators of spaCy, stands out for its active learning capabilities. It intelligently suggests the most informative examples to label next, significantly reducing annotation effort. Prodigy's strength lies in its customizability, allowing users to define annotation workflows with Python code and seamlessly integrate them with machine learning models, especially within the spaCy ecosystem. It's an excellent choice for projects that require complex annotation tasks, have a budget for a premium tool, and value the efficiency gains of active learning.

Label Studio is a versatile, open source option that caters to a wide array of data types, including text, images, audio, and video. Its user-friendly visual interface and customizable labeling configurations make it accessible to annotators of all levels. Label Studio also supports collaboration and offers various export formats, making it compatible with diverse machine learning platforms. It's a strong contender for projects needing a flexible, free solution that supports multiple data types and requires a collaborative annotation environment.

Doccano is a specialized, open source tool designed explicitly for text annotation in machine learning. It excels in tasks such as sequence labeling, text classification, and sequence-to-sequence labeling. Doccano features a simple and intuitive interface, supports multiple users, and provides an API for integration with machine learning pipelines. It's the go-to choice for projects solely focused on text annotation that need a straightforward, free solution and desire seamless integration with their existing machine learning workflows.

Here's an example of how you might integrate annotations from Doccano into a Python workflow:

```python
import json
from transformers import (
    AutoTokenizer, AutoModelForTokenClassification)

def load_doccano_ner(file_path):
    with open(file_path, 'r') as f:
        data = [json.loads(line) for line in f]
    return data

doccano_data = load_doccano_ner('doccano_export.jsonl')
```

```
tokenizer = AutoTokenizer.from_pretrained("bert-base-uncased")
model = AutoModelForTokenClassification.from_pretrained(
    "bert-base-uncased")

for item in doccano_data:
    text = item['text']
    labels = item['labels']

    # Process annotations and prepare for model input
    tokens = tokenizer.tokenize(text)
    ner_tags = ['O'] * len(tokens)
    for start, end, label in labels:
        start_token = len(tokenizer.tokenize(text[:start]))
        end_token = len(tokenizer.tokenize(text[:end]))
        ner_tags[start_token] = f'B-{label}'
        for i in range(start_token + 1, end_token):
            ner_tags[i] = f'I-{label}'

    # Now you can use tokens and ner_tags for model training or
inference
```

This code loads NER annotations from a Doccano export file and processes them into a format suitable for training a BERT-based token classification model. The tokens and `ner_tags` in the following example show a sample format:

```
text = "The majestic Bengal tiger prowled through the Sundarbans, a
habitat it shares with spotted deer."
labels = [[13, 25, "ANIMAL"], [47, 57, "GPE"], [81, 93, "ANIMAL"]]

tokens = ['The', 'majestic', 'Bengal', 'tiger', 'prowled', 'through',
    'the', 'Sundarbans', ',', 'a', 'habitat', 'it', 'shares', 'with',
    'spotted', 'deer', '.']

ner_tags = ['O', 'O', 'B-ANIMAL', 'I-ANIMAL', 'O', 'O', 'O', 'B-GPE',
    'O', 'O', 'O', 'O', 'O', 'O', 'B-ANIMAL', 'I-ANIMAL', 'O']
```

This example demonstrates NER for identifying and classifying animal names within a text. The text contains a sentence about a Bengal tiger and spotted deer in the Sundarbans. The `labels` list provides the start and end indices of the animal entities ("Bengal tiger", "spotted deer") and their corresponding type ("ANIMAL"), as well as the geopolitical entity, i.e., "Sundarbans" ("GPE"). The `tokens` list is the word-level segmentation of the text. Finally, the `ner_tags` list represents the NER annotations in the BIO (Begin-Inside-Outside) format, where "B-ANIMAL" marks the beginning of an animal entity, "I-ANIMAL" marks subsequent words within the same animal entity, "B-GPE" marks the beginning of a geopolitical entity, and "O" signifies tokens that are not part of any named entity.

Managing annotation quality

To ensure high-quality annotations, we need to implement a robust quality assurance process.

Let's look at some of the approaches to measure annotation quality:

- **Inter-annotator agreement**: Calculate agreement scores between annotators using metrics such as **Cohen's Kappa**. Cohen's Kappa is a statistical measure that evaluates inter-rater reliability between two annotators by comparing their observed agreement to what would be expected by chance, accounting for the possibility of random agreements and producing a score between -1 and 1, where 1 indicates perfect agreement, 0 indicates agreement equivalent to chance, and negative values indicate agreement less than chance.

  The following code calculates Cohen's Kappa coefficient to quantify the agreement between two sets of categorical ratings:

  ```python
  from sklearn.metrics import cohen_kappa_score

  annotator1 = [0, 1, 2, 0, 1]
  annotator2 = [0, 1, 1, 0, 1]

  kappa = cohen_kappa_score(annotator1, annotator2)
  print(f"Cohen's Kappa: {kappa}")
  ```

- **Gold standard comparison**: Compare annotations against a gold standard dataset. A gold standard dataset in the context of machine learning and data annotation is a set of data that has been manually labeled or annotated by expert humans. It's considered the "ground truth" or the most accurate representation of the correct answers. This dataset is used as a benchmark to evaluate the performance of machine learning models or to assess the quality of annotations done by other annotators.

  The following Python function, `calculate_accuracy`, computes the agreement between a set of true labels (the `gold_standard`) and a set of predicted or annotated labels (annotations):

  ```python
  def calculate_accuracy(gold_standard, annotations):
      return sum(
          g == a for g, a in zip(
              gold_standard, annotations
          )
      ) / len(gold_standard)

  gold_standard = [0, 1, 2, 0, 1]
  annotator_result = [0, 1, 1, 0, 1]

  accuracy = calculate_accuracy(gold_standard, annotator_result)
  print(f"Accuracy: {accuracy}")
  ```

While Cohen's Kappa and accuracy against a gold standard are fundamental, other metrics provide deeper insights into annotation quality. For instance, Krippendorff's Alpha offers a versatile approach, accommodating various data types and handling missing data, making it suitable for complex annotation tasks. In scenarios involving multiple annotators, Fleiss' Kappa extends Cohen's Kappa, providing an overall assessment of agreement across the group.

For tasks such as object detection or image segmentation, **intersection over union** (**IoU**) becomes crucial, quantifying the overlap between predicted and ground truth bounding boxes or masks. Furthermore, especially when dealing with imbalanced datasets or specific error types that are more costly, precision, recall, and the F1-score provide a nuanced evaluation, particularly useful in tasks such as NER.

- **Sensitivity and specificity**: These metrics, often used in medical diagnosis or binary classification, are also valuable for annotation quality assessment. Sensitivity (also known as recall or true positive rate) measures the proportion of actual positives that are correctly identified, while specificity (true negative rate) measures the proportion of actual negatives that are correctly identified.

- **Root mean square error** (**RMSE**) **and mean absolute error** (**MAE**): For tasks involving numerical or continuous annotations (e.g., rating scales, bounding box coordinates, etc.), RMSE and MAE can quantify the difference between the annotated values and the true values. RMSE gives higher weight to larger errors, while MAE treats all errors equally.

- **Time-based metrics**: Besides the quality of labels, the efficiency of the annotation process is also important. Tracking the time spent per annotation, especially when correlated with accuracy or agreement scores, can reveal areas for process improvement or identify annotators who might need additional training. Also, analyzing the distribution of annotation times can help identify unusually difficult or ambiguous instances.

Ultimately, a holistic approach to annotation quality involves considering a combination of relevant metrics, tailored to the specific task and project goals. Regular monitoring, feedback loops, and iterative refinement of guidelines and training are essential to maintain high standards throughout the annotation process. Remember that the choice of metrics should align with the nature of the data, the complexity of the task, and the desired outcomes of the machine learning project.

An effective alternative for scaling annotation efforts is the use of crowdsourcing.

Crowdsourcing annotations – benefits and challenges

Crowdsourcing can be an effective way to scale annotation efforts. Platforms such as Amazon Mechanical Turk or Appen (formerly Figure Eight) provide access to a large workforce. However, ensuring quality can be challenging. Here's an example of how you might aggregate crowd-sourced annotations:

```
from collections import Counter

def aggregate_annotations(annotations):
    return Counter(annotations).most_common(1)[0][0]
```

```
crowd_annotations = [
    ['PERSON', 'PERSON', 'ORG', 'PERSON'],
    ['PERSON', 'ORG', 'ORG', 'PERSON'],
    ['PERSON', 'PERSON', 'ORG', 'LOC']
]

aggregated = [aggregate_annotations(annot)
    for annot in zip(*crowd_annotations)]
print(f"Aggregated annotations: {aggregated}")
```

This code uses a simple majority voting scheme to aggregate annotations from multiple annotators. While this approach is effective in many cases, tie-breakers are needed for situations with equal votes, and additional strategies such as assigning weights based on annotator reliability or leveraging machine-learning-based reconciliation models can further improve quality.

Next, we'll delve into semi-automated annotation techniques, where machine learning models assist human annotators to accelerate labeling tasks.

Semi-automated annotation techniques

Semi-automated annotation combines machine learning with human verification to speed up the annotation process. Here's a simple example using spaCy:

```
import spacy

nlp = spacy.load("en_core_web_sm")

def semi_automated_ner(text):
    doc = nlp(text)
    return [(ent.start_char, ent.end_char, ent.label_)
    for ent in doc.ents]

text = "Apple Inc. was founded by Steve Jobs in Cupertino."
auto_annotations = semi_automated_ner(text)
print(f"Auto-generated annotations: {auto_annotations}")

# Human annotator would then verify and correct these annotations
```

This code uses a pre-trained spaCy model to generate initial NER annotations, which can then be verified and corrected by human annotators.

Next, we explore a couple of strategies for scaling annotation workflows to handle large-scale language datasets.

Scaling annotation processes for massive language datasets

For massive datasets, consider the following strategies:

- **Distributed processing**: Use libraries such as **Dask** or **PySpark** for distributed annotation processing. Dask and PySpark are powerful libraries that can be used for distributed data annotation processing, enabling teams to handle large-scale annotation tasks efficiently. These libraries allow you to parallelize annotation workflows across multiple cores or even clusters of computers, significantly speeding up the process for massive datasets. With Dask, you can scale existing Python-based annotation scripts to run on distributed systems, while PySpark offers robust data processing capabilities within the Apache Spark ecosystem. Both libraries provide familiar APIs that make it easier to transition from local annotation pipelines to distributed ones, allowing annotation teams to process and manage datasets that are too large for a single machine.

- **Active learning**: This technique involves iteratively selecting the most informative samples for human labeling, based on model uncertainty or expected impact. Starting with a small, labeled dataset, it trains a model, uses it to identify valuable unlabeled samples, has humans annotate these, and then updates the model. This cycle repeats, optimizing annotation efforts and improving model performance efficiently.

  Here's a simple active learning example:

  ```
  import numpy as np
  from sklearn.ensemble import RandomForestClassifier
  from modAL.models import ActiveLearner

  # Simulated unlabeled dataset
  X_pool = np.random.rand(1000, 10)

  # Initialize active learner
  learner = ActiveLearner(
      estimator=RandomForestClassifier(),
      X_training=X_pool[:10],
      y_training=np.random.randint(0, 2, 10)
  )

  # Active learning loop
  n_queries = 100
  for _ in range(n_queries):
      query_idx, query_inst = learner.query(X_pool)
      # In real scenario, get human annotation here
  ```

```
        y_new = np.random.randint(0, 2, 1)
        learner.teach(X_pool[query_idx], y_new)
        X_pool = np.delete(X_pool, query_idx, axis=0)

    print(
        f"Model accuracy after active learning: "
        f"{learner.score(
            X_pool, np.random.randint(0, 2, len(X_pool)))}"
    )
```

This example demonstrates a basic active learning loop, where the model selects the most informative samples for annotation, potentially reducing the total number of annotations needed.

Now that we've visited some annotation techniques, let's check out some of the biases that may occur while performing annotation and how we can avoid them.

Annotation biases and mitigation strategies

Annotation biases are systematic errors or prejudices that can creep into labeled datasets during the annotation process. These biases can significantly impact the performance and fairness of machine learning models trained on this data, leading to models that are inaccurate or exhibit discriminatory behavior. Recognizing and mitigating these biases is crucial for building robust and ethical AI systems.

Types of annotation bias include the following:

- **Selection bias**: This occurs when the data selected for annotation is not representative of the true distribution of data the model will encounter in the real world. For instance, if a dataset for facial recognition primarily contains images of people with lighter skin tones, the model trained on it will likely perform poorly on people with darker skin tones.

- **Labeling bias**: This arises from the subjective interpretations, cultural backgrounds, or personal beliefs of the annotators. For example, in sentiment analysis, annotators from different cultures might label the same text with different sentiment polarities. Similarly, an annotator's personal biases might lead them to label certain groups or individuals more negatively or positively than others.

- **Confirmation bias**: Annotators might unconsciously favor labels that confirm their pre-existing beliefs or hypotheses about the data.

- **Automation bias**: Over-reliance on suggestions from pre-trained models or active learning systems can lead annotators to accept incorrect labels without sufficient scrutiny.

- **Ambiguity in guidelines**: If the annotation guidelines are unclear or incomplete, it can lead to inconsistent labeling across annotators, introducing noise and bias into the dataset.

Here are some strategies to mitigate bias:

- **Diverse and representative data**: Ensure that the data selected for annotation is diverse and representative of the target population and use cases. This may involve oversampling underrepresented groups or collecting data from multiple sources.

- **Clear and comprehensive guidelines**: Develop detailed annotation guidelines that clearly define the labeling criteria and provide examples for each label. Address potential ambiguities and edge cases in the guidelines. Regularly review and update the guidelines based on annotator feedback and emerging issues.

- **Annotator training and calibration**: Provide thorough training to annotators on the task, guidelines, and potential biases they should be aware of. Conduct calibration sessions where annotators label the same data and discuss any discrepancies to ensure consistency.

- **Multiple annotators and inter-annotator agreement**: Use multiple annotators for each data point and measure **inter-annotator agreement** (**IAA**) using metrics such as Cohen's Kappa or Fleiss' Kappa. A high IAA indicates good consistency, while a low IAA suggests issues with the guidelines, training, or the task itself.

- **Adjudication process**: Establish a process for resolving disagreements between annotators. This might involve having a senior annotator or expert review and make the final decision.

- **Active learning with bias awareness**: When using active learning, be mindful of potential biases in the model's suggestions. Encourage annotators to critically evaluate the suggestions and not blindly accept them.

- **Bias auditing and evaluation**: Regularly audit the labeled data and the trained models for potential biases. Evaluate model performance across different demographic groups or categories to identify any disparities.

- **Diverse annotation teams**: Assemble annotation teams with diverse backgrounds, perspectives, and experiences to mitigate the influence of individual biases.

By implementing these mitigation strategies, you can significantly reduce the impact of annotation biases, leading to more accurate, fair, and reliable machine learning models. It's important to remember that bias mitigation is an ongoing process that requires continuous monitoring, evaluation, and refinement throughout the entire machine learning life cycle.

Summary

From this design pattern, you learned about advanced techniques for dataset annotation and labeling in LLM development. You now understand the crucial importance of high-quality annotations in improving model performance and generalization. You've gained insights into various annotation strategies for different LLM tasks, including text classification, NER, and question answering.

In this chapter, we introduced you to tools and platforms for large-scale text annotation, methods for managing annotation quality, and the pros and cons of crowdsourcing annotations. You also learned about semi-automated annotation techniques and strategies for scaling annotation processes for massive language datasets, such as distributed processing and active learning. We provided practical examples using libraries such as spaCy, transformers, and scikit-learn, which helped you grasp key concepts and implementation approaches.

In the next chapter, you'll explore how to build efficient and scalable pipelines for training LLMs. This includes exploring best practices for data preprocessing, key considerations for designing model architectures, and strategies to optimize performance and scalability.

Subscribe for a free eBook

New frameworks, evolving architectures, research drops, production breakdowns—AI_Distilled filters the noise into a weekly briefing for engineers and researchers working hands-on with LLMs and GenAI systems. Subscribe now and receive a free eBook, along with weekly insights that help you stay focused and informed. Subscribe at `https://packt.link/80z6Y` or scan the QR code below.

Part 2:
Training and Optimization of Large Language Models

This part delves into the processes required to train and optimize LLMs effectively. We guide you through designing robust training pipelines that balance modularity and scalability. You will learn how to tune hyperparameters to maximize performance, implement regularization techniques to stabilize training, and integrate efficient checkpointing and recovery methods for long-running training sessions. Additionally, we explore advanced topics such as pruning and quantization, which enable you to reduce model size and computational requirements without sacrificing performance. Fine-tuning techniques for adapting pre-trained models to specific tasks or domains are also covered in detail. By the end of this part, you will be equipped to build, train, and optimize LLMs capable of meeting the challenges of real-world applications.

This part has the following chapters:

- *Chapter 7, Training Pipeline*
- *Chapter 8, Hyperparameter Tuning*
- *Chapter 9, Regularization*
- *Chapter 10, Checkpointing and Recovery*
- *Chapter 11, Fine-Tuning*
- *Chapter 12, Model Pruning*
- *Chapter 13, Quantization*

7

Training Pipeline

In this chapter, we'll explore the key components of an LLM training pipeline, from data ingestion and preprocessing to model architecture and optimization strategies.

You'll gain insights into implementing effective monitoring and logging systems, ensuring you can track your model's progress and make data-driven decisions throughout the training process.

In this chapter, we'll be covering the following topics:

- Components of a training pipeline
- Data input and preprocessing
- LLM architecture design considerations
- Loss functions and optimization strategies
- Logging
- Pipeline modularity and reusability
- Scaling your training pipeline for larger models

Components of a training pipeline

An LLM training pipeline consists of several interconnected steps, each playing a role in the model's development. We'll present a basic pipeline here and explore many of these components in further depth as we progress through the chapter:

- **Dataset creation**: Builds preprocessed data into a format suitable for training, often involving shuffling and batching.
- **Model architecture**: Defines the structure of the LLM, including the number of layers, attention mechanisms, and other architectural choices.
- **Training loop**: The core of the pipeline where the model learns from the data through forward and backward passes.

- **Optimization**: Handles parameter updates based on calculated gradients and chosen optimization strategies.

- **Evaluation**: Regularly assesses model performance on validation data to track progress and prevent overfitting. We will cover this topic in more detail in *Chapter 14*.

- **Checkpointing**: Periodically saves model states to resume training or use for inference. We will cover this topic in detail in *Chapter 10*.

- **Logging and monitoring**: Continuously tracks training metrics and resource utilization.

We'll implement a basic LLM training pipeline using PyTorch and the Transformers library:

```
from torch.utils.data import DataLoader
from transformers import (
    AutoTokenizer, AutoModelForCausalLM, AdamW,
    get_linear_schedule_with_warmup
from datasets import load_dataset
import torch
from torch.nn import functional as F
import wandb
```

PyTorch is a popular deep learning framework that enables building neural networks through a dynamic computational graph, while the Transformers library implements the popular transformer architecture we discussed in *Chapter 1*.

The following code block demonstrates the loading of a Wikipedia dataset and the tokenization of its text content using a pre-trained GPT-2 tokenizer:

```
# Dataset Creation: Ingestion and Preprocessing
dataset = load_dataset("wikipedia", "20220301.en", split="train")
tokenizer = AutoTokenizer.from_pretrained("gpt2")

def preprocess_function(examples):
    return tokenizer(examples["text"], truncation=True,
        max_length=512, padding="max_length")

tokenized_dataset = dataset.map(preprocess_function,
    batched=True, remove_columns=dataset.column_names)
```

In the preceding code block, we're setting up the data ingestion and preprocessing components of our pipeline. We use the Hugging Face Datasets library to load a Wikipedia dataset, which provides a large corpus of text suitable for training an LLM. We then initialize a tokenizer based on the **GPT-2 model**, which will be used to preprocess our text data.

The `preprocess_function` defined above takes raw text examples and tokenizes them, truncating to a maximum length of 512 tokens and padding shorter sequences to this length. This ensures all our input sequences have the same length, which is necessary for efficient batch processing. We choose a `max_length` value of `512` as a balance between context length and memory efficiency. Longer sequences provide more context but require more memory and computation. Some recent LLM models, such as **Gemini 1.5 Pro**, can get as many as 2 million tokens in content length (`https://cloud.google.com/vertex-ai/generative-ai/docs/long-context`).

Next, we create our training DataLoader, which will handle batching and shuffling of our dataset during training:

```
# Dataset Creation: Loading
train_dataloader = DataLoader(
    tokenized_dataset, shuffle=True, batch_size=8)
```

We set the batch size to 8, which is chosen as a balance between memory usage and training efficiency. Larger batch sizes can lead to faster training but require more GPU memory. For LLMs, which often have a large number of parameters, smaller batch sizes are often necessary to fit the model and data in GPU memory.

We then initialize our model architecture using the pre-trained GPT-2 model. This gives us a strong starting point for our LLM, leveraging the knowledge already captured in the pre-trained weights. Using a pre-trained model as a starting point is a common practice in transfer learning, allowing us to benefit from the general language understanding learned by the model on a large corpus of text. See the following code:

```
# Model Architecture
model = AutoModelForCausalLM.from_pretrained("gpt2")

# Optimization
optimizer = AdamW(model.parameters(), lr=5e-5)
```

As shown in the preceding code, for optimization, we use the **AdamW optimizer**, which is an improved version of Adam that implements weight decay correctly. We set the learning rate (`lr`) to `5e-5`, which is a common choice for fine-tuning pre-trained models. The learning rate is a hyperparameter that determines the size of the adjustments made to the model's weights during training, influencing how quickly and effectively the model learns.

This learning rate offers a good balance between learning speed and stability. It's small enough to allow for fine-grained updates to the pre-trained weights, but large enough to allow meaningful learning to occur.

The subsequent code blocks outline the essential stages of training a language model, including setting up the training process, initializing a logging tool, executing the main training loop with forward and backward passes, performing evaluation to assess model performance, and saving checkpoints of the model's parameters during training.

1. We start by setting up the training loop:

```
num_epochs = 3
num_training_steps = num_epochs * len(train_dataloader)
lr_scheduler = get_linear_schedule_with_warmup(
    optimizer, num_warmup_steps=100,
    num_training_steps=num_training_steps)
```

2. Then, we initialize the Weights & Biases (wandb) library for experiment tracking and logging of training metrics:

```
wandb.init(project="llm_training", name="gpt2_finetune")

device = torch.device("cuda" if torch.cuda.is_available()
    else "cpu")
model.to(device)

for epoch in range(num_epochs):
    model.train()
    for batch in train_dataloader:
        batch = {k: v.to(device) for k, v in batch.items()}
        outputs = model(batch)
        loss = outputs.loss
        loss.backward()

        optimizer.step()
        lr_scheduler.step()
        optimizer.zero_grad()

        wandb.log({"loss": loss.item()})
```

3. We next implement an evaluation phase to assess the model's performance on the training data:

```
model.eval()
eval_loss = 0
with torch.no_grad():
    for batch in train_dataloader:  # Using training data
for simplicity
        batch = {k: v.to(device) for k, v in batch.items()}
```

```
            outputs = model(batch)
            eval_loss += outputs.loss.item()
        eval_loss /= len(train_dataloader)
        wandb.log({"eval_loss": eval_loss})
```

4. Finally, we save a checkpoint of the model's state dictionary at the end of each epoch:

```
        torch.save(model.state_dict(),
            f"model_checkpoint_epoch_{epoch}.pt")


    wandb.finish()
```

These snippets implement the training loop, evaluation, checkpointing, and logging components of our pipeline:

We set the number of training epochs to 3, which means the model will iterate through the entire dataset three times during training. This hyperparameter can be adjusted based on your specific needs – increasing it may lead to better model performance if the model is underfitting, and decreasing it can help prevent overfitting and reduce training time. Monitor validation loss during training to determine the optimal number of epochs for your particular dataset and model architecture.

The learning rate scheduler implements a linear decay with warmup, which helps stabilize training in the early stages and then gradually reduces the learning rate to fine-tune the model more precisely. The learning rate controls how much a model adjusts its internal parameters during training – a higher rate means bigger adjustments but potential overshooting, while a lower rate means more precise but slower learning.

We use **Weights & Biases** (wandb) for logging, which allows us to track our training progress in real time and compare different runs (https://wandb.ai/site). This is crucial for monitoring the training process and making informed decisions about hyperparameter tuning and model architecture changes.

The training loop iterates over our data for the specified number of epochs. In each iteration, we do the following:

1. Move the batch to the appropriate device (GPU if available)

2. Perform a forward pass through the model

3. Calculate the loss

4. Perform backpropagation

5. Update the model parameters

6. Update the learning rate scheduler

7. Log the training loss

After each epoch, we perform a simple evaluation of the training data (in a real scenario, you'd use a separate validation set), log the evaluation loss, and save a checkpoint of the model. Checkpointing is needed for long-running training processes, allowing us to resume training from a saved state if needed.

As we've seen, the training pipeline involves several essential steps. Before the model architecture and training loop can function effectively, however, we must address data input and preprocessing, which we will discuss next.

Data input and preprocessing

Efficient data handling is crucial for LLM training, as we discussed in *Part 1* of this book. Here, let's explore advanced techniques for data input and preprocessing:

1. Import the required Python packages:

    ```
    from datasets import load_dataset, concatenate_datasets
    from transformers import AutoTokenizer
    from torch.utils.data import DataLoader
    import numpy as np
    ```

2. Load and combine multiple datasets:

    ```
    wiki_dataset = load_dataset("wikipedia", "20220301.en",
    split="train")
    books_dataset = load_dataset("bookcorpus", split="train")

    # Combine datasets
    combined_dataset = concatenate_
        datasets([wiki_dataset, books_dataset])
    ```

3. Initialize the tokenizer and perform preprocess:

    ```
    tokenizer = AutoTokenizer.from_pretrained("gpt2")

    def preprocess_function(examples):
        # Tokenize the texts
        tokenized = tokenizer(
            examples["text"], truncation=True, max_length=1024)

        # Create input_ids and attention_mask
        input_ids = tokenized["input_ids"]
        attention_mask = tokenized["attention_mask"]

        # Create labels for causal language modeling
        labels = [
            ids[1:] + [tokenizer.eos_token_id] for ids in input_ids]
    ```

```
            return {"input_ids": input_ids,
                "attention_mask": attention_mask, "labels": labels}

    # Apply preprocessing
    tokenized_dataset = combined_dataset.map(
        preprocess_function,
        batched=True,
        remove_columns=combined_dataset.column_names,
        num_proc=4   # Adjust based on your CPU cores
    )
```

4. Create the DataLoader:

```
    train_dataloader = DataLoader(
        tokenized_dataset,
        shuffle=True,
        batch_size=16,
        collate_fn=lambda x: {k: np.stack([xi[k] for xi in x])
            for k in x[0]}
    )
```

In this enhanced preprocessing pipeline, we're loading multiple datasets to increase the diversity of our training data. This is needed for LLMs, as a diverse dataset helps the model learn a broader range of language patterns and knowledge.

We use a longer `max_length` value of `1024` tokens to provide more context to the model. This increased context length allows the model to capture longer-range dependencies in the text, which can be beneficial for many language-understanding tasks. However, it also increases memory usage and computational requirements, so there's a trade-off to consider.

The `preprocess_function` now creates labels for causal language modeling by shifting the input sequences. This is a common approach for training language models, where the model's task is to predict the next token given the previous tokens. During preprocessing, handling edge cases such as emojis, URLs, and non-standard characters can enhance model performance. Emojis can convey nuanced emotions and context, requiring appropriate encoding or tokenization to preserve their meaning without introducing noise. URLs often contain valuable information but can vary widely in structure, so they might be replaced with placeholder tokens to maintain consistency while preventing the model from overfitting to specific links. Non-standard characters, including symbols from different languages or special punctuation, need careful normalization or removal to reduce complexity and avoid confusion during training. By addressing these edge cases through strategies such as normalization, token replacement, and selective filtering, preprocessing pipelines can better prepare diverse and complex data, enhancing the robustness and accuracy of the resulting language models.

We use multiprocessing (`num_proc=4`) to speed up the preprocessing. The number of processes should be adjusted based on your CPU cores and available memory. Multiprocessing can significantly reduce preprocessing time, especially for large datasets.

The batch size is increased to `16`, which is more suitable for larger GPU memory. The custom `collate_fn` in the DataLoader ensures proper batching of our preprocessed data. This function stacks the arrays for each key in the batch, creating tensor-like structures that can be efficiently processed by PyTorch.

With the data appropriately prepared, we now turn our attention to the LLM architecture design considerations, which dictate the model's capacity to effectively learn from and understand data input.

LLM architecture design considerations

When designing the architecture for an LLM, several factors come into play.

Here are the key factors influencing LLM architecture:

- **Vocabulary size**: Determines the size of the input and output embedding layers
- **Maximum sequence length (context size)**: Defines the amount of preceding text the model can consider
- **Embedding dimension**: Specifies the size of each token's vector representation, influencing the model's ability to capture information
- **Number of transformer layers**: Represents the depth of the network, impacting the complexity of patterns the model can learn
- **Number of attention heads**: Allows the model to attend to different parts of the input simultaneously
- **Model size (number of parameters)**: Overall capacity of the model, influenced by embedding dimension, number of layers, and attention heads
- **Dataset size**: The amount and diversity of training data
- **Number of training steps**: The duration of the optimization process
- **Computational resources**: Hardware constraints that affect model size, training speed, and overall feasibility.
- **Risk of overfitting**: Higher with larger models and smaller datasets
- **Data quality**: The cleanliness and relevance of the training data
- **Efficiency of model architecture**: Design choices that can improve performance without drastically increasing model size
- **Training algorithms**: Optimization techniques and strategies
- **Data curation practices**: Methods for selecting and preparing training data
- **Test time compute**: Computational resources available during inference

In the following code block, we provide examples of configuring some of these factors using a GPT-2 style language model, specifying key architectural parameters.

```
from transformers import GPT2Config, GPT2LMHeadModel

# Define custom model configuration
config = GPT2Config(
    vocab_size=50257,   # GPT-2 vocabulary size
    n_positions=1024,   # Maximum sequence length
    n_ctx=1024,         # Context size
    n_embd=768,         # Embedding dimension
    n_layer=12,         # Number of transformer layers
    n_head=12           # Number of attention heads
)

# Initialize the model with custom configuration
model = GPT2LMHeadModel(config)

print(f"Model parameters: {model.num_parameters():,}")
```

This configuration creates a GPT-2 style model with 12 layers and 12 attention heads. Let's break down the key parameters:

- vocab_size: Set to 50257, which is the vocabulary size of the original GPT-2 model. This determines the size of the embedding layer and the output layer.

- n_positions and n_ctx: Both are set to 1024, matching our preprocessing step. This defines the maximum sequence length the model can handle.

- n_embd: The embedding dimension, set to 768. This determines the size of the hidden states throughout the model.

- n_layer: The number of transformer layers, set to 12. More layers can capture more complex patterns but increase computational requirements.

- n_head: The number of attention heads, set to 12. Multiple attention heads allow the model to focus on different aspects of the input simultaneously.

The embedding dimension of 768 and the 12 layers provide a balanced trade-off between model capacity and computational efficiency. This configuration results in a model with about 124 million parameters, which is substantial but still trainable on common GPU hardware.

For larger models, you might increase n_layer, n_embd, and n_head. However, this would also increase the computational requirements and the risk of overfitting, especially on smaller datasets. When scaling up, consider techniques such as gradient accumulation, mixed precision training, and distributed training to manage the increased computational load.

In a broader scope, **scaling laws** can be considered. The scaling laws for LLMs describe how performance improves predictably as three key factors increase: model size (number of parameters), dataset size (amount of training data), and the number of training steps (optimization iterations). Specifically, larger models tend to capture more complex patterns and exhibit better generalization, larger datasets provide more diverse information for learning, and more training steps allow the model to refine its understanding and reduce errors. For optimal performance, these factors should scale proportionally – for instance, increasing the model size should be matched by a corresponding increase in dataset size and training steps. This balanced scaling ensures that each component supports the others, preventing bottlenecks such as overfitting smaller models on vast datasets or undertraining large models with insufficient data.

However, recent advancements and practical challenges have shown that simply scaling these factors is not always sufficient for continual performance improvements. Issues such as diminishing returns, where each additional parameter or data point contributes less to overall performance, have become more apparent. Additionally, the immense computational and energy resources required for training increasingly large models raise sustainability and accessibility concerns. Data quality also becomes a critical factor, as larger datasets may introduce more noise and biases, potentially degrading model performance. For more details about this, please see the article at `https://www.pcgamer.com/software/ai/open-ai-co-founder-reckons-ai-training-has-hit-a-wall-forcing-ai-labs-to-train-their-models-smarter-not-just-bigger/`.

To address these challenges, researchers are exploring more efficient model architectures, improved training algorithms, better data curation practices, and test time compute. See my Medium article for more details on test time compute: `https://kenhuangus.medium.com/test-time-compute-3633a4c55716`

At the beginning of 2025, DeepSeek (an AI startup in China) announced some model training innovations by introducing a suite of techniques aimed at significantly increasing efficiency and reducing costs, while simultaneously enhancing the model's reasoning capabilities (`https://arxiv.org/abs/2501.12948`). Unlike traditional approaches that rely heavily on vast computational resources and human-supervised fine-tuning, DeepSeek leverages large-scale reinforcement learning focused on reasoning tasks, using automated reward systems rather than human feedback. Key innovations include multi-token prediction, which allows the model to learn from multiple future tokens at once, increasing sample efficiency, and speeding up training. DeepSeek also employs a mixture-of-experts architecture to activate only relevant sub-networks for each task, thus reducing computational load. By optimizing both algorithms and hardware, DeepSeek has managed to train highly capable models at a fraction of the cost and time required by competitors, setting new standards for open, efficient, and powerful AI development.

Having explored the architectural design considerations and model training innovations for LLMs — along with a code example demonstrating how to configure model training parameters — we are now ready to examine how these architectural choices are actually learned during training. In this next section, we will discuss the loss function and optimization strategies, which serve as the engine that drives the model to adjust its internal parameters based on both the training data and the architecture we have defined.

Loss functions and optimization strategies

LLMs typically use **cross-entropy loss** for training. This approach measures the difference between the model's predicted probability distribution of words and the actual distribution in the training data. By minimizing this loss, LLMs learn to generate more accurate and contextually appropriate text. Cross-entropy loss is particularly well-suited for language tasks due to its ability to handle the high dimensionality and discrete nature of textual data.

Let's implement this along with some advanced optimization techniques:

1. First, we import the required PyTorch libraries and specific modules from the Transformers library for optimization:

    ```
    import torch
    from torch.optim import AdamW
    from transformers import get_linear_schedule_with_warmup
    ```

2. Next, we configure the AdamW optimizer with a specified learning rate and weight decay:

    ```
    optimizer = AdamW(model.parameters(), lr=5e-5,
        weight_decay=0.01)
    ```

3. Then, we define a linear learning rate scheduler with a warm-up period:

    ```
    num_epochs = 3
    total_steps = len(train_dataloader) * num_epochs
    scheduler = get_linear_schedule_with_warmup(
        optimizer,
        num_warmup_steps=100,
        num_training_steps=total_steps
    )
    ```

4. Subsequently, we set up the training device and initiate the main training loop:

```
device = torch.device("cuda" if torch.cuda.is_available()
    else "cpu")
model.to(device)

for epoch in range(num_epochs):
    model.train()
    for batch in train_dataloader:
        batch = {k: torch.tensor(v).to(device)
            for k, v in batch.items()
        }
        outputs = model(batch)
        loss = outputs.loss
        loss.backward()
```

5. Finally, we implement gradient clipping to prevent exploding gradients during training:

```
torch.nn.utils.clip_grad_norm_(model.parameters(), max_norm=1.0)

        optimizer.step()
        scheduler.step()
        optimizer.zero_grad()
```

In this optimization setup, we use the AdamW optimizer with a learning rate of 5e-5 and weight decay of 0.01. The algorithm adapts the learning rate for each parameter based on the first and second moments of the gradients, allowing it to handle sparse gradients effectively. This makes AdamW particularly useful for training large neural networks.

The weight decay of 0.01 adds a small regularization term to the loss function, which can help prevent overfitting by penalizing large weight values.

We implement a **learning rate scheduler** with warmup. The warmup phase helps stabilize training in the early stages by gradually increasing the learning rate from a very small value. After the warmup phase, the learning rate decreases linearly. This schedule can help the model converge to a better optimum.

In the training loop, we implement **gradient clipping** with a max_norm value of 1.0. Gradient clipping prevents exploding gradients by scaling down gradient values that exceed a certain threshold. This is particularly important for LLMs, which can be prone to unstable gradients due to their depth and the long-range dependencies they capture.

In this section, we learned about AdamW optimization, learning rate scheduling with warmup, and gradient clipping for stable LLM training. Next, we talk about logging the training process, which is crucial for monitoring progress and using tools like **TensorBoard** to gain insights for improvement.

Logging

Effective logging can be useful for tracking the progress of LLM training.

The following code blocks demonstrate how to integrate TensorBoard for effective logging during the training of an LLM using PyTorch. Let's break down each part.

1. We first initialize the TensorBoard `SummaryWriter` for logging training progress:

    ```
    from torch.utils.tensorboard import SummaryWriter
    import time

    # Initialize TensorBoard writer
    writer = SummaryWriter()
    ```

2. Then, we set the model to training mode, initialize variables for tracking loss, define the logging interval, and record the start time to monitor training performance:

    ```
    model.train()
    total_loss = 0
    log_interval = 100
    start_time = time.time()
    ```

3. Then, we move on to the training loop. We process each batch by moving data to the appropriate device, performing forward and backward passes, applying gradient clipping, and updating the model's parameters using the optimizer and scheduler:

    ```
    for i, batch in enumerate(train_dataloader):
        batch = {k: torch.tensor(v).to(device)
            for k, v in batch.items()}
        outputs = model(batch)
        loss = outputs.loss
        total_loss += loss.item()

        loss.backward()
        torch.nn.utils.clip_grad_norm_(model.parameters(),
            max_norm=1.0)
        optimizer.step()
        scheduler.step()
        optimizer.zero_grad()
    ```

4. We log the training metrics to TensorBoard at specified intervals, calculate the average loss, measure the elapsed time, print the progress to the console, and reset the tracking variables for the next interval:

```
if (i + 1) % log_interval == 0:
    cur_loss = total_loss / log_interval
    elapsed = time.time() - start_time
    writer.add_scalar(
        'training_loss', cur_loss, global_step=i
    )
    writer.add_scalar(
        'learning_rate', scheduler.get_last_lr()[0],
        global_step=i
    )
    print(
        f'| epoch {epoch:3d} '
        f'| {i:5d}/{len(train_dataloader):5d} batches | '
        f'lr {scheduler.get_last_lr()[0]:02.2f} | '
        f'ms/batch {elapsed * 1000 / log_interval:5.2f} | '
        f'loss {cur_loss:5.2f}'
    )
    total_loss = 0
    start_time = time.time()

writer.close()
```

This enhanced training loop uses TensorBoard for logging training loss and learning rate. TensorBoard is a powerful tool for visualizing training progress and comparing different runs. We log the following metrics:

- **Training loss**: This is the average loss over the last `log_interval` batches. A decreasing trend in this metric indicates that the model is learning.

- **Learning rate**: We log the current learning rate to visualize how it changes over time due to our learning rate scheduler.

We set `log_interval` to `100`, meaning we log and print out progress information every 100 batches. This interval strikes a balance between getting frequent updates and not slowing down training too much with logging operations. You may need to adjust this based on your dataset size and training speed.

The output or log information includes the following:

- Current epoch and batch number
- Current learning rate

- Time per batch (in milliseconds)
- Current loss

This detailed logging allows you to monitor the training process closely, helping you identify issues such as unstable loss, learning rate problems, or unexpectedly slow training.

Pipeline modularity and reusability

Modularity and **reusability** are fundamental principles for building efficient pipelines because they make code more maintainable, adaptable, and reliable. By breaking down a pipeline into independent, reusable modules (such as data preprocessing, model training, and evaluation components), developers can easily modify individual parts without affecting others, test each component separately, and reuse proven code across different projects.

This approach not only saves development time but also ensures consistency in operations, reduces the chance of errors, and makes it easier for teams to collaborate by working on separate modules while maintaining clear interfaces between components. In the case of training pipelines, encapsulating processes in reusable classes allows for flexible configuration, seamless integration with different datasets, and straightforward sharing of standardized implementations across multiple projects.

To make our pipeline more modular and reusable, let's encapsulate our training process in a class:

1. We start with class definition:

```
class LLMTrainer:
    def __init__(self, model, train_dataloader, optimizer,
    scheduler, device
    ):
        self.model = model
        self.train_dataloader = train_dataloader
        self.optimizer = optimizer
        self.scheduler = scheduler
        self.device = device
        self.writer = SummaryWriter()
```

2. Then, we define the train epoch function. The function sets the model to training mode and iterates over the training data, processing each batch by computing the loss, performing backpropagation with gradient clipping, and updating the model parameters using the optimizer and scheduler:

```
def train_epoch(self):
    self.model.train()
    total_loss = 0
    log_interval = 100
```

```
start_time = time.time()
for i, batch in enumerate(self.train_dataloader):
    batch = {k: torch.tensor(v).to(self.device)
        for k, v in batch.items()
    }
    outputs = self.model(batch)
    loss = outputs.loss
    total_loss += loss.item()

    loss.backward()
    torch.nn.utils.clip_grad_norm_(
        self.model.parameters(), max_norm=1.0)
    self.optimizer.step()
    self.scheduler.step()
    self.optimizer.zero_grad()
```

3. Next, we periodically log the training progress to both TensorBoard and the console by checking if the current batch index is a multiple of the `log_interval`; if it is, we calculate the average loss and elapsed time since the last log, record the training loss and learning rate to TensorBoard using the `SummaryWriter`, print a formatted progress update including batch number, learning rate, milliseconds per batch, and current loss to the console, and then reset the accumulated `total_loss` and `start_time` for the next logging interval:

```
if (i + 1) % log_interval == 0:
    cur_loss = total_loss / log_interval
    elapsed = time.time() - start_time
    self.writer.add_scalar(
        'training_loss', cur_loss, global_step=i
    )
    self.writer.add_scalar(
        'learning_rate',
        self.scheduler.get_last_lr()[0],
        global_step=i
    )

    print(
        f'| {i:5d}/'
        f'{len(self.train_dataloader):5d} '
        f'batches | '
        f'lr '
        f'{self.scheduler.get_last_lr()'
        f'[0]:02.2f} | '
        f'ms/batch '
        f'{elapsed * 1000 / log_interval:5.2f} '
```

```
                              f'| '
                              f'loss '
                              f'{cur_loss:5.2f}'
                          )
                  total_loss = 0
                  start_time = time.time()
```

4. Next, the `train` function orchestrates the training process by looping through the specified number of epochs, printing a message at the start of each epoch, invoking the `train_epoch` method to perform training for that epoch, and, finally, closing the writer once all epochs are completed. It serves as the main entry point for training, providing a structure where additional features such as validation and checkpointing can be integrated as needed:

```python
def train(self, num_epochs):
    for epoch in range(num_epochs):
        print(f'Starting epoch {epoch+1}')
        self.train_epoch()
        # Here you could add validation, checkpointing, etc.

    self.writer.close()
```

5. Lastly, we instantiate the `LLMTrainer` class with the specified model, training data loader, optimizer, scheduler, and device. Then, the training process is started by calling the `train` method to execute three full training epochs, thereby initiating and managing the model's learning cycle:

```python
trainer = LLMTrainer(model, train_dataloader,
    optimizer, scheduler, device)
trainer.train(num_epochs=3)
```

This modular design offers several advantages:

- **Encapsulation**: All the training logic is contained within the `LLMTrainer` class, making it easier to manage and understand.

- **Reusability**: You can easily use this trainer for different models or datasets by creating a new instance with different parameters.

- **Extensibility**: The class structure makes it easy to add new functionality. For example, you could add methods for validation, checkpointing, or early stopping.

- **Separation of concerns**: The training logic is separated from the model definition and data preparation, following good software engineering principles.

The following log demonstrates the training process over 3 epochs, with periodic logging every 100 batches. Each log entry includes the current batch number, total batches, learning rate, milliseconds per batch, and the average loss:

```
Starting epoch 1
|    100/1000 batches | lr 0.01  | ms/batch 45.67 | loss 2.35
|    200/1000 batches | lr 0.01  | ms/batch 44.89 | loss 2.10
|    300/1000 batches | lr 0.01  | ms/batch 46.12 | loss 1.95
|    400/1000 batches | lr 0.01  | ms/batch 45.50 | loss 1.80
|    500/1000 batches | lr 0.01  | ms/batch 44.75 | loss 1.65
|    600/1000 batches | lr 0.009 | ms/batch 45.30 | loss 1.50
|    700/1000 batches | lr 0.009 | ms/batch 44.95 | loss 1.40
|    800/1000 batches | lr 0.009 | ms/batch 45.10 | loss 1.30
|    900/1000 batches | lr 0.009 | ms/batch 45.00 | loss 1.25
|   1000/1000 batches | lr 0.009 | ms/batch 44.80 | loss 1.20


Starting epoch 2
|    100/1000 batches | lr 0.009 | ms/batch 44.60 | loss 1.18
|    200/1000 batches | lr 0.009 | ms/batch 44.70 | loss 1.15
|    300/1000 batches | lr 0.009 | ms/batch 44.80 | loss 1.12
|    400/1000 batches | lr 0.008 | ms/batch 44.50 | loss 1.10
|    500/1000 batches | lr 0.008 | ms/batch 44.60 | loss 1.08
|    600/1000 batches | lr 0.008 | ms/batch 44.55 | loss 1.05
|    700/1000 batches | lr 0.008 | ms/batch 44.65 | loss 1.03
|    800/1000 batches | lr 0.007 | ms/batch 44.50 | loss 1.00
|    900/1000 batches | lr 0.007 | ms/batch 44.60 | loss 0.98
|   1000/1000 batches | lr 0.007 | ms/batch 44.55 | loss 0.95


Starting epoch 3
|    100/1000 batches | lr 0.007 | ms/batch 44.50 | loss 0.93
|    200/1000 batches | lr 0.007 | ms/batch 44.60 | loss 0.90
|    300/1000 batches | lr 0.006 | ms/batch 44.55 | loss 0.88
|    400/1000 batches | lr 0.006 | ms/batch 44.50 | loss 0.85
|    500/1000 batches | lr 0.006 | ms/batch 44.60 | loss 0.83
|    600/1000 batches | lr 0.006 | ms/batch 44.55 | loss 0.80
|    700/1000 batches | lr 0.005 | ms/batch 44.50 | loss 0.78
|    800/1000 batches | lr 0.005 | ms/batch 44.60 | loss 0.75
|    900/1000 batches | lr 0.005 | ms/batch 44.55 | loss 0.73
|   1000/1000 batches | lr 0.005 | ms/batch 44.50 | loss 0.70
Training completed. Writer closed.
```

Here is an explanation of the above simulated log:

- **Epoch start**: Each epoch begins with a message such as `Starting epoch 1`, indicating the commencement of a new training cycle

- **Batch logging**: Every 100 batches, the following information is logged:

  - **Batch progress**: Displays the current batch number out of the total batches, such as `100/1000 batches`

  - **Learning rate (lr)**: Shows the current learning rate, which may decrease over epochs due to the scheduler, such as `lr 0.01`

  - **Milliseconds per batch (ms/batch)**: Indicates the time taken to process each batch, such as `ms/batch 45.67`

  - **Loss**: Represents the average loss over the last 100 batches, showing the model's performance, such as `loss 2.35`

- **Learning rate schedule**: Notice how the learning rate decreases over epochs, reflecting the scheduler's adjustments to facilitate better convergence

- **Training completion**: After all epochs are completed, a final message (`Training completed. Writer closed.`) indicates the end of the training process and the closure of the logging writer

The log provides a clear overview of the training dynamics, allowing developers and researchers to monitor the model's learning progress, adjust hyperparameters if necessary, and ensure that the training is proceeding as expected.

Scaling your training pipeline for larger models

To train larger models, we need to employ techniques such as gradient accumulation and mixed precision training.

To train very large language models that might not fit on a single GPU, the following code introduces a special `LargeScaleLLMTrainer`. It uses two main tricks to handle this:

First, gradient accumulation allows us to simulate having access to a larger GPU. Instead of updating the model's parameters after every small batch of data, we process several small batches, accumulating their gradients along the way. Only after a predefined number of batches do we perform an actual update to the model's parameters. This technique enables the model to learn as if it had seen a much larger batch of data, without requiring the memory capacity of an extremely large GPU.

Second, it employs mixed precision training, a technique where the computer performs many calculations using smaller, lower-precision numbers (which require less memory and are faster to compute), while reserving higher-precision numbers for situations where accuracy is critical. This approach accelerates training and reduces overall memory usage. To mitigate potential issues that can arise from using lower-precision values, GradScaler is used to maintain numerical stability during backpropagation.

The following code defines how this special trainer works, including how it processes data, calculates the loss, and updates the model's learning using these tricks. It also still includes important steps like making sure the gradients (how the model should change) don't get too big and logging progress so we can see how the training is going. Finally, it shows a simple example of how to use this special trainer. Now, let us break it into several parts:

1. Let us start by importing the relevant Python package and defining the class:

```python
import torch.cuda.amp as amp

class LargeScaleLLMTrainer(LLMTrainer):
    def __init__(self, model, train_dataloader,
        optimizer, scheduler, device, accumulation_steps=4
    ):
        super().__init__(model, train_dataloader,
            optimizer, scheduler, device)
        self.accumulation_steps = accumulation_steps
        self.scaler = amp.GradScaler()
```

2. We can then define the training epoch:

```python
def train_epoch(self):
    self.model.train()
    total_loss = 0
    log_interval = 100
    start_time = time.time()

    for i, batch in enumerate(self.train_dataloader):
        batch = {
            k: torch.tensor(v).to(self.device)
            for k, v in batch.items()
        }

        with amp.autocast():
            outputs = self.model(batch)
            loss = outputs.loss / self.accumulation_steps

        self.scaler.scale(loss).backward()
```

3. Then, we implement the following code block, which updates the model's parameters, learning rate, and gradient scaler only after processing a defined number of batches (accumulation_steps), effectively simulating a larger batch size while managing memory constraints:

```python
if (i + 1) % self.accumulation_steps == 0:
    self.scaler.unscale_(self.optimizer)
    torch.nn.utils.clip_grad_norm_(
        self.model.parameters(), max_norm=1.0
    )
```

```
                self.scaler.step(self.optimizer)
                self.scaler.update()
                self.scheduler.step()
                self.optimizer.zero_grad()

            total_loss += loss.item() * self.accumulation_steps
```

4. We then periodically calculate and log the average training loss and learning rate to TensorBoard, while also printing a summary of the current training progress to the console at intervals defined by `log_interval`:

```
            if (i + 1) % log_interval == 0:
                cur_loss = total_loss / log_interval
                elapsed = time.time() start_time
                self.writer.add_scalar('training_loss',
                    cur_loss, global_step=i)
                self.writer.add_scalar('learning_rate',
                    self.scheduler.get_last_lr()[0],
                    global_step=i)
                print(
                    f'| {i:5d}/{len(self.train_dataloader):5d}
                        batches | '
                    f'lr {self.scheduler.get_last_lr()[0]:02.2f}
                        | '
                    f'ms/batch {elapsed * 1000 /
                        log_interval:5.2f} | '
                    f'loss {cur_loss:5.2f}'
                )
                total_loss = 0
                start_time = time.time()
```

5. We demonstrate the initialization and execution of a large-scale language model training process:

```
large_trainer = LargeScaleLLMTrainer(
    model, train_dataloader, optimizer, scheduler, device)
large_trainer.train(num_epochs=3)
```

This enhanced trainer uses two key techniques for scaling to larger models:

*   **Gradient accumulation**: We update weights every four batches (set by `accumulation_steps`). This allows us to effectively increase the batch size without increasing memory usage, which is effective for training large models on limited GPU memory. We divide the loss by `accumulation_steps` to maintain the same effective learning rate.

*   **Mixed precision training**: We use PyTorch's **Automatic Mixed Precision** (**AMP**) to perform computations in `float16`, where possible, while maintaining `float32` master weights. This can significantly speed up training and reduce memory usage, especially on modern GPUs with tensor cores.

GradScaler is used to prevent underflow in float16 calculations. It scales the loss to prevent small gradient values, then unscales before the optimizer step.

We still apply gradient clipping, but now it's done after unscaling the gradients to ensure we're clipping the true gradient values.

For even larger models, you might consider techniques such as **model parallelism** (splitting the model across multiple GPUs), **pipeline parallelism** (splitting the model into stages), or using specialized libraries such as **DeepSpeed** or **Megatron-LM**. These advanced techniques allow the training of models with billions of parameters across multiple GPUs or even multiple machines. Memory offloading can be a good alternative when GPU memory is insufficient to handle vast amounts of data and model parameters. Memory offloading involves transferring parts of the model's data or computations to alternative memory storage, such as **Non-Volatile Memory Express** (**NVMe**) SSDs. By leveraging NVMe memory, which offers high-speed data access compared to traditional storage, systems can effectively manage and store intermediate activations, gradients, and model states that exceed GPU memory capacity. This approach allows for training larger models or using higher batch sizes without requiring immediate GPU memory expansion. However, it introduces additional latency due to data transfer between the GPU and NVMe storage, which can impact training speed. Optimizing data access patterns and utilizing efficient offloading strategies can minimize performance overhead and maintain effective training workflows when employing memory offloading techniques.

Summary

In this chapter, you learned about a practical pattern of pipeline design for training LLMs. You learned how to create efficient data preprocessing workflows, implement model architectures, and apply advanced optimization strategies. You now understand how to set up effective logging systems to track your model's progress. You also explored techniques for building modular and reusable pipelines and discovered methods for scaling your training process to accommodate larger models. With these skills, you're well equipped to train state-of-the-art language models efficiently and effectively.

In the next chapter, we'll explore the hyperparameter tuning pattern.

8

Hyperparameter Tuning

In this chapter, you'll learn about the hyperparameters in LLMs and strategies for optimizing them efficiently. We'll explore both manual and automated tuning approaches, including grid search, random search, and more advanced methods, such as Bayesian optimization and population-based training. You'll also gain insights into handling multi-objective optimization scenarios common in LLM development.

By the end, you'll be equipped with practical tools and techniques to fine-tune your LLMs for optimal performance across various tasks and domains.

In this chapter, we'll be covering the following topics:

- Understanding hyperparameters
- Manual versus automated tuning
- Grid and random search
- Bayesian optimization
- Population-based methods
- Multi-objective hyperparameter optimization
- Hyperparameter tuning at scale – challenges and solutions

Understanding hyperparameters

Hyperparameters are settings that are set before the machine learning training process begins and are not learned from the data. They control various aspects of the learning algorithm itself, such as the model's complexity, learning rate, and the overall training process. Data scientists manually choose and tune these hyperparameters to optimize the model's performance.

Hyperparameters in LLMs can be broadly categorized into three groups: architectural, optimization, and regularization hyperparameters:

- **Architectural hyperparameters**: These define the design and structure of the model, determining how it processes and represents data. They are critical because they directly influence the model's capacity to learn complex patterns and relationships in the data. The right architecture balances computational efficiency with performance, enabling the model to generalize well to unseen data.

  Parameters within this category include the following:

  - Number of layers

  - Hidden size

  - Number of attention heads

  - Feed-forward dimension

  - Vocabulary size

- **Optimization hyperparameters**: These govern how the model learns during training by adjusting the parameters to minimize the loss function. They are important because they control the rate and manner of updates, affecting convergence speed, stability, and the model's ability to reach an optimal solution. Proper tuning ensures efficient training without divergence or underfitting.

  Parameters within this category include the following (we covered these in *Chapter 7*):

  - Learning rate

  - Batch size

  - Number of training steps

  - Warmup steps

  - Learning rate schedule

- **Regularization hyperparameters**: These introduce mechanisms to prevent the model from overfitting to the training data, ensuring it generalizes to new data. They are crucial because models with high capacity can easily memorize the training data, leading to poor performance on unseen data. Regularization techniques enforce constraints that encourage simplicity and robustness.

  Parameters within this category include the following (see *Chapter 9* for more):

  - Dropout rate

  - Weight decay

  - Label smoothing

Let's implement a function to create an LLM with configurable hyperparameters:

```
from transformers import GPT2Config, GPT2LMHeadModel

def create_llm(
    num_layers, hidden_size, num_heads, ff_dim, vocab_size
):
    config = GPT2Config(
        n_layer=num_layers,
        n_embd=hidden_size,
        n_head=num_heads,
        n_inner=ff_dim,
        vocab_size=vocab_size
    )
    model = GPT2LMHeadModel(config)
    return model

# Example usage
model = create_llm(num_layers=12, hidden_size=768,
    num_heads=12, ff_dim=3072, vocab_size=50257)
print(f"Model parameters: {model.num_parameters():,}")
```

In this code, we define a function, `create_llm`, that allows us to easily create LLMs with different architectural hyperparameters. The function takes the following parameters:

- `num_layers`: The number of transformer layers in the model. More layers can capture more complex patterns, but they increase computational requirements.

- `hidden_size`: The dimension of the hidden states throughout the model. This affects the model's capacity to capture information.

- `num_heads`: The number of attention heads in each layer. Multiple heads allow the model to focus on different aspects of the input simultaneously.

- `ff_dim`: The dimension of the feed-forward layer in each transformer block. This is typically set to four times the `hidden_size`.

- `vocab_size`: The size of the model's vocabulary. This determines the size of the embedding layer and the output layer.

We use these parameters to create a `GPT2Config` object, which is then used to initialize a `GPT2LMHeadModel`. This approach allows us to easily experiment with different model architectures.

Manual versus automated tuning

Manual tuning involves adjusting hyperparameters based on intuition, experience, and gradual experimentation. Manual tuning allows you to leverage domain knowledge to explore tailored configurations systematically, but it is time-intensive, prone to suboptimal results, and inefficient in exploring large hyperparameter spaces.

Automated tuning, on the other hand, uses algorithms to systematically explore the hyperparameter space. Automated tuning efficiently explores large hyperparameter spaces using algorithms to optimize performance, saving time and effort compared to manual tuning, but it can be computationally expensive and may require expertise to configure properly.

Manual tuning is useful when domain knowledge or intuition can guide a small, targeted search space, especially in resource-constrained settings or for simpler models. Automated tuning is better for large, complex hyperparameter spaces where systematic exploration and optimization are required, as it can find better configurations more efficiently despite higher computational costs.

Let's implement both approaches.

Manual tuning

First, we'll implement manual tuning:

1. Start with the imports:

    ```
    import numpy as np
    from transformers import Trainer, TrainingArguments
    from datasets import load_dataset
    ```

2. Load a sample dataset:

    ```
    dataset = load_dataset(
        "wikitext", "wikitext-2-raw-v1", split="train")

    def tokenize_function(examples):
        return tokenizer(
            examples["text"], truncation=True, max_length=512)

    tokenized_dataset = dataset.map(tokenize_function,
        batched=True, remove_columns=dataset.column_names)
    ```

3. Set up the manual tuning hyperparameters:

    ```
    manual_hyperparameters = [
        {"num_layers": 6, "hidden_size": 512, "num_heads": 8, "ff_
    dim": 2048},
    ```

```
            {"num_layers": 12, "hidden_size": 768, "num_heads": 12, "ff_
      dim": 3072},
            {"num_layers": 24, "hidden_size": 1024, "num_heads": 16,
      "ff_dim": 4096}
      ]
```

4. Conduct training with `manual_hyperparameters`:

```
for hp in manual_hyperparameters:
    model = create_llm(hp, vocab_size=50257)

    training_args = TrainingArguments(
        output_dir=(
            f"./results_{hp['num_layers']}_"
            f"{hp['hidden_size']}"
        ),
        num_train_epochs=3,
        per_device_train_batch_size=8,
        logging_dir=(
            f"./logs_{hp['num_layers']}_"
            f"{hp['hidden_size']}"
        ),
    )

    trainer = Trainer(
        model=model,
        args=training_args,
        train_dataset=tokenized_dataset,
    )

    trainer.train()
```

5. Evaluate the model:

```
eval_results = trainer.evaluate()
print(f"Hyperparameters: {hp}")
print(f"Evaluation results: {eval_results}")
```

In this manual tuning example, we define a list of hyperparameter configurations to try. We then iterate through these configurations, creating a model for each, training it, and evaluating its performance. This approach allows us to systematically explore different model sizes and architectures.

The manual tuning process can be guided by domain knowledge and intuition. For example, we might start with a small model (6 layers, 512 hidden size) and gradually increase the size to see how it affects performance. We choose these specific configurations based on common practices in transformer-based models:

- The smallest configuration (6 layers, 512 hidden size) represents a compact model suitable for faster training and deployment

- The medium configuration (12 layers, 768 hidden size) is similar to the base GPT-2 model, known to perform well on many tasks

- The largest configuration (24 layers, 1,024 hidden size) represents a more powerful model that might capture more complex patterns but requires more computational resources

Automated tuning

Now, let's implement a simple automated tuning approach using random search (we will show a more advanced random search in the next section):

1. Add the `import` statement and set up the random parameters:

```
import random

def random_hp_search(num_trials=10):
    best_eval_loss = float('inf')
    best_hp = None

    for _ in range(num_trials):
        hp = {
            "num_layers": random.choice([6, 12, 24]),
            "hidden_size": random.choice([512, 768, 1024]),
            "num_heads": random.choice([8, 12, 16]),
            "ff_dim": random.choice([2048, 3072, 4096])
        }
```

2. Conduct training:

```
        model = create_llm(hp, vocab_size=50257)

        training_args = TrainingArguments(
            output_dir=f"./results_random_{_}",
            num_train_epochs=3,
            per_device_train_batch_size=8,
            logging_dir=f"./logs_random_{_}",
```

```
        )

        trainer = Trainer(
            model=model,
            args=training_args,
            train_dataset=tokenized_dataset,
        )

        trainer.train()
```

3. Evaluate and print out the results:

```
        eval_results = trainer.evaluate()
        eval_loss = eval_results['eval_loss']

        if eval_loss < best_eval_loss:
            best_eval_loss = eval_loss
            best_hp = hp

        print(
            f"Trial {_ + 1}: "
            f"Hyperparameters: {hp}, "
            f"Eval Loss: {eval_loss}"
        )

    print(
        f"Best Hyperparameters: {best_hp}, "
        f"Best Eval Loss: {best_eval_loss}"
    )

random_hp_search()
```

This random search implementation randomly selects hyperparameters from predefined options for each trial (no manual intervention during trials). Predefined options refer to the specified ranges, sets, or distributions from which random values for hyperparameters are sampled during the search process. For example, discrete hyperparameters such as the number of layers might be chosen from a set [6, 12, 24], while continuous hyperparameters such as learning rate could be sampled from a uniform or log-uniform distribution, such as $10^{(-5)}$ to $10^{(-3)}$. These options define the boundaries and possible values for each hyperparameter, guiding the random sampling process.

We choose to search over a discrete set of values for each hyperparameter to limit the search space and ensure that we're exploring configurations that are known to work well for transformer models. The number of trials (10 in this case) is a balance between exploration and computational resources. More trials increase the chance of finding a good configuration but also increase the computational cost.

In the subsequent sections, we will introduce other automated turning techniques such as grid search and more advanced random search, Bayesian optimization, the population-based method, and multi-objective hyperparameter optimization.

Grid and random search

Grid search and **random search** are two common methods for hyperparameter tuning. We covered random search in the previous section. In this section, we implement grid search and a more advanced version of random search.

1. Add the import and set up the grid search parameters:

    ```
    import itertools

    def grid_search():
        hp_grid = {
            "num_layers": [6, 12, 24],
            "hidden_size": [512, 768, 1024],
            "num_heads": [8, 12, 16],
            "ff_dim": [2048, 3072, 4096]
        }

        best_eval_loss = float('inf')
        best_hp = None
    ```

2. Train the model with the defined hyperparameters:

    ```
    for hp in itertools.product(*hp_grid.values()):
        hp_dict = dict(zip(hp_grid.keys(),hp))

        model = create_llm(
            hp_dict["num_layers"],
            hp_dict["hidden_size"],
            hp_dict["num_heads"],
            hp_dict["ff_dim"],
            vocab_size=50257
        )

        training_args = TrainingArguments(
            output_dir=(
                f"./results_grid_{hp_dict['num_layers']}_"
                f"{hp_dict['hidden_size']}"
            ),
            num_train_epochs=3,
            per_device_train_batch_size=8,
    ```

```
        logging_dir=(
            f"./logs_grid_{hp_dict['num_layers']}_"
            f"{hp_dict['hidden_size']}"
        ),
    )

    trainer = Trainer(
        model=model,
        args=training_args,
        train_dataset=tokenized_dataset,
    )

    trainer.train()
```

3. Evaluate and print out the results:

```
        eval_results = trainer.evaluate()
        eval_loss = eval_results['eval_loss']

        if eval_loss < best_eval_loss:
            best_eval_loss = eval_loss
            best_hp = hp_dict

        print(
            f"Hyperparameters: {hp_dict}, "
            f"Eval Loss: {eval_loss}"
        )

    print(
        f"Best Hyperparameters: {best_hp}, "
        f"Best Eval Loss: {best_eval_loss}"
    )

grid_search()
```

Grid search exhaustively explores all combinations of hyperparameters. This approach is thorough but can be computationally expensive, especially for LLMs with many hyperparameters. In this implementation, we're exploring $3^4 = 81$ different configurations, which could take a significant amount of time and resources.

The hyperparameter ranges are chosen to cover a reasonable space of model sizes, from relatively small (6 layers, 512 hidden size) to quite large (24 layers, 1,024 hidden size). This allows us to explore the trade-off between model size and performance.

Now, let's implement a more sophisticated random search that also includes optimization hyperparameters:

1. Add the `import` statement and set up the `advanced_random_search` hyperparameters:

```
import random

def advanced_random_search(num_trials=20):
    best_eval_loss = float('inf')
    best_hp = None
    for _ in range(num_trials):
        hp = {
            "num_layers": random.choice([6, 12, 24]),
            "hidden_size": random.choice([512, 768, 1024]),
            "num_heads": random.choice([8, 12, 16]),
            "ff_dim": random.choice([2048, 3072, 4096]),
            "learning_rate": 10random.uniform(-5, -3),
            "batch_size": random.choice([8, 16, 32]),
            "num_epochs": random.randint(2, 5),
            "warmup_steps": random.randint(100, 1000),
            "weight_decay": random.uniform(0, 0.2)
        }
```

2. Conduct the training:

```
        model = create_llm(
            num_layers=hp['num_layers'],
                hidden_size=hp['hidden_size'],
            num_heads=hp['num_heads'], ff_dim=hp['ff_dim'],
                vocab_size=50257)

        training_args = TrainingArguments(
            output_dir=f"./results_advanced_random_{_}",
            num_train_epochs=hp['num_epochs'],
            per_device_train_batch_size=hp['batch_size'],
            learning_rate=hp['learning_rate'],
            warmup_steps=hp['warmup_steps'],
            weight_decay=hp['weight_decay'],
            logging_dir=f"./logs_advanced_random_{_}",
        )

        trainer = Trainer(
            model=model,
            args=training_args,
            train_dataset=tokenized_dataset,
```

```
        )

        trainer.train()
```

3. Evaluate and print out the results:

```
        eval_results = trainer.evaluate()
        eval_loss = eval_results['eval_loss']

        if eval_loss < best_eval_loss:
            best_eval_loss = eval_loss
            best_hp = hp

        print(
            f"Trial {_ + 1}: Hyperparameters: {hp}, "
            f"Eval Loss: {eval_loss}"
        )

    print(
        f"Best Hyperparameters: {best_hp}, "
        f"Best Eval Loss: {best_eval_loss}"
    )
```

This advanced random search includes both architectural and optimization hyperparameters. We use `random.uniform` for **continuous hyperparameters** (parameters that can take any real number value within a range, such as `0.001`, `0.0015`, or `0.002`) such as learning rate and weight decay, and `random.choice` or `random.randint` for **discrete hyperparameters** (parameters that can only take specific predefined values or integers, such as choosing between `32`, `64`, and `128` for batch size or selecting from a fixed set of options).

The ranges for each hyperparameter are chosen based on common practices in LLM training (see also *Chapter 7*):

- **Learning rate**: We use a log-uniform distribution between `1e-5` and `1e-3`, as learning rates for LLMs are typically in this range
- **Batch size**: We choose from `8`, `16`, and `32`, which are common batch sizes that balance between computational efficiency and stability
- **Number of epochs**: We allow `2` to `5` epochs, as LLMs often converge within a few epochs on large datasets
- **Warmup steps**: We choose between `100` and `1,000` steps, which can help stabilize early training
- **Weight decay**: We use a uniform distribution between `0` and `0.2`, as small amounts of weight decay can help prevent overfitting

Advanced random search is better than grid search because it explores the hyperparameter space more efficiently by sampling randomly instead of exhaustively evaluating every possible combination. This flexibility allows it to focus on key hyperparameters that significantly impact performance, preventing redundant evaluations of less impactful ones. It can handle continuous parameters directly by sampling from distributions, unlike grid search, which requires discretization and exponentially grows in computational cost as the parameter space increases. By limiting the number of trials to a predefined budget, advanced random search can discover effective configurations faster and with less computational expense, making it more practical for large and complex models.

Bayesian optimization

Bayesian optimization is a more sophisticated approach to hyperparameter tuning that can be particularly effective for LLMs. It uses a probabilistic model to predict the performance of different hyperparameter configurations and intelligently selects the next configuration to try.

Let's implement Bayesian optimization using the `optuna` library. **Optuna** is an open source hyperparameter optimization framework for automating the process of finding optimal parameters for algorithms and models. It employs advanced Bayesian optimization techniques, primarily the **Tree-structured Parzen Estimator** (TPE) algorithm, to efficiently search complex parameter spaces:

1. Import optuna and set up the hyperparameters:

```python
import optuna
from transformers import Trainer, TrainingArguments
import torch

def objective(trial):
    # Define the hyperparameters to optimize
    hp = {
        "num_layers": trial.suggest_int("num_layers", 6, 24),
        "hidden_size": trial.suggest_categorical(
            "hidden_size", [512, 768, 1024]
        ,
        "num_heads": trial.suggest_categorical(
            "num_heads", [8, 12, 16]
        ),
        "ff_dim": trial.suggest_categorical(
            "ff_dim", [2048, 3072, 4096]
        ),
        "learning_rate": trial.suggest_loguniform(
            "learning_rate", 1e-5, 1e-3
        ),
        "batch_size": trial.suggest_categorical(
            "batch_size", [8, 16, 32]
```

```
        ),
        "num_epochs": trial.suggest_int("num_epochs", 2, 5),
        "warmup_steps": trial.suggest_int(
        "warmup_steps", 100, 1000),
        "weight_decay": trial.suggest_uniform(
        "weight_decay", 0, 0.2)
    }

    model = create_llm(
        num_layers=hp['num_layers'],
        hidden_size=hp['hidden_size'],
        num_heads=hp['num_heads'], ff_dim=hp['ff_dim'],
        vocab_size=50257
    )
```

2. Conduct training:

```
    training_args = TrainingArguments(
        output_dir=f"./results_bayesian_{trial.number}",
        num_train_epochs=hp['num_epochs'],
        per_device_train_batch_size=hp['batch_size'],
        learning_rate=hp['learning_rate'],
        warmup_steps=hp['warmup_steps'],
        weight_decay=hp['weight_decay'],
        logging_dir=f"./logs_bayesian_{trial.number}",
    )

    trainer = Trainer(
        model=model,
        args=training_args,
        train_dataset=tokenized_dataset,
    )

    trainer.train()

    eval_results = trainer.evaluate()
    return eval_results['eval_loss']
```

3. Run the optimization:

```
study = optuna.create_study(direction="minimize")
study.optimize(objective, n_trials=20)

print("Best trial:")
```

```
trial = study.best_trial
print(f"Value: {trial.value}")
print("Params: ")
for key, value in trial.params.items():
    print(f"    {key}: {value}")
```

In this implementation, we define an `objective` function that Optuna will optimize. The function creates and trains a model with the hyperparameters suggested by Optuna and then returns the evaluation loss.

We use Optuna's suggestion methods to define the search space:

- `suggest_int` for integer hyperparameters such as `num_layers` and `num_epochs`
- `suggest_categorical` for hyperparameters with discrete options such as `hidden_size` and `num_heads`
- `suggest_loguniform` for the learning rate, as we want to search this space logarithmically
- `suggest_uniform` for weight decay, as we want to search this space uniformly

The ranges for each hyperparameter are similar to those in our random search implementation based on common practices in LLM training.

Bayesian optimization can be more efficient than grid or random search, especially for expensive-to-evaluate functions such as training LLMs. It uses the results of previous trials to inform the selection of future trials, potentially finding good configurations more quickly.

Population-based methods

Population-based training (**PBT**) is a powerful technique that combines parallel search with adaptive hyperparameter tuning during the training process. PBT is particularly effective for problems where training can be paused and resumed efficiently. This is because PBT periodically evaluates and updates hyperparameters and model weights across a population, requiring seamless pause-and-resume capabilities. This adaptability ensures optimal use of computational resources and makes PBT ideal for tasks such as neural architecture search, reinforcement learning, and hyperparameter tuning, where iterative optimization is computationally intensive.

Here, we'll implement a simplified version of PBT to illustrate its core concepts and functionality.

We'll start by creating a `SimplePBT` class that encapsulates the core functionality of the PBT algorithm. Let's break down the implementation:

1. First, initialize the class:

```
import random
import copy
```

```
class SimplePBT:
    def __init__(self, population_size=4, num_generations=5):
        self.population_size = population_size
        self.num_generations = num_generations
        self.population = []
```

The `SimplePBT` class is initialized with two main parameters:

- `population_size`: The number of different hyperparameter configurations to maintain (the default is 4)

- `num_generations`: The number of iterations the PBT algorithm will run (the default is 5)

The `population` list will store dictionaries representing each individual in the population, containing hyperparameters and their corresponding performance scores.

2. Initialize the population: The `initialize_population` method creates the initial set of hyperparameter configurations:

```
def initialize_population(self):
    for _ in range(self.population_size):
        hp = {
            "num_layers": random.choice([6, 12, 24]),
            "hidden_size": random.choice([512, 768, 1024]),
            "num_heads": random.choice([8, 12, 16]),
            "ff_dim": random.choice([2048, 3072, 4096]),
            "learning_rate": 10random.uniform(-5, -3),
            "batch_size": random.choice([8, 16, 32]),
            "weight_decay": random.uniform(0, 0.2)
        }
        self.population.append({"hp": hp, "score": None})
```

For each individual in the population, do the following:

- **Categorical hyperparameters**, which are a subset of **discrete hyperparameters** (e.g., `num_layers`, `hidden_size`), are randomly selected from predefined options. These hyperparameters are categorical because they represent distinct, individual choices rather than values along a continuum.

- **Continuous hyperparameters** (e.g., `learning_rate`, `weight_decay`) are sampled from specified ranges.

Each configuration is added to the `population` list with an initial score of `None`.

3. Train and evaluate: The `train_and_evaluate` method is responsible for creating an LLM with the given hyperparameters, setting up training arguments, initializing a trainer with the model and arguments, training the model, evaluating the model, and returning the evaluation loss:

```
def train_and_evaluate(self, hp):
    model = create_llm(num_layers=hp['num_layers'],
        hidden_size=hp['hidden_size'],
        num_heads=hp['num_heads'],
        ff_dim=hp['ff_dim'], vocab_size=50257)

    training_args = TrainingArguments(
        output_dir=f"./results_pbt_{random.randint(0, 1000)}",
        num_train_epochs=3,
        per_device_train_batch_size=hp['batch_size'],
        learning_rate=hp['learning_rate'],
        weight_decay=hp['weight_decay'],
        logging_dir=f"./logs_pbt_{random.randint(0, 1000)}",
    )

    trainer = Trainer(
        model=model,
        args=training_args,
        train_dataset=tokenized_dataset,
    )

    trainer.train()

    eval_results = trainer.evaluate()
    return eval_results['eval_loss']
```

This method assumes the existence of `create_llm`, `TrainingArguments`, and `Trainer` classes, which would typically be provided by a deep learning framework such as Hugging Face Transformers.

4. Exploit and explore: The `exploit_and_explore` method implements the core PBT algorithm:

```
def exploit_and_explore(self):
    # Sort population by score
    self.population.sort(key=lambda x: x['score'])

    # Replace bottom half with mutated versions of top half
    for i in range(self.population_size // 2):
        self.population[i + self.population_size // 2]['hp'] =\
            self.mutate(
                copy.deepcopy(self.population[i]['hp'])
            )
```

It sorts the population based on their scores (a lower score indicates less loss). The bottom-performing half of the population is replaced with mutated versions of the top-performing half. This approach balances **exploitation** (keeping good configurations) with **exploration** (trying new variations).

5. Mutate: The `mutate` method introduces variations in the hyperparameters:

```python
def mutate(self, hp):
    # Randomly mutate one hyperparameter
    param_to_mutate = random.choice(list(hp.keys()))
    if param_to_mutate in [
        'num_layers', 'hidden_size', 'num_heads', 'ff_dim',
        'batch_size'
    ]:
        hp[param_to_mutate] = random.choice(
            [6, 12, 24]
            if param_to_mutate == "num_layers" else
            [512, 768, 1024]
            if param_to_mutate == "hidden_size" else
            [8, 12, 16]
            if param_to_mutate == "num_heads" else
            [2048, 3072, 4096]
            if param_to_mutate == "ff_dim" else
            [8, 16, 32]
        )
    elif param_to_mutate == 'learning_rate':
        hp[param_to_mutate] *= random.uniform(0.8, 1.2)
    elif param_to_mutate == 'weight_decay':
        hp[param_to_mutate] = min(
            max(hp[param_to_mutate]
                + random.uniform(-0.05, 0.05), 0), 0.2
        )
    return hp
```

It randomly selects one hyperparameter to mutate. For categorical parameters, it chooses a new value from predefined options. For continuous parameters like learning rate, it perturbs the current value within a certain range. For weight decay, it adds a small random value while keeping it within [0, 0.2].

This mutation strategy allows both small and large changes in the hyperparameters, promoting diverse exploration of the hyperparameter space.

6. Run the PBT process:

```python
def run(self):
    self.initialize_population()

    for generation in range(self.num_generations):
        print(f"Generation {generation + 1}")

        for i, individual in enumerate(self.population):
            individual['score'] = \
                self.train_and_evaluate(individual['hp'])
            print(
                f"Individual {i + 1}:
                Score = {individual['score']}"
            )

        self.exploit_and_explore()

    best_individual = min(self.population,
        key=lambda x: x['score'])
    print("\nBest Hyperparameters:")
    print(best_individual['hp'])
    print(f"Best Score: {best_individual['score']}")
```

The run method orchestrates the entire PBT process:

I.   It initializes the population.

II. For each generation, it trains and evaluates each individual in the population and it performs exploitation and exploration to update the population.

III. After all generations, it prints the best hyperparameters and the score found.

7. Use the SimplePBT class: To use the SimplePBT class, you can simply create an instance and run it:

```python
# Run PBT
pbt = SimplePBT()
pbt.run()
```

This will start the PBT process with the default population size of 4 and 5 generations. You can adjust these parameters when creating the SimplePBT instance to suit your specific needs.

Multi-objective hyperparameter optimization

In LLM development, we often need to balance multiple objectives, such as model performance, inference speed, and model size. Let's implement multi-objective optimization using Optuna:

1. Add the `import` statement and set up the hyperparameters:

```python
import optuna
def objective(trial):
    hp = {
        "num_layers": trial.suggest_int("num_layers", 6, 24),
        "hidden_size": trial.suggest_categorical(
            "hidden_size", [512, 768, 1024]),
        "num_heads": trial.suggest_categorical(
            "num_heads", [8, 12, 16]),
        "ff_dim": trial.suggest_categorical(
            "ff_dim", [2048, 3072, 4096]),
        "learning_rate": trial.suggest_loguniform(
            "learning_rate", 1e-5, 1e-3),
        "batch_size": trial.suggest_categorical(
            "batch_size", [8, 16, 32]),
        "weight_decay": trial.suggest_uniform(
            "weight_decay", 0, 0.2)
    }

    model = create_llm(
        num_layers=hp['num_layers'],
        hidden_size=hp['hidden_size'],
        num_heads=hp['num_heads'],
        ff_dim=hp['ff_dim'],
        vocab_size=50257
    )
```

2. Conduct the training:

```python
    training_args = TrainingArguments(
        output_dir=f"./results_multi_objective_{trial.number}",
        num_train_epochs=3,
        per_device_train_batch_size=hp['batch_size'],
        learning_rate=hp['learning_rate'],
        weight_decay=hp['weight_decay'],
        logging_dir=f"./logs_multi_objective_{trial.number}",
    )
    trainer = Trainer(
        model=model,
```

```
        args=training_args,
        train_dataset=tokenized_dataset,
    )

    trainer.train()
```

3. Carry out the evaluation:

```
    eval_results = trainer.evaluate()
    eval_loss = eval_results['eval_loss']

    # Calculate model size in MB
    model_size = sum(p.numel() for p in model.parameters())
        * 4 / 1024 / 1024  # assuming float32

    # Simulate inference time (this would be more accurate if
actually measured)
    inference_time = 0.001 * hp['num_layers']
        * (hp['hidden_size'] / 512) 2

    return eval_loss, model_size, inference_time
```

4. Run the multi-objective optimization:

```
study = optuna.create_study(
    directions=["minimize", "minimize", "minimize"])
study.optimize(objective, n_trials=50)

print("Pareto front:")
for trial in study.best_trials:
    print(f"Trial {trial.number}")
    print(f"  Value: Loss={trial.values[0]:.4f},
        Size={trial.values[1]:.2f}MB,
        Inference Time={trial.values[2]:.4f}s")
    print("  Params:")
    for key, value in trial.params.items():
        print(f"    {key}: {value}")
```

In this multi-objective optimization, we're trying to minimize three objectives simultaneously:

- Evaluation loss (model performance)
- Model size (in MB)
- Inference time (simulated based on model architecture)

We use Optuna's multi-objective optimization capability by specifying multiple directions in `create_study`. The optimization process will try to find the **Pareto front** (the set of solutions where improving any one objective necessitates degrading at least one other objective) of these objectives' configurations, where improving one objective would necessarily worsen another.

The `objective` function now returns three values corresponding to our three objectives. For model size, we calculate the total number of parameters and convert it to MB. For inference time, we use a simple heuristic based on the model's architecture in a real scenario, you would want to measure this.

This approach allows us to explore trade-offs between model performance, size, and speed. It's particularly useful for LLM development, where we often need to balance these factors for different deployment scenarios.

Hyperparameter tuning at scale – challenges and solutions

When tuning hyperparameters for LLMs, we face several challenges:

- **Computational cost**: Training LLMs is expensive, limiting the number of trials we can run
- **Long training times**: Each trial can take days or weeks, making the entire process very time-consuming
- **Large search space**: LLMs have many hyperparameters, creating a vast search space
- **Sensitivity to initialization**: LLM performance can vary significantly with different random seeds

To address these challenges, we can employ several strategies:

- **Use smaller proxy tasks**: Instead of tuning on the full task, use a smaller dataset or fewer training steps to get a quick estimate of performance
- **Leverage pre-trained models**: Start from pre-trained weights and focus on tuning fine-tuning hyperparameters
- **Use multi-fidelity optimization**: Start with low-fidelity evaluations (e.g., few training steps) and gradually increase fidelity for promising configurations
- **Distributed hyperparameter tuning**: Use multiple machines to explore different hyperparameters in parallel

Let's implement a simple multi-fidelity optimization approach:

1. Add the `import` statement and set up the hyperparameters:

```
import optuna
def objective(trial):
    hp = {
        "num_layers": trial.suggest_int("num_layers", 6, 24),
        "hidden_size": trial.suggest_categorical(
            "hidden_size", [512, 768, 1024]),
        "num_heads": trial.suggest_categorical(
            "num_heads", [8, 12, 16]),
        "ff_dim": trial.suggest_categorical(
            "ff_dim", [2048, 3072, 4096]),
        "learning_rate": trial.suggest_loguniform(
            "learning_rate", 1e-5, 1e-3),
        "batch_size": trial.suggest_categorical(
            "batch_size", [8, 16, 32]),
        "weight_decay": trial.suggest_uniform(
            "weight_decay", 0, 0.2)
    }

    model = create_llm(
        num_layers=hp['num_layers'],
        hidden_size=hp['hidden_size'],
        num_heads=hp['num_heads'], ff_dim=hp['ff_dim'],
        vocab_size=50257)
```

2. Use a multi-fidelity strategy to train, starting with a small number of steps:

```
    for steps in [100, 500, 2000]:
        training_args = TrainingArguments(
            output_dir= \
                f"./results_multi_fidelity_{trial.number}_
                {steps}",
            max_steps=steps,
            per_device_train_batch_size=hp['batch_size'],
            learning_rate=hp['learning_rate'],
            weight_decay=hp['weight_decay'],
            logging_dir=\
                f"./logs_multi_fidelity_{trial.number}_{steps}",
        )
```

```
            trainer = Trainer(
                model=model,
                args=training_args,
                train_dataset=tokenized_dataset,
            )

            trainer.train()
```

3. Conduct evaluation:

```
            eval_results = trainer.evaluate()
            eval_loss =

            eval_results = trainer.evaluate()
            eval_loss = eval_results['eval_loss']

            trial.report(eval_loss, step=steps)
```

4. Prune the unpromising trials:

```
            if trial.should_prune():
                raise optuna.TrialPruned()

        return eval_loss
```

5. Run the multi-fidelity optimization:

```
    study = optuna.create_study(
        pruner=optuna.pruners.MedianPruner())
    study.optimize(objective, n_trials=30)

    print("Best trial:")
    trial = study.best_trial
    print(f"Value: {trial.value}")
    print("Params: ")
    for key, value in trial.params.items():
        print(f"    {key}: {value}")
```

There are a few aspects of this multi-fidelity approach that we should look at:

- We start by training each model configuration for only 100 steps, which gives a quick initial estimate of performance

- We then increase the number of training steps to 500 and then 2,000 for promising configurations

- We use Optuna's pruning mechanism to early-stop unpromising trials, saving computational resources

`MedianPruner` stops a trial if its performance is worse than the median of previous trials at the same step. This allows us to focus our computational resources on the most promising hyperparameter configurations.

This approach helps to address the challenges of hyperparameter tuning at scale:

- It reduces the computational cost by quickly eliminating poor configurations

- It shortens the overall tuning time by using shorter training runs for initial evaluation

- It allows us to explore a larger search space by running more trials in the same amount of time

However, there are still limitations to this approach. The performance after a small number of steps may not always correlate well with the final performance, especially for LLMs that often require long training times to converge.

To further improve hyperparameter tuning at scale, consider the following advanced techniques:

- **Distributed hyperparameter tuning**: This setup allows multiple machines to contribute to the same hyperparameter search, greatly speeding up the process:

```python
import optuna

def objective(trial):
    # ... (same as before) ...

# Create a study object with MySQL storage for distributed
optimization
storage = optuna.storages.RDBStorage(
    "mysql://user:password@host/database",
    engine_kwargs={"pool_size": 20, "max_overflow": 0}
)
study = optuna.create_study(
    storage=storage, pruner=optuna.pruners.MedianPruner())

# This can be run on multiple machines
study.optimize(objective, n_trials=10)
```

- **Leveraging pre-trained models**: This approach starts from pre-trained models and focuses on tuning the fine-tuning hyperparameters and model size, which can be more efficient than training from scratch:

```python
from transformers import AutoModelForCausalLM, AutoTokenizer

def create_pretrained_llm(model_name, num_layers=None):
    model = AutoModelForCausalLM.from_pretrained(model_name)
    if num_layers is not None:
        # Adjust the number of layers (this is a simplified
approach)
```

```
        model.transformer.h = model.transformer.h[:num_layers]
    return model

def objective(trial):
    hp = {
        "model_name": trial.suggest_categorical(
            "model_name",
            ["gpt2", "gpt2-medium", "gpt2-large"]),
        "num_layers": trial.suggest_int("num_layers", 6, 24),
        "learning_rate": trial.suggest_loguniform(
            "learning_rate", 1e-5, 1e-3),
        "batch_size": trial.suggest_categorical(
            "batch_size", [8, 16, 32]),
        "weight_decay": trial.suggest_uniform(
            "weight_decay", 0, 0.2)
    }

    model = create_pretrained_llm(
        hp['model_name'], hp['num_layers'])

    # ... (rest of the objective function) ...

study = optuna.create_study(
        pruner=optuna.pruners.MedianPruner())
study.optimize(objective, n_trials=30)
```

- **Bayesian optimization with Gaussian processes**: For problems where we can only afford a small number of trials, Gaussian process-based Bayesian optimization can be more sample-efficient than tree-based methods such as TPE (which is Optuna's default):

```
import optuna

sampler = optuna.samplers.GPSampler()
study = optuna.create_study(sampler=sampler)
study.optimize(objective, n_trials=50)
```

This approach can be particularly useful for LLM tuning where each trial is very expensive.

- **Asynchronous Successive Halving Algorithm** (**ASHA**): ASHA is a bandit-based algorithm that can be more efficient than simple pruning methods:

```
from optuna.pruners import SuccessiveHalvingPruner

pruner = SuccessiveHalvingPruner(
    min_resource=100, reduction_factor=3,
        min_early_stopping_rate=0)
study = optuna.create_study(pruner=pruner)
study.optimize(objective, n_trials=100)
```

ASHA is particularly well-suited for large-scale hyperparameter optimization as it can handle asynchronous parallel optimization efficiently.

Summary

Hyperparameter tuning for LLMs presents unique challenges due to the scale and complexity of these models. By leveraging techniques such as multi-fidelity optimization, distributed tuning, and advanced algorithms such as Bayesian optimization and ASHA, we can make this process more efficient and effective. However, it's important to remember that there's often no one-size-fits-all solution, and the best approach may depend on your specific use case, available resources, and the characteristics of your LLM task.

In the next chapter, we'll focus on LLM regularization.

Subscribe for a free eBook

New frameworks, evolving architectures, research drops, production breakdowns—AI_Distilled filters the noise into a weekly briefing for engineers and researchers working hands-on with LLMs and GenAI systems. Subscribe now and receive a free eBook, along with weekly insights that help you stay focused and informed. Subscribe at `https://packt.link/8Oz6Y` or scan the QR code below.

9

Regularization

Regularization is a set of methods that constrain or modify the learning process to prevent the model from memorizing training data too precisely, encouraging it to learn more robust and generalizable patterns instead.

Regularization is a crucial aspect of training LLMs to prevent overfitting and improve generalization. Overfitting is detrimental because it causes a model to perform exceptionally well on training data while failing miserably on new, unseen data. When a model overfits, it essentially memorizes the noise and peculiarities of the training dataset, rather than learning generalizable patterns and relationships. This creates an illusion of high accuracy during development but leads to poor real-world performance, rendering the model ineffective for its intended purpose of making accurate predictions on novel inputs.

In this chapter, you'll learn about different regularization techniques specifically tailored to LLMs. We'll explore methods such as layer-wise adaptive regularization, regularization in fine-tuning, and the combination of multiple techniques. You'll gain insights into implementing these strategies and understanding their impact on model performance.

In this chapter, we'll be covering the following topics:

- L2 regularization (Ridge regression)
- Dropout
- Layer-wise adaptive regularization
- Gradient clipping and noise injection
- Regularization in transfer learning and fine-tuning scenarios
- Emerging regularization techniques for next-generation LLMs

L2 regularization (Ridge regression)

L2 regularization, also known as ridge regression or weight decay, is a technique used to prevent overfitting in machine learning models. It works by adding a penalty term to the loss function, which is proportional to the square of the model's weights. This penalty term discourages the model from assigning large weights to individual features, leading to a simpler and more generalized model. By minimizing the combined loss function, which includes both the original loss and the penalty term, the model finds a balance between fitting the training data well and keeping the weights small, ultimately improving its ability to generalize to new, unseen data

Here's how to use it:

```
from torch.optim import AdamW

def train_with_weight_decay(
    model, train_dataloader, weight_decay=0.01, lr=5e-5, epochs=3
):
    optimizer = AdamW(model.parameters(), lr=lr,
        weight_decay=weight_decay)

    for epoch in range(epochs):
        model.train()
        total_loss = 0
        for batch in train_dataloader:
            optimizer.zero_grad()
            outputs = model(batch)
            loss = outputs.loss
            loss.backward()
            optimizer.step()
            total_loss += loss.item()
        print(
            f"Epoch {epoch + 1}, "
            f"Loss: {total_loss / len(train_dataloader):.4f}"
        )

# Assuming you have a train_dataloader
# train_with_weight_decay(model, train_dataloader)
```

In this implementation, we use the AdamW optimizer that we discussed in *Chapter 7*, which correctly implements weight decay. The `weight_decay` parameter controls the strength of regularization. A typical value is `0.01`, but you may need to adjust this based on your specific model and dataset.

Dropout

Dropout is another powerful regularization technique that randomly "drops out" a portion of neurons during training.

Dropout helps combat overfitting by randomly deactivating a fraction of neurons during each training iteration, forcing the network to develop redundant pathways for information flow. This technique prevents neurons from becoming overly dependent on each other by creating a form of ensemble learning within a single network, where different subnetworks handle similar tasks. The result is a more robust model that relies on distributed representations rather than memorizing specific patterns, ultimately improving generalization to unseen data when all neurons are active during inference.

It's particularly effective in large neural networks such as LLMs. Here's how to implement dropout in a transformer-based LLM:

```python
class TransformerWithDropout(nn.Module):
    def __init__(
    self, vocab_size, d_model, nhead, num_layers, dropout=0.1
):
        super().__init__()
        self.embedding = nn.Embedding(vocab_size, d_model)
        self.pos_encoder = nn.Embedding(1000, d_model)  # Simplified
positional encoding
        self.transformer = nn.TransformerEncoder(
            nn.TransformerEncoderLayer(d_model, nhead,
                dim_feedforward=4*d_model, dropout=dropout),
            num_layers
        )
        self.fc_out = nn.Linear(d_model, vocab_size)
        self.dropout = nn.Dropout(dropout)

    def forward(self, x):
        x = self.embedding(x) + self.pos_encoder(
            torch.arange(x.size(1), device=x.device))
        x = self.dropout(x)
        x = x.transpose(0, 1)  # Transform to shape expected by
transformer
        x = self.transformer(x)
        x = x.transpose(0, 1)  # Transform back
        return self.fc_out(x)

model = TransformerWithDropout(vocab_size=50257,
    d_model=768, nhead=12, num_layers=12, dropout=0.1)
```

```
print(
    f"Model parameters: "
    f"{sum(p.numel() for p in model.parameters()):,}"
)
```

In this implementation, dropout is applied after the embedding layer and within each transformer layer. The dropout rate of 0.1 is typical, but you may need to adjust this based on your specific use case.

Keep in mind that dropout is only applied during training, not during inference (when the model is being used to make predictions).

During training, neurons are randomly "dropped" (deactivated) with a specified probability (e.g., 0.5 means each neuron has a 50% chance of being turned off for that training batch). This forces the network to learn more robust features since it can't rely on any single neuron always being present.

During inference (testing, evaluation, or deployment), dropout is disabled and all neurons are active. However, the weights are typically scaled by the dropout rate to account for the fact that more neurons are active than during training. This scaling ensures the expected output magnitude remains consistent.

This training-only application of dropout is a key part of what makes it effective as a regularization technique – it creates a form of ensemble learning during training while still allowing for full network capacity during actual use.

Layer-wise adaptive regularization

Layer-wise adaptive regularization involves applying different regularization strengths to different layers of the model. This can be particularly effective for LLMs, where lower layers may benefit from less regularization to capture fundamental patterns, while higher layers might need stronger regularization to prevent overfitting.

The following Python code defines a LayerwiseAdaptiveRegularization class, which is a PyTorch nn.Module designed to wrap a base transformer model and apply a dropout rate that increases linearly with the depth of the model's layers:

```
class LayerwiseAdaptiveRegularization(nn.Module):
    def __init__(
        self, base_model, num_layers, base_dropout=0.1,
        dropout_increase_per_layer=0.02
    ):
        super().__init__()
        self.base_model = base_model
        self.num_layers = num_layers
        self.base_dropout = base_dropout
        self.dropout_increase_per_layer = dropout_increase_per_layer
        self.set_layerwise_dropout()
```

```
    def set_layerwise_dropout(self):
        for i, layer in enumerate(self.base_model.transformer.h):
            dropout = self.base_dropout
                    + i * self.dropout_increase_per_layer
            layer.attn.dropout.p = dropout
            layer.mlp.dropout.p = dropout

    def forward(self, *args, kwargs):
        return self.base_model(*args, kwargs)

base_model = create_lm_model()
model = LayerwiseAdaptiveRegularization(base_model, num_layers=12)
```

The `LayerwiseAdaptiveRegularization` class initializes with a base model, the number of layers, a starting dropout probability, and an increment for each subsequent layer. It then configures the dropout probabilities within the attention and MLP sub-layers of the transformer blocks. Finally, its forward method simply passes the input through the wrapped base model. An example of its usage is shown by wrapping a `create_lm_model()` with this layer-wise dropout regularization.

This implementation wraps a base GPT-2 model and applies increasing dropout rates to higher layers. The base dropout rate is `0.1`, and it increases by `0.02` for each subsequent layer.

Gradient clipping and noise injection

Gradient clipping and noise injection are techniques used to improve the training stability and generalization of LLMs.

Gradient clipping, while primarily employed for optimization stability (see *Chapter 7*), can indirectly contribute to regularization. By limiting the magnitude of gradients, it can constrain the updates to model parameters, potentially leading to a smoother optimization path and preventing overfitting. In some cases, gradient clipping can effectively reduce the impact of certain parameters, especially when gradients for those parameters are consistently clipped. This can lead to a form of implicit sparsity, where less important parameters are effectively downweighted.

Noise injection is a regularization technique commonly used to improve the generalization of machine learning models. By adding a small amount of noise to the input data, weights, or activation functions, noise injection helps prevent overfitting. The technique forces the model to be less reliant on specific patterns in the training data, encouraging it to learn more robust, general features that apply across different datasets. This approach is particularly useful in neural networks, where noise such as the following can be injected at various stages:

- **Input noise**: Adds noise directly to the input data, helping the model become more robust to variations in the input

- **Weight noise**: Perturbs the weights during training, encouraging the model to generalize better

- **Activation noise**: Adds noise to the activation functions, leading to smoother decision boundaries and reducing overfitting

These methods help prevent overfitting, reduce the impact of outliers, and encourage the model to explore a wider range of solutions, ultimately leading to more robust and reliable language models.

Here's how to implement gradient clipping and noise injection:

```python
import torch.nn.functional as F


def train_with_grad_clip_and_noise(
    model, train_dataloader, grad_clip=1.0,
    noise_factor=0.01, lr=5e-5, epochs=3
):
    optimizer = AdamW(model.parameters(), lr=lr)

    for epoch in range(epochs):
        model.train()
        total_loss = 0
        for batch in train_dataloader:
            optimizer.zero_grad()

            # Add noise to inputs
            input_ids = batch['input_ids']
            noise = torch.randn_like(
                input_ids, dtype=torch.float) * noise_factor
            noisy_inputs = input_ids.float() + noise
            noisy_inputs = noisy_inputs.long().clamp(
                min=0, max=model.config.vocab_size - 1)

            outputs = model(input_ids=noisy_inputs, labels=input_ids)
            loss = outputs.loss
            loss.backward()

            clip_grad_norm_(model.parameters(), grad_clip)
            optimizer.step()
            total_loss += loss.item()

        print(
            f"Epoch {epoch + 1}, "
            f"Loss: {total_loss / len(train_dataloader):.4f}"
        )
```

```
# Assuming you have a train_dataloader
# train_with_grad_clip_and_noise(model, train_dataloader)
```

This implementation applies gradient clipping to prevent exploding gradients and adds small amounts of noise to the input to improve robustness. `noise_factor` controls the amount of noise added; you may need to adjust this based on your specific use case.

The function initializes an **AdamW optimizer** and iterates over the dataset for a specified number of epochs. During each training step, it clears old gradients, adds noise to input tokens (ensuring values remain within the vocabulary range), and feeds the noisy input into the model for forward and backward passes. **Gradient clipping** prevents exploding gradients, ensuring stable training. The optimizer updates the model parameters, and the loss is tracked to monitor progress. Finally, the function prints the average loss per epoch.

Next, let us explore regularization in transfer learning and fine-tuning scenarios.

Regularization in transfer learning and fine-tuning scenarios

When fine-tuning pre-trained LLMs, it's important to carefully adjust regularization to avoid hindering task-specific adaptation while still preventing overfitting. Here's an approach to fine-tuning with adaptive regularization:

```
from transformers import GPT2LMHeadModel, GPT2Tokenizer

def fine_tune_with_adaptive_regularization(
    pretrained_model_name, train_dataloader,
    initial_dropout=0.1, epochs=3
):
    model = GPT2LMHeadModel.from_pretrained(pretrained_model_name)
    tokenizer = GPT2Tokenizer.from_pretrained(pretrained_model_name)

    optimizer = AdamW(model.parameters(), lr=5e-5, weight_decay=0.01)

    for epoch in range(epochs):
        model.train()
        total_loss = 0
        current_dropout = initial_dropout * (1 - epoch / epochs)

        for module in model.modules():
            if isinstance(module, nn.Dropout):
                module.p = current_dropout
```

```
        for batch in train_dataloader:
            optimizer.zero_grad()
            outputs = model(batch)
            loss = outputs.loss
            loss.backward()
            optimizer.step()
            total_loss += loss.item()

        print(
            f"Epoch {epoch + 1}, "
            f"Loss: {total_loss / len(train_dataloader):.4f}, "
            f"Dropout: {current_dropout:.4f}"
        )

    # Assuming you have a train_dataloader
    # fine_tune_with_adaptive_regularization('gpt2', train_dataloader)
```

This implementation starts with a higher dropout rate and gradually decreases it over the course of fine-tuning. This allows the model to adapt to the new task while still maintaining some regularization to prevent overfitting. This approach is also called adaptive dropout.

Adaptive dropout works well because it dynamically adjusts dropout rates based on neuron importance, rather than applying uniform dropout across the network. By selectively dropping less critical neurons more frequently while preserving important feature detectors, adaptive dropout creates an optimal balance between regularization and information preservation. This targeted approach prevents overfitting more efficiently than standard dropout, as it maintains the network's capacity to learn complex patterns through important neurons while aggressively regularizing redundant or noise-sensitive parts, resulting in models that generalize better with less performance sacrifice on critical features.

Emerging regularization techniques

Recent years have seen the emergence of sophisticated techniques that address the complex challenges of modern deep learning architectures. These new approaches go beyond simply preventing overfitting – they aim to improve model robustness, find better optima in the loss landscape, and enhance generalization through innovative training strategies. From geometrically motivated methods such as **sharpness-aware minimization** (**SAM**) to advanced optimization strategies such as **stochastic weight averaging** (**SWA**), these emerging regularization techniques are reshaping how we approach model training and generalization.

Stochastic weight averaging

SWA is a technique that improves neural network generalization by averaging weights from multiple points along the optimization trajectory, effectively finding flatter, more robust minima that perform better on unseen data than the typically sharp minima found by conventional optimization methods. **Stochastic gradient descent (SGD)** is a fundamental optimization algorithm that updates model parameters by following the negative gradient of the loss function computed on randomly selected small batches of training data, enabling efficient training of large models such as neural networks by approximating the full gradient computation while introducing beneficial noise that helps escape poor local minima.

WA involves averaging multiple points along the trajectory of SGD with a modified learning rate schedule. It improves generalization by finding broader optima. Here is a code example:

```
from torch.optim.swa_utils import AveragedModel, SWALR

# Create SWA model and scheduler
swa_model = AveragedModel(model)
swa_scheduler = SWALR(optimizer, swa_lr=0.05)

# Training loop with SWA
for epoch in range(100):
    if epoch > 75:  # Start SWA after epoch 75
        swa_model.update_parameters(model)
        swa_scheduler.step()
```

Sharpness-aware minimization

SAM seeks parameters that lie in neighborhoods with uniformly low loss values, leading to better generalization. Its key features are the following:

- Looks for "flat" minima instead of sharp ones

- Improves robustness against input perturbations

- Generally provides better generalization than standard SGD

Let us implement the SAM class in the following Python code:

```
class SAM(torch.optim.Optimizer):
    def __init__(self, params, base_optimizer, rho=0.05):
        self.rho = rho
        self.base_optimizer = base_optimizer(params)

    def step(self):
        # First forward-backward pass
        grad_norm = self._grad_norm()
        scale = self.rho / (grad_norm + 1e-12)
```

```
            # Perturb weights
            for group in self.param_groups:
                for p in group['params']:
                    e_w = p.grad * scale
                    p.add_(e_w)


            # Second forward-backward pass
            self.base_optimizer.step()
```

Differential privacy-based regularization

Differential privacy (DP) is a technique that adds carefully calibrated noise to data or computations to protect individual privacy while still allowing useful insights, ensuring that the inclusion or exclusion of any single data point does not significantly affect model performance.

DP-based regularization is a technique used to enhance model privacy by adding noise to the model's training process, which protects individual data points from being exposed in model outputs or learned representations. By introducing controlled randomness, DP-based regularization limits the model's reliance on any specific data sample, thereby reducing the risk of overfitting and making the model less sensitive to variations in individual data points. This method is particularly valuable in privacy-sensitive applications, as it ensures that models can learn generalizable patterns without revealing specific information about the training data, making it useful in healthcare, finance, and other areas requiring data confidentiality.

The following code snippet implements the DPOptimizer class:

```
class DPOptimizer(torch.optim.Optimizer):
    def __init__(
        self, params, noise_multiplier=1.0, max_grad_norm=1.0
    ):
        self.noise_multiplier = noise_multiplier
        self.max_grad_norm = max_grad_norm


    def step(self):
        # Clip gradients
        torch.nn.utils.clip_grad_norm_(self.param_groups[0]['params'],
                                       self.max_grad_norm)


        # Add noise
        for p in self.param_groups[0]['params']:
            noise = torch.randn_like(p.grad) * self.noise_multiplier
            p.grad.add_(noise)
```

Fast gradient sign method

The **fast gradient sign method** (**FGSM**) is a technique for creating adversarial examples by adding a small, targeted perturbation to input data, pushing the model to misclassify. It works by calculating the gradient of the loss function with respect to the input and applying a slight adjustment in the direction that maximizes the model's error. The input data is slightly changed by a small amount, controlled by a factor called ϵ, to create an "adversarial example" that can fool a machine learning model. FGSM is commonly used to test model robustness and for adversarial training, where models are trained on adversarial examples to enhance security. However, FGSM's one-step nature makes it fast but less effective against strong defenses, unlike iterative methods that achieve higher attack success.

Let us see how it is implemented here:

```
def fgsm_attack(image, epsilon, data_grad):
    sign_data_grad = data_grad.sign()
    perturbed_image = image + epsilon * sign_data_grad
    perturbed_image = torch.clamp(perturbed_image, 0, 1)
    return perturbed_image
```

Lookahead optimizer

The lookahead optimizer is an innovative optimization technique that enhances the training stability and convergence of traditional optimizers, such as Adam or SGD, by maintaining two sets of parameters: fast weights and slow weights. The fast weights are updated frequently using a standard optimizer, while the slow weights are updated less frequently by synchronizing them with the fast weights. This approach allows for better exploration of the loss landscape, as the optimizer can escape local minima and smooth out oscillations in the optimization trajectory. By leveraging the strengths of both the base optimizer and the lookahead mechanism, this optimizer leads to faster convergence and improved generalization, making it a valuable addition to deep learning model training.

The following code snippet shows how the lookahead optimizer can be implemented:

```
class Lookahead(torch.optim.Optimizer):
    def __init__(self, optimizer, k=5, alpha=0.5):
        self.optimizer = optimizer
        self.k = k
        self.alpha = alpha
        self.step_counter = 0
        self.slow_weights = [
            [p.clone().detach() for p in group['params']]

            for group in optimizer.param_groups
        ]
```

```
def step(self):
    self.step_counter += 1
    self.optimizer.step()

    if self.step_counter % self.k == 0:
        for group, slow_weights in zip(
            self.optimizer.param_groups, self.slow_weights
        ):
            for p, q in zip(group['params'], slow_weights):
                p.data.mul_(self.alpha).add_(
                    q, alpha=1.0 - self.alpha)
                q.data.copy_(p.data)
```

Summary

In this chapter, we covered fundamental concepts such as weight decay and L2 regularization, dropout methods, layer-wise adaptive regularization, and combining multiple regularization approaches. We also discussed regularization strategies for transfer learning and fine-tuning scenarios, as well as techniques for enhancing model stability, such as gradient clipping and noise injection. Additionally, we introduced various emerging regularization methods.

In the next chapter, we'll explore checkpointing and recovery and investigate why these techniques are essential for managing long-running training processes.

10

Checkpointing and Recovery

Checkpointing and **recovery** refer to the process of saving the state of a system, application, or model at specific intervals (checkpointing) and restoring it from a saved state in case of failure (recovery). In machine learning, checkpointing involves periodically saving model parameters, optimizer states, and training progress so that training can resume from the last checkpoint instead of starting over. This is especially useful for long-running tasks, where interruptions due to system crashes, power failures, or preempted cloud instances can otherwise result in significant losses.

Checkpointing and recovery are crucial for ensuring **fault tolerance**, **efficiency**, and **reproducibility** in training large-scale models. Without checkpointing, an unexpected failure could waste hours or even days of computation. Additionally, it allows for **experiment reproducibility**, enabling researchers to revisit and fine-tune models from intermediate states, rather than redoing entire training runs. Efficient checkpointing strategies (e.g., saving at fixed intervals or when validation performance improves) help balance storage overhead while minimizing retraining costs.

In this chapter, we'll explore strategies for determining optimal checkpoint frequency, efficient storage formats for large models, and techniques for recovering from various types of failures. You'll also gain insights into checkpointing in distributed training scenarios and version control for model checkpoints.

In this chapter, we'll be covering the following topics:

- Why is checkpointing important?
- Checkpoint frequency and storage strategies
- Efficient checkpoint formats
- Recovering from failures
- Checkpointing in distributed LLM training
- Version control for LLM checkpoints
- Automated checkpointing and recovery systems

Why is checkpointing important?

Checkpointing is a common practice in LLM training due to the long duration and resource-intensive nature of the LLM training process.

Let's implement a basic checkpointing system:

```python
import torch
from transformers import GPT2LMHeadModel, GPT2Config
import os

class LLMTrainer:
    def __init__(
        self, model, optimizer, checkpoint_dir='checkpoints'
    ):
        self.model = model
        self.optimizer = optimizer
        self.checkpoint_dir = checkpoint_dir
        os.makedirs(checkpoint_dir, exist_ok=True)

    def save_checkpoint(self, epoch, step, loss):
        checkpoint = {
            'epoch': epoch,
            'step': step,
            'model_state_dict': self.model.state_dict(),
            'optimizer_state_dict': self.optimizer.state_dict(),
            'loss': loss
        }
        checkpoint_path = os.path.join(self.checkpoint_dir,
            f'checkpoint_epoch_{epoch}_step_{step}.pt')
        torch.save(checkpoint, checkpoint_path)
        print(f"Checkpoint saved: {checkpoint_path}")

    def load_checkpoint(self, checkpoint_path):
        checkpoint = torch.load(checkpoint_path)
        self.model.load_state_dict(checkpoint['model_state_dict'])
        self.optimizer.load_state_dict(
            checkpoint['optimizer_state_dict'])
        return (
            checkpoint['epoch'], checkpoint['step'],
            checkpoint['loss']
        )
```

```
# Simulating training loop
for epoch in range(10):
    for step in range(1000):
        # ... training code ...
        if step % 100 == 0:
            trainer.save_checkpoint(epoch, step, loss.item())

# Loading a checkpoint
epoch, step, loss = trainer.load_checkpoint(
    'checkpoints/checkpoint_epoch_5_step_500.pt')
print(f"Resumed training from epoch {epoch}, step {step}, with loss
{loss}")
```

This implementation demonstrates the basic structure of a checkpointing system. The `save_checkpoint` method saves the model state, optimizer state, and training progress information. The `load_checkpoint` method allows you to resume training from a saved checkpoint.

Checkpoint frequency and storage strategies

Determining the optimal checkpoint frequency involves striking a balance between *safety* and *efficiency*. Let's explore different strategies and their implementation:

```
import time
import shutil

class AdvancedLLMTrainer(LLMTrainer):
    def __init__(
        self, model, optimizer, checkpoint_dir='checkpoints',
        max_checkpoints=5
    ):
        super().__init__(model, optimizer, checkpoint_dir)
        self.max_checkpoints = max_checkpoints
        self.checkpoints = []

    def save_checkpoint(self, epoch, step, loss):
        checkpoint_path = super().save_checkpoint(epoch, step, loss)
        self.checkpoints.append(checkpoint_path)

        if len(self.checkpoints) > self.max_checkpoints:
            oldest_checkpoint = self.checkpoints.pop(0)
            os.remove(oldest_checkpoint)
            print(f"Removed old checkpoint: {oldest_checkpoint}")
```

```
        def save_checkpoint_by_time(
            self, epoch, step, loss, interval_minutes=60
        ):
            current_time = time.time()
            if (
                not hasattr(self, 'last_checkpoint_time') or
                current_time - self.last_checkpoint_time >=
                interval_minutes * 60
            ):
                self.save_checkpoint(epoch, step, loss)
                self.last_checkpoint_time = current_time

        def save_best_checkpoint(self, epoch, step, loss):
            if not hasattr(self, 'best_loss') or loss < self.best_loss:
                self.best_loss = loss
                checkpoint_path = os.path.join(
                    self.checkpoint_dir, 'best_model.pt')
                torch.save({
                    'epoch': epoch,
                    'step': step,
                    'model_state_dict': self.model.state_dict(),
                    'optimizer_state_dict': self.optimizer.state_dict(),
                    'loss': loss
                }, checkpoint_path)
                print(f"Best model saved: {checkpoint_path}")

# Usage example
trainer = AdvancedLLMTrainer(model, optimizer)

for epoch in range(10):
    for step in range(1000):
        # ... training code ...
        trainer.save_checkpoint_by_time(epoch, step, loss.item(),
            interval_minutes=30)
        trainer.save_best_checkpoint(epoch, step, loss.item())
```

This implementation introduces several checkpointing strategies:

- **Regular checkpointing with a maximum number of checkpoints**: This prevents excessive disk usage by removing old checkpoints when the limit is reached

- **Time-based checkpointing**: This saves checkpoints at regular time intervals, which can be useful for long-running training processes

- **Best model checkpointing**: This saves the model with the best performance (lowest loss in this case), which is useful for model selection

Here's a trade-off analysis of the three checkpointing strategies:

- **Regular checkpointing with a maximum number of checkpoints**:

  - **Pros**: Prevents excessive storage usage and ensures periodic snapshots of training progress

  - **Cons**: Might overwrite useful older checkpoints, potentially losing good models if performance fluctuates

  - **Best use case**: When storage is a constraint and periodic snapshots are needed for resumption

- **Time-based checkpointing**:

  - **Pros**: Ensures checkpoints are spaced out over time, which is useful for monitoring long training runs

  - **Cons**: Can be inefficient if checkpoints are saved too frequently (wasting storage) or too infrequently (missing critical states)

  - **Best use case**: For long-running training processes where consistent snapshots are needed for debugging or rollback

- **Best model checkpointing**:

  - **Pros**: Retains the most promising model, which is useful for final model selection.

  - **Cons**: If loss is noisy, a single "best" checkpoint may not be truly representative. Can fail to capture intermediate learning dynamics.

  - **Best use case**: When selecting the most performant model is the priority over periodic snapshots.

Here are some factors to consider when selecting the strategy you wish to adopt:

- **Computational cost**: Frequent checkpointing increases disk I/O and CPU overhead

- **Failure recovery**: Regular and time-based checkpointing help resume training after interruptions, whereas best-model checkpointing may not provide recent progress

- **Storage constraints**: Maintaining many checkpoints consumes storage; regular checkpointing with a limit is most efficient in managing this

- **Rate of model improvement**: If the model improves rapidly, frequent checkpoints may be useful; if the progress is slow, fewer but more strategic checkpoints may suffice

The recommended approach for checkpointing LLMs is to combine strategies:

- Use regular checkpointing (e.g., every few hours) to ensure progress is saved

- Use best model checkpointing to retain the best-performing model

- Use a rolling window of recent checkpoints to balance storage efficiency and recovery options

Efficient checkpoint formats

For LLMs with billions of parameters, checkpoint size can become a significant concern. Let's explore some strategies for efficient checkpoint storage:

1. Import the necessary libraries and implement `EfficientLLMTrainer`:

```python
import torch
import io
import zipfile

class EfficientLLMTrainer(AdvancedLLMTrainer):
    def save_checkpoint_efficient(self, epoch, step, loss):
        checkpoint = {
            'epoch': epoch,
            'step': step,
            'model_state_dict': self.model.state_dict(),
            'optimizer_state_dict': self.optimizer.state_dict(),
            'loss': loss
        }

        checkpoint_path = os.path.join(
            self.checkpoint_dir,
                f'checkpoint_epoch_{epoch}_step_{step}.zip')

        with zipfile.ZipFile(checkpoint_path,
            'w', zipfile.ZIP_DEFLATED
        ) as zipf:
            for key, value in checkpoint.items():
                if isinstance(value, dict):  # For model and
    optimizer state_dicts
                    buffer = io.BytesIO()
                    torch.save(value, buffer)
                    zipf.writestr(f'{key}.pt',
                    buffer.getvalue())
                else:
                    zipf.writestr(f'{key}.txt', str(value))

        print(f"Efficient checkpoint saved: {checkpoint_path}")
```

This code defines an `EfficientLLMTrainer` class that extends `AdvancedLLMTrainer` (presumably a pre-existing class for training LLMs). The key function implemented is `save_checkpoint_efficient`, which efficiently saves model checkpoints in a compressed ZIP format.

2. Let's define the function (`load_checkpoint_efficient`) to load the checkpoint in ZIP format:

```python
def load_checkpoint_efficient(self, checkpoint_path):
    checkpoint = {}
    with zipfile.ZipFile(checkpoint_path, 'r') as zipf:
        for filename in zipf.namelist():
            if filename.endswith('.pt'):
                with zipf.open(filename) as f:
                    key = filename[:-3]
                    # Remove .pt extension
                    checkpoint[key] = torch.load(
                        io.BytesIO(f.read()))
            else:
                with zipf.open(filename) as f:
                    key = filename[:-4]
                    # Remove .txt extension
                    value = f.read().decode('utf-8')
                    checkpoint[key] = (
                        int(value) if key in
                        ['epoch', 'step']
                        else float(value)
                    )

    self.model.load_state_dict(
        checkpoint['model_state_dict'])
    self.optimizer.load_state_
        dict(checkpoint['optimizer_state_dict'])
    return (
        checkpoint['epoch'], checkpoint['step'],
        checkpoint['loss']
    )
```

This function, `load_checkpoint_efficient`, is responsible for loading a previously saved checkpoint from a ZIP file and restoring the model and optimizer states. See the following example usage.

3. Example usage:

```python
trainer = EfficientLLMTrainer(model, optimizer)
trainer.save_checkpoint_efficient(epoch, step, loss.item())
epoch, step, loss = trainer.load_checkpoint_ efficient(
    'checkpoints/checkpoint_epoch_5_step_500.zip')
```

This implementation uses ZIP compression to reduce the size of checkpoints. It also separates the model and optimizer state dictionaries from other metadata, allowing for more efficient storage and loading.

Other strategies for efficient checkpoint storage include the following:

- **Quantization**: Reducing the precision of model weights (e.g., from float32 to float16) can significantly reduce the checkpoint size (see more about this strategy in *Chapter 13*)

- **Incremental checkpointing**: Only save the changes since the last checkpoint, rather than the entire model state

- **Distributed storage**: In multi-GPU or multi-node setups, distribute the checkpoint across multiple storage devices

- **Cloud storage**: Use cloud storage solutions that offer fast I/O and automatic compression

For very large models, you might also consider more advanced techniques, such as **model sharding**, where different parts of the model are saved separately and can be loaded on demand.

Recovering from failures

Robust recovery mechanisms are crucial for LLM training. Let's implement a system that can handle various types of failures:

```python
import signal
import sys

class RobustLLMTrainer(EfficientLLMTrainer):
    def __init__(
        self, model, optimizer, checkpoint_dir='checkpoints',
        autosave_interval=15
    ):
        super().__init__(model, optimizer, checkpoint_dir)
        self.autosave_interval = autosave_interval
        self.setup_signal_handlers()

    def setup_signal_handlers(self):
        signal.signal(signal.SIGINT, self.handle_interrupt)
        signal.signal(signal.SIGTERM, self.handle_interrupt)

    def handle_interrupt(self, signum, frame):
        print("Interrupted! Saving checkpoint before exiting...")
        self.save_checkpoint_efficient(self.current_epoch,
            self.current_step, self.current_loss)
        sys.exit(0)
```

```
    def train(self, epochs, steps_per_epoch, train_fn):
        try:
            start_epoch, start_step = 0, 0
            latest_checkpoint = self.get_latest_checkpoint()
            if latest_checkpoint:
                start_epoch, start_step, _ = \
                self.load_checkpoint_efficient(latest_checkpoint)
                print(
                    f"Resuming from epoch {start_epoch}, "
                    f"step {start_step}"
                )

            for epoch in range(start_epoch, epochs):
                self.current_epoch = epoch
                for step in range(start_step, steps_per_epoch):
                    self.current_step = step
                    self.current_loss = train_fn(
                        self.model, epoch, step)

                    if step % self.autosave_interval == 0:
                        self.save_checkpoint_efficient(
                            epoch, step, self.current_loss)

                start_step = 0  # Reset step counter at the start of
each epoch

        except Exception as e:
            print(f"Error occurred: {e}")
            print("Saving checkpoint before exiting...")
            self.save_checkpoint_efficient(self.current_epoch,
                self.current_step, self.current_loss)
            raise

    def get_latest_checkpoint(self):
        checkpoints = sorted(os.listdir(self.checkpoint_dir))
        return (
            os.path.join(self.checkpoint_dir, checkpoints[-1])
            if checkpoints
            else None
        )
```

```
# Usage
def train_step(model, epoch, step):
    # Simulated training step
    loss = 1 / (epoch + 1 + step + 1)   # Dummy loss that decreases
over time
    return loss

trainer = RobustLLMTrainer(model, optimizer)
trainer.train(epochs=10, steps_per_epoch=1000, train_fn=train_step)
```

The RobustLLMTrainer class extends EfficientLLMTrainer to add resilience by handling interruptions (such as SIGINT for *Ctrl + C* and SIGTERM for termination) and saving checkpoints to prevent data loss. It initializes with a model, optimizer, checkpoint directory, and auto-save interval, then sets up signal handlers to trigger a graceful shutdown by saving progress before exiting.

During training, it attempts to resume from the latest checkpoint if available. It loops through epochs and steps, running train_fn to compute loss and periodically saving checkpoints based on autosave_interval. If an exception occurs, it catches the error, saves the progress, and re-raises the exception to avoid silent failures.

The get_latest_checkpoint() method retrieves the most recent checkpoint by sorting files in the checkpoint directory (though os is missing and should be imported). The script concludes with an example usage where a dummy loss function is defined, and training is started with trainer. train(epochs=10, steps_per_epoch=1000, train_fn=train_step).

This implementation includes several robustness features:

- **Signal handling**: The trainer catches interrupt signals (*Ctrl + C*) and gracefully saves a checkpoint before exiting

- **Automatic resumption**: The trainer automatically finds and loads the latest checkpoint when starting training

- **Regular auto-saves**: Checkpoints are saved at regular intervals during training

- **Exception handling**: If an error occurs during training, a checkpoint is saved before the exception is re-raised

These features help recover from various types of failures:

- **System crashes or power outages**: Regular auto-saves ensure that not too much progress is lost

- **User interruptions**: Signal handling allows for graceful exits with the state saved

- **Code errors**: Exception handling ensures that progress is saved even if an unexpected error occurs

For even more robust recovery, consider implementing the following:

- **Checkpoint validation**: Verify the integrity of checkpoints before loading them
- **Multiple backup checkpoints**: Keep several recent checkpoints in case the latest one is corrupted
- **Distributed checkpointing**: In multi-node setups, ensure that checkpoints are consistent across all nodes

Checkpointing in distributed LLM training

Distributed training introduces additional complexity to checkpointing.

Let's break down the implementation of a basic distributed checkpointing system and understand each component:

1. We first define the `DistributedLLMTrainer` class, which inherits from `RobustLLMTrainer`. The `DistributedLLMTrainer` class is designed for the distributed training of LLMs using PyTorch's `torch.distributed` framework. It ensures that the model is trained across multiple devices (e.g., GPUs) or nodes efficiently:

    ```
    import torch.distributed as dist

    class DistributedLLMTrainer(RobustLLMTrainer):
        def __init__(
            self, model, optimizer, checkpoint_dir='checkpoints',
            autosave_interval=15
        ):
            super().__init__(model, optimizer, checkpoint_dir,
                autosave_interval)
            self.rank = dist.get_rank()
            self.world_size = dist.get_world_size()
    ```

    The initialization does the following:

    I.   Calls the parent class initializer.

    II. Sets up distributed training attributes:

        i.   `self.rank`: Identifies the current process

        ii. `self.world_size`: Indicates the total number of processes

2. We then use the following methods to save and load checkpoints during distributed training:

    ```
    def save_checkpoint_distributed(self, epoch, step, loss):
        if self.rank == 0:  # Only the main process saves
    checkpoints
            self.save_checkpoint_efficient(epoch, step, loss)
    ```

```
          dist.barrier()  # Synchronize all processes

    def load_checkpoint_distributed(self, checkpoint_path):
        if self.rank == 0:
            epoch, step, loss = \
                self.load_checkpoint_efficient(checkpoint_path)
        else:
            epoch, step, loss = 0, 0, 0.0

        # Broadcast the loaded data to all processes
        epoch = torch.tensor(epoch).to(self.rank)
        step = torch.tensor(step).to(self.rank)
        loss = torch.tensor(loss).to(self.rank)

        dist.broadcast(epoch, 0)
        dist.broadcast(step, 0)
        dist.broadcast(loss, 0)

        # Make sure all processes have loaded the checkpoint
        dist.barrier()

        return epoch.item(), step.item(), loss.item()
```

The following methods handle distributed checkpointing:

- save_checkpoint_distributed: Only the main process (rank 0) saves the checkpoint to avoid redundant writes, reduce disk I/O, and ensure consistency across processes. If all ranks are saved independently, it could lead to storage inefficiencies and potential race conditions. After saving, dist.barrier() synchronizes all processes to ensure they wait for the checkpoint to be written. When loading, only rank 0 reads the checkpoint to prevent redundant disk access; then, it broadcasts the loaded values to all other ranks using dist. broadcast(), ensuring every process starts from the same state before resuming training.

- load_checkpoint_distributed:

  - Only the main process loads the checkpoint

  - It broadcasts the loaded values to all other processes

  - It ensures all processes have the same checkpoint data

3. Next, we implement distributed training:

```
    def train_distributed(self, epochs, steps_per_epoch, train_fn):
        try:
            start_epoch, start_step = 0, 0
```

```
            if self.rank == 0:
                latest_checkpoint = self.get_latest_checkpoint()
                if latest_checkpoint:
                    start_epoch, start_step, _ = \
                        self.load_checkpoint_efficient(
                        latest_checkpoint)

            # Broadcast the starting epoch and step to all processes
            start_epoch = torch.tensor(start_epoch).to(self.rank)
            start_step = torch.tensor(start_step).to(self.rank)
            dist.broadcast(start_epoch, 0)
            dist.broadcast(start_step, 0)
            start_epoch = start_epoch.item()
            start_step = start_step.item()

            if self.rank == 0:
                print(
                    f"Resuming from epoch {start_epoch}, "
                    f"step {start_step}"
                )

            for epoch in range(start_epoch, epochs):
                self.current_epoch = epoch
                for step in range(start_step, steps_per_epoch):
                    self.current_step = step
                    self.current_loss = train_fn(
                        self.model, epoch, step)

                    if step % self.autosave_interval == 0:
                        self.save_checkpoint_distributed(
                            epoch, step, self.current_loss)

                start_step = 0  # Reset step counter at the start of
each epoch

        except Exception as e:
            print(f"Error occurred on rank {self.rank}: {e}")
            self.save_checkpoint_distributed(self.current_epoch,
                self.current_step, self.current_loss)
            dist.destroy_process_group()
            raise
```

The `train_distributed` method does the following:

I.   Determines the starting point (epoch and step)

II.   Broadcasts this information to all processes

III.   Runs the training loop with periodic checkpointing

IV.   Handles exceptions by saving a final checkpoint and cleaning up

4. We then employ the following code to initialize distributed training with PyTorch, set up your model for parallel execution, and perform a simple distributed training loop:

```python
def init_distributed():
    dist.init_process_group(backend='nccl')
    rank = dist.get_rank()
    torch.cuda.set_device(rank)
    return rank

def distributed_train_step(model, epoch, step):
    # Simulated distributed training step
    loss = 1 / (epoch + 1 + step + 1)  # Dummy loss that
decreases over time
    return loss

def main():
    rank = init_distributed()
    model = GPT2LMHeadModel(GPT2Config()).to(rank)
    model = torch.nn.parallel.DistributedDataParallel(
        model, device_ids=[rank])
    optimizer = torch.optim.AdamW(model.parameters(), lr=5e-5)

    trainer = DistributedLLMTrainer(model, optimizer)
    trainer.train_distributed(epochs=10, steps_per_epoch=1000,
        train_fn=distributed_train_step)

if __name__ == "__main__":
    main()
```

This code includes the following:

• `init_distributed`: Initializes the distributed training environment

• `distributed_train_step`: A dummy training function for demonstration

• `main`: Shows how to use `DistributedLLMTrainer` in practice

Key considerations for distributed checkpointing include maintaining consistency by synchronizing all processes using barriers during checkpointing, ensuring that only the main process handles I/O operations to avoid conflicts, and effectively sharing important data by broadcasting it from the main process to the other processes. Additionally, the system incorporates robust error handling, allowing it to gracefully save checkpoints and clean up distributed resources in case of failures.

Next, let us focus on the version control aspect.

Version control for LLM checkpoints

Version control for LLM checkpoints can help with managing different versions of your model during the development process. Here's a simple implementation:

```python
import os
import json
import shutil

class VersionControlledLLMTrainer(DistributedLLMTrainer):
    def __init__(
        self, model, optimizer, checkpoint_dir='checkpoints',
        version_file='versions.json'
    ):
        super().__init__(model, optimizer, checkpoint_dir)
        self.version_file = version_file
        self.versions = self.load_versions()

    def load_versions(self):
        if os.path.exists(self.version_file):
            with open(self.version_file, 'r') as f:
                return json.load(f)
        return {}

    def save_versions(self):
        with open(self.version_file, 'w') as f:
            json.dump(self.versions, f, indent=2)

    def save_checkpoint_versioned(
        self, epoch, step, loss, version_name
    ):
        checkpoint_path = self.save_checkpoint_efficient(
            epoch, step, loss)
        self.versions[version_name] = {
            'path': checkpoint_path,
            'epoch': epoch,
```

```
                    'step': step,
                    'loss': loss
            }
            self.save_versions()
            print(f"Saved version '{version_name}': {checkpoint_path}")

    def load_checkpoint_versioned(self, version_name):
        if version_name not in self.versions:
            raise ValueError(f"Version '{version_name}' not found")
        version_info = self.versions[version_name]
        return self.load_checkpoint_efficient(version_info['path'])

    def create_branch(self, base_version, new_version):
        if base_version not in self.versions:
            raise ValueError(
                f"Base version '{base_version}' not found")
        base_info = self.versions[base_version]
        new_path = f"{self.checkpoint_dir}/branch_{new_version}.pt"
        shutil.copy(base_info['path'], new_path)
        self.versions[new_version] = {
            'path': new_path,
            'epoch': base_info['epoch'],
            'step': base_info['step'],
            'loss': base_info['loss'],
            'branched_from': base_version
        }
        self.save_versions()
        print(f"Created branch '{new_version}' from '{base_version}'")

# Usage
trainer = VersionControlledLLMTrainer(model, optimizer)
trainer.save_checkpoint_versioned(epoch=10, step=500,
    loss=0.1, version_name="v1.0")
trainer.create_branch("v1.0", "experimental_branch")
epoch, step, loss = trainer.load_checkpoint_versioned(
    "experimental_branch")
```

This implementation provides basic version control features:

- **Version tracking**: Each saved checkpoint can be associated with a version name
- **Branching**: You can create new branches from existing checkpoints, allowing for experimentation
- **Version history**: The version information is stored in a JSON file for easy inspection and management

The key benefits of version control for LLM checkpoints are as follows:

- **Experimentation**: You can easily try different training strategies or hyperparameters from a common starting point
- **Collaboration**: Team members can share and work on different versions of the model
- **Reproducibility**: Specific versions of the model can be referenced and recreated

Automated checkpointing and recovery systems

To make the checkpointing and recovery process more robust and hands-off, we can implement an automated system:

1. First, import the required modules:

    ```
    import threading
    import time
    ```

    We imported two key modules here:

    - `threading`: Enables the creation of threads for running tasks (such as auto-save and health checks) concurrently with the main training process
    - `time`: Used to manage intervals between auto-saves and health checks, as well as timestamping saved checkpoints

2. Next, we define and initialize the class:

    ```
    class AutomatedLLMTrainer(VersionControlledLLMTrainer):
        def __init__(
            self, model, optimizer, checkpoint_dir='checkpoints',
            autosave_interval=15, version_file='versions.json',
            health_check_interval=60
        ):
            super().__init__(model, optimizer, checkpoint_dir,
                version_file)
            self.autosave_interval = autosave_interval
            self.health_check_interval = health_check_interval
            self.training_active = False
    ```

The `AutomatedLLMTrainer` class inherits from a base class, `VersionControlledLLMTrainer`, which handles basic checkpointing logic. This class introduces automation for checkpointing and system health monitoring.

The following is a list of parameters that manage auto-saving, system health checks, and training execution control:

- `autosave_interval`: The time (in seconds) between auto-save checkpoints.

- `health_check_interval`: The time between system health checks.

- `training_active`: A flag to indicate whether the training is ongoing. It is used to control the threads' execution.

The constructor calls `super().__init__()` to inherit functionality from the parent class and sets up intervals for auto-saving and health checks.

3. Auto-save the thread for checkpointing:

```
def start_autosave_thread(self):
    def autosave_loop():
        while self.training_active:
            time.sleep(self.autosave_interval)
            if self.training_active:
                self.save_checkpoint_versioned(
                    self.current_epoch, self.current_step,
                    self.current_loss,
                    f"autosave_{time.time()}")
    self.autosave_thread = threading.Thread(
        target=autosave_loop)
    self.autosave_thread.start()
```

This method starts a separate thread that periodically saves a checkpoint during training.

The following is a list of components responsible for handling periodic auto-saving during training:

- `autosave_loop`: A function that continuously runs while `training_active` is True. Every `autosave_interval` seconds, it calls the `save_checkpoint_versioned()` method to save the current state.

- `threading.Thread`: The thread runs `autosave_loop` in the background, ensuring that auto-saves happen concurrently with the training process.

4. Next, we implement a health check thread. This method starts a health check thread that monitors system performance at regular intervals:

```
def start_health_check_thread(self):
    def health_check_loop():
        while self.training_active:
            time.sleep(self.health_check_interval)
            if self.training_active:
                if not self.check_system_health():
                    print("System health check failed.
```

```
            Initiating recovery...")
        self.initiate_recovery()
    self.health_check_thread = threading.Thread(
        target=health_check_loop)
    self.health_check_thread.start()
```

Here are the main elements of the preceding snippet:

- `health_check_loop`: A function that continuously runs during training. Every `health_check_interval` seconds, it checks the system health by calling `check_system_health()`. If a problem is detected, it triggers the recovery process.

- `check_system_health()`: This method needs to be defined to check the system's performance metrics (e.g., GPU memory or CPU usage). If the health check fails, it calls `initiate_recovery()`.

5. We perform system health check and recovery. The following placeholder method is where the system health checks will be implemented, for example, checking GPU memory, CPU utilization, disk space, or any other resource critical to the training process. It returns `True` if everything is fine, and `False` if there's a problem:

```
def check_system_health(self):
    # Implement system health checks here
    # For example, check GPU memory, CPU usage, disk space, etc.
    return True  # Return False if health check fails
```

The following method will contain logic for what to do if the system health check fails. It could, for instance, reload the last checkpoint, reduce the batch size, or take other corrective actions depending on the issue detected:

```
def initiate_recovery(self):
    # Implement recovery logic here
    # For example, reload from the last checkpoint, reduce batch
size, etc.
    pass
```

6. Finally, we conduct automated training with checkpointing and health checks. This method manages the overall training process with automation. It activates the auto-save and health check threads and initiates distributed training via the parent class's `train_distributed()` method:

```
def train_with_automation(
    self, epochs, steps_per_epoch, train_fn):
    self.training_active = True
    self.start_autosave_thread()
    self.start_health_check_thread()
```

```
try:
    super().train_distributed(epochs, steps_per_epoch,
        train_fn)
finally:
    self.training_active = False
    self.autosave_thread.join()
    self.health_check_thread.join()
```

Here's a breakdown of the main code elements:

- `self.training_active`: Set to `True` to indicate that training is running

- `try-finally block`: Ensures that no matter how the training ends (whether it completes or crashes), the `training_active` flag is set to `False` and both threads are properly terminated

This approach reduces manual intervention, enhances reliability, and offers flexibility in defining recovery logic based on the specific training needs.

Summary

Implementing robust checkpointing and recovery systems is common practice for successful LLM training. By incorporating these techniques, you can ensure that your long-running training processes are resilient to failures, easily manageable, and conducive to experimentation and collaboration.

To expand our discussion, *Table 10.1* lists checkpointing strategies, trade-offs, and use cases:

Checkpointing Strategy	Description	Trade-Offs	Use Cases
Regular (with max limit)	Saves at intervals (steps/epochs); keeps a maximum number.	Pros: Saves storage; periodic snapshots. Cons: Might overwrite good checkpoints.	Iterative model development; monitoring training progress; preventing complete data loss during long training runs.
Time-based	Saves at specified intervals (e.g., every 30 minutes).	Pros: Time-spaced snapshots. Cons: Inefficient if the interval is too short/long.	Long-running experiments where consistent, time-stamped checkpoints are crucial for debugging and analysis; ensuring recoverability in case of system failures.

Checkpointing Strategy	Description	Trade-Offs	Use Cases
Best model	Saves only when the model achieves the best performance.	Pros: Retains the best model. Cons: May not be representative if loss is noisy; no intermediate snapshots.	Selecting the most performant model.
Efficient (compression)	Uses compression (e.g., ZIP) to reduce size.	Storage-constrained environments; handling large models where storage is a primary concern; archiving models for long-term storage.	Storage-constrained environments; archiving models for long-term storage.
Efficient (quantization)	Reduces precision of weights (e.g., float32 to float16).	Pros: Reduces size. Cons: Potential accuracy loss.	Deploying models on resource-limited devices; reducing checkpoint size for faster transfer and storage; accelerating model loading.
Efficient (incremental)	Saves only changes since the last checkpoint.	Pros: Can significantly reduce size. Cons: Complex; potentially fragile.	Training models with gradual parameter updates; large models where frequent full checkpoints are impractical; continuous learning scenarios.
Distributed	In distributed training, only the main process (rank 0) saves; data is broadcast to others.	Pros: Avoids redundant writes; ensures consistency. Cons: Requires coordination.	Large-scale distributed training jobs; ensuring consistent model states across multiple workers; minimizing network overhead.

Checkpointing Strategy	Description	Trade-Offs	Use Cases
Version-controlled	Associates checkpoints with versions; supports branching.	Pros: Experimentation; reproducibility; rollback. Cons: Adds complexity.	Collaborative model development; tracking experimental variations; ensuring reproducibility for scientific research; managing model evolution.
Automated (with health checks)	Auto-saves checkpoints; performs health checks; can initiate recovery.	Pros: Reduces manual work; enhances reliability. Cons: Requires health check/recovery implementation.	Mission-critical training jobs; automated recovery from failures; long-running experiments requiring high reliability.

Table 10.1 – Checkpointing strategies, trade-offs, and use cases

In the next chapter, we'll explore effective techniques for adapting pre-trained language models to specific tasks or domains.

Subscribe for a free eBook

New frameworks, evolving architectures, research drops, production breakdowns—AI_Distilled filters the noise into a weekly briefing for engineers and researchers working hands-on with LLMs and GenAI systems. Subscribe now and receive a free eBook, along with weekly insights that help you stay focused and informed. Subscribe at `https://packt.link/8Oz6Y` or scan the QR code below.

11
Fine-Tuning

In this design pattern, you'll learn about effective strategies for **fine-tuning** pre-trained language models.

Fine-tuning LLMs addresses a fundamental optimization problem in transfer learning: Pre-training on large datasets helps LLMs learn general language skills and knowledge, but the differences between the pre-training data and the data for specific tasks can reduce performance. Fine-tuning uses a smaller, carefully chosen dataset for the task to update the model, making it better suited to the task's needs. This process retains useful knowledge from pre-training while refining the model's ability to perform effectively on the target task.

In this chapter, we'll be covering the following topics:

- Implementing transfer learning and fine-tuning
- Strategies for freezing and unfreezing layers
- Learning rate scheduling
- Domain-specific techniques
- Few-shot and zero-shot fine-tuning
- Continual fine-tuning and catastrophic forgetting

Implementing transfer learning and fine-tuning

We will use the following code blocks to demonstrate transfer learning with GPT-2, handling model initialization, data processing, and the fine-tuning workflow. We will use the Transformers library and WikiText dataset to fine-tune a pre-trained language model:

1. First, we load and initialize the GPT-2 model and tokenizer with configured padding:

    ```
    def load_model_and_tokenizer(model_name="gpt2"):
        model = GPT2LMHeadModel.from_pretrained(model_name)
        tokenizer = GPT2Tokenizer.from_pretrained(model_name)
        tokenizer.pad_token = tokenizer.eos_token
        return model, tokenizer
    ```

2. Then, the following code block manages dataset loading and text tokenization with a sequence length of 512:

    ```
    def prepare_dataset(dataset_name="wikitext",
        dataset_config="wikitext-2-raw-v1"
    ):
        dataset = load_dataset(dataset_name, dataset_config)
        return dataset

    def tokenize_function(examples, tokenizer):
        return tokenizer(
            examples["text"], truncation=True,
            padding="max_length", max_length=512)
    ```

3. Finally, we set up our training configuration, initialize the trainer, and execute fine-tuning:

    ```
    def fine_tune_lm(model, tokenizer,
        dataset, output_dir="./fine_tuned_model"
    ):
        tokenized_dataset = dataset.map(
            lambda examples: tokenize_function(examples, tokenizer),
            batched=True)
        training_args = TrainingArguments(
            output_dir=output_dir,
            num_train_epochs=3,
            per_device_train_batch_size=8,
            per_device_eval_batch_size=8,
            warmup_steps=500,
            weight_decay=0.01,
            logging_dir="./logs",
        )
    ```

```
trainer = Trainer(
    model=model,
    args=training_args,
    train_dataset=tokenized_dataset["train"],
    eval_dataset=tokenized_dataset["validation"],
)
trainer.train()
trainer.save_model()
```

The code sets up a `fine_tune_lm` function that prepares and executes language model fine-tuning. It first tokenizes the dataset using batched processing, then configures training parameters including epochs, batch sizes, warmup steps, and weight decay. Next, it initializes a trainer with the model, arguments, and datasets, runs the training process, and finally saves the fine-tuned model.

Batch size has a significant impact on both training stability and performance. Larger batch sizes allow for more parallelization and faster training on capable hardware but require more memory. They can provide more stable gradient estimates by averaging over more examples, potentially leading to better convergence. However, very large batches may generalize poorly compared to smaller ones, as they can cause the model to converge to sharper minima. Smaller batch sizes introduce more noise in gradient updates, which can help escape local minima and potentially find better solutions, but training takes longer. Finding the optimal batch size involves balancing hardware constraints, convergence stability, and generalization performance for your specific model and dataset.

When fine-tuning LLMs, we often don't need to update all the model's parameters. Selectively **freezing** and **unfreezing** layers can lead to more efficient and effective fine-tuning.

Strategies for freezing and unfreezing layers

The idea behind selectively freezing and unfreezing layers is rooted in how knowledge is structured and distributed across a deep neural network. Lower layers in LLMs tend to capture more general language representations—such as syntax, part-of-speech, and morphology—while higher layers are more specialized and task-dependent. This hierarchical organization allows us to leverage the general-purpose linguistic knowledge already encoded in the early layers while fine-tuning only the task-specific portions of the network.

By freezing the lower layers, we preserve their pre-trained capabilities and prevent catastrophic forgetting, which can occur if the entire model is updated indiscriminately on a narrow domain dataset. This also drastically reduces the number of trainable parameters, leading to lower memory usage and faster convergence. Meanwhile, selectively unfreezing the upper layers allows the model to adapt its representations for new tasks or domains without disturbing its core language understanding capabilities.

Let's look at how we can implement this:

1. First, we implement selective layer freezing by disabling gradients for all layers except the specified number of final layers:

```
def freeze_layers(model, num_layers_to_freeze):
    for param in model.base_model.parameters():
        param.requires_grad = False

    for i, layer in enumerate(model.base_model.transformer.h):
        if i >= len(model.base_model.transformer.h) -\
            num_layers_to_freeze:
            for param in layer.parameters():
                param.requires_grad = True
```

2. Then, we manage progressive layer unfreezing across training epochs:

```
def gradual_unfreeze(model, trainer, num_epochs, total_layers):
    layers_per_epoch = total_layers // num_epochs

    for epoch in range(num_epochs):
        freeze_layers(model, (epoch + 1) * layers_per_epoch)
        trainer.train(resume_from_checkpoint=True)
```

3. Finally, we configure optimized training parameters for the gradual unfreezing process:

```
training_args = TrainingArguments(
    output_dir="./fine_tuned_model",
    num_train_epochs=5,  # Increased epochs for better learning
    per_device_train_batch_size=16,  # Larger batch size
    per_device_eval_batch_size=16,
    warmup_steps=1000,  # More warmup steps
    learning_rate=2e-5,  # Added learning rate
    weight_decay=0.1,  # Increased weight decay
    logging_dir="./logs",
    save_steps=500,  # Added save frequency
    eval_steps=500   # Added evaluation frequency
)
trainer = Trainer(
    model=model,
    args=training_args,
    train_dataset=tokenized_dataset["train"],
    eval_dataset=tokenized_dataset["validation"],
)
```

This implementation introduces two key strategies:

- `freeze_layers`: This function freezes all layers except for the last `num_layers_to_freeze`
- `gradual_unfreeze`: This function gradually unfreezes layers over the course of training

The gradual unfreezing approach allows the model to adapt its higher-level features first, then progressively fine-tune lower-level features. This can lead to better performance and help prevent catastrophic forgetting.

Catastrophic forgetting is reduced because of the following reasons:

- Layer freezing preserves knowledge in earlier layers by disabling gradient updates for them, maintaining the fundamental representations learned during pre-training while only adapting task-specific later layers. This retains the model's general knowledge while allowing adaptation to new tasks.

- Gradual unfreezing implements a staged approach where training begins with only the final layers unfrozen (which contain more task-specific representations), then progressively unfreezes earlier layers. This allows the model to adapt higher-level features first before making more fundamental changes, providing a gentle transition that helps maintain previously learned patterns.

- The training configuration supports these approaches with a carefully balanced learning rate, increased warmup steps, and higher weight decay that further prevents drastic parameter shifts. The increased epochs allow for more gradual adaptation while save and evaluation checkpoints provide monitoring to prevent overfitting during the unfreezing process.

Together, these techniques create a more controlled fine-tuning process that preserves general knowledge while effectively adapting to new tasks.

Finetuning performance can be significantly improved by applying appropriate learning rate scheduling, which we'll visit next.

Learning rate scheduling

As mentioned, proper **learning rate scheduling** is often used for effective fine-tuning. The following code demonstrates common learning rate scheduling techniques for LLM fine-tuning, offering both **linear** and **cosine warmup** strategies to optimize training:

1. First, we set up the scheduling framework with the required imports and function initialization:

```
from transformers import (
    get_linear_schedule_with_warmup,
    get_cosine_schedule_with_warmup)
```

```
def fine_tune_with_lr_scheduling(
    model, tokenizer, dataset, scheduler_type="linear",
    num_epochs=3
):
    tokenized_dataset = dataset.map(
        lambda examples: tokenize_function(examples, tokenizer),
        batched=True)
```

2.   Next, we configure optimized training parameters with improved defaults:

```
training_args = TrainingArguments(
    output_dir="./fine_tuned_model",
    num_train_epochs=3,
    per_device_train_batch_size=32,   # Increased batch size
    per_device_eval_batch_size=32,
    weight_decay=0.1,   # Increased weight decay
    logging_dir="./logs",
    learning_rate=2e-5,   # Adjusted learning rate
    warmup_ratio=0.1,    # Added warmup ratio
    eval_steps=100,       # Added evaluation frequency
    save_steps=100        # Added save frequency
)
trainer = Trainer(
    model=model,
    args=training_args,
    train_dataset=tokenized_dataset["train"],
    eval_dataset=tokenized_dataset["validation"],
)
```

3.   Finally, we implement learning rate scheduling with dynamic warmup steps calculation:

```
num_training_steps = len(tokenized_dataset["train"]) //
    training_args.per_device_train_batch_size * num_epochs

if scheduler_type == "linear":
    scheduler = get_linear_schedule_with_warmup(
        trainer.optimizer,
        num_warmup_steps=num_training_steps // 10,   # 10% warmup
        num_training_steps=num_training_steps
    )
elif scheduler_type == "cosine":
    scheduler = get_cosine_schedule_with_warmup(
        trainer.optimizer,
        num_warmup_steps=num_training_steps // 10,   # 10% warmup
        num_training_steps=num_training_steps
```

```
    )
else:
    raise ValueError("Unsupported scheduler type")
```

This implementation provides two common learning rate scheduling strategies:

- **Linear schedule with warmup**: The learning rate increases linearly from 0 to the initial `lr` during warmup, then decreases linearly to 0. We discussed this in *Chapter 7* under the *Loss functions and optimization strategies* section. However, it is important to note that we need to use the same warmup schedule for fine-tuning as well. Warmup helps prevent sudden weight updates early in training, ensuring smoother convergence.

- **Cosine schedule with warmup**: Similar to the linear schedule, but in this case, the decrease follows a cosine curve.

These scheduling strategies can help stabilize training and potentially lead to better convergence.

Domain-specific fine-tuning techniques

When fine-tuning LLMs for specific domains, we often need to adapt our approach. Let's look at an example of domain-specific fine-tuning for a scientific corpus. The following code implements domain-specific fine-tuning for scientific text using custom dataset preparation and training configuration:

1. First, we set up the dataset preparation for scientific text with a specified block size and language modeling collator:

```
import torch
from transformers import (
    TextDataset, DataCollatorForLanguageModeling )

def prepare_scientific_dataset(file_path, tokenizer):
    dataset = TextDataset(
        tokenizer=tokenizer,
        file_path=file_path,
        block_size=128,
    )
    data_collator = DataCollatorForLanguageModeling(
        tokenizer=tokenizer, mlm=False,
    )
    return dataset, data_collator
```

2. Next, we handle dataset preparation for both training and evaluation:

```
def fine_tune_for_scientific_domain(
    model, tokenizer, train_file, eval_file,
    output_dir="./scientific_model"
):
```

```
        train_dataset, data_collator =
            prepare_scientific_dataset(train_file, tokenizer)
        eval_dataset, _ = prepare_scientific_dataset(
            eval_file, tokenizer)
```

3. Finally, we configure optimized training parameters for scientific domain adaptation:

```
training_args = TrainingArguments(
    output_dir=output_dir,
    num_train_epochs=3,                # Reduced epochs
    per_device_train_batch_size=8,  # Increased batch size
    per_device_eval_batch_size=8,
    warmup_steps=1000,                 # Increased warmup
    weight_decay=0.1,                  # Increased weight decay
    learning_rate=3e-5,                # Added learning rate
    logging_dir="./logs",
    evaluation_strategy="steps",       # Changed to steps
    eval_steps=500,                    # Added eval frequency
    save_steps=500,                    # Added save frequency
    gradient_accumulation_steps=4   # Added gradient accumulation
)
```

This implementation includes several domain-specific considerations:

- **Custom dataset preparation**: We use `TextDataset` to handle domain-specific text files

- **Smaller batch size**: Scientific texts often have longer sequences, so we reduce the batch size

- **More epochs**: Domain adaptation might require more training iterations

- **Regular evaluation**: After each epoch, we evaluate the model to track validation loss and key domain-specific metrics, ensuring proper adaptation

When fine-tuning for specific domains, consider the following steps:

- Adapting the vocabulary for domain-specific terms

- Using domain-specific evaluation metrics

- Potentially modifying the model architecture for domain-specific features

In the following section, we'll explore a couple of strategies for fine-tuning models with little to no labeled data from the target domain.

Few-shot and zero-shot fine-tuning

Few-shot and **zero-shot learning** are powerful techniques for adapting LLMs to new tasks with minimal or no task-specific training data. Let's implement a few-shot fine-tuning approach:

1. We create a prompt that includes a few examples of the task:

```
def prepare_few_shot_dataset(examples, tokenizer, num_shots=5):
    few_shot_examples = examples[:num_shots]
    prompt = "\n\n".join(
        [
            f"Input: {ex['input']}\n"
            f"Output: {ex['output']}"
            for ex in few_shot_examples
        ]
    )
    prompt += "\n\nInput: {input}\nOutput:"

    def tokenize_function(example):
        full_prompt = prompt.format(input=example['input'])
        tokenized_prompt = tokenizer(full_prompt,
            truncation=True,
            padding="max_length", max_length=512)
        tokenized_output = tokenizer(
            example['output'], truncation=True,
            padding="max_length", max_length=512)

        tokenized_prompt['labels'] = \
            [-100] * len(tokenized_prompt['input_ids'])
            + tokenized_output['input_ids']
        return tokenized_prompt

    return examples.map(tokenize_function)
```

2. The model is then fine-tuned on this prompt-based dataset:

```
def few_shot_fine_tune(
    model, tokenizer, dataset, num_shots=5, num_epochs=3
):
    few_shot_dataset = prepare_few_shot_dataset(dataset,
        tokenizer, num_shots)

    training_args = TrainingArguments(
        output_dir="./few_shot_model",
        num_train_epochs=num_epochs,
```

```
        per_device_train_batch_size=4,
        per_device_eval_batch_size=4,
        warmup_steps=100,
        weight_decay=0.01,
        logging_dir="./logs",
    )

    trainer = Trainer(
        model=model,
        args=training_args,
        train_dataset=few_shot_dataset,
    )

    trainer.train()
    return trainer
```

The `few_shot_fine_tune` function implements few-shot fine-tuning, which adapts a pre-trained model to new tasks using minimal examples. It takes a model, tokenizer, dataset, and configuration parameters (num_shots=5, num_epochs=3), then prepares a small subset of the data with `prepare_few_shot_dataset`, configures training with `TrainingArguments` (specifying output locations, batch sizes, and optimization parameters), initializes a `Trainer` object with these components, executes the training process via `trainer.train()`, and finally returns the trained model wrapped in the `Trainer` object—all using the Hugging Face Transformers library framework commonly used for language models.

3. The fine-tuned model can then generalize to new instances of the task:

```
# Usage
model, tokenizer = load_model_and_tokenizer()
dataset = load_dataset("your_dataset")  # Load your few-shot
dataset
few_shot_trainer = few_shot_fine_tune(model, tokenizer, dataset)
```

This implementation demonstrates few-shot fine-tuning.

For zero-shot learning, you would typically rely on the pre-trained model's ability to understand task descriptions without any task-specific examples or fine-tuning.

Continual fine-tuning and catastrophic forgetting

Continual fine-tuning involves adapting a model to new tasks while retaining performance on previous tasks. However, this can lead to **catastrophic forgetting**. Catastrophic forgetting in LLMs refers to the phenomenon where a model loses previously learned information when fine-tuned on new tasks or data without appropriate mechanisms to preserve prior knowledge.

Let's implement a simple strategy to mitigate this:

1. First, we calculate parameter importance and implement **elastic weight consolidation** (**EWC**) loss for preserving critical weights:

```
import copy

def ewc_loss(model, old_model, importance, loss):
    ewc_lambda = 0.01
    for n, p in model.named_parameters():
        if n in importance:
            loss += ewc_lambda * importance[n]
                * (p - old_model[n]).pow(2).sum()
    return loss

def compute_importance(model, dataset):
    importance = {}
    model.eval()
    for batch in dataset:
        model.zero_grad()
        output = model(batch)
        loss = output.loss
        loss.backward()
        for n, p in model.named_parameters():
            if p.grad is not None:
                if n not in importance:
                    importance[n] = p.grad.data.clone().pow(2)
                else:
                    importance[n] += p.grad.data.clone().pow(2)
    return importance
```

2. We then implement the following code, which manages sequential training on multiple tasks while maintaining previous knowledge:

```
def continual_fine_tune(
        model, tokenizer, datasets, num_epochs=3
):
    old_model = None
    importance = None
    for i, dataset in enumerate(datasets):
        if old_model is not None:
            importance = compute_importance(
                old_model, datasets[i-1])
        old_model = copy.deepcopy(model)
        tokenized_dataset = dataset.map(
```

```
                    lambda examples: tokenize_function(examples,
                        tokenizer),
                    batched=True)
```

3.   Finally, we define optimized training parameters for continual learning:

```
training_args = TrainingArguments(
    output_dir=f"./continual_fine_tuned_model_task_{i+1}",
    num_train_epochs=8,                    # Increased epochs
    per_device_train_batch_size=20,    # Increased batch size
    per_device_eval_batch_size=20,
    warmup_steps=2000,                     # Increased warmup
    weight_decay=0.2,                      # Increased weight decay
    learning_rate=2e-5,                    # Added learning rate
    logging_dir="./logs",
    evaluation_strategy="steps",    # Added evaluation strategy
    eval_steps=1000,                    # Added evaluation frequency
    save_steps=1000                      # Added save frequency
)
```

This implementation introduces several key concepts for continual fine-tuning:

- **EWC**: We implement a simplified version of EWC, which adds a penalty term to the loss function to prevent drastic changes to important parameters for previous tasks

- **Importance computation**: We calculate the importance of each parameter based on its gradient magnitude on the previous task

- **Continual fine-tuning loop**: We fine-tune the model on each task sequentially, using EWC to mitigate forgetting

- **Evaluation on all tasks**: After fine-tuning on each new task, we evaluate the model's performance on all previous tasks to monitor forgetting

The key considerations for continual fine-tuning are as follows:

- **Balance between plasticity and stability**: EWC helps maintain this balance, allowing the model to learn new tasks while preserving knowledge of previous ones

- **Computational overhead**: Computing importance and applying EWC increases the computational cost of training

- **Task similarity**: The effectiveness of continual fine-tuning can depend on the similarity between tasks

Additional strategies to consider for mitigating catastrophic forgetting include the following:

- **Gradient episodic memory (GEM)**: In this approach, a small episodic memory of data from previous tasks is stored and used to constrain the gradient updates on new tasks, as follows:

```python
def project(gradient, memories):
    for memory in memories:
        if torch.dot(gradient, memory) < 0:
            gradient -= (
                torch.dot(gradient, memory) / torch.dot(
                    memory, memory)
            ) * memory
    return gradient


# This would be integrated into the training loop
```

- **Progressive neural networks**: Here, a new "column" of layers for each new task is created, while lateral connections to previously learned features are maintained.

- **Learning without Forgetting (LwF)**: In this approach, knowledge distillation is employed to preserve the model's performance on previous tasks:

```python
def lwf_loss(
    model, old_model, new_data, old_data, temperature=2
):
    # Compute standard loss on new data
    new_loss = compute_loss(model, new_data)

    # Compute distillation loss on old data
    old_outputs = old_model(old_data)
    new_outputs = model(old_data)
    distillation_loss = F.kl_div(
        F.log_softmax(new_outputs / temperature, dim=1),
        F.softmax(old_outputs / temperature, dim=1),
        reduction='batchmean'
    ) * (temperature  2)

    return new_loss + distillation_loss


# This would replace the standard loss in the training loop
```

These advanced techniques can be particularly useful when fine-tuning LLMs across a diverse range of tasks or domains.

Summary

Fine-tuning patterns for LLMs encompass a wide range of techniques, from basic transfer learning to advanced continual learning strategies. By mastering these patterns, you can effectively adapt pre-trained models to new tasks and domains, optimize performance, and mitigate issues such as catastrophic forgetting. As the field of LLMs continues to evolve, staying updated with the latest fine-tuning techniques will be crucial for developing state-of-the-art language models tailored to specific applications.

Here are the key takeaways from this chapter:

- **Fine-tuning adapts pre-trained LLMs**: Fine-tuning is the key process for adapting general-purpose, pre-trained LLMs to specific tasks and datasets, bridging the gap between general language understanding and specialized performance

- **Layer management is crucial**: Strategically freezing and unfreezing layers (especially gradual unfreezing) is critical for balancing the preservation of pre-trained knowledge with adaptation to the new task

- **Learning rate scheduling stabilizes training**: Using learning rate schedules with warmup (linear or cosine) is essential for stable and effective fine-tuning, preventing drastic early updates and promoting convergence

- **Domain/task specificity matters**: Techniques such as domain-specific vocabulary adaptation, custom data handling, and few-shot/zero-shot approaches are vital for maximizing performance on specialized tasks

- **Catastrophic forgetting must be addressed**: In continual learning scenarios, techniques such as EWC, GEM, and others are necessary to prevent the model from losing previously learned information when trained on new tasks

We will explore model pruning in the next chapter. Model pruning systematically removes redundant or less important neural connections in LLMs while preserving core functionality, essentially creating a lighter, more efficient version that maintains similar performance but requires fewer computational resources.

12

Model Pruning

In this chapter, we'll explore **model pruning** techniques designed to reduce model size while maintaining performance.

Model pruning refers to the systematic elimination of unnecessary parameters from a neural network while maintaining performance. For LLMs, this typically involves identifying and removing redundant or less important weights, neurons, or attention heads based on criteria such as magnitude, sensitivity analysis, or gradient-based importance.

You'll learn how to implement various pruning methods, from magnitude-based pruning to iterative techniques, and the trade-offs involved in size reduction versus performance. Additionally, this chapter will help you decide whether to prune during or after training, ensuring your LLMs remain efficient and effective.

In this chapter, we'll be covering the following topics:

- Magnitude-based pruning
- Structured versus unstructured pruning
- Iterative pruning techniques
- Pruning during training versus post-training pruning
- Balancing pruning and model performance
- Combining pruning with other compression techniques

Magnitude-based pruning

Magnitude-based pruning is one of the simplest and most widely used pruning techniques. The idea behind this method is to remove weights in the neural network that contribute least to the model's overall function, typically, these are weights with the smallest magnitude (absolute value). By pruning such weights, the model becomes more compact and faster, with minimal impact on accuracy:

```
import torch
import torch.nn.utils.prune as prune


# Assume model is an instance of a pre-trained LLM
model = ...  # Load or define your LLM model


# Prune 30% of the lowest magnitude weights in all Linear layers
for name, module in model.named_modules():
    if isinstance(module, torch.nn.Linear):
        prune.l1_unstructured(module, name='weight', amount=0.3)


# Remove the pruning reparameterization
for name, module in model.named_modules():
    if isinstance(module, torch.nn.Linear):
        prune.remove(module, 'weight')
```

In this code example, magnitude-based pruning removes 30% of the lowest-magnitude weights in all linear layers of an LLM. The prune.l1_unstructured function specifies that weights with the smallest L1 norm will be pruned.

The following code snippet implements the prune.l1_unstructured function for unstructured L1-norm-based pruning on a given parameter tensor within a PyTorch module by zeroing out weights with the smallest absolute values:

```
    def prune.l1_unstructured(module, name, amount):
    """Prunes weights with lowest L1 norm magnitude in a module's
tensor"""
    # Get the parameter to prune
    tensor = getattr(module, name)

    # Calculate number of parameters to prune
    n_params_to_prune = int(amount * tensor.numel())

    # Get magnitude threshold (kth smallest absolute value)
    threshold = torch.kthvalue(
        tensor.abs().view(-1), n_params_to_prune
    ).values
```

```
# Create and apply mask (zeros out weights below threshold)
mask = tensor.abs() > threshold
pruned_tensor = tensor.clone() * mask

# Update parameter and register mask
setattr(module, name, torch.nn.Parameter(pruned_tensor))
module.register_buffer(f'{name}_mask', mask)

# Add hook to maintain pruning during updates
module.register_forward_pre_hook(
    lambda m, _: setattr(
        m, name,
        torch.nn.Parameter(
            getattr(m, name) * getattr(m, f'{name}_mask')
        )
    )
)

return mask
```

Here, the function begins by extracting the target tensor from the module and determining how many of its elements should be pruned based on the specified proportion amount. It identifies a pruning threshold by computing the k-th smallest absolute value in the tensor, where k corresponds to the number of parameters to prune. A binary mask is then created, where values above the threshold are retained while those below the threshold are set to zero. This mask is applied to produce a pruned version of the tensor, which replaces the original parameter in the module. The mask is stored as a buffer to persist across model operations, and a forward pre-hook is registered to ensure that pruning is enforced before every forward pass, preserving the sparsity pattern even if the underlying weights are updated during training.

In model pruning, the L1 norm is used to evaluate the importance of weights or parameters in a model by summing the absolute values of their components, with lower L1 norm values often indicating less significant parameters that can be removed to reduce model size while maintaining performance.

After pruning, the prune.remove method is called to remove the pruning reparameterization and make the changes permanent.

Magnitude-based pruning is particularly effective for models with many small weights that contribute little to overall performance, but it may not be sufficient when applied alone for large-scale pruning.

Structured versus unstructured pruning

When pruning LLMs, you can either prune weights individually (unstructured pruning) or remove entire structures, such as filters, channels, or attention heads (structured pruning):

- **Unstructured pruning**: This involves removing individual weights based on magnitude or other criteria. It provides more granularity but can result in sparse matrices, which are harder to optimize on standard hardware, as demonstrated in the `prune.l1_unstructured` function described earlier.

- **Structured pruning**: Entire sections of the model, such as neurons, channels, or layers, are pruned. This approach is easier to implement on modern hardware and often leads to better speedups in inference time, even though it may have a larger immediate effect on model performance.

Structured pruning in LLMs can be implemented using PyTorch's built-in utilities, as shown in the following code. Here, we apply L2-norm structured pruning to remove 30% of neurons across linear layers, targeting entire rows of weight matrices to effectively eliminate complete neurons rather than just individual connections:

```
import torch.nn.utils.prune as prune

# Structured pruning of entire neurons in a layer
for name, module in model.named_modules():
    if isinstance(module, torch.nn.Linear):
        prune.ln_structured(
            module, name='weight', amount=0.3, n=2, dim=0
        )
```

In this structured pruning example, the `ln_structured` function removes entire neurons from the linear layer based on the L2 norm across all weights in a given dimension. The choice of structured pruning can significantly reduce computational complexity while also making the model more suitable for deployment on standard hardware architectures.

Next, we'll see how to prune a small fraction of weights at a time over multiple training steps instead of pruning large portions of the model in a single pass.

Iterative pruning techniques

Here, we'll talk about **iterative pruning**, which allows you to prune a small fraction of weights at a time over multiple training steps. This method reduces the risk of drastic performance drops and provides more opportunities for the model to recover and adjust to the pruning.

The iterative approach also allows for fine-tuning after each pruning step, enabling the model to "heal" from the weight reduction:

```
# Iteratively prune 10% of the model after every 10 epochs
for epoch in range(1, num_epochs+1):
    train(model, train_loader, optimizer)  # Regular training step
    if epoch % 10 == 0:
        for name, module in model.named_modules():
            if isinstance(module, torch.nn.Linear):
                prune.l1_unstructured(module, name='weight',
                    amount=0.1)
                prune.remove(module, 'weight')  # Remove pruning mask
after each step
    validate(model, val_loader)
```

In this example, 10% of the weights are pruned after every 10 epochs. The gradual removal of weights ensures that the model has enough time to adjust between each pruning step. Iterative pruning, combined with validation steps, can help find a more optimal balance between model size and performance.

Pruning during training versus post-training pruning

A key decision in applying pruning is whether to prune the model during training or after training is complete:

- **Pruning during training**: This approach allows the model to adjust to the pruned structure over time by iteratively pruning weights as it learns. The model can compensate for pruned weights, potentially resulting in better final performance. However, it requires more computational resources and training time.

  Here's an example of this approach:

  ```
  import torch
  import torch.nn.utils.prune as prune

  # Assuming model is a pre-trained LLM
  model = ...  # Load or define your LLM model
  optimizer = torch.optim.Adam(model.parameters(), lr=0.001)
  criterion = torch.nn.CrossEntropyLoss()

  def train(model, train_loader, optimizer):
      model.train()
      for batch in train_loader:
          inputs, targets = batch
          optimizer.zero_grad()
          outputs = model(inputs)
  ```

```
            loss = criterion(outputs, targets)
            loss.backward()
            optimizer.step()

# Prune 20% of the weights every 5 epochs during training
for epoch in range(1, 20):
    train(model, train_loader, optimizer)

    # Apply pruning every 5 epochs
    if epoch % 5 == 0:
        for name, module in model.named_modules():
            if isinstance(module, torch.nn.Linear):
                prune.l1_unstructured(module, name='weight',
                    amount=0.2)
                prune.remove(module, 'weight')  # Remove
reparameterization after each pruning
```

- **Post-training pruning**: In this approach, pruning is performed after the model has been fully trained. This method is computationally efficient since it doesn't require modifications during the training process, and you can optionally fine-tune the model afterward. However, it may result in a larger accuracy drop compared to pruning during training.

  Let's take a look at an example of post-training pruning:

```
# Assuming the model has already been fully trained
model = ...  # Load or define your trained LLM model

# Prune 30% of the weights in all Linear layers after training
for name, module in model.named_modules():
    if isinstance(module, torch.nn.Linear):
        prune.l1_unstructured(module, name='weight', amount=0.3)

# Optionally, fine-tune the model after pruning
fine_tune_epochs = 3
for epoch in range(fine_tune_epochs):
    train(model, train_loader, optimizer)  # Fine-tuning the
pruned model
```

The choice between these two depends on your performance constraints and available resources. Pruning during training often leads to more stable models, while post-training pruning is faster and more resource-efficient.

Balancing pruning and model performance

Finding the right balance between pruning and model performance is critical. Aggressive pruning can lead to significant performance degradation, while too little pruning may not yield enough benefits. The key is to identify which parts of the model can be pruned with minimal impact on accuracy. This requires careful validation after each pruning step and close monitoring of key performance metrics. These metrics include parameter reduction rates, inference speed gains, memory footprint reduction, changes in perplexity, and task-specific performance. Throughout the process, it's crucial to balance the accuracy-efficiency trade-off to ensure the pruned model retains acceptable performance despite having fewer parameters

A common strategy is to apply fine-tuning after pruning to restore some of the lost performance. Fine-tuning allows the model to adjust to the pruned structure and recover its original capabilities:

```python
import torch.nn.utils.prune as prune

# Assuming model has been trained and pruned
model = ...  # Pruned LLM model

# Apply fine-tuning to restore performance after pruning
optimizer = torch.optim.Adam(model.parameters(), lr=1e-5)  # Lower
learning rate for fine-tuning
fine_tune_epochs = 5

for epoch in range(fine_tune_epochs):
    train(model, train_loader, optimizer)  # Reuse the train function
from earlier
    validate(model, val_loader)  # Validation step to monitor
performance
```

In this example, after pruning a portion of the weights, the model is fine-tuned with a lower learning rate to restore performance. A lower learning rate allows the model to adjust gradually to the new pruned structure, preventing the destabilization of learned features. Validation is performed after each fine-tuning step to monitor the model's progress and ensure that pruning has not significantly degraded performance.

Let's see how we can combine pruning with other model compression techniques.

Combining pruning with other compression techniques

Pruning can be combined with other model compression techniques, such as quantization or distillation, to achieve even greater reductions in model size and complexity. Combining these techniques often results in more compact models that maintain high performance.

Pruning and quantization

Pruning followed by **quantization** can lead to significant reductions in model size and faster inference speeds, especially for resource-constrained environments:

```python
import torch
import torch.nn.utils.prune as prune
import torch.quantization as quant

# Prune the model first
model = ...  # Pre-trained LLM
for name, module in model.named_modules():
    if isinstance(module, torch.nn.Linear):
        prune.l1_unstructured(module, name='weight', amount=0.4)
        prune.remove(module, 'weight')

# Apply dynamic quantization after pruning
quantized_model = quant.quantize_dynamic(
    model, {torch.nn.Linear}, dtype=torch.qint8
)

# Check the size reduction
print("Original model size:", torch.cuda.memory_allocated())
print("Quantized model size:", torch.cuda.memory_allocated())
```

Pruning and knowledge distillation

You can also combine pruning with **knowledge distillation**, where a smaller, pruned **student model** is trained to mimic the behavior of a larger, well-trained **teacher model**:

```python
# Teacher and student models for knowledge distillation
teacher_model = ...  # Larger, fully trained model
student_model = ...  # Smaller model to be distilled and pruned

def distillation_loss(student_outputs, teacher_outputs, temperature):
    return torch.nn.KLDivLoss()(
        torch.nn.functional.log_softmax(
            student_outputs / temperature
        ),
        torch.nn.functional.softmax(
            teacher_outputs / temperature
        )
    )
```

```
# Train the smaller, pruned model using knowledge distillation
temperature = 2.0
optimizer = torch.optim.Adam(student_model.parameters(), lr=1e-4)

for batch in train_loader:
    inputs, _ = batch
    teacher_outputs = teacher_model(inputs)
    student_outputs = student_model(inputs)

    loss = distillation_loss(
        student_outputs, teacher_outputs, temperature
    )
    loss.backward()
    optimizer.step()
```

This approach allows the student model to achieve high performance with fewer parameters. Knowledge distillation helps compensate for accuracy loss caused by pruning by transferring high-level representations from the unpruned teacher model.

These examples illustrate how pruning can be applied during or after training, balanced with performance requirements, and combined with other compression techniques such as quantization and knowledge distillation to create more efficient LLMs.

Summary

In this chapter, we explored various model pruning techniques for LLMs, including magnitude-based pruning, structured versus unstructured pruning, and iterative pruning methods. We discussed the trade-offs involved in pruning during training versus post-training, and the importance of fine-tuning after pruning to recover lost performance. By combining pruning with other compression techniques, such as quantization and distillation, you can create more efficient LLMs suitable for deployment in resource-constrained environments.

In the next chapter, we'll explore quantization techniques for LLMs, focusing on reducing numerical precision to improve model efficiency while maintaining performance. You'll learn how to apply post-training and quantization-aware training to optimize your LLMs further.

Subscribe for a free eBook

New frameworks, evolving architectures, research drops, production breakdowns—AI_Distilled filters the noise into a weekly briefing for engineers and researchers working hands-on with LLMs and GenAI systems. Subscribe now and receive a free eBook, along with weekly insights that help you stay focused and informed. Subscribe at `https://packt.link/8Oz6Y` or scan the QR code below.

13

Quantization

In this chapter, we'll dive into **quantization** methods that can optimize LLMs for deployment on resource-constrained devices, such as mobile phones, embedded systems, or edge computing environments.

Quantization is a technique that reduces the precision of numerical representations, thus shrinking the model's size and improving its inference speed without heavily compromising its performance.

Quantization is particularly beneficial in the following scenarios:

- **Resource-constrained deployment**: When deploying models on devices with limited memory, storage, or computational power, such as mobile phones, IoT devices, or edge computing platforms

- **Latency-sensitive applications**: When real-time or near-real-time responses are required, quantization can significantly reduce inference time

- **Large-scale deployment**: When deploying models at scale, even modest reductions in model size and inference time can translate to substantial cost savings in infrastructure and energy consumption

- **Bandwidth-limited scenarios**: When models need to be downloaded to devices over limited bandwidth connections, smaller quantized models reduce transmission time and data usage

- **Models with redundant precision**: When many LLMs are trained with higher precision than necessary for good performance, they become excellent candidates for quantization.

However, quantization may not be suitable in some cases, such as the following:

- **Highly precision-sensitive tasks**: For applications where even minor degradation in accuracy is unacceptable, such as certain medical diagnostics or critical financial models

- **Models already optimized for low precision**: If a model was specifically designed or trained to operate efficiently at lower precisions, further quantization may cause significant performance drops

- **Small models**: For already compact models, the overhead of quantization operations might outweigh the benefits in some hardware configurations

- **Development and fine-tuning phases**: During active development and experimentation, working with full-precision models is often preferable for maximum flexibility and to avoid masking potential issues

- **Hardware incompatibility**: Target hardware may lack efficient support for the specific quantized formats you're planning to use (e.g., some devices may not have optimized INT8 or INT4 computation capabilities)

- **Complex architectures with varying sensitivity**: Some parts of an LLM architecture (such as attention mechanisms) may be more sensitive to quantization than others, requiring more sophisticated mixed-precision approaches rather than naive quantization

By understanding these considerations, you can make informed decisions about whether and how to apply quantization techniques to your LLM deployments, balancing performance requirements against resource constraints.

In this chapter, you will learn about different quantization strategies, and by the end of this chapter, you'll be able to apply quantization methods to make your LLMs more efficient, while ensuring that any reduction in precision has minimal impact on the model's performance.

In this chapter, we'll be covering the following topics:

- Understanding the basics
- Mixed-precision quantization
- Hardware-specific considerations
- Comparing quantization strategies
- Combining quantization with other optimization techniques

Understanding the basics

Quantization refers to reducing the precision of the weights and activations of a model, typically from **32-bit floating point** (**FP32**) to lower precision formats such as **16-bit** (**FP16**) or even **8-bit integers** (**INT8**). The goal is to decrease memory usage, speed up computation, and make the model more deployable on hardware with limited computational capacity. While quantization can lead to performance degradation, carefully tuned quantization schemes usually result in only minor losses in accuracy, especially for LLMs with robust architectures.

There are two primary quantization methods: **dynamic quantization** and **static quantization**.

- **Dynamic quantization**: Calculates quantization parameters on the fly during inference based on the actual input values. This adapts better to varying data distributions but introduces some computational overhead compared to static approaches.

In the following example, we use `torch.quantization.quantize_dynamic` to dynamically quantize the linear layers of a pre-trained LLM:

```python
import torch
from torch.quantization import quantize_dynamic

# Assume 'model' is a pre-trained LLM (e.g., transformer-based
model)
model = ...

# Apply dynamic quantization on linear layers for INT8 precision
quantized_model = quantize_dynamic(
    model, {torch.nn.Linear}, dtype=torch.qint8
)

# Check size reduction
print(f"Original model size: {torch.cuda.memory_allocated()}
bytes")
print(f"Quantized model size: {torch.cuda.memory_allocated()}
bytes")
```

This immediately reduces memory requirements and increases inference speed.

- **Static quantization**: Converts weights to lower precision using pre-computed scaling factors determined during a calibration phase with representative data. Once quantized, these parameters remain fixed during inference, providing consistent performance and maximum speedup.

In the following example, we statically quantize a simple model using `torch.quantization.prepare` and `torch.quantization.convert`:

```python
import torch
import torch.nn as nn
import torch.quantization

# Define a simple model
class SimpleModel(nn.Module):
    def __init__(self):
        super().__init__()
        self.fc = nn.Linear(784, 256)
        self.relu = nn.ReLU()
        self.out = nn.Linear(256, 10)

    def forward(self, x):
        x = self.relu(self.fc(x))
        return self.out(x)
```

```
# Create and prepare model for static quantization
model_fp32 = SimpleModel()
model_fp32.eval()
model_fp32.qconfig = torch.quantization.get_default_qconfig(
    'fbgemm')
prepared_model = torch.quantization.prepare(model_fp32)

# Calibration step: run representative data through the model
# (This example uses random data; replace with real samples)
for _ in range(100):
    sample_input = torch.randn(1, 784)
    prepared_model(sample_input)

# Convert to quantized version
quantized_model = torch.quantization.convert(prepared_model)

# Model is now statically quantized and ready for inference
print(quantized_model
```

This statically quantized model uses fixed scale and zero-point parameters for each quantized tensor, allowing hardware accelerators to achieve higher inference efficiency.

In contrast to dynamic quantization, static quantization requires a calibration phase with representative data before inference. During this phase, the model is run in evaluation mode to collect activation statistics, which are then used to compute quantization parameters. The weights and activations are then quantized ahead of time and remain fixed during inference, allowing for faster execution and more predictable performance.

There are also two main quantization approaches based on when quantization is applied:

- **Post-training quantization (PTQ)**: Applies quantization after the model has been fully trained, with minimal or no additional training. Can be implemented as either static (with calibration) or dynamic.

- **Quantization-aware training (QAT)**: Simulates quantization effects during training by adding fake quantization operations in the forward pass while keeping gradients in full precision. Typically results in static quantization for deployment.

PTQ

PTQ is the most straightforward form of quantization and is applied after a model has been fully trained. It doesn't require model retraining and works by converting the high-precision weights and activations into lower-precision formats, typically INT8. PTQ is ideal for models where retraining is expensive or impractical, and it works best for tasks that are not overly sensitive to precision loss.

Keep in mind that some PTQ methods often require a calibration step on a representative dataset to determine optimal quantization parameters such as scaling factors and zero points, capture activation distributions during inference, and minimize the error between original and quantized model outputs. This calibration process helps the quantization algorithm understand the numerical range and distribution of weights and activations across the network, allowing more accurate mapping from higher precision formats (such as FP32) to lower precision formats (such as INT8 or INT4), ultimately preserving model accuracy while reducing memory footprint and computational requirements for deployment.

This example demonstrates static PTQ:

```
import torch
import torch.quantization as quant

# Load pre-trained model
model = ...

# Convert model to quantization-ready state
model.eval()
model.qconfig = torch.quantization.default_qconfig

# Prepare for static quantization
model_prepared = quant.prepare(model)

# Apply quantization
model_quantized = quant.convert(model_prepared)
```

The model is first put in evaluation mode using `.eval()`, then prepared for quantization using the `.prepare()` method, and finally converted into a quantized model. This method provides an efficient means of deploying LLMs on low-power devices with minimal overhead.

QAT

QAT goes beyond simple PTQ by incorporating the effects of quantization into the training process itself. This allows the model to learn how to compensate for the quantization-induced noise, often resulting in better performance than PTQ, particularly for more complex tasks.

During QAT, both weights and activations are simulated at lower precision during training but are kept at higher precision for gradient calculations. This method is particularly useful when the application requires high performance with aggressive quantization.

In the following example, we configure the model for QAT using `get_default_qat_qconfig()`, which simulates the quantized behavior during the training phase:

```
import torch.quantization as quant

# Set up QAT
model.train()
model.qconfig = torch.quantization.get_default_qat_qconfig('fbgemm')

# Prepare for QAT
model_prepared = quant.prepare_qat(model)

# Training loop (for simplicity, only showing initialization)
for epoch in range(num_epochs):
    train_one_epoch(model_prepared, train_loader, optimizer)
    validate(model_prepared, val_loader)

# Convert to quantized version
model_quantized = quant.convert(model_prepared.eval())
```

Once the model has been trained, it is converted to a quantized version suitable for deployment. QAT typically results in better model accuracy compared to PTQ, particularly for more complex or critical applications.

Mixed-precision quantization

Mixed-precision quantization is a more flexible approach that leverages multiple levels of numerical precision within a single model. For instance, less critical layers of the model can use INT8, while more sensitive layers remain in FP16 or FP32. This allows greater control over the trade-off between performance and precision. Using mixed-precision quantization can significantly reduce model size and inference time while keeping critical aspects of the LLM intact.

The following code demonstrates an example of quantization to optimize memory usage and speed in LLM training or inference:

```
from torch.cuda.amp import autocast

# Mixed precision in LLM training or inference
model = ...

# Use FP16 where possible, fall back to FP32 for sensitive
computations
with autocast():
    output = model(input_data)
```

In this example, we use the `autocast()` function from PyTorch's **Automatic Mixed Precision (AMP)** library to enable FP16 computation in parts of the model where precision is less critical, while FP32 is retained for more sensitive layers. This method helps reduce memory usage and inference time without severely affecting performance.

Hardware-specific considerations

Different hardware platforms—such as GPUs, CPUs, or specialized accelerators such as TPUs—can have vastly different capabilities and performance characteristics when it comes to handling quantized models. For instance, some hardware may natively support INT8 operations, while others are optimized for FP16.

Understanding the target deployment hardware is crucial for selecting the right quantization technique. For example, NVIDIA GPUs are well-suited to FP16 computations due to their support for mixed-precision training and inference, while CPUs often perform better with INT8 quantization because of hardware-accelerated integer operations.

When deploying LLMs in production, it is important to experiment with quantization strategies tailored to your specific hardware and ensure that your model leverages the strengths of the platform.

Comparing quantization strategies

When comparing different quantization strategies, each approach offers distinct advantages and challenges, which can be measured through factors such as implementation complexity, accuracy preservation, performance impact, and resource requirements.

In terms of implementation complexity, PTQ is the simplest to execute, requiring minimal additional work beyond the training of the original model. Dynamic quantization is more complex, as it involves more runtime considerations due to the dynamic handling of activations. Mixed-precision quantization introduces more complexity since it requires a granular, layer-by-layer assessment of precision sensitivity and potentially custom kernel development for optimized execution. QAT ranks as the most complex, requiring the integration of fake quantization nodes into the training graph and extended training times to account for the noise introduced by quantization.

When it comes to accuracy preservation, QAT performs the best, maintaining accuracy within a small margin of floating-point performance, especially when targeting aggressive quantization (sub-8-bit). Mixed-precision quantization also ranks high in accuracy retention since it allows critical layers to remain in higher precision, balancing performance and accuracy well. PTQ generally maintains accuracy within acceptable limits, though more complex architectures may suffer higher losses in precision. Dynamic quantization typically retains better accuracy than PTQ in RNN-based models, but struggles in CNN architectures, particularly when activations are sensitive to input distribution changes.

In terms of resource requirements, PTQ demands the fewest resources, making it ideal for fast deployment scenarios with limited computational availability. Dynamic quantization ranks slightly higher in resource consumption because it handles activation quantization at runtime, though this is offset by the reduced burden on memory and storage. Mixed-precision quantization, while requiring more resources during implementation due to sensitivity analysis, can be efficient during inference, particularly on hardware that supports multiple precisions. QAT is the most resource-intensive, as it necessitates additional training time, higher memory usage during training, and more compute resources to adapt the model to quantization.

From a performance perspective, PTQ offers considerable improvements in memory savings and computational speedup, typically reducing storage by 75% and achieving 2–4x acceleration on compatible hardware. However, QAT, while similar in compression ratio, adds overhead during training but compensates by producing models that can handle more aggressive quantization without significant performance loss. Dynamic quantization provides similar memory savings as PTQ, but its compute acceleration is generally lower due to runtime overhead. Mixed-precision quantization can offer near-floating-point performance, with speedups dependent on how efficiently the hardware can execute models with varying precision levels.

The decision framework for choosing the optimal quantization strategy hinges on specific project requirements. PTQ is appropriate when fast deployment is a priority, the model architecture is relatively simple, and slight accuracy loss is acceptable. QAT is the best choice when accuracy is paramount, retraining resources are available, and aggressive quantization is needed. Dynamic quantization fits scenarios that require runtime flexibility and the handling of varying input distributions, especially in RNN-based architectures. Mixed-precision quantization is optimal for complex models with varying precision needs, where both high accuracy and performance are required, and where the hardware can efficiently manage multiple precision formats.

Each quantization strategy serves a different purpose based on the trade-off between accuracy, complexity, performance, and resources, allowing users to tailor their approach to the specific needs of their deployment environment.

Table 13.1 compares each strategy.

Strategy	Accuracy	Complexity	Performance	Resources
PTQ	Good for simple models; declines with complexity	Low; minimal setup	75% storage reduction; 2–4x speedup	Low; minimal compute needed
QAT	Highest; best for sub-8-bit	High; requires extended training	High compression with the best accuracy	High; intensive training needs

Strategy	Accuracy	Complexity	Performance	Resources
Dynamic	Good for RNNs; weak for CNNs	Medium; runtime overhead	Good memory savings; slower compute	Medium; runtime processing
Mixed-Precision	High; flexible precision options	Medium-high; layer-specific tuning	Hardware-dependent speedup	Medium-high during setup

Table 13.1 – Comparison of quantization strategies

In practice, some scenarios may benefit from combining strategies. For example, you might initially apply PTQ to achieve quick deployment, then use QAT selectively on accuracy-sensitive layers. Another approach could involve using mixed-precision for specific layers while applying dynamic quantization for activations to balance runtime flexibility and performance.

Combining quantization with other optimization techniques

Quantization can be combined with other optimization techniques, such as pruning and knowledge distillation, to create highly efficient models that are suitable for deployment on resource-constrained devices. By leveraging multiple methods, you can significantly reduce model size while maintaining or minimally impacting performance. This is especially useful when deploying LLMs on edge devices or mobile platforms where computational and memory resources are limited.

Pruning and quantization

One of the most effective combinations is **pruning** followed by quantization. First, pruning removes redundant weights from the model, reducing the number of parameters. Quantization then reduces the precision of the remaining weights, which further decreases the model size and improves inference speed. Here's an example:

```
import torch
import torch.nn.utils.prune as prune
import torch.quantization as quant

# Step 1: Prune the model
model = ...  # Pre-trained LLM model
for name, module in model.named_modules():
    if isinstance(module, torch.nn.Linear):
        prune.l1_unstructured(module, name='weight', amount=0.5)
        # Prune 50% of the weights
        prune.remove(module, 'weight')
```

```
# Step 2: Apply dynamic quantization to the pruned model
quantized_model = quant.quantize_dynamic(
    model, {torch.nn.Linear}, dtype=torch.qint8  # Convert to INT8
precision
)

# Check size reduction
print("Original model size:", torch.cuda.memory_allocated())
print("Quantized model size:", torch.cuda.memory_allocated())
```

In this example, pruning is applied to remove 50% of the weights in all linear layers, and dynamic quantization reduces the precision of the remaining weights to INT8 for further size reduction.

The result is a compact, highly optimized model that consumes fewer computational resources, making it suitable for deployment on devices with limited hardware capabilities.

Knowledge distillation and quantization

Another powerful combination is knowledge distillation followed by quantization. In this scenario, a smaller student model is trained to replicate the behavior of a larger teacher model. Once the student model is trained, quantization is applied to further optimize the student model for deployment. This combination is particularly useful when you need to maintain high performance with minimal computational overhead.

Let's look at an example step by step:

1. Define teacher and student models:

    ```
    import torch
    import torch.nn.functional as F
    teacher_model = ...  # Larger, fully trained model
    student_model = ...  # Smaller model to be trained through
    distillation
    ```

2. Define a knowledge distillation loss function:

    ```
    def distillation_loss(
        student_outputs, teacher_outputs, temperature=2.0
    ):
        teacher_probs = F.softmax(
            teacher_outputs / temperature, dim=1)
        student_probs = F.log_softmax(
            student_outputs / temperature, dim=1)
        return F.kl_div(student_probs, teacher_probs,
            reduction='batchmean')
    ```

3. Add a training loop for knowledge distillation:

```
optimizer = torch.optim.Adam(student_model.parameters(),
    lr=1e-4)

for batch in train_loader:
    inputs, _ = batch
    optimizer.zero_grad()
```

4. Forward pass through the teacher and student models:

```
teacher_outputs = teacher_model(inputs)
student_outputs = student_model(inputs)
```

The forward pass through both the teacher and student models generates their respective output logits for the same input data. This parallel inference step is necessary to compute the distillation loss, which quantifies how closely the student replicates the teacher's behavior. By comparing these outputs, the training process can guide the student to internalize the teacher's knowledge without requiring the original labels.

5. Compute the distillation loss:

```
loss = distillation_loss(student_outputs, teacher_outputs)
loss.backward()
optimizer.step()
```

Computing the distillation loss allows the student model to learn from the teacher by minimizing the discrepancy between their output distributions. This guides the student to approximate the behavior of the larger, more accurate teacher model while maintaining its own compact structure. By backpropagating this loss and updating the model parameters through optimization, the student progressively aligns its predictions with the teacher, leading to improved performance with reduced model complexity.

6. Quantize the distilled student model:

```
quantized_student_model = quant.quantize_dynamic(
    student_model, {torch.nn.Linear}, dtype=torch.qint8
)
```

7. Check size and efficiency improvements:

```
print("Quantized student model size:",
    torch.cuda.memory_allocated())
```

Knowledge distillation is used to train a smaller student model that mimics the behavior of the larger teacher model, and quantization is applied to the student model, reducing the precision of its weights to further optimize it for deployment.

This method helps maintain performance while drastically reducing the model's size, making it well-suited for low-power or real-time applications.

By combining quantization with pruning and knowledge distillation, you can achieve highly optimized models that balance size, efficiency, and performance. These models are especially useful for deployment on edge devices or environments with stringent resource constraints.

Summary

In this chapter, we explored different quantization techniques for optimizing LLMs, including PTQ, QAT, and mixed-precision quantization. We also covered hardware-specific considerations and methods for evaluating quantized models. By combining quantization with other optimization methods, such as pruning or knowledge distillation, LLMs can be made both efficient and powerful for real-world applications.

In the next chapter, we will delve into the process of evaluating LLMs, focusing on metrics for text generation, language understanding, and dialogue systems. Understanding these evaluation methods is key to ensuring your optimized models perform as expected across diverse tasks.

Part 3:
Evaluation and Interpretation
of Large Language Models

In this part, we focus on methods for evaluating and interpreting LLMs to ensure that they meet performance expectations and align with the intended use cases. You will learn how to use evaluation metrics tailored to various NLP tasks and apply cross-validation techniques to reliably assess your models. We explore interpretability methods that allow you to understand the inner workings of LLMs, as well as techniques for identifying and addressing biases in their outputs. Adversarial robustness is another key area covered, helping you defend models against attacks. Additionally, we introduce Reinforcement Learning from Human Feedback (RLHF) as a powerful method for aligning LLMs with user preferences. By mastering these evaluation and interpretation techniques, you will be able to fine-tune your models to achieve transparency, fairness, and reliability.

This part has the following chapters:

- *Chapter 14, Evaluation Metrics*

- *Chapter 15, Cross-Validation*

- *Chapter 16, Interpretability*

- *Chapter 17, Fairness and Bias Detection*

- *Chapter 18, Adversarial Robustness*

- *Chapter 19, Reinforcement Learning from Human Feedback*

14

Evaluation Metrics

In this chapter, we will explore the most recent and commonly used benchmarks for evaluating LLMs across various domains. We'll delve into metrics for **natural language understanding** (NLU), reasoning and problem solving, coding and programming, conversational ability, and commonsense reasoning.

You'll learn how to apply these benchmarks to assess your LLM's performance comprehensively. By the end of this chapter, you'll be equipped to design robust evaluation strategies for your LLM projects, compare models effectively, and make data-driven decisions to improve your models based on state-of-the-art evaluation techniques.

In this chapter we'll be covering the following topics:

- NLU benchmarks
- Reasoning and problem-solving metrics
- Coding and programming evaluation
- Conversational ability assessment
- Commonsense and general knowledge benchmarks
- Other commonly used benchmarks
- Developing custom metrics and benchmarks
- Interpreting and comparing LLM evaluation results

NLU benchmarks

NLU is a crucial capability of LLMs. Let's explore some of the most recent and widely used benchmarks in this domain.

Massive multitask language understanding

Massive multitask language understanding (MMLU) is a comprehensive benchmark that tests models across 57 subjects, including science, mathematics, engineering, and more. It's designed to assess both breadth and depth of knowledge.

Here's an example of how you might evaluate an LLM on MMLU using the `lm-evaluation-harness` library:

```
from lm_eval import tasks, evaluator

def evaluate_mmlu(model):
    task_list = tasks.get_task_dict(["mmlu"])
    results = evaluator.simple_evaluate(
        model=model,
        task_list=task_list,
        num_fewshot=5,
        batch_size=1
    )
    return results

# Assuming you have a pre-trained model
model = load_your_model()  # Replace with actual model loading
mmlu_results = evaluate_mmlu(model)
print(f"MMLU Score: {mmlu_results['mmlu']['acc']}")
```

This code evaluates the model on MMLU tasks with five-shot learning (learning by using 5 examples). The score represents the average accuracy across all subjects.

SuperGLUE

SuperGLUE is a benchmark designed to be more challenging than its predecessor, **GLUE**. It includes tasks that require more complex reasoning.

GLUE and SuperGLUE are benchmarks designed to evaluate NLU models across a range of tasks. GLUE includes tasks such as sentiment analysis, linguistic acceptability, paraphrase detection, and semantic similarity, with datasets such as SST-2, CoLA, MRPC, and STS-B. SuperGLUE extends GLUE by adding more challenging tasks such as question answering, coreference resolution, and logical reasoning, with datasets such as **Boolean Questions** (**BoolQ**), **Reading Comprehension with Commonsense Reasoning Dataset** (**ReCoRD**), and the Winograd schema challenge. Together, they provide a comprehensive assessment of a model's ability to handle diverse and complex language tasks.

SuperGLUE significantly extends the complexity level beyond GLUE by deliberately incorporating tasks that demand sophisticated reasoning capabilities, including challenging commonsense inference problems such as **Word-in-Context** (**WiC**) and BoolQ, causal reasoning assessments in **Choice of Plausible Alternatives** (**COPA**), and more nuanced reading comprehension challenges through ReCoRD and **Multi-Sentence Reading Comprehension** (**MultiRC**)—all requiring models to demonstrate deeper linguistic understanding and logical thinking than GLUE's primarily classification-based tasks that focus on more straightforward linguistic phenomena such as grammatical acceptability, sentiment analysis, and textual entailment.

Here's how you might evaluate on SuperGLUE.

First, here are the necessary imports for working with datasets and transformer models:

```
from datasets import load_dataset
from transformers import (
    AutoModelForSequenceClassification, AutoTokenizer,
    Trainer, TrainingArguments)
```

The following code example contains the main evaluation function for SuperGLUE. It handles model initialization, dataset loading, preprocessing, and training setup:

```
def evaluate_superglue(model_name, task="cb"):
    model = AutoModelForSequenceClassification.from_pretrained(
        model_name)
    tokenizer = AutoTokenizer.from_pretrained(model_name)

    dataset = load_dataset("super_glue", task)

    def tokenize_function(examples):
        return tokenizer(
            examples["premise"], examples["hypothesis"],
            truncation=True)

    tokenized_datasets = dataset.map(tokenize_function, batched=True)

    training_args = TrainingArguments(
        output_dir="./results",
        evaluation_strategy="epoch",
        num_train_epochs=3,
    )

    trainer = Trainer(
        model=model,
        args=training_args,
        train_dataset=tokenized_datasets["train"],
```

```
        eval_dataset=tokenized_datasets["validation"],
    )

    results = trainer.evaluate()
    return results
```

This code defines an `evaluate_superglue` function that takes a pre-trained language model name and an optional SuperGLUE task name (defaulting to `"cb"`) as input. It loads the specified pre-trained model and its tokenizer, then loads the corresponding SuperGLUE dataset. It tokenizes the premise and hypothesis of the examples in the dataset, prepares training arguments for evaluation, initializes a `Trainer` object with the model, training arguments, and tokenized training and validation datasets, and finally evaluates the model on the validation set, returning the evaluation results.

In the next code block, we use the **CommitmentBank (CB)** dataset. CB is an NLU dataset and benchmark task that focuses on determining whether a speaker is committed to the truth of a hypothesis given a premise statement, essentially measuring a model's ability to understand textual entailment and speaker commitment.

For example, given a premise such as *I think it's going to rain today* and a hypothesis of *It will rain today*, the task is to determine whether the speaker is fully committed to the hypothesis (entailment), denies it (contradiction), or remains uncommitted (neither)—in this case, the use of *I think* indicates the speaker isn't fully committed to the claim. This task is particularly challenging as it requires models to understand subtle linguistic features such as reported speech, modal expressions, hedging language, and embedded clauses, making it a valuable tool for evaluating language models' grasp of semantic nuances and speaker commitment levels in natural communication.

Here's a code block showing how to run the evaluation with a specific model on the CB task:

```
model_name = "bert-base-uncased"  # Replace with your model
results = evaluate_superglue(model_name)
print(f"SuperGLUE {task} Score: {results['eval_accuracy']}")
```

TruthfulQA

TruthfulQA is designed to measure a model's tendency to reproduce falsehoods commonly believed by humans. It's crucial for assessing the reliability of LLMs in real-world applications.

Here's an example of a falsehood that TruthfulQA might test:

Claim: *Cracking your knuckles will give you arthritis.*

This claim is a common belief, but research suggests that knuckle cracking (also known as knuckle popping) is not a significant risk factor for developing arthritis. While it may have other effects, such as joint instability or weakened grip strength, the link to arthritis is not strongly supported.

Here's a simplified approach to evaluate on TruthfulQA:

```python
def evaluate_truthfulqa(model, tokenizer, data_path):
    with open(data_path, 'r') as f:
        data = json.load(f)

    correct = 0
    total = 0

    for item in data:
        question = item['question']
        correct_answers = item['correct_answers']

        input_ids = tokenizer.encode(question, return_tensors='pt')
        output = model.generate(input_ids, max_length=50)
        response = tokenizer.decode(output[0],
            skip_special_tokens=True)

        if any(
            answer.lower() in response.lower()
            for answer in correct_answers
        ):
            correct += 1
        total += 1

    accuracy = correct / total
    return accuracy
```

The `evaluate_truthfulqa` Python function takes a pre-trained language `model`, its corresponding `tokenizer`, and the `data_path` to a JSON file containing TruthfulQA questions and their correct answers. It reads the data, iterates through each question, tokenizes the question, generates a response from the model, decodes the response, and checks if any of the correct answers (case-insensitive) are present in the generated response. Finally, it calculates and returns the accuracy of the model on the provided TruthfulQA dataset.

To run the evaluation code, use the following:

```python
model_name = "gpt2"  # Replace with your model
model = AutoModelForCausalLM.from_pretrained(model_name)
tokenizer = AutoTokenizer.from_pretrained(model_name)

accuracy = evaluate_truthfulqa(model, tokenizer,
    "path/to/truthfulqa_data.json")
print(f"TruthfulQA Accuracy: {accuracy}")
```

This code assumes you have the TruthfulQA dataset in a JSON format. It generates responses to questions and checks whether they contain any of the correct answers.

Now, we will shift our focus to reasoning and problem-solving metrics to examine how effectively LLMs can perform tasks requiring logical thought and problem-solving skills.

Reasoning and problem-solving metrics

Evaluating an LLM's ability to reason and solve problems is crucial for many applications. Let's look at some key benchmarks in this area.

AI2 Reasoning Challenge

AI2 Reasoning Challenge (ARC) is designed to test grade-school-level science questions that require reasoning. See also: `https://huggingface.co/datasets/allenai/ai2_arc`

Here is an example of an ARC question:

> One year, the oak trees in a park began producing more acorns than usual. The next year, the population of chipmunks in the park also increased. Which best explains why there were more chipmunks the next year?
>
> A.   Shady areas increased
>
> B.   Food sources increased
>
> C.   Oxygen levels increased
>
> D.   Available water increased

Correct answer: *B. Food sources increased*

This question requires the student to reason about the relationship between the increase in acorns (a food source for chipmunks) and the subsequent rise in the chipmunk population, rather than simply recalling a fact.

ARC serves as a strong benchmark to distinguish models that rely on pattern recognition from those capable of true reasoning, making it valuable for assessing AI robustness, comparing performance against humans, and developing more capable reasoning-based AI models.

Here's how you might evaluate on ARC:

```
def evaluate_arc(model_name):
    model = AutoModelForMultipleChoice.from_pretrained(model_name)
    tokenizer = AutoTokenizer.from_pretrained(model_name)

    dataset = load_dataset("ai2_arc", "ARC-Challenge")
```

```python
def preprocess_function(examples):
    first_sentences = [
        [[context] * 4 for context in examples["question"]
    ]
    second_sentences = [
        [examples["choices"]["text"][i][j] for j in range(4)]
        for i in range(len(examples["question"]))
    ]

    tokenized_examples = tokenizer(
        first_sentences, second_sentences,
        truncation=True, padding=True
    )
    tokenized_examples["label"] = [
        examples["choices"]["label"].index(
            examples["answerKey"][i]
        ) for i in range(len(examples["question"]))
    ]
    return tokenized_examples

tokenized_datasets = dataset.map(
    preprocess_function, batched=True,
    remove_columns=dataset["train"].column_names
)

training_args = TrainingArguments(
    output_dir="./results",
    evaluation_strategy="epoch",
    num_train_epochs=3,
)

trainer = Trainer(
    model=model,
    args=training_args,
    train_dataset=tokenized_datasets["train"],
    eval_dataset=tokenized_datasets["test"],
)

results = trainer.evaluate()
return results
```

This code provides a standardized way to assess the multiple-choice reasoning capabilities of a given pre-trained language model on a challenging science question-answering benchmark. By tokenizing each question-choice pair separately and training/evaluating with a multiple-choice head, the process directly measures the model's ability to select the correct answer from a set of plausible alternatives, offering insights into its understanding and reasoning over scientific concepts.

To run the evaluation code, use the following:

```
model_name = "bert-base-uncased"  # Replace with your model
results = evaluate_arc(model_name)
print(f"ARC-Challenge Score: {results['eval_accuracy']}")
```

This code evaluates a model on the **ARC-Challenge** dataset, which contains the more difficult questions from ARC.

Grade School Math 8K

Grade School Math 8K (GSM8K) is a dataset of 8.5K grade school math word problems (https://github.com/openai/grade-school-math). It's designed to test an LLM's ability to solve multi-step math problems. Here's a simplified evaluation approach:

```
def extract_answer(text):
    match = re.search(r'(\d+)(?=\s*$)', text)
    return int(match.group(1)) if match else None


def evaluate_gsm8k(model, tokenizer, dataset):
    correct = 0
    total = 0

    for item in dataset:
        question = item['question']
        true_answer = item['answer']

        input_ids = tokenizer.encode(question, return_tensors='pt')
        output = model.generate(input_ids, max_length=200)
        response = tokenizer.decode(output[0],
            skip_special_tokens=True)

        predicted_answer = extract_answer(response)
        if predicted_answer == true_answer:
            correct += 1
        total += 1

    accuracy = correct / total
    return accuracy
```

This Python code defines two functions:

- `extract_answer`: This function uses a regular expression to find and extract the last numerical value from a given text string. If a number is found at the end of the string, it is returned as an integer. If no such number is found, the function returns `None`.

- `evaluate_gsm8k`: This function takes a language model, its tokenizer, and a dataset of math word problems. It iterates through each problem, encodes the question, generates a response from the model, decodes the response, extracts the predicted numerical answer using `extract_answer`, and compares it to the true answer to calculate the accuracy of the model on the provided GSM8k dataset.

This evaluation approach specifically targets the model's ability to solve math word problems and, importantly, to produce the final numerical answer in a format that can be easily extracted. The `extract_answer` function highlights an assumption that the correct answer will be the last number mentioned in the model's response. While this may not always hold true, it serves as a practical heuristic for this dataset. The overall process measures the model's combined capabilities in understanding the problem, performing the necessary calculations, and presenting the result in an expected format.

To run the evaluation code, use the following:

```
model_name = "gpt2"  # Replace with your model
model = AutoModelForCausalLM.from_pretrained(model_name)
tokenizer = AutoTokenizer.from_pretrained(model_name)

# Assume you've loaded the GSM8K dataset
gsm8k_dataset = load_gsm8k_dataset()  # Replace with actual dataset
loading
accuracy = evaluate_gsm8k(model, tokenizer, gsm8k_dataset)
print(f"GSM8K Accuracy: {accuracy}")
```

This code generates responses to GSM8K problems and extracts the final numerical answer for comparison with the ground truth.

Next, we'll explore coding and programming evaluation to see how we can measure the code generation and code execution abilities of an LLM; this is becoming increasingly vital in software development.

Coding and programming evaluation

Evaluating an LLM's coding abilities is becoming increasingly important. Let's look at how we can use HumanEval to evaluate this:

HumanEval is a benchmark for evaluating code generation capabilities. It includes a set of programming problems with unit tests.

Here's a simplified approach to evaluate on HumanEval:

1. The following code snippet sets up the core execution functionality. It defines a `run_code` function that takes generated code and a test case, combines them, and executes them in a safe subprocess with a timeout. It handles execution errors and timeouts gracefully, making it robust for evaluating potentially problematic code:

```python
import json
import subprocess

def run_code(code, test_case):
    full_code = f"{code}\n\nprint({test_case})"
    try:
        result = subprocess.run(
            ['python', '-c', full_code],
            capture_output=True, text=True, timeout=5
        )
        return result.stdout.strip()
    except subprocess.TimeoutExpired:
        return "Timeout"
    except Exception as e:
        return str(e)
```

2. The following code example contains the main evaluation function that implements the HumanEval benchmark. It loads coding problems from a JSON file, uses a model to generate solutions for each problem, runs the solutions against test cases, and calculates the overall accuracy of the model's performance:

```python
def evaluate_humaneval(model, tokenizer, data_path):
    with open(data_path, 'r') as f:
        problems = json.load(f)

    correct = 0
    total = 0

    for problem in problems:
        prompt = problem['prompt']
        test_cases = problem['test_cases']

        input_ids = tokenizer.encode(prompt,
            return_tensors='pt')
        output = model.generate(input_ids, max_length=500)
        generated_code = tokenizer.decode(output[0],
            skip_special_tokens=True)
```

```
        all_tests_passed = True
        for test_case, expected_output in test_cases:
            result = run_code(generated_code, test_case)
            if result != expected_output:
                all_tests_passed = False
                break

        if all_tests_passed:
            correct += 1
        total += 1

    accuracy = correct / total
    return accuracy
```

3. Here's a code snippet showing the usage of the evaluation framework. It's a template for loading a specific code generation model and its tokenizer, then running the HumanEval evaluation on that model and printing the results. This section would need to be customized with actual model loading code depending on the specific model being used:

```
model_name = "codex"  # Replace with your code-generation model
model = load_your_model(model_name)  # Replace with actual model
loading
tokenizer = load_your_tokenizer(model_name)  # Replace with
actual tokenizer loading
accuracy = evaluate_humaneval(
    model, tokenizer, "path/to/humaneval_data.json")
print(f"HumanEval Accuracy: {accuracy}")
```

We now turn to evaluating the conversational abilities of LLMs (LLMs), focusing on their performance in interactive dialogue—a critical capability for applications such as chatbots.

Conversational ability assessment

Evaluating the conversational abilities of LLMs is crucial for chatbot and dialogue system applications. Let's look at a key benchmark in this area: MT-Bench.

MT-Bench is a benchmark for evaluating multi-turn conversations. It assesses the model's ability to maintain context and provide coherent responses over multiple turns.

MT-Bench evaluations often combine automated scoring with human assessments to ensure a more comprehensive evaluation of AI models, particularly for tasks requiring nuanced reasoning, coherence, and contextual understanding. While automated metrics provide consistency and scalability, human evaluations help capture qualitative aspects such as reasoning depth, relevance, and fluency, which may not be fully captured by automated methods alone.

Here's a simplified approach to evaluate on MT-Bench:

```python
import json

def evaluate_mt_bench(model, tokenizer, data_path):
    with open(data_path, 'r') as f:
        conversations = json.load(f)

    scores = []

    for conversation in conversations:
        context = ""
        for turn in conversation['turns']:
            human_msg = turn['human']
            context += f"Human: {human_msg}\n"

            input_ids = tokenizer.encode(context, return_tensors='pt')
            output = model.generate(input_ids, max_length=200)
            response = tokenizer.decode(output[0],
                skip_special_tokens=True)

            context += f"AI: {response}\n"

            # Simplified scoring: check if keywords are present
            score = sum(keyword in response.lower()
                for keyword in turn['keywords'])
            scores.append(score / len(turn['keywords']))

    average_score = sum(scores) / len(scores)
    return average_score
```

This function provides a basic framework for evaluating a conversational model based on its ability to incorporate context and generate relevant responses as judged by the presence of specific keywords. The simplified scoring method offers a coarse-grained assessment of the model's output. A more sophisticated evaluation of MT-Bench typically involves human evaluation or more nuanced automated metrics that consider factors such as coherence, helpfulness, and correctness, which this simplified keyword-based approach does not capture. Therefore, the returned average score should be interpreted as a very preliminary indicator of performance based solely on the presence of specified keywords.

The following code snippet shows how to use the evaluation framework with a specific model. It demonstrates loading the model and tokenizer, and then running the evaluation:

```
model_name = "gpt2"  # Replace with your model
model = AutoModelForCausalLM.from_pretrained(model_name)
tokenizer = AutoTokenizer.from_pretrained(model_name)
score = evaluate_mt_bench(model, tokenizer,
    "path/to/mt_bench_data.json")
print(f"MT-Bench Score: {score}")
```

This code simulates multi-turn conversations and scores responses based on the presence of expected keywords. In practice, MT-Bench often involves human evaluation or more sophisticated automated metrics.

To evaluate LLMs in real-world applications, we must also assess their commonsense and general knowledge benchmarks. Let's look at how to do so.

Commonsense and general knowledge benchmarks

Assessing an LLM's commonsense reasoning and general knowledge is crucial for many real-world applications. Let's look at a key benchmark in this area: WinoGrande.

WinoGrande is a large-scale dataset of schemas, designed to test commonsense reasoning about complex situations described in natural language.

Here's how you might evaluate on WinoGrande:

```
def evaluate_winogrande(model_name):
 model = AutoModelForMultipleChoice.from_pretrained(model_name)
 tokenizer = AutoTokenizer.from_pretrained(model_name)

 dataset = load_dataset("winogrande", "winogrande_xl")

 def preprocess_function(examples):
     first_sentences = [[context] * 2
             for context in examples["sentence"]]
     second_sentences = [
         [
             examples["option1"][i], examples["option2"][i]
         ] for i in range(len(examples["sentence"]))
     ]

     tokenized_examples = tokenizer(
         first_sentences, second_sentences, truncation=True,
         padding=True
```

```
    )
    tokenized_examples["label"] = [int(label) - 1
        for label in examples["answer"]]
    return tokenized_examples

tokenized_datasets = dataset.map(
    preprocess_function, batched=True,
    remove_columns=dataset["train"].column_names
)

training_args = TrainingArguments(
    output_dir="./results",
    evaluation_strategy="epoch",
    num_train_epochs=3,
)

trainer = Trainer(
    model=model,
    args=training_args,
    train_dataset=tokenized_datasets["train"],
    eval_dataset=tokenized_datasets["validation"],
)

results = trainer.evaluate()
return results
```

This function specifically assesses a language model's ability to perform pronoun resolution, a crucial aspect of natural language understanding that requires contextual reasoning. By presenting pairs of sentences differing only in the pronoun and its antecedent, the Winogrande benchmark challenges models to identify the correct referent. Evaluating on this task provides insight into a model's capacity to understand subtle semantic relationships and handle ambiguities in text, which is essential for more complex language processing tasks.

Here's a code example showing how to run the evaluation with a specific model:

```
model_name = "bert-base-uncased"  # Replace with your model
results = evaluate_winogrande(model_name)
print(f"WinoGrande Score: {results['eval_accuracy']}")
```

This code evaluates a model on the WinoGrande dataset, testing its ability to resolve ambiguities in sentences that require commonsense reasoning.

Other commonly used benchmarks

Other commonly used benchmarks provide diverse ways to evaluate the performance and capabilities of language models in various domains and task complexities:

- **Instruction Following Evaluation (IFEval):** This benchmark assesses a model's ability to follow natural language instructions across diverse tasks. It evaluates both task completion and instruction adherence.

- **Big Bench Hard (BBH):** BBH is a subset of the larger BIG-Bench benchmark, focusing on particularly challenging tasks that even LLMs struggle with. It covers areas such as logical reasoning, common sense, and abstract thinking.

- **Massive Multitask Language Understanding – Professional (MMLU-PRO):** This is an expanded version of the original MMLU benchmark, with a focus on professional and specialized knowledge domains. It tests models on subjects such as law, medicine, engineering, and other expert fields.

Here's a comparison of IFEval, BBH, and MMLU-PRO:

- IFEval focuses on evaluating a model's ability to follow natural language instructions across various tasks, emphasizing task completion and instruction adherence rather than domain-specific knowledge or reasoning complexity

- BBH is a subset of BIG-Bench that targets especially difficult reasoning tasks, making it a strong test for logical reasoning, abstract thinking, and common sense—areas where LLMs typically struggle

- MMLU-PRO extends MMLU to professional and specialized fields, assessing a model's expertise in law, medicine, engineering, and other technical domains, making it ideal for evaluating domain-specific proficiency rather than general reasoning or instruction-following

Each benchmark serves a distinct purpose: IFEval for instruction-following, BBH for reasoning under difficulty, and MMLU-PRO for professional knowledge assessment.

Developing custom metrics and benchmarks

Custom metrics are essential because commonly used benchmarks such as MMLU, HumanEval, and SuperGLUE often provide a general evaluation framework but may not align with the specific requirements of a particular application. Custom metrics provide a more tailored and meaningful evaluation, allowing developers to align models with their specific performance goals.

When creating custom metrics or benchmarks, consider the following best practices:

- **Define clear objectives**: Determine exactly what aspects of model performance you want to measure. This could be task-specific accuracy, reasoning ability, or adherence to certain constraints.

- **Ensure dataset quality**: Curate a high-quality, diverse dataset that represents the full spectrum of challenges in your domain of interest. Consider factors such as the following:

  - Balanced representation of different categories or difficulty levels

  - Removal of biased or problematic examples

  - Inclusion of edge cases and rare scenarios

- **Design robust evaluation criteria**: Develop clear, quantifiable metrics for assessing performance. This might involve the following:

  - Creating rubrics for human evaluation

  - Defining automated scoring mechanisms

  - Establishing baselines for comparison

- **Consider multiple dimensions**: Don't rely on a single metric. Evaluate models across various dimensions such as the following:

  - Accuracy

  - Consistency

  - Safety and bias mitigation

  - Efficiency (e.g., inference time and resource usage)

- **Implement rigorous testing protocols**: Establish standardized procedures for running benchmarks, including the following:

  - Consistent model configurations and prompts

  - Multiple runs to account for variability

  - Statistical analysis of results

- **Iterate and refine**: Continuously improve your benchmark based on feedback and emerging challenges in the field. This might involve the following:

  - Adding new test cases

  - Adjusting scoring methods

  - Incorporating insights from the research community

Interpreting and comparing LLM evaluation results

When interpreting and comparing results across these diverse benchmarks, it's important to consider the strengths and limitations of each metric. It is also important to consider differences in model size, training data, and fine-tuning approaches. Here's an example of how you might visualize and compare results across multiple benchmarks:

```python
def compare_models(model1_scores, model2_scores, benchmarks):
    df = pd.DataFrame({
        'Model1': model1_scores,
        'Model2': model2_scores
    }, index=benchmarks)

    ax = df.plot(kind='bar', figsize=(12, 6), width=0.8)
    plt.title('Model Comparison Across Benchmarks')
    plt.xlabel('Benchmarks')
    plt.ylabel('Scores')
    plt.legend(['Model1', 'Model2'])
    plt.xticks(rotation=45, ha='right')

    for container in ax.containers:
        ax.bar_label(container, fmt='%.2f')

    plt.tight_layout()
    plt.show()

# Example scores (replace with actual results)
model1_scores = [0.75, 0.82, 0.68, 0.70, 0.77, 0.65, 0.80]
model2_scores = [0.80, 0.79, 0.72, 0.75, 0.81, 0.68, 0.78]
benchmarks = ['MMLU', 'SuperGLUE', 'TruthfulQA', 'ARC', 'GSM8K',
    'HumanEval', 'WinoGrande']

compare_models(model1_scores, model2_scores, benchmarks)
```

This code creates a bar chart comparing two models across different benchmarks, providing a visual aid for interpreting results.

When interpreting these results, consider the following:

- **Task specificity**: Some benchmarks (e.g., GSM8K for math and HumanEval for coding) test specific capabilities. A model might excel in one area but underperform in others.

- **Generalization**: Look for consistent performance across diverse tasks. This indicates good generalization abilities.

- **Improvement margins**: Consider where the largest improvements can be made. This can guide future fine-tuning or training efforts.

- **Real-world relevance**: Prioritize benchmarks that align closely with your intended use case.

- **Limitations**: Be aware of each benchmark's limitations. For example, automated metrics might not capture nuanced aspects of language understanding or generation.

Here's an example of how you might summarize and interpret these results:

```python
def interpret_results(model1_scores, model2_scores, benchmarks):
    for benchmark, score1, score2 in zip(
        benchmarks, model1_scores, model2_scores
    ):
        print(f"\n{benchmark}:")
        print(f"Model1: {score1:.2f}, Model2: {score2:.2f}")

        if score1 > score2:
            print(f"Model1 outperforms Model2 by {(score1 - score2) *
100:.2f}%")
        elif score2 > score1:
            print(f"Model2 outperforms Model1 by {(score2 - score1) *
100:.2f}%")
        else:
            print("Both models perform equally")

        if benchmark == 'MMLU':
            print("This indicates overall language understanding
across diverse subjects.")
        elif benchmark == 'GSM8K':
            print("This reflects mathematical reasoning
capabilities.")
        # Add similar interpretations for other benchmarks

interpret_results(model1_scores, model2_scores, benchmarks)
```

This function provides a textual interpretation of the results, highlighting performance differences and their implications.

Summary

Evaluating LLMs requires a variety of benchmarks. By understanding and effectively using these evaluation techniques, you can make informed decisions about model performance and guide further improvements in your LLM projects.

As we move forward, the next chapter will delve into cross-validation techniques specifically tailored for LLMs. We'll explore methods for creating appropriate data splits for pre-training and fine-tuning, as well as strategies for few-shot and zero-shot evaluation. This will build upon the evaluation metrics we've discussed here, providing a more comprehensive framework for assessing LLM performance and generalization capabilities across different domains and tasks.

Subscribe for a free eBook

New frameworks, evolving architectures, research drops, production breakdowns—AI_Distilled filters the noise into a weekly briefing for engineers and researchers working hands-on with LLMs and GenAI systems. Subscribe now and receive a free eBook, along with weekly insights that help you stay focused and informed. Subscribe at `https://packt.link/8Oz6Y` or scan the QR code below.

15
Cross-Validation

Cross-validation is a statistical technique used to assess how well a machine learning model generalizes to unseen data. It involves partitioning a dataset into multiple subsets or "folds," training the model on some of these subsets while testing it on the remaining ones. This process is repeated to ensure a reliable performance estimate. This helps detect overfitting and provides a more robust evaluation than a single train-test split. In the context of LLMs, cross-validation must be adapted to address the complexities of pre-training, fine-tuning, few-shot learning, and domain generalization, making it an essential tool for evaluating model performance across varied tasks and data distributions.

In this chapter, you will explore cross-validation strategies specifically designed for LLMs. We'll delve into methods for creating appropriate data splits for pre-training and fine-tuning, as well as strategies for few-shot and zero-shot evaluation. You'll learn how to assess domain and task generalization in LLMs and handle the unique challenges of cross-validation in the context of LLMs.

By the end of this chapter, you'll be equipped with robust cross-validation techniques to reliably assess your LLM's performance and generalization capabilities across various domains and tasks.

In this chapter, we'll be covering the following topics:

- Pre-training and fine-tuning data splits
- Few-shot and zero-shot evaluation strategies
- Domain and task generalization
- Continual learning evaluation
- Cross-validation challenges and best practices

Pre-training and fine-tuning data splits

In LLMs, data splits refer to the division of datasets into training, validation, and test sets to ensure the model learns generalizable patterns rather than memorizing data. This is essential for evaluating performance fairly, tuning model parameters, and preventing data leakage. Proper splitting is especially important in LLMs due to their scale, the diversity of tasks, and the need to assess domain and task generalization.

Stratified sampling for pre-training data

Stratified sampling is a sampling method that first divides the population into smaller subgroups (**strata**) based on shared characteristics and then randomly samples from within each stratum to ensure proportional representation of all groups in the final sample. This is particularly useful when dealing with imbalanced datasets.

When creating data splits for pre-training, it's important to ensure that each split represents the diversity of the entire dataset. Here's an example of how you might implement **stratified sampling** for pre-training data:

```
import pandas as pd
from sklearn.model_selection import StratifiedShuffleSplit

def stratified_pretraining_split(
    data, text_column, label_column, test_size=0.1, random_state=42
):
    sss = StratifiedShuffleSplit(
        n_splits=1, test_size=test_size, random_state=random_state)

    for train_index, test_index in sss.split(
        data[text_column], data[label_column]
    ):
        train_data = data.iloc[train_index]
        test_data = data.iloc[test_index]

    return train_data, test_data

# Example usage
data = pd.read_csv('your_pretraining_data.csv')
train_data, test_data = stratified_pretraining_split(
    data, 'text', 'domain')

print(f"Training set size: {len(train_data)}")
print(f"Test set size: {len(test_data)}")
```

This code uses `StratifiedShuffleSplit` to create a stratified split of the pre-training data, ensuring that the distribution of domains (or any other relevant categorical variable) is similar in both the training and test sets.

Time-based splitting for fine-tuning data

For fine-tuning tasks that involve time-sensitive data, it's often beneficial to use **time-based splitting**.

Time-based splitting is a data partitioning strategy where the dataset is divided according to chronological order, ensuring that earlier data is used for training and later data for validation or testing. This approach is especially important for fine-tuning tasks involving time-sensitive data—such as financial forecasting, user behavior modeling, or event prediction—where future information should not influence past training. By preserving the natural temporal sequence, time-based splitting helps evaluate how well a model can generalize to future, unseen scenarios, closely mimicking real-world deployment.

This approach helps evaluate how well the model generalizes to future data:

```
import pandas as pd

def time_based_finetuning_split(data, timestamp_column, split_date):
    data[timestamp_column] = pd.to_datetime(data[timestamp_column])
    train_data = data[data[timestamp_column] < split_date]
    test_data = data[data[timestamp_column] >= split_date]
    return train_data, test_data

# Example usage
data = pd.read_csv('your_finetuning_data.csv')
split_date = '2023-01-01'
train_data, test_data = time_based_finetuning_split(
    data, 'timestamp', split_date)

print(f"Training set size: {len(train_data)}")
print(f"Test set size: {len(test_data)}")
```

This function splits the data based on a specified date, which is particularly useful for tasks where the model needs to generalize to future events or trends.

Oversampling and weighting techniques for data balancing

When working with datasets that have an uneven distribution of categories, such as imbalanced domains or label frequencies, **oversampling** and **weighting techniques** can help ensure that the model learns effectively from all classes. Oversampling involves replicating examples from underrepresented categories to increase their presence in the training data, preventing the model from ignoring them. This can be done using methods such as random oversampling or synthetic data generation (e.g., SMOTE for structured data). On the other hand, weighting techniques adjust the loss function by assigning higher importance to underrepresented categories, so the model learns from them without necessarily increasing the dataset size. Both approaches help mitigate bias, improving the model's ability to generalize across all categories, rather than favoring the most frequent ones.

Here's a short code example demonstrating oversampling and class weighting techniques using PyTorch and sklearn, applied to a text classification task:

```python
from sklearn.utils.class_weight import compute_class_weight
from torch.utils.data import DataLoader, WeightedRandomSampler
import torch
import numpy as np

# Example class distribution (e.g., from dataset labels)
labels = [0, 0, 0, 1, 1, 2]   # Class 2 is underrepresented

# --- 1. Class Weighting ---
# Compute weights inversely proportional to class frequencies
class_weights = compute_class_weight(
    'balanced', classes=np.unique(labels), y=labels)
class_weights = torch.tensor(class_weights, dtype=torch.float)

# Pass weights to loss function
loss_fn = torch.nn.CrossEntropyLoss(weight=class_weights)

# --- 2. Oversampling with Weighted Sampler ---
# Create sample weights: inverse of class frequency for each label
label_counts = np.bincount(labels)
sample_weights = [1.0 / label_counts[label] for label in labels]

# Create sampler for DataLoader
sampler = WeightedRandomSampler(
    weights=sample_weights, num_samples=len(labels), replacement=True
)

# Use the sampler in your DataLoader
# Assuming `train_dataset` is a PyTorch Dataset object
train_loader = DataLoader(train_dataset, sampler=sampler,
    batch_size=4)
```

The code demonstrates two common techniques for addressing class imbalance in classification tasks: class weighting and oversampling. First, it uses `compute_class_weight` of `sklearn` to calculate weights inversely proportional to class frequencies, assigning higher importance to underrepresented classes (e.g., class 2, which appears less often). These weights are passed to PyTorch's `CrossEntropyLoss`, so that during training, misclassifying rare classes penalizes the model more than misclassifying common ones. Second, it performs oversampling by computing a per-sample weight based on the inverse frequency of each sample's class, which ensures that samples from minority classes have a higher probability of being selected during training. These sample weights are used to initialize PyTorch's `WeightedRandomSampler`, which enables the `DataLoader` to sample training data in a balanced way across classes without having to physically duplicate data. Together, these techniques help the model learn to treat all classes fairly, improving its generalization on imbalanced datasets.

Few-shot and zero-shot evaluation strategies

Few-shot and zero-shot evaluation strategies enable LLMs to generalize across tasks without requiring extensive retraining. Zero-shot learning is useful for tasks where no labeled examples are available, while few-shot learning enhances performance by providing limited guidance. These methods are key to making LLMs adaptable and scalable for real-world applications.

Here is a comparison between the two strategies:

Aspect	Zero-shot	Few-shot
Description	No examples; model must infer task from prompt alone	Provides a small number of labeled examples in the prompt
Strengths	No labeled data needed, highly flexible	Higher accuracy, better task comprehension
Weaknesses	Lower accuracy, risk of ambiguity	Requires careful example selection, still less effective than fine-tuning
Use Cases	Open-ended Q&A, commonsense reasoning, general-knowledge tasks	Text classification, translation, summarization, code generation

Table 15.1 – Few-shot vs. zero-shot

Let's see how to implement each of these strategies.

Few-shot evaluation

In **few-shot evaluation**, we provide the model with a small number of examples before asking it to perform a task. Here's an example of how you might implement few-shot evaluation:

```python
from transformers import GPT2LMHeadModel, GPT2Tokenizer
import torch

def few_shot_evaluate(
    model, tokenizer, task_description, examples, test_instance
):
    prompt = f"{task_description}\n\nExamples:\n"
    for example in examples:
        prompt += (
            f"Input: {example['input']}\n"
            f"Output: {example['output']}\n\n"
        )

    prompt += f"Input: {test_instance}\nOutput:"

    input_ids = tokenizer.encode(prompt, return_tensors='pt')

    with torch.no_grad():
        output = model.generate(input_ids, max_length=100,
            num_return_sequences=1)

    generated_text = tokenizer.decode(output[0],
        skip_special_tokens=True)
    return generated_text.split("Output:")[-1].strip()

# Example usage
model = GPT2LMHeadModel.from_pretrained('gpt2-large')
tokenizer = GPT2Tokenizer.from_pretrained('gpt2-large')

task_description = "Classify the sentiment of the following movie
reviews as positive or negative."
examples = [
    {"input": "This movie was fantastic!", "output": "Positive"},
    {"input": "I hated every minute of it.", "output": "Negative"}
]
test_instance = "The acting was superb, but the plot was confusing."

result = few_shot_evaluate(
    model, tokenizer, task_description, examples, test_instance
```

```
)
print(f"Few-shot evaluation result: {result}")
```

This code demonstrates how to perform few-shot evaluation on a sentiment analysis task using a pre-trained GPT-2 model.

The `few_shot_evaluate` function takes a GPT-2 model, tokenizer, task description, examples, and a test instance as input. It constructs a **few-shot prompt** by formatting the task description and adding multiple input-output example pairs to help the model understand the task. The function then appends the test instance, leaving the output blank so the model can complete it. The prompt is tokenized using `tokenizer.encode`, converting it into numerical tokens suitable for the model. The function then uses `model.generate` inside a `torch.no_grad()` block to generate text without computing gradients, making inference more efficient. The model generates a response with a maximum length of `100` tokens, ensuring it stays concise. The generated text is then decoded using `tokenizer.decode`, with `skip_special_tokens=True` to remove unwanted tokens. Finally, the function extracts the part of the response after the last occurrence of `"Output: "` to isolate the model's generated answer, trimming any extra whitespace. This approach effectively enables **few-shot learning**, where the model leverages provided examples to make a more informed prediction.

Zero-shot evaluation

Zero-shot evaluation tests a model's ability to perform a task without any specific examples. Here's how you might implement zero-shot evaluation:

```
def zero_shot_evaluate(
    model, tokenizer, task_description, test_instance
):
    prompt = f"{task_description}\n\nInput: {test_instance}\nOutput:"

    input_ids = tokenizer.encode(prompt, return_tensors='pt')

    with torch.no_grad():
        output = model.generate(
            input_ids, max_length=100, num_return_sequences=1
        )

    generated_text = tokenizer.decode(output[0],
        skip_special_tokens=True)
    return generated_text.split("Output:")[-1].strip()

# Example usage
task_description = "Classify the following text into one of these
categories: Science, Politics, Sports, Entertainment."
test_instance = "NASA's Mars rover has discovered traces of ancient
microbial life."
```

```
result = zero_shot_evaluate(
    model, tokenizer, task_description, test_instance
)
print(f"Zero-shot evaluation result: {result}")
```

This function demonstrates zero-shot evaluation on a text classification task.

The `zero_shot_evaluate` function performs **zero-shot inference** using a pre-trained language model by constructing a prompt that describes the task and presents an input without any labeled examples. It first formats the prompt by combining `task_description` with `test_instance`, ensuring that the model understands the task and what it needs to classify. The phrase `"Output:"` is appended to signal where the model should generate its response. The prompt is then tokenized using tokenizer.encode, converting it into numerical input tensors that the model can process. The function uses `torch.no_grad()` to disable gradient computation, making inference more efficient. The `model.generate` function takes the tokenized prompt and generates an output sequence with a maximum length of 100 tokens while returning only one sequence. The generated output is then decoded back into text using `tokenizer.decode`, ensuring that any special tokens are removed. Finally, the function extracts and returns the portion of the generated text that appears after `"Output:"`, which represents the model's predicted classification. In the example usage, the function is applied to a classification task where the model is asked to categorize a given text snippet—`"NASA's Mars rover has discovered traces of ancient microbial life."`—into one of the predefined categories: `Science`, `Politics`, `Sports`, or `Entertainment`. The model, without seeing any labeled examples, infers the correct category based on its prior knowledge. The output is then printed, demonstrating the model's zero-shot classification ability.

Domain and task generalization

Assessing how well an LLM generalizes across different domains and tasks is crucial for understanding its true capabilities. Let's explore some techniques for this purpose.

Evaluating domain adaptation

To evaluate **domain adaptation**, we can test the model on data from a different domain than it was trained on. Here's an example:

```
def evaluate_domain_adaptation(
    model, tokenizer, source_domain_data, target_domain_data
):
    def predict(text):
        inputs = tokenizer(
            text, return_tensors='pt', truncation=True, padding=True
        )
```

```
        outputs = model(inputs)
        return torch.argmax(outputs.logits, dim=1).item()

    # Evaluate on source domain
    source_predictions = [
        predict(text) for text in source_domain_data['text']
    ]
    source_accuracy = accuracy_score(
        source_domain_data['label'], source_predictions
)

    # Evaluate on target domain
    target_predictions = [
        predict(text) for text in target_domain_data['text']
    ]
    target_accuracy = accuracy_score(
        target_domain_data['label'], target_predictions
)

    return {
        'source_accuracy': source_accuracy,
        'target_accuracy': target_accuracy,
        'adaptation_drop': source_accuracy - target_accuracy
    }
```

The following is how we evaluate domain adaptation and print out the result:

```
source_domain_data = load_source_domain_data()  # Replace with actual
data loading
target_domain_data = load_target_domain_data()  # Replace with actual
data loading

results = evaluate_domain_adaptation(
    model, tokenizer, source_domain_data, target_domain_data
)
print(f"Source domain accuracy: {results['source_accuracy']:.2f}")
print(f"Target domain accuracy: {results['target_accuracy']:.2f}")
print(f"Adaptation drop: {results['adaptation_drop']:.2f}")
```

Putting it together, we can use the preceding code to evaluate the model's performance on both the source domain (what it was trained on) and the target domain, calculating the drop in performance as a measure of domain adaptation.

Evaluating task generalization

To assess **task generalization**, we can evaluate the model on a variety of tasks it wasn't specifically fine-tuned for. Here's an example using the GLUE benchmark (which we discussed in *Chapter 14*):

```python
def evaluate_task_generalization(
    model_name, tasks=['mnli', 'qqp', 'qnli', 'sst2']
):
    results = {}

    for task in tasks:
        model = \
            AutoModelForSequenceClassification.from_pretrained(
            model_name)
        tokenizer = AutoTokenizer.from_pretrained(model_name)

        dataset = load_dataset('glue', task)

        def tokenize_function(examples):
            return tokenizer(
                examples['sentence'], truncation=True, padding=True)

        tokenized_datasets = dataset.map(tokenize_function,
            batched=True)

        training_args = TrainingArguments(
            output_dir=f"./results_{task}",
            evaluation_strategy="epoch",
            num_train_epochs=1,
        )

        trainer = Trainer(
            model=model,
            args=training_args,
            train_dataset=tokenized_datasets['train'],
            eval_dataset=tokenized_datasets['validation'],
        )

        eval_results = trainer.evaluate()
        results[task] = eval_results['eval_accuracy']

    return results
```

The following is how to run the evaluation based on the previously defined function:

```
model_name = "bert-base-uncased"  # Replace with your model
generalization_results = evaluate_task_generalization(model_name)

for task, accuracy in generalization_results.items():
    print(f"{task} accuracy: {accuracy:.2f}")
```

Putting together the preceding code, we can evaluate the model on multiple GLUE tasks to assess its ability to generalize across different NLP tasks.

Continual learning evaluation

Continual learning is the ability of a model to learn new tasks without forgetting previously learned ones. Here's an example of how you might evaluate continual learning in LLMs:

1. Set up our continual learning framework by initializing the model, the tokenizer, and the main function structure:

```
def evaluate_continual_learning(
    model_name, tasks=['sst2', 'qnli', 'qqp'], num_epochs=3
):
    model = \
        AutoModelForSequenceClassification.from_
        pretrained(model_name)
    tokenizer = AutoTokenizer.from_pretrained(model_name)
    results = {}
```

2. Define the preprocessing function that handles different input formats for various GLUE tasks:

```
def preprocess_function(examples, task):
    # Different tasks have different input formats
    if task == 'qqp':
        texts = (examples['question1'], examples['question2'])
    elif task == 'qnli':
        texts = (examples['question'], examples['sentence'])
    else:  # sst2
        texts = (examples['sentence'], None)

    tokenized = tokenizer(*texts, padding=True, truncation=True)
    tokenized['labels'] = examples['label']
    return tokenized
```

3. Preprocess and prepare the dataset for each task:

```
for task in tasks:
    dataset = load_dataset('glue', task)
    tokenized_dataset = dataset.map(
        lambda x: preprocess_function(x, task),
        batched=True,
        remove_columns=dataset['train'].column_names
    )
    model.config.num_labels = 3 if task == 'mnli' else 2
```

4. Provide the training setup and execution for each task:

```
trainer = Trainer(
    model=model,
    args=TrainingArguments(
        output_dir=f"./results_{task}",
        num_train_epochs=num_epochs,
        learning_rate=2e-5,
        per_device_train_batch_size=16,
        per_device_eval_batch_size=16,
        evaluation_strategy="epoch"
    ),
    train_dataset=tokenized_dataset['train'],
    eval_dataset=tokenized_dataset['validation']
)
trainer.train()
```

5. Conduct an evaluation across all previously seen tasks:

```
task_results = {}
for eval_task in tasks[:tasks.index(task)+1]:
    eval_dataset = load_dataset('glue', eval_task)['validation']
    eval_tokenized = eval_dataset.map(
        lambda x: preprocess_function(x, eval_task),
        batched=True,
        remove_columns=eval_dataset.column_names
    )
    eval_results = trainer.evaluate(eval_dataset=eval_tokenized)
    task_results[eval_task] = eval_results['eval_accuracy']
results[task] = task_results
```

6. Run the evaluation and display the results:

```
model_name = "bert-base-uncased"  # Replace with your model
cl_results = evaluate_continual_learning(model_name)
for task, task_results in cl_results.items():
    print(f"\nAfter training on {task}:")
    for eval_task, accuracy in task_results.items():
        print(f"  {eval_task} accuracy: {accuracy:.2f}")
```

Putting the preceding code blocks together, we show how to fine-tune the model on a sequence of tasks and evaluate its performance on all previously seen tasks after each fine-tuning step, allowing us to assess how well it retains knowledge of earlier tasks.

Cross-validation challenges and best practices

LLMs present unique challenges for cross-validation due to their scale and the nature of their training data. Here are some key challenges:

- **Data contamination**: Avoiding test set overlap with pre-training data is difficult given the vast and diverse web data LLMs are trained on, making it hard to ensure a truly unseen validation set

- **Computational cost**: Traditional methods such as k-fold cross-validation are often infeasible due to the immense computational resources required for models of this scale

- **Domain shift**: LLMs may show inconsistent performance when exposed to data from underrepresented or entirely new domains, complicating the evaluation of generalizability

- **Prompt sensitivity**: The performance of LLMs can vary significantly based on subtle differences in prompt wording, adding another layer of variability to the validation process

Based on these challenges, here are some best practices for LLM cross-validation:

- **Mitigate data contamination**: Use rigorous data deduplication methods to identify and remove overlaps between the pre-training corpus and validation datasets. Tools such as MinHash or Bloom filters can efficiently detect near-duplicates in large datasets.

MinHash

MinHash is a probabilistic technique for quickly estimating how similar two sets are by converting large sets into smaller, representative fingerprints (**hashes**) where the probability of hash collision is proportional to the similarity between the original sets, making it particularly useful for detecting near-duplicate content in large datasets.

MinHashLSH is based on MinHash and **locality-sensitive hashing** (**LSH**), which groups similar items into the same "buckets" to enable fast lookup and comparison.

The following code example demonstrates data deduplication using MinHash and MinHashLSH for detecting near-duplicates in datasets:

```
from datasketch import MinHash, MinHashLSH
import numpy as np

def deduplicate_data(texts, threshold=0.8):
    # Initialize LSH index for fast similarity search
    lsh = MinHashLSH(threshold=threshold, num_perm=128)
    unique_texts = []

    for idx, text in enumerate(texts):
        minhash = MinHash(num_perm=128)
        for ngram in get_ngrams(text):
            minhash.update(ngram.encode('utf8'))

        if not lsh.query(minhash):  # Check if similar text
exists
            lsh.insert(str(idx), minhash)
            unique_texts.append(text)
    return unique_texts
```

- **Reduce computational cost**: Use stratified sampling or a single-split validation (e.g., train-validation-test) approach to minimize computational overhead. Alternatively, employ smaller model checkpoints or distilled versions of the LLM during experimentation before scaling up.

The following code example shows stratified sampling for efficient validation:

```
from sklearn.model_selection import StratifiedKFold
from collections import defaultdict

def create_efficient_splits(data, labels, n_splits=5):
    # Group data by domain
    domain_data = defaultdict(list)
    for text, domain in zip(data, labels):
        domain_data[domain].append(text)

    # Create stratified splits
    skf = StratifiedKFold(n_splits=n_splits, shuffle=True)
    splits = []
    for train_idx, val_idx in skf.split(data, labels):
        splits.append((train_idx, val_idx))
    return splits
```

- **Handle domain shift**: Construct validation datasets with explicit representation from diverse domains. Fine-tune models with representative domain-specific data to reduce performance gaps in underrepresented areas.

This code example demonstrates handling domain shift through domain-specific validation:

```
def evaluate_domain_performance(model, tokenizer, eval_data):
    domain_scores = defaultdict(list)

    for text, domain in eval_data:
        inputs = tokenizer(text, return_tensors='pt')
        with torch.no_grad():
            outputs = model(inputs)
            score = outputs.logits.mean().item()
            domain_scores[domain].append(score)

    # Calculate domain-specific metrics
    return {domain: np.mean(scores)
        for domain, scores in domain_scores.items()}
```

- **Address prompt sensitivity**: Perform prompt engineering systematically. Use techniques such as prompt paraphrasing, instruction tuning, or ensemble evaluation across multiple prompts to ensure robustness and minimize the variability introduced by prompt changes.

The following code example shows systematic prompt engineering with multiple variants:

```
def evaluate_with_prompt_ensemble(
    model, tokenizer, text, base_prompt
):
    prompt_variants = [
        f"{base_prompt}: {text}",
        f"Please {base_prompt.lower()}: {text}",
        f"I want you to {base_prompt.lower()}: {text}"
    ]

    responses = []
    for prompt in prompt_variants:
        inputs = tokenizer(prompt, return_tensors='pt')
        with torch.no_grad():
            output = model.generate(inputs, max_length=100)
            responses.append(tokenizer.decode(output[0]))

    # Aggregate responses (e.g., by voting or averaging)
    return aggregate_responses(responses)
```

The following code example shows how to combine all these approaches into a single evaluation pipeline:

```
def robust_evaluation_pipeline(model, data, domains):
    # First deduplicate the data
    clean_data = deduplicate_data(data)

    # Create efficient splits
    splits = create_efficient_splits(clean_data, domains)

    # Evaluate across domains with prompt ensembles
    results = defaultdict(dict)
    for domain in domains:
        domain_data = [d for d, dom in zip(clean_data, domains)
            if dom == domain]
        scores = evaluate_with_prompt_ensemble(model, tokenizer,
            domain_data, "analyze")
        results[domain] = scores

    return results
```

Summary

Cross-validation for LLMs requires careful consideration of their unique characteristics and capabilities. By implementing these advanced techniques and best practices, you can obtain a more robust and comprehensive assessment of your LLM's performance across various domains and tasks.

As we move forward, the next chapter will delve into the crucial topic of interpretability in LLMs. We'll explore techniques for understanding and explaining the outputs and behaviors of LLMs.

Get This Book's PDF Version and Exclusive Extras

UNLOCK NOW

Scan the QR code (or go to packtpub.com/unlock). Search for this book by name, confirm the edition, and then follow the steps on the page.

Note: Keep your invoice handly. Purchase made directly from packt don't require one.

16
Interpretability

Interpretability in LLMs refers to the model's ability to understand and explain how the model processes inputs and generates outputs.

Interpretability is needed for LLMs for several reasons:

- **Trust and transparency**: Understanding how LLMs arrive at their outputs builds trust among users and stakeholders
- **Debugging and improvement**: Interpretability techniques can help identify model weaknesses and guide improvements
- **Ethical considerations**: Interpretable models allow for better assessment of potential biases and fairness issues
- **Regulatory compliance**: In some domains, interpretable AI models may be required for regulatory compliance

In this chapter, we will explore advanced techniques for understanding and explaining the outputs and behaviors of LLMs. We'll discuss how to apply these techniques to transformer-based LLMs and examine the trade-offs between model performance and interpretability.

In this chapter, we'll be covering the following topics:

- Attention visualization techniques
- Probing methods
- Explaining LLM predictions with attribution methods
- Interpretability in transformer-based LLMs
- Mechanistic interpretability
- Trade-offs between interpretability and performance

Attention visualization techniques

Attention mechanisms are a key component of transformer-based LLMs (see *Chapter 1*). Visualizing attention patterns can provide insights into how the model processes and attends to different parts of the input.

Here's an example of how to visualize attention in a transformer-based model:

```python
import torch
from transformers import BertTokenizer, BertModel
import matplotlib.pyplot as plt
import seaborn as sns

def visualize_attention(model, tokenizer, text):
    inputs = tokenizer(text, return_tensors="pt")
    outputs = model(inputs, output_attentions=True)

    attention = outputs.attentions[-1].squeeze().detach().numpy()

    tokens = tokenizer.convert_ids_to_tokens(inputs["input_ids"][0])

    plt.figure(figsize=(10, 8))
    sns.heatmap(attention, xticklabels=tokens,
        yticklabels=tokens, cmap="YlGnBu")
    plt.title("Attention Visualization")
    plt.show()

# Example usage
model_name = "bert-base-uncased"
model = BertModel.from_pretrained(model_name)
tokenizer = BertTokenizer.from_pretrained(model_name)

text = "The cat sat on the mat."
visualize_attention(model, tokenizer, text)
```

This code provides a simple way to visualize the attention mechanism of a BERT model when processing a given input sentence. It begins by importing necessary libraries: PyTorch for model handling, Hugging Face's `transformers` library for loading the BERT model and tokenizer, and Matplotlib and Seaborn for visualization. The `visualize_attention` function takes a BERT model, tokenizer, and input text. It first tokenizes the input using the tokenizer and feeds the tokenized input into the model with `output_attentions=True` to retrieve the attention weights. From the returned outputs, it extracts the attention matrix from the last layer (i.e., `outputs.attentions[-1]`), detaches it from the computation graph, and converts it to a NumPy array. This matrix represents how much attention each token in the sequence gives to every other token. The token IDs are then converted back to readable tokens for labeling the axes of a heatmap. Using Seaborn's `heatmap`, the attention scores are visualized as a color-coded matrix, making it easier to interpret which words the model focuses on while processing each token. Finally, the code loads the pre-trained BERT base model and tokenizer, defines a sample sentence, and calls the visualization function to display the attention map, offering insights into BERT's inner workings.

Keep in mind that attention maps do not always correlate with model reasoning in LLMs. While they show where the model focuses, they don't necessarily explain why a decision is made. Attention can be diffused, inconsistent, or misleading, sometimes highlighting irrelevant tokens while still producing correct outputs. Since LLMs encode information in distributed representations, reasoning often occurs beyond direct attention, involving deep latent transformations across layers. Research also shows that attention maps can be manipulated without changing model behavior, proving they are not a definitive explanation of reasoning. For better interpretability, they should be combined with gradient-based methods, probing techniques, and causal analysis.

Probing methods

Probing involves training simple models on the internal representations of an LLM to assess what linguistic properties are captured at different layers.

Different layers in a transformer specialize in different linguistic properties. Lower layers capture syntax and token identity; middle layers handle grammar and sentence structure; and higher layers focus on semantics, reasoning, and factual recall. This hierarchy emerges naturally during training, with lower layers excelling in syntactic tasks and higher layers in semantic reasoning. Probing studies confirm this specialization, aiding interpretability, fine-tuning, and model compression for task-specific optimizations.

Here's an example of how to implement a probing task:

```
import torch
from transformers import BertTokenizer, BertModel
from sklearn.model_selection import train_test_split
from sklearn.linear_model import LogisticRegression
from sklearn.metrics import accuracy_score

def probe_bert_layers(model, tokenizer, texts, labels, layer_nums):
    # Get BERT embeddings for each layer
    def get_embeddings(text):
        inputs = tokenizer(text, return_tensors="pt",
            padding=True, truncation=True)
        with torch.no_grad():
            outputs = model(inputs, output_hidden_states=True)
        return outputs.hidden_states
```

```
    results = {}
    for layer in layer_nums:
        embeddings = [
            get_embeddings(text)[layer]
            .squeeze()
            .mean(dim=0)
            .numpy() for text in texts
        ]

        # Split data
        X_train, X_test, y_train, y_test = train_test_split(
        embeddings, labels, test_size=0.2, random_state=42
    )

        # Train and evaluate probe
        probe = LogisticRegression(random_state=42)
        probe.fit(X_train, y_train)
        y_pred = probe.predict(X_test)
        accuracy = accuracy_score(y_test, y_pred)

        results[f"Layer_{layer}"] = accuracy

    return results

# Example usage
model_name = "bert-base-uncased"
model = BertModel.from_pretrained(model_name)
tokenizer = BertTokenizer.from_pretrained(model_name)

texts = ["The cat sat on the mat.", "The dog chased the ball.",
...]  # Add more examples
labels = [0, 1, ...]  # Corresponding labels (e.g., 0 for simple, 1
for complex sentences)

layer_nums = [1, 6, 12]  # Layers to probe
probe_results = probe_bert_layers(model, tokenizer, texts, labels,
    layer_nums)

for layer, accuracy in probe_results.items():
    print(f"{layer} Accuracy: {accuracy:.2f}")
```

This code implements a simple probing task to assess how well different layers of a BERT model capture a specific linguistic property (in this case, sentence complexity).

Explaining LLM predictions with attribution methods

Attribution methods aim to identify which input features contribute most to a model's prediction.

We need to discuss attribution methods because understanding why a model produces a particular prediction is critical for both interpretability and trustworthiness in real-world applications. Attribution methods provide a systematic way to trace the influence of specific input tokens on the model's output, which is particularly important in LLMs where predictions are often made from complex, high-dimensional token embeddings and non-linear interactions across multiple attention layers. Without attribution, users and developers are left with a black-box model that produces outputs without any transparent rationale, making it difficult to validate decisions, debug behaviors, or ensure alignment with intended use cases.

One popular attribution method is **integrated gradients**.

Integrated gradients is an attribution method used to explain the predictions of neural networks by quantifying the contribution of each input feature to the model's output. It computes feature attributions by integrating the gradients of the model's output with respect to the input, along a straight path from a baseline to the actual input.

Keep in mind that gradient-based methods in LLMs can be noisy due to sensitivity to input perturbations, mini-batch variance, and gradient saturation, affecting both training stability and interpretability. In optimization, noise can cause oscillations or suboptimal convergence, while in interpretability, methods such as integrated gradients can produce inconsistent attributions across runs. This instability reduces trust in model insights, especially for similar inputs. Techniques such as gradient smoothing, averaging, and second-order optimization help mitigate noise but add computational overhead, creating a trade-off between efficiency and precision in LLM development.

Here's an example of how to implement integrated gradients for a transformer-based model:

```
import torch
from transformers import BertTokenizer, BertForSequenceClassification
import numpy as np
import matplotlib.pyplot as plt


def integrated_gradients(
    model, tokenizer, text, target_class, steps=50
):
    input_ids = tokenizer.encode(text, return_tensors="pt")
    baseline_ids = torch.zeros_like(input_ids)

    alphas = torch.linspace(0, 1, steps)
    delta = input_ids - baseline_ids

    accumulated_grads = 0
```

```
    for alpha in alphas:
        interpolated_ids = baseline_ids + alpha * delta
        interpolated_ids.requires_grad_()

        outputs = model(interpolated_ids)
        pred = outputs.logits[:, target_class]

        model.zero_grad()
        pred.backward()

        accumulated_grads += interpolated_ids.grad

    attributions = \
        (input_ids - baseline_ids) * accumulated_grads / steps
    return attributions.squeeze().detach().numpy()

# Example usage
model_name = "bert-base-uncased"
model = BertForSequenceClassification.from_pretrained(model_name)
tokenizer = BertTokenizer.from_pretrained(model_name)

text = "This movie was fantastic!"
target_class = 1  # Assuming 1 is the positive sentiment class

attributions = integrated_gradients(model, tokenizer, text,
    target_class)

# Visualize attributions
tokens = tokenizer.convert_ids_to_tokens(tokenizer.encode(text))
plt.figure(figsize=(10, 5))
plt.bar(range(len(tokens)), attributions)
plt.xticks(range(len(tokens)), tokens, rotation=45)
plt.title("Integrated Gradients Attribution")
plt.show()
```

This code demonstrates how to use the integrated gradients method to interpret a BERT-based sequence classification model by attributing the model's prediction to individual input tokens. The integrated_gradients function works by first encoding the input text into token IDs using the tokenizer and creating a baseline input of the same shape filled with zeros. It then interpolates between the baseline and actual input in small steps (default is 50) to compute gradients along this path. For each interpolated input, it calculates the model's output for the specified target class, performs backpropagation to get the gradient with respect to the input, and accumulates these gradients. Finally, it computes the average of these gradients and multiplies it by the input difference (*input – baseline*) to get the attributions—this quantifies how much each input token contributes to the prediction. After defining the model and tokenizer, the code runs the attribution method on an example text and displays the results as a bar plot, where each bar corresponds to a token and its importance for the target prediction. This technique offers a more principled and model-aware way to understand which parts of the input were most influential, making it a powerful tool for interpretability and trust in model predictions.

Interpretability in transformer-based LLMs

Transformer-based LLMs present unique challenges and opportunities for interpretability. Some key areas to consider are as follows:

- **Multi-head attention**: Analyzing individual attention heads to reveal specialized functions
- **Positional embeddings**: Understanding how models use positional information
- **Layer-wise analysis**: Examining how different linguistic features are captured across layers

Here's an example of analyzing multi-head attention:

```python
import torch
from transformers import BertTokenizer, BertModel
import matplotlib.pyplot as plt

def analyze_multihead_attention(model, tokenizer, text):
    inputs = tokenizer(text, return_tensors="pt")
    outputs = model(inputs, output_attentions=True)

    attention = outputs.attentions[-1].squeeze().detach().numpy()

    tokens = tokenizer.convert_ids_to_tokens(inputs["input_ids"][0])

    num_heads = attention.shape[0]
    fig, axs = plt.subplots(2, 4, figsize=(20, 10))
    axs = axs.ravel()

    for i in range(num_heads):
        sns.heatmap(attention[i], xticklabels=tokens,
            yticklabels=tokens, ax=axs[i], cmap="YlGnBu")
        axs[i].set_title(f"Head {i+1}")

    plt.tight_layout()
    plt.show()
```

```
# Example usage
model_name = "bert-base-uncased"
model = BertModel.from_pretrained(model_name)
tokenizer = BertTokenizer.from_pretrained(model_name)

text = "The president of the United States visited Paris last week."
analyze_multihead_attention(model, tokenizer, text)
```

This code visualizes the attention patterns of different heads in the last layer of a BERT model, allowing for comparison of their specialized functions.

Mechanistic interpretability

Mechanistic interpretability (MI) is an emerging field that aims to understand how neural networks process information at a detailed, component level—similar to how we might reverse-engineer a mechanical device. Rather than just observing inputs and outputs, MI seeks to trace how information flows through the network, identify specific computational patterns, and understand how different parts of the network (such as individual neurons or attention heads) contribute to the model's behavior.

MI is important because it goes beyond surface-level explanations to uncover the internal mechanisms of how neural networks, particularly complex models like LLMs, actually work. By analyzing how specific components—like neurons, layers, or attention heads—process and transform information, MI helps researchers build a deeper, more principled understanding of model behavior. This insight is crucial for several reasons: it enhances trust by making models more transparent; it enables precise debugging and targeted improvements; it helps uncover and mitigate hidden biases or vulnerabilities; and it supports the development of safer, more controllable AI systems. Ultimately, MI brings us closer to treating neural networks not as black boxes, but as understandable systems that can be analyzed, interpreted, and refined with greater confidence.

Let's build this up step by step:

1. First, let's create a simple interpretable model structure:

   ```
   import torch
   import torch.nn as nn

   class InterpretableTransformer(nn.Module):
       def __init__(self, vocab_size, d_model, nhead, num_layers):
           super().__init__()
           self.embedding = nn.Embedding(vocab_size, d_model)
           encoder_layer = nn.TransformerEncoderLayer(
               d_model, nhead, batch_first=True
           )
   ```

```
self.transformer = nn.TransformerEncoder(encoder_layer,
    num_layers)
self.fc = nn.Linear(d_model, vocab_size)
```

2. Now, let's add a method to extract attention patterns, which are crucial for understanding how the model processes relationships between tokens:

```
def get_attention_patterns(self, x):
    """Extract attention weights from each layer"""
    x = self.embedding(x)
    attention_patterns = []

    for layer in self.transformer.layers:
        # Register a hook to capture attention weights
        attention_weights = None
        def hook(module, input, output):
            nonlocal attention_weights
            attention_weights = output[1]   # attention weights

        handle = layer.self_attn.register_forward_hook(hook)
        x = layer(x)
        attention_patterns.append(attention_weights)
        handle.remove()

    return attention_patterns
```

3. Let's add a neuron activation analysis to understand which neurons are most active for specific inputs:

```
def analyze_neuron_activations(self, x, layer_idx):
    """Analyze individual neuron activations in a specific
layer"""
    activations = []

    def hook(module, input, output):
        activations.append(output.detach())

    # Register hook on specific layer
    handle = list(self.transformer.layers)[layer_idx]\
        .register_forward_hook(hook)

    # Forward pass
    with torch.no_grad():
        self(x)
```

```
handle.remove()
layer_activations = activations[0]

# Find most active neurons
mean_activation = layer_activations.mean(dim=(0,1))   #
Average across batch and sequence
top_neurons = torch.topk(mean_activation, k=10)

return top_neurons.indices, top_neurons.values
```

4. We can add a method for causal intervention—temporarily modifying specific neurons to see how it affects the output:

```
def intervention_study(self, x, layer_idx, neuron_idx):
    """Study how zeroing out specific neurons affects the
output"""
    original_output = None
    modified_output = None

    def hook_original(module, input, output):
        nonlocal original_output
        original_output = output.detach()

    def hook_modified(module, input, output):
        nonlocal modified_output
        modified = output.clone()
        modified[:,:,neuron_idx] = 0  # Zero out specific neuron
        modified_output = modified
        return modified

    layer = list(self.transformer.layers)[layer_idx]

    # Get original output
    handle = layer.register_forward_hook(hook_original)
    self(x)
    handle.remove()

    # Get modified output
    handle = layer.register_forward_hook(hook_modified)
    self(x)
    handle.remove()

    return original_output, modified_output
```

5. Finally, let's add a visualization helper:

```python
import matplotlib.pyplot as plt

def visualize_attention(attention_weights, tokens=None):
    """Visualize attention patterns"""
    plt.figure(figsize=(10, 8))
    plt.imshow(attention_weights[0].cpu(), cmap='viridis')

    if tokens is not None:
        plt.xticks(range(len(tokens)), tokens, rotation=45)
        plt.yticks(range(len(tokens)), tokens)

    plt.colorbar()
    plt.title('Attention Pattern')
    plt.show()
```

Here's how to use these tools together:

```python
# Initialize model
model = InterpretableTransformer(vocab_size=1000,
    d_model=256, nhead=8, num_layers=4)

# Sample input
input_ids = torch.randint(0, 1000, (1, 20))  # Batch size 1, sequence
length 20

# Get attention patterns
attention_patterns = model.get_attention_patterns(input_ids)

# Analyze neuron activations
top_neurons, activation_values = model.analyze_neuron_activations(
    input_ids, layer_idx=0
)

# Perform intervention study
original, modified = model.intervention_study(input_ids,
    layer_idx=0, neuron_idx=42)

# Visualize attention
visualize_attention(attention_patterns[0])  # Visualize first layer's
attention
```

Each component helps us understand different aspects of the model:

- Attention patterns show how the model relates different tokens to each other
- The neuron activation analysis reveals which neurons are most important for processing specific inputs
- Causal intervention helps us understand the role of specific neurons by observing how the output changes when we modify them
- Visualization tools help us interpret these patterns more intuitively

This is a basic implementation—real MI research often involves more sophisticated techniques, such as circuit analysis, activation patching, and detailed studies of how specific capabilities (such as induction or negation) are implemented in the network.

Trade-offs between interpretability and performance

There's often a tension between model performance and interpretability. More complex models tend to perform better but are harder to interpret. Some approaches to balance this trade-off include the following:

- **Distillation**: Training smaller, more interpretable models to mimic larger LLMs
- **Sparse models**: Encouraging sparsity in model weights or activations for easier interpretation
- **Modular architectures**: Designing models with interpretable components

Here's a simple example of model distillation:

```
import torch
from transformers import (
    BertForSequenceClassification,
    DistilBertForSequenceClassification,
    BertTokenizer)

def distill_bert(
    teacher_model, student_model, tokenizer, texts, temperature=2.0
):
    teacher_model.eval()
    student_model.train()

    optimizer = torch.optim.Adam(student_model.parameters(), lr=1e-4)
    loss_fn = torch.nn.KLDivLoss(reduction="batchmean")

    for text in texts:
        inputs = tokenizer(
```

```
        text, return_tensors="pt", padding=True, truncation=True
    )

    with torch.no_grad():
        teacher_outputs = teacher_model(inputs)
        teacher_logits = teacher_outputs.logits / temperature

    student_outputs = student_model(inputs)
    student_logits = student_outputs.logits / temperature

    loss = loss_fn(torch.log_softmax(student_logits, dim=-1),
                   torch.softmax(teacher_logits, dim=-1))

    optimizer.zero_grad()
    loss.backward()
    optimizer.step()

    return student_model

# Example usage
teacher_model = BertForSequenceClassification.from_pretrained(
    "bert-base-uncased")
student_model = DistilBertForSequenceClassification.from_pretrained(
    "distilbert-base-uncased"
)
tokenizer = BertTokenizer.from_pretrained("bert-base-uncased")

texts = ["This movie was great!", "I didn't like the book.", ...]  #
Add more examples

distilled_model = distill_bert(
    teacher_model, student_model, tokenizer, texts
)
```

This code demonstrates a simple distillation process, where a smaller DistilBERT model learns to mimic the behavior of a larger BERT model.

In addition, we need to keep in mind trade-offs between compression and interpretability, which revolve around balancing efficiency, accuracy, and transparency. Compression techniques such as quantization, pruning, and knowledge distillation significantly reduce model size and inference latency, enabling LLMs to run on edge devices or with lower computational costs. However, these methods can degrade performance, particularly in long-context reasoning, rare token prediction, or domain-specific tasks, where preserving intricate weight structures is crucial. Moreover, heavily compressed models often become less interpretable since removing neurons or attention heads or reducing precision obscures the model's internal representations, making it harder to analyze why certain outputs are generated.

Conversely, interpretability techniques, such as feature attribution, attention visualization, and probing, help researchers and users understand how LLMs process information, detect bias, or debug failures, but they typically require access to the full, unmodified model. Larger, uncompressed models retain more internal knowledge and nuanced representations, making them easier to analyze but harder to deploy efficiently. Furthermore, highly interpretable architectures sometimes impose constraints on model flexibility, limiting their ability to generalize across diverse tasks.

The key challenge is finding the optimal balance—for example, **Low-Rank Adaptation** (**LoRA**) allows for fine-tuning without modifying full model weights, helping maintain some interpretability while enabling efficient deployment. As LLMs scale, developers must weigh efficiency gains from compression against the risks of reduced transparency, especially in high-stakes applications such as healthcare, law, and AI safety, where understanding model decisions is as critical as performance.

Summary

In this chapter, we equipped you with a toolkit of interpretability techniques to gain insights into your LLMs' decision-making processes, which is crucial for developing more transparent and trustworthy AI systems.

As LLMs continue to grow in size and capability, interpretability research will play a crucial role in ensuring these powerful models can be understood, trusted, and safely deployed in real-world applications. Some key challenges and future directions in interpretability will include scaling such techniques for large models, understanding causal relationships, enabling interactive explorations, and developing techniques for specific downstream tasks.

In the next chapter, we will explore techniques for assessing and mitigating fairness and bias in LLMs. This is a critical aspect of responsible AI development, building on the interpretability methods we've discussed to ensure that LLMs are not only powerful and interpretable but also fair and unbiased in their outputs and decision-making processes.

Subscribe for a free eBook

New frameworks, evolving architectures, research drops, production breakdowns—AI_Distilled filters the noise into a weekly briefing for engineers and researchers working hands-on with LLMs and GenAI systems. Subscribe now and receive a free eBook, along with weekly insights that help you stay focused and informed. Subscribe at `https://packt.link/8Oz6Y` or scan the QR code below.

17
Fairness and Bias Detection

Fairness in LLMs involves ensuring that the model's outputs and decisions do not discriminate against or unfairly treat individuals or groups based on protected attributes such as race, gender, age, or religion. It's a complex concept that goes beyond just avoiding explicit bias.

There are several definitions of fairness in machine learning:

- **Demographic parity**: The probability of a positive outcome should be the same for all groups
- **Equal opportunity**: The true positive rates should be the same for all groups
- **Equalized odds**: Both true positive and false positive rates should be the same for all groups

For LLMs, fairness often involves ensuring that the model's language generation and understanding capabilities are equitable across different demographic groups and do not perpetuate or amplify societal bias.

In this chapter, you'll learn about different types of bias that can emerge in LLMs and techniques for detecting them.

In this chapter, we'll be covering the following topics:

- Types of bias
- Fairness metrics for LLM text generation and understanding
- Detecting bias
- Debiasing strategies
- Fairness-aware training
- Ethical considerations

Types of bias

LLMs can exhibit various types of bias:

- **Representation bias**: The underrepresentation or misrepresentation of certain groups in training data—for example, a facial recognition system trained primarily on lighter-skinned faces may exhibit significantly higher error rates when identifying individuals with darker skin tones, due to inadequate representation in the training set.

- **Linguistic bias**: The language used by AI systems to describe different groups—for instance, an AI system as may label men as "assertive" and women as "aggressive when referring to the same behaviors across genders, reinforcing subtle discriminatory patterns.

- **Allocation bias**: The unfair distribution of resources or opportunities based on model predictions, as seen when an automated hiring system systematically ranks candidates from certain universities higher, regardless of their qualifications, thereby disproportionately allocating interview opportunities to graduates from these institutions.

- **Quality of service bias**: Variations in model performance across different groups, as illustrated by a machine translation system that provides significantly more accurate translations for mainstream languages like English, Spanish, and Mandarin while delivering lower-quality translations for languages with fewer speakers or less representation in the training data.

- **Stereotypical bias**: The reinforcement of societal stereotypes through language generation, as demonstrated when an AI writing assistant automatically suggests stereotypical career paths when completing stories about characters of different backgrounds – suggesting careers in sports or entertainment for characters from certain racial backgrounds while suggesting professional careers like doctors or lawyers for others.

- **Explicit and implicit bias**: Explicit bias in LLMs arises from overt patterns in training data, such as stereotypes present in text sources, leading to clearly identifiable bias in outputs. Implicit bias, on the other hand, is more subtle and emerges from underlying statistical correlations in data, shaping responses in ways that may reinforce hidden bias without direct intention. While explicit bias can often be detected and mitigated through filtering or fine-tuning, implicit bias is harder to identify and requires deeper intervention, such as bias-aware training techniques and regular auditing of model outputs.

- **Hidden bias**: Hidden bias in LLMs arises when training data, model design, or deployment choices subtly skew responses, reinforcing stereotypes or excluding perspectives. This can manifest in gendered language, cultural favoritism, or political slants, often due to overrepresented viewpoints in training data. Algorithmic processing can further amplify these biases, making responses inconsistent or skewed based on prompt phrasing. To mitigate this, diverse datasets, bias audits, and ethical fine-tuning are essential, ensuring models generate balanced and fair outputs while allowing user-aware adjustments within ethical constraints.

Here's an example of how to check for representation bias in a dataset (we will just show one example to limit the size of this chapter):

```python
import pandas as pd
from collections import Counter

def analyze_representation(texts, attribute_list):
    attribute_counts = Counter()
    for text in texts:
        for attribute in attribute_list:
            if attribute.lower() in text.lower():
                attribute_counts[attribute] += 1

    total = sum(attribute_counts.values())
    percentages = {attr: count/total*100
        for attr, count in attribute_counts.items()}

    return pd.DataFrame({
        'Attribute': percentages.keys(),
        'Percentage': percentages.values()
    }).sort_values('Percentage', ascending=False)

# Example usage
texts = [
    "The CEO announced a new policy.",
    "The nurse took care of the patient.",
    "The engineer designed the bridge.",
    # ... more texts
]

gender_attributes = ['he', 'she', 'his', 'her', 'him', 'her']
representation_analysis = analyze_representation(
    texts, gender_attributes
)
print(representation_analysis)
```

This code analyzes the representation of gender-related terms in a corpus of texts, which can help identify potential gender bias in the dataset.

Fairness metrics for LLM text generation and understanding

Fairness metrics often focus on comparing model performance or outputs across different demographic groups.

Here are some examples:

- **Demographic parity difference for text classification**: This metric measures the difference in positive prediction rates between the most and least favored groups:

```python
from sklearn.metrics import confusion_matrix
import numpy as np

def demographic_parity_difference(
    y_true, y_pred, protected_attribute
):
    groups = np.unique(protected_attribute)

    dps = []
    for group in groups:
        mask = protected_attribute == group
        cm = confusion_matrix(y_true[mask], y_pred[mask])
        dp = (cm[1, 0] + cm[1, 1]) / cm.sum()
        dps.append(dp)

    return max(dps) - min(dps)

# Example usage
y_true = [0, 1, 1, 0, 1, 0, 1, 1]
y_pred = [0, 1, 0, 0, 1, 1, 1, 1]
protected_attribute = ['A', 'A', 'B', 'B', 'A', 'B', 'A', 'B']

dpd = demographic_parity_difference(
    y_true, y_pred, protected_attribute
)
print(f"Demographic Parity Difference: {dpd}")
```

The code defines a `demographic_parity_difference` function that computes the difference in demographic parity between groups defined by a protected attribute. It takes true labels (`y_true`), predicted labels (`y_pred`), and the protected attribute values as input. For each unique group in the protected attribute, it creates a Boolean mask to isolate the corresponding subset of predictions and computes the confusion matrix for that group. The demographic parity (DP) for each group is then calculated as the proportion of positive predictions—true or false—out of all predictions for that group, specifically using (`cm[1, 0] + cm[1, 1]`) / `cm.sum()`, which corresponds to the number of actual positives (both misclassified and correctly classified) over the total. It stores these DP values and finally returns the maximum difference between them, indicating the disparity in treatment across groups. The example demonstrates this using dummy data, printing out the DP difference between groups `'A'` and `'B'`.

- **Equal opportunity difference for text classification**: This metric measures the difference in true positive rates between the most and least favored groups:

```
def equal_opportunity_difference(
    y_true, y_pred, protected_attribute
):
    groups = np.unique(protected_attribute)

    tprs = []
    for group in groups:
        mask = (protected_attribute == group) & (y_true == 1)
        tpr = np.mean(y_pred[mask] == y_true[mask])
        tprs.append(tpr)

    return max(tprs) - min(tprs)

# Example usage
eod = equal_opportunity_difference(y_true, y_pred,
    protected_attribute)
print(f"Equal Opportunity Difference: {eod}")
```

This code calculates the difference in true positive rates between groups defined by a protected attribute, measuring how equally the model correctly identifies positive cases across those groups.

Now that we've explored a couple of metrics for measuring fairness in model outputs and understanding capabilities, we'll move on to learning techniques to actually detect bias in practice, building on these metrics to develop systematic testing approaches.

Detecting bias

Detecting bias in LLMs often involves analyzing model outputs across different demographic groups or for different types of inputs. Here are some techniques:

- **Word embeddings**: This code measures gender bias in word embeddings by comparing the projection of profession words onto the gender direction:

```python
from gensim.models import KeyedVectors
import numpy as np

def word_embedding_bias(
    model, male_words, female_words, profession_words
):
    male_vectors = [model[word] for word in male_words if word
in model.key_to_index]
    female_vectors = [model[word] for word in female_words
        if word in model.key_to_index]

    male_center = np.mean(male_vectors, axis=0)
    female_center = np.mean(female_vectors, axis=0)

    gender_direction = male_center - female_center

    biases = []
    for profession in profession_words:
        if profession in model.key_to_index:
            bias = np.dot(model[profession], gender_direction)
            biases.append((profession, bias))

    return sorted(biases, key=lambda x: x[1], reverse=True)

# Example usage
model = KeyedVectors.load_word2vec_format(
    'path_to_your_embeddings.bin', binary=True
)

male_words = ['he', 'man', 'boy', 'male', 'gentleman']
female_words = ['she', 'woman', 'girl', 'female', 'lady']
profession_words = ['doctor', 'nurse', 'engineer', 'teacher',
    'CEO']

biases = word_embedding_bias(
    model, male_words, female_words, profession_words
```

```
)
for profession, bias in biases:
    print(f"{profession}: {bias:.4f}")
```

This code measures gender bias in word embeddings by first creating average vectors for male and female terms, calculating a gender direction vector between them, and then measuring how closely different profession words align with this gender axis through dot product calculations. The function returns professions sorted by their bias score, where positive values indicate male association and negative values indicate female association, allowing users to quantify gender stereotypes embedded in the language model.

- **Sentiment analysis:** You can analyze sentiment across different groups to detect potential bias:

```
from transformers import pipeline

def analyze_sentiment_bias(
    texts, groups,
model_name="distilbert-base-uncased-finetuned-sst-2-english"):
    sentiment_analyzer = pipeline(
        "sentiment-analysis", model=model_name
    )

    results = {group: {'positive': 0, 'negative': 0}
        for group in set(groups)}

    for text, group in zip(texts, groups):
        sentiment = sentiment_analyzer(text)[0]
        results[group][sentiment['label'].lower()] += 1

    for group in results:
        total = results[group]['positive'] \
            + results[group]['negative']
        results[group]['positive_ratio'] = \
            results[group]['positive'] / total

    return results

# Example usage
texts = [
    "The man is very intelligent.",
    "The woman is very intelligent.",
    "The man is a great leader.",
    "The woman is a great leader.",
]
groups = ['male', 'female', 'male', 'female']
```

```
bias_results = analyze_sentiment_bias(texts, groups)
print(bias_results)
```

This code analyzes sentiment bias across different demographic groups by using a pre-trained sentiment analysis model from the `transformers` library. It takes a list of texts and their corresponding group labels, processes each text through a sentiment analyzer, and tallies positive and negative sentiment counts for each group. The function then calculates a "positive ratio" for each group (the proportion of texts classified as positive), allowing comparison of sentiment distribution across different groups. In the example, it's specifically examining potential gender bias by analyzing how identical statements about intelligence and leadership are classified when attributed to men versus women, which could reveal if the underlying language model treats identical qualities differently based on gender association.

- **Coreference resolution**: You can analyze coreference resolution to detect potential occupation-gender bias:

```
import spacy

def analyze_coreference_bias(texts, occupations, genders):
    nlp = spacy.load("en_core_web_sm")

    results = {gender: {occ: 0 for occ in occupations}
        for gender in genders}
    counts = {gender: 0 for gender in genders}

    for text in texts:
        doc = nlp(text)
        occupation = None
        gender = None

        for token in doc:
            if token.text.lower() in occupations:
                occupation = token.text.lower()
            if token.text.lower() in genders:
                gender = token.text.lower()

        if occupation and gender:
            results[gender][occupation] += 1
            counts[gender] += 1

    for gender in results:
        for occ in results[gender]:
            results[gender][occ] /= counts[gender]
```

```
        return results

# Example usage
texts = [
    "The doctor examined her patient. She prescribed some
medication.",
    "The nurse took care of his patients. He worked a long
shift.",
    # ... more texts
]
occupations = ['doctor', 'nurse', 'engineer', 'teacher']
genders = ['he', 'she']

bias_results = analyze_coreference_bias(texts, occupations,
    genders)
print(bias_results)
```

The code defines an `analyze_coreference_bias` function that uses spaCy's NLP pipeline to assess potential gender bias in text by analyzing how often specific gendered pronouns (like "he" and "she") co-occur with certain occupations (e.g., "doctor", "nurse"). It initializes a spaCy language model and creates a nested dictionary to count occurrences of each gender-occupation pair, as well as a separate count for each gender. For each input text, it tokenizes the content, identifies if any of the predefined occupations and gendered pronouns appear, and if both are present, it increments the relevant counters. After processing all texts, it normalizes the occupation counts for each gender by the total number of gender mentions, effectively yielding a proportion that reflects the relative association of each occupation with each gender in the given dataset. The function returns this normalized result, which is then printed in the example usage.

Next, we'll build on this detection knowledge to explore practical strategies for reducing bias, helping us move from diagnosis to treatment.

Debiasing strategies

Debiasing LLMs is an active area of research. Here are some strategies:

- **Data augmentation** (see *Chapter 3*): In the following code, we augment the dataset by swapping gendered words, helping to balance gender representation:

```
import random

def augment_data(texts, male_words, female_words):
    augmented_texts = []
    for text in texts:
```

```
            words = text.split()
            for i, word in enumerate(words):
                if word.lower() in male_words:
                    female_equivalent = female_words[
                        male_words.index(word.lower())
                    ]
                    new_text = ' '.join(words[:i]
                        + [female_equivalent] + words[i+1:])
                    augmented_texts.append(new_text)
                elif word.lower() in female_words:
                    male_equivalent = male_words[
                        female_words.index(word.lower())
                    ]
                    new_text = ' '.join(words[:i]
                        + [male_equivalent] + words[i+1:])
                    augmented_texts.append(new_text)
        return texts + augmented_texts

# Example usage
texts = [
    "The doctor examined his patient.",
    "The nurse took care of her patients.",
]
male_words = ['he', 'his', 'him']
female_words = ['she', 'her', 'her']

augmented_texts = augment_data(texts, male_words, female_words)
print(augmented_texts)
```

- **Bias fine-tuning**: In the following code, we fine-tune a language model to replace biased words with more neutral alternatives:

```
from transformers import (
    AutoModelForCausalLM, AutoTokenizer,
    TrainingArguments, Trainer)
import torch

def create_debiasing_dataset(biased_words, neutral_words):
    inputs = [f"The {biased} person" for biased in biased_words]
    targets = [f"The {neutral} person"
        for neutral in neutral_words]
```

```
    return inputs, targets

def fine_tune_for_debiasing(
    model, tokenizer, inputs, targets, epochs=3
):
    input_encodings = tokenizer(inputs, truncation=True,
        padding=True)
    target_encodings = tokenizer(targets, truncation=True,
        padding=True)

    dataset = torch.utils.data.TensorDataset(
        torch.tensor(input_encodings['input_ids']),
        torch.tensor(input_encodings['attention_mask']),
        torch.tensor(target_encodings['input_ids'])
    )

    training_args = TrainingArguments(
        output_dir='./results',
        num_train_epochs=epochs,
        per_device_train_batch_size=8,
        warmup_steps=500,
        weight_decay=0.01,
        logging_dir='./logs',
    )

    trainer = Trainer(
        model=model,
        args=training_args,
        train_dataset=dataset,
    )

    trainer.train()
    return model

# Example usage
model_name = "gpt2"
model = AutoModelForCausalLM.from_pretrained(model_name)
tokenizer = AutoTokenizer.from_pretrained(model_name)

biased_words = ['bossy', 'emotional', 'hysterical']
neutral_words = ['assertive', 'passionate', 'intense']
```

```
inputs, targets = create_debiasing_dataset(
    biased_words, neutral_words
)
debiased_model = fine_tune_for_debiasing(
    model, tokenizer, inputs, targets
)
```

Fairness-aware training

Fairness constraints in machine learning are mathematical formulations that quantify and enforce specific notions of fairness by ensuring that model predictions maintain desired statistical properties across different demographic groups. These constraints typically express conditions such as demographic parity (equal positive prediction rates across groups), equalized odds (equal true positive and false positive rates), or individual fairness (similar individuals receive similar predictions). They can be incorporated directly into model optimization as regularization terms or enforced as post-processing steps. By explicitly modeling these constraints, developers can mitigate algorithmic bias and ensure more equitable outcomes across protected attributes like race, gender, or age—balancing the traditional goal of accuracy with ethical considerations about how predictive systems impact different populations.

Incorporating fairness constraints directly into the training process can help produce fairer models. Here's a simplified example:

```
import torch
import torch.nn as nn
import torch.optim as optim

class FairClassifier(nn.Module):
    def __init__(self, input_size, hidden_size, num_classes):
        super(FairClassifier, self).__init__()
        self.fc1 = nn.Linear(input_size, hidden_size)
        self.fc2 = nn.Linear(hidden_size, num_classes)

    def forward(self, x):
        x = torch.relu(self.fc1(x))
        return self.fc2(x)

def fair_loss(
    outputs, targets, protected_attributes, lambda_fairness=0.1
):
    criterion = nn.CrossEntropyLoss()
    task_loss = criterion(outputs, targets)
```

```
    # Demographic parity
    group_0_pred = outputs[protected_attributes == 0].mean(dim=0)
    group_1_pred = outputs[protected_attributes == 1].mean(dim=0)
    fairness_loss = torch.norm(group_0_pred - group_1_pred, p=1)

    return task_loss + lambda_fairness * fairness_loss

def train_fair_model(
    model, train_loader, epochs=10, lr=0.001,
    lambda_fairness=0.1
):
    optimizer = optim.Adam(model.parameters(), lr=lr)

    for epoch in range(epochs):
        for inputs, targets, protected_attributes in train_loader:
            optimizer.zero_grad()
            outputs = model(inputs)
            loss = fair_loss(
                outputs, targets,
                protected_attributes, lambda_fairness
            )
            loss.backward()
            optimizer.step()

        print(f'Epoch {epoch+1}/{epochs}, Loss: {loss.item():.4f}')

    return model

# Example usage (assuming you have prepared your data)
input_size = 10
hidden_size = 50
num_classes = 2

model = FairClassifier(input_size, hidden_size, num_classes)
train_loader = ...   # Your DataLoader here

fair_model = train_fair_model(model, train_loader)
```

This code implements a neural network classifier that aims to be fair with respect to protected attributes such as race or gender. The FairClassifier class defines a simple two-layer neural network, while the fair_loss function combines standard classification loss with a fairness constraint that penalizes the model when predictions differ between demographic groups. The train_fair_model function handles the training loop, applying this combined loss to optimize the model parameters while balancing accuracy and fairness.

By incorporating a fairness penalty term in the loss function (weighted by `lambda_fairness`), the model is explicitly trained to make similar predictions across different protected groups, addressing potential bias. This represents a "constraint-based" approach to fair machine learning, where the fairness objective is directly incorporated into the optimization process rather than applied as a post-processing step. The trade-off between task performance and fairness can be tuned through the `lambda_fairness` hyperparameter.

Ethical considerations

Developing fair and unbiased LLMs is not just a technical challenge but also an ethical imperative. Some key ethical considerations include the following:

- **Transparency**: Be open about the model's limitations and potential bias.

- **Diverse development teams**: Ensure diverse perspectives in the development process to help identify and mitigate potential bias.

- **Regular auditing**: Implement regular bias and fairness audits of your LLM throughout its life cycle.

- **Contextual deployment**: Consider the specific context and potential impacts of deploying your LLM in different applications.

- **Ongoing research**: Stay informed about the latest research in AI ethics and fairness and continuously work to improve your models.

- **User education**: Educate users about the capabilities and limitations of your LLM, including potential bias.

- **Feedback mechanisms**: Implement robust feedback mechanisms to identify and address unfair or biased outputs in deployed models. Keep in mind that feedback loops can reinforce bias by amplifying patterns in data, leading to self-perpetuating errors. If an AI system's outputs influence future inputs—whether in content recommendations, hiring, or risk assessments—small biases can compound over time, narrowing diversity, reinforcing stereotypes, and skewing decision-making.

Here's an example of how you might implement a simple feedback system:

```python
pythonCopyimport sqlite3
from datetime import datetime

class FeedbackSystem:
    def __init__(self, db_name='feedback.db'):
        self.conn = sqlite3.connect(db_name)
        self.cursor = self.conn.cursor()
        self.cursor.execute('''
            CREATE TABLE IF NOT EXISTS feedback
```

```
                (id INTEGER PRIMARY KEY AUTOINCREMENT,
                 model_output TEXT,
                 user_feedback TEXT,
                 timestamp DATETIME)
        ''')
        self.conn.commit()

    def record_feedback(self, model_output, user_feedback):
        self.cursor.execute('''
            INSERT INTO feedback (model_output, user_feedback,
timestamp)
            VALUES (?, ?, ?)
        ''', (model_output, user_feedback, datetime.now()))
        self.conn.commit()

    def get_recent_feedback(self, limit=10):
        self.cursor.execute('''
            SELECT model_output, user_feedback, timestamp
            FROM feedback
            ORDER BY timestamp DESC
            LIMIT ?
        ''', (limit,))
        return self.cursor.fetchall()

    def close(self):
        self.conn.close()

# Example usage
feedback_system = FeedbackSystem()

# Simulating model output and user feedback
model_output = "The CEO made her decision."
user_feedback = "Biased: assumes CEO is female"
feedback_system.record_feedback(model_output, user_feedback)

# Retrieving recent feedback
recent_feedback = feedback_system.get_recent_feedback()
for output, feedback, timestamp in recent_feedback:
    print(f"Output: {output}")
    print(f"Feedback: {feedback}")
    print(f"Time: {timestamp}")
    print()

feedback_system.close()
```

This code sets up a simple SQLite database to store user feedback on model outputs, which can be regularly reviewed to identify potential biases or issues.

Summary

In this chapter, we learned about fairness and bias in LLMs, focusing on understanding different fairness definitions, such as demographic parity, equal opportunity, and equalized odds. We explored the types of bias that can emerge in LLMs, including representation, linguistic, allocation, quality of service, and stereotypical, along with techniques for detecting and quantifying them through metrics such as demographic parity difference and equal opportunity difference.

We used practical coding examples to show you how to analyze bias. Debiasing strategies such as data augmentation, bias-aware fine-tuning, and fairness-aware training were also covered, providing actionable ways to mitigate bias. Finally, we gained insights into ethical considerations, including transparency, diverse development teams, regular auditing, and user feedback systems. These skills will help you detect, measure, and address bias in LLMs while building more equitable and transparent AI systems.

Keep in mind that fairness metrics in LLMs often conflict because they prioritize different aspects of equitable treatment. For example, *demographic parity* (equal outcomes across groups) can clash with *equalized odds*, which ensures similar false positive and false negative rates across groups, particularly when base rates differ. Similarly, *calibration* (ensuring predicted probabilities reflect actual outcomes) can contradict *equalized odds*, as a model that is well calibrated might still have unequal error rates. Additionally, *individual fairness* (treating similar individuals similarly) can be at odds with *group fairness*, which enforces equity across demographic groups, sometimes requiring differential treatment. These conflicts highlight the challenge of balancing fairness objectives in AI models.

As we move forward, the next chapter will explore advanced prompt engineering techniques for LLMs.

18

Adversarial Robustness

Adversarial attacks on LLMs are designed to manipulate the model's output by making small, often imperceptible changes to the input. These attacks can expose vulnerabilities in LLMs and potentially lead to security risks or unintended behaviors in real-world applications.

In this chapter, we'll discover techniques for creating and defending against **adversarial examples** in LLMs. Adversarial examples are carefully crafted inputs designed to intentionally mislead the model into producing incorrect or unexpected outputs. You'll learn about textual adversarial attacks, methods to generate these examples, and techniques to make your models more robust. We'll also cover evaluation methods and discuss the real-world implications of adversarial attacks on LLMs.

In this chapter, we'll be covering the following topics:

- Types of textual adversarial attacks
- Adversarial training techniques
- Evaluating robustness
- Trade-offs in the adversarial training of LLMs
- Real-world implications

Types of textual adversarial attacks

Textual adversarial attacks involve subtly modifying text inputs to mislead models into making incorrect predictions, often with changes imperceptible to humans.

There are three levels of attacks to keep in mind:

- **Character-level attacks**: Modifying individual characters in words
- **Word-level attacks**: Replacing words with synonyms or similar words
- **Sentence-level attacks**: Modifying sentence structure while preserving meaning

In addition, a fourth type of attack to consider involves **universal adversarial triggers**, which are specific phrases that, when added, cause the model to behave incorrectly across various inputs.

Here are some illustrative examples of universal adversarial triggers:

- **For sentiment analysis**: Imagine a sentiment analysis model trained to classify movie reviews as "positive" or "negative." A universal adversarial trigger might be a seemingly nonsensical phrase such as "invisible carpet notebook". If this trigger is appended to various positive reviews, such as "This movie was fantastic," resulting in "This movie was fantastic invisible carpet notebook," the model might incorrectly classify them as "negative." Similarly, adding the same trigger to other positive reviews such as "I really enjoyed the acting" could also flip its prediction to "negative."

- **For text classification (e.g., topic identification)**: Consider a model classifying news articles into categories such as "Sports," "Politics," or "Technology." A universal adversarial trigger could be "the the grand elephant". Appending this trigger to a "Sports" article such as "The team won the championship" to get "The team won the championship the the grand elephant" might cause the model to misclassify it as "Politics." Likewise, adding it to a "Technology" article about a new gadget could also lead to an incorrect classification.

- **For natural language inference (NLI)**: In NLI, a model determines the relationship between two sentences (e.g., *entailment*, *contradiction*, *neutral*). A trigger such as "always dance quickly" might be designed to consistently force an "entailment" prediction. For example, given the premise "A person is walking," and the hypothesis "A person is moving," the model would correctly predict "entailment." However, if the trigger is added to the premise, "A person is walking always dance quickly," the model might be tricked into still predicting "entailment" even if the relationship becomes less clear or even nonsensical.

For simplicity, in this section, we will discuss two types of attacks. First, let's implement a simple character-level attack:

```python
import random
import string

def character_level_attack(text, prob=0.1):
    def modify_char(c):
        if random.random() < prob:
            return random.choice(string.ascii_letters) if c.isalpha()
else c
        return c
    return ''.join(modify_char(c) for c in text)

# Example usage
original_text = "The quick brown fox jumps over the lazy dog."
```

```
attacked_text = character_level_attack(original_text)
print(f"Original: {original_text}")
print(f"Attacked: {attacked_text}")
```

This code defines a `character_level_attack` function that aims to create a slightly altered version of an input text by randomly modifying individual characters. For each character in the input text, there is a probability (set by the `prob` parameter, defaulting to `0.1`) that it will be changed. If a character is selected for modification and it is an alphabetic character, it will be replaced by a random lowercase or uppercase letter. Non-alphabetic characters (such as spaces and punctuation) are left unchanged. The function then joins the potentially modified characters back into a string, producing the "attacked" text.

The output of this code will display two lines. The first line, labeled `"Original:"`, will show the initial input text: `"The quick brown fox jumps over the lazy dog."`. The second line, labeled `"Attacked:"`, will present the modified text. Due to the random nature of the character replacement based on the `prob` value, the `"Attacked:"` text will likely have some of its alphabetic characters replaced by other random letters. For example, "The" might become "Tge", "quick" could be "quicj", and so on. The number and specific locations of these changes will vary each time the code is executed because of the random selection process.

Next, as another example, let's implement a more sophisticated word-level attack using synonym replacement:

```
import nltk
from nltk.corpus import wordnet

nltk.download('wordnet')
nltk.download('averaged_perceptron_tagger')

def get_synonyms(word, pos):
    synonyms = set()
    for syn in wordnet.synsets(word):
        if syn.pos() == pos:
            synonyms.update(
                lemma.name()
                for lemma in syn.lemmas()
                if lemma.name() != word
        )
    return list(synonyms)
```

This function retrieves synonyms for a given word based on its part of speech. It uses WordNet, a lexical database for the English language, to find synonyms while ensuring they are different from the original word.

Now, let's implement a word-level attack:

```
def word_level_attack(text, prob=0.2):
    words = nltk.word_tokenize(text)
    pos_tags = nltk.pos_tag(words)

    attacked_words = []
    for word, pos in pos_tags:
        if random.random() < prob:
            wordnet_pos = {'NN': 'n', 'JJ': 'a', 'VB': 'v',
                'RB': 'r'}.get(pos[:2])
            if wordnet_pos:
                synonyms = get_synonyms(word, wordnet_pos)
                if synonyms:
                    attacked_words.append(random.choice(synonyms))
                    continue
        attacked_words.append(word)

    return ' '.join(attacked_words)

# Example usage
original_text = "The intelligent scientist conducted groundbreaking
research."
attacked_text = word_level_attack(original_text)
print(f"Original: {original_text}")
print(f"Attacked: {attacked_text}")
```

This code snippet defines a function `word_level_attack` that attempts to create a subtly altered version of an input text by randomly replacing some words with their synonyms. It first tokenizes the input text into individual words and then determines the part-of-speech (POS) tag for each word. For each word, there's a probability (set by the `prob` parameter, defaulting to `0.2`) that the word will be targeted for replacement. If a word is chosen, its POS tag is used to find potential synonyms from the WordNet lexical database. If synonyms are found, a random synonym replaces the original word in the output; otherwise, the original word is kept.

The output of this code will display two lines. The first line, labeled `"Original:"`, will show the initial input text: `"The intelligent scientist conducted groundbreaking research."`. The second line, labeled `"Attacked:"`, will present the modified text. Due to the random nature of the word replacement based on the prob value, the `"Attacked:"` text will likely have some words replaced by their synonyms. For instance, "intelligent" might be replaced by "smart" or "clever," "conducted" by "carried_out" or "did," and "groundbreaking" by "innovative" or "pioneering." The specific changes will vary each time the code is executed because of the random selection of words and their synonyms.

Adversarial training techniques

Adversarial training involves exposing the model to adversarial examples during the training process to improve its robustness. Here's a simplified example of how you might implement adversarial training for an LLM:

```python
import torch

def adversarial_train_step(model, inputs, labels, epsilon=0.1):
    embeds = model.get_input_embeddings()(inputs["input_ids"])
    embeds.requires_grad = True

    outputs = model(inputs, inputs_embeds=embeds)
    loss = torch.nn.functional.cross_entropy(outputs.logits, labels)

    loss.backward()
    perturb = epsilon * embeds.grad.detach().sign()
    adv_embeds = embeds + perturb

    adv_outputs = model(inputs_embeds=adv_embeds)
    adv_loss = torch.nn.functional.cross_entropy(
        adv_outputs.logits, labels
    )

    return 0.5 * (loss + adv_loss)
```

This function performs a single step of adversarial training. It generates adversarial perturbations using the **Fast Gradient Sign Method** (**FGSM**) and combines the loss from both clean and adversarial inputs. FGSM is a single-step adversarial attack that efficiently generates adversarial examples by calculating the gradient of the loss function with respect to the input data and then adding a small perturbation in the direction of the gradient's sign. This perturbation, scaled by a small epsilon, aims to maximize the model's prediction error, causing misclassification while being almost imperceptible to humans.

To use this in a full training loop, employ the following function:

```python
def adversarial_train(
    model, train_dataloader, optimizer, num_epochs=3
):
    for epoch in range(num_epochs):
        for batch in train_dataloader:
            inputs, labels = batch
            loss = adversarial_train_step(model, inputs, labels)
            optimizer.zero_grad()
            loss.backward()
            optimizer.step()
    return model
```

This function iterates over the training data, performing adversarial training steps for each batch. It updates the model parameters using the combined loss from clean and adversarial inputs.

Evaluating robustness

To evaluate the robustness of an LLM, we can measure its performance on both clean and adversarial inputs:

```
def evaluate_robustness(
    model, tokenizer, test_dataset, attack_function
):
    model.eval()
    clean_preds, adv_preds, labels = [], [], []

    for item in test_dataset:
        inputs = tokenizer(item['text'], return_tensors='pt',
            padding=True, truncation=True)
        with torch.no_grad():
            clean_output = model(inputs).logits
        clean_preds.append(torch.argmax(clean_output, dim=1).item())

        adv_text = attack_function(item['text'])
        adv_inputs = tokenizer(adv_text, return_tensors='pt',
            padding=True, truncation=True
        )
        with torch.no_grad():
            adv_output = model(adv_inputs).logits
        adv_preds.append(torch.argmax(adv_output, dim=1).item())

        labels.append(item['label'])

    return calculate_metrics(labels, clean_preds, adv_preds)
```

This function evaluates the model's performance on both clean and adversarially attacked inputs. It processes each item in the test dataset, generating predictions for both the original and attacked versions of the input.

You should also calculate the evaluation metrics:

```
from sklearn.metrics import accuracy_score, f1_score

def calculate_metrics(labels, clean_preds, adv_preds):
    return {
        'clean_accuracy': accuracy_score(labels, clean_preds),
        'adv_accuracy': accuracy_score(labels, adv_preds),
        'clean_f1': f1_score(labels, clean_preds, average='weighted'),
        'adv_f1': f1_score(labels, adv_preds, average='weighted')
    }
```

The provided Python code defines a function called `calculate_metrics` that takes three arguments: the true labels of the test data, the model's predictions on the original (clean) test data, and the model's predictions on the adversarially attacked versions of the test data. Inside the function, it utilizes the `accuracy_score` and `f1_score` functions from the `sklearn.metrics` library to calculate four key evaluation metrics:

- The accuracy of the model's predictions on the clean data (`clean_accuracy`)

- The accuracy on the adversarial data (`adv_accuracy`)

- The weighted F1 score on the clean data (`clean_f1`)

- The weighted F1 score on the adversarial data (`adv_f1`)

The function then returns these four scores as a dictionary, where each metric's name is the key and its calculated value is the corresponding value.

Each of the calculated scores provides a different perspective on the model's performance. Accuracy represents the overall proportion of correctly classified instances out of the total number of instances. A high accuracy on clean data indicates the model performs well on original, unperturbed inputs, while a low accuracy suggests poor general performance. Conversely, a high accuracy on adversarial data implies the model is robust against the specific type of attack used, meaning the attacks are not very effective at fooling the model. A low accuracy on adversarial data, despite potentially high clean accuracy, highlights the model's vulnerability to these attacks. The F1 score, particularly the weighted version used here to account for potential class imbalance, provides a balanced measure of precision and recall. A high F1 score on clean data signifies good performance in terms of both correctly identifying positive instances and avoiding false positives. Similarly, a high F1 score on adversarial data indicates robustness, as the model maintains good precision and recall even under attack. A low F1 score on either clean or adversarial data suggests the model struggles with either precision or recall, or both, in those respective conditions. Comparing the clean and adversarial scores reveals the extent to which the attacks degrade the model's performance; a significant drop indicates a lack of robustness.

Trade-offs in the adversarial training of LLMs

Adversarial training can improve model robustness, but it often comes with trade-offs:

- **Increased computational cost**: Generating adversarial examples during training is computationally expensive

- **Potential decrease in clean accuracy**: Focusing on adversarial robustness might slightly reduce performance on clean inputs

- **Generalization to unseen attacks**: Models might become robust to specific types of attacks but remain vulnerable to others

To visualize these trade-offs, you could create a plot comparing clean and adversarial accuracy across different levels of adversarial training:

```python
import matplotlib.pyplot as plt

def plot_robustness_tradeoff(
    clean_accuracies, adv_accuracies, epsilon_values
):
    plt.figure(figsize=(10, 6))
    plt.plot(epsilon_values, clean_accuracies, label='Clean Accuracy')
    plt.plot(epsilon_values, adv_accuracies,
        label='Adversarial Accuracy')
    plt.xlabel('Epsilon (Adversarial Perturbation Strength)')
    plt.ylabel('Accuracy')
    plt.title('Robustness Trade-off in Adversarial Training')
    plt.legend()
    plt.show()
```

This function creates a plot to visualize how increasing the strength of adversarial training (epsilon) affects both clean and adversarial accuracy.

Real-world implications

Understanding the real-world implications of adversarial attacks on LLMs is crucial for responsible deployment:

- **Security risks**: Adversarial attacks could be used to bypass content filters or manipulate model outputs in security-critical applications

- **Misinformation**: Attackers could potentially use adversarial techniques to generate fake news or misleading content that evades detection systems

- **User trust**: If LLMs are easily fooled by adversarial inputs, it could erode user trust in AI systems

- **Legal and ethical concerns**: The ability to manipulate LLM outputs raises ethical questions about responsibility and accountability in AI-driven decision-making

- **Robustness in diverse environments**: Real-world deployment of LLMs requires evaluating their performance under diverse adverse conditions, rather than relying solely on clean laboratory settings

To address these implications, consider implementing robust deployment practices and red teaming exercises:

```
class RobustLLMDeployment:
    def __init__(self, model, tokenizer, attack_detector):
        self.model = model
        self.tokenizer = tokenizer
        self.attack_detector = attack_detector

    def process_input(self, text):
        if self.attack_detector(text):
            return "Potential adversarial input detected. Please try
 again."
        inputs = self.tokenizer(
            text, return_tensors='pt', padding=True,
            truncation=True
        )
        with torch.no_grad():
            outputs = self.model(inputs)
        return self.post_process_output(outputs)

    def post_process_output(self, outputs):
        # Implement post-processing logic here
        pass

    def log_interaction(self, input_text, output_text):
        # Implement logging for auditing and monitoring
        pass
```

This class encapsulates best practices for deploying robust LLMs, including input validation, attack detection, and output post-processing.

Summary

Addressing adversarial robustness in LLMs is crucial for their safe and reliable deployment in real-world applications. By implementing the techniques and considerations discussed in this chapter, you can work toward developing LLMs that are more resilient to adversarial attacks while maintaining high performance on clean inputs.

In the upcoming chapter, we will explore **Reinforcement Learning from Human Feedback (RLHF)** for LLM training.

Subscribe for a free eBook

New frameworks, evolving architectures, research drops, production breakdowns—AI_Distilled filters the noise into a weekly briefing for engineers and researchers working hands-on with LLMs and GenAI systems. Subscribe now and receive a free eBook, along with weekly insights that help you stay focused and informed. Subscribe at `https://packt.link/8Oz6Y` or scan the QR code below.

19

Reinforcement Learning from Human Feedback

In this chapter, we'll dive into **Reinforcement Learning from Human Feedback (RLHF)**, a powerful technique for aligning LLMs with human preferences. RLHF combines reinforcement learning with human feedback to fine-tune language models. It aims to align the model's outputs with human preferences, improving the quality and safety of generated text.

RLHF differs from standard supervised fine-tuning by optimizing for human preferences rather than predefined correct answers. While supervised learning minimizes loss against labeled examples, RLHF creates a reward model from human comparisons between model outputs and then uses this reward function (typically with **proximal policy optimization (PPO)**) to update the model's policy. The process typically employs a divergence penalty to prevent excessive drift from the initial model distribution.

The key benefits of RLHF are as follows:

- Improved alignment of models with human values and preferences
- Enhanced control over model outputs
- Reduction of harmful or biased content
- Ability to optimize for specific task performance

By the end of this chapter, you'll be able to implement RLHF techniques to improve the alignment and output quality of your LLMs.

In this chapter, we'll be covering the following topics:

- Components of RLHF systems
- Scaling RLHF
- Limitations of RLHF in language modeling
- Applications of RLHF

Components of RLHF systems

A typical RLHF system for LLMs consists of three main components:

- **Base language model**: The pre-trained LLM to be fine-tuned
- **Reward model**: A model trained on human preferences to provide feedback
- **Policy optimization**: The process of updating the base model using the reward signal

The base language model serves as the starting point. This is the general-purpose large language model that has already undergone extensive pre-training on large-scale corpora using self-supervised objectives such as next-token prediction. At this stage, the model is capable of generating coherent language and demonstrating broad linguistic competence. However, it lacks alignment with human preferences, task-specific objectives, or context-dependent behavior expected in real-world deployment. This pre-trained model is the substrate upon which subsequent tuning is performed. Its architecture, training regime, and scaling have already been well-documented in literature, and since RLHF builds upon it without altering its fundamental structure, further detailing it is unnecessary here.

Instead, let us focus on the reward model and the policy optimization component, which work together to guide and reshape the output distribution of the base model based on human-aligned criteria. These two parts introduce the core mechanisms of feedback-driven adaptation and reinforcement tuning and will be examined in the following sections.

Reward model

Let's implement a basic structure for the reward model:

```python
import torch
from transformers import AutoModelForCausalLM, AutoTokenizer

class RLHFSystem:
    def __init__(self, base_model_name, reward_model_name):
        self.base_model = AutoModelForCausalLM.from_pretrained(
            base_model_name)
        self.reward_model = \
            AutoModelForSequenceClassification.from_pretrained(
            reward_model_name
        )
        self.tokenizer = AutoTokenizer.from_pretrained(
            base_model_name)

    def generate_text(self, prompt):
        inputs = self.tokenizer(prompt, return_tensors="pt")
        outputs = self.base_model.generate(inputs, max_length=100)
```

```
            return self.tokenizer.decode(outputs[0],
                skip_special_tokens=True)

    def get_reward(self, text):
        inputs = self.tokenizer(text, return_tensors="pt")
        with torch.no_grad():
            outputs = self.reward_model(inputs)
        return outputs.logits.item()
```

This class sets up the basic structure for an RLHF system, including the base language model and the reward model. The generate_text method produces text from a given prompt, while get_reward estimates the reward for a given text using the reward model.

The reward model is central to the RLHF process, as it translates human preferences into a learnable signal. Trained on datasets consisting of human comparisons between model outputs—where evaluators choose the better of two responses—it learns to predict how a human might rate any given response. During the reinforcement learning phase, this reward model serves as an automated proxy for human judgment, allowing the base model to receive immediate feedback on thousands of generated outputs. The policy model (the language model being optimized) then learns to maximize these predicted reward scores through techniques such as PPO, gradually shifting its behavior toward generating responses that better align with human preferences while maintaining coherence and capabilities through divergence constraints. This creates a powerful feedback loop that enables continuous alignment with human values, something that would be impossible with static supervised datasets.

Here's a simple implementation of reward model training:

```
from torch.utils.data import DataLoader, Dataset
from transformers import Trainer, TrainingArguments

class FeedbackDataset(Dataset):
    def __init__(self, texts, labels):
        self.texts = texts
        self.labels = labels

    def __len__(self):
        return len(self.texts)

    def __getitem__(self, idx):
        return {"text": self.texts[idx], "label": self.labels[idx]}

    def train_reward_model(model, tokenizer, texts, labels):
        dataset = FeedbackDataset(texts, labels)
```

```
def tokenize_function(examples):
    return tokenizer(examples["text"], padding="max_length",
        truncation=True)

tokenized_dataset = dataset.map(tokenize_function, batched=True)

training_args = TrainingArguments(
    output_dir="./results",
    num_train_epochs=3,
    per_device_train_batch_size=8,
    learning_rate=2e-5,
)

trainer = Trainer(
    model=model,
    args=training_args,
    train_dataset=tokenized_dataset,
)

trainer.train()
return model
```

This code sets up a dataset of human feedback and trains the reward model using the Hugging Face Trainer API. The reward model learns to predict human preferences based on the provided labels.

Policy optimization

Policy optimization is the process of updating the base language model using the rewards from the reward model. A common approach is PPO, which strikes a balance between ease of implementation, sample efficiency, and reliable performance. The term "proximal" in PPO refers to its key innovation: limiting how much the policy can change in each training step to prevent harmful large updates. It does this by using a "clipped" objective function that discourages updates that would move the policy too far from its previous version. PPO has become especially popular in AI alignment and RLHF because it's more stable than other policy gradient methods – it helps with avoiding the problem where model updates become too aggressive and destroy previously learned good behaviors. When used in language models, PPO helps gradually shift the model's outputs to better match human preferences while maintaining coherent and fluent text generation.

Here's a simplified implementation of PPO for LLMs:

```
def ppo_step(
    base_model, reward_model, optimizer, prompt, num_iterations=5
):
```

```
for _ in range(num_iterations):
    # Generate text
    outputs = base_model.generate(prompt, max_length=100,
        return_dict_in_generate=True, output_scores=True
    )
    generated_text = tokenizer.decode(
        outputs.sequences[0], skip_special_tokens=True
    )

    # Get reward
    reward = reward_model(generated_text)

    # Compute policy loss
    log_probs = outputs.scores[0].log_softmax(dim=-1)
    policy_loss = -log_probs * reward

    # Update model
    optimizer.zero_grad()
    policy_loss.mean().backward()
    optimizer.step()

return base_model
```

This function performs a single step of PPO, generating text, computing rewards, and updating the base model's parameters to maximize the expected reward. Keep in mind that this PPO code is illustrative; actual implementations may require more around rewards and safety checks.

Direct preference optimization (**DPO**) is another approach in RLHF that focuses on aligning models with human preferences by directly optimizing for preferred outcomes. Unlike traditional RL methods, which often rely on reward models to guide learning, DPO simplifies the process by using pairs of preferred and dispreferred outputs to adjust the model's behavior. This method enhances efficiency and effectiveness in training models so that they generate outputs that align more closely with human expectations.

DPO might be preferred over PPO when computational efficiency and implementation simplicity are priorities. This is because DPO eliminates the need for separate reward model training and complex reinforcement learning optimization loops. It offers a more streamlined approach by directly updating policy parameters from preference data, which can be particularly valuable in scenarios with limited resources or when PPO training exhibits instability or reward hacking. DPO can also make better use of limited human preference datasets without the intermediate step of reward modeling. Additionally, it provides a cleaner experimental setup for studying how preferences directly impact model behavior without the confounding factors introduced by separate reward models and reinforcement learning optimization.

Here's a short code example demonstrating how to implement DPO using Python:

```python
from transformers import AutoModelForCausalLM, AutoTokenizer
from trl import DPOTrainer

# Load a pre-trained language model and tokenizer
model_name = "gpt2"
model = AutoModelForCausalLM.from_pretrained(model_name)
tokenizer = AutoTokenizer.from_pretrained(model_name)

# Define the dataset containing human preference pairs
# Each entry in the dataset is a tuple (prompt, preferred_completion,
dispreferred_completion)
dataset = [
    ("Prompt 1", "Preferred Completion 1", "Dispreferred Completion
1"),
    ("Prompt 2", "Preferred Completion 2", "Dispreferred Completion
2"),
    # Add more data as needed
]

# Initialize the DPO Trainer
trainer = DPOTrainer(
    model=model,
    tokenizer=tokenizer,
    dataset=dataset,
    beta=0.1  # Hyperparameter controlling the strength of preference
optimization
)

# Train the model using DPO
trainer.train()

# Save the fine-tuned model
model.save_pretrained("fine-tuned-model")
tokenizer.save_pretrained("fine-tuned-model")
```

This code snippet demonstrates how to set up and train a language model using DPO, allowing it to better align with human feedback by directly optimizing for preferred completions.

Having discussed PPO and DPO, next, we'll examine scaling strategies for RLHF regarding large-scale models.

Scaling RLHF

Scaling RLHF to large models presents challenges due to computational requirements. Here are some strategies that can be implemented:

- **Distributed training**: This involves partitioning the training workload across multiple devices – typically GPUs or TPUs – by employing data parallelism, model parallelism, or pipeline parallelism. In data parallelism, the same model is replicated across devices, and each replica processes a different mini-batch of data. Gradients are averaged and synchronized after each step. On the other hand, model parallelism splits the model itself across multiple devices, enabling the training of architectures that are too large to fit on a single device. Finally, pipeline parallelism further divides the model into sequential stages across devices, which are then trained in a pipelined fashion to improve throughput. Frameworks such as DeepSpeed and Megatron-LM provide infrastructure for managing these complex parallelization schemes and optimizing communication overheads.

- **Gradient checkpointing**: This reduces memory usage by selectively storing only a subset of intermediate activations during the forward pass. During backpropagation, the missing activations are recomputed as needed, trading compute for memory. This technique is particularly useful when training large transformer models, where memory consumption due to storing full activation histories becomes prohibitive. Popular libraries such as PyTorch's `torch.utils.checkpoint` or TensorFlow's recomputation wrappers make it possible to apply this technique without having to rewrite model architectures.

- **Mixed-precision training**: This utilizes 16-bit floating-point (FP16 or BF16) formats instead of the standard 32-bit (FP32) for most computations. This reduces memory footprint and increases throughput due to faster arithmetic and lower memory bandwidth usage. To maintain model accuracy and numerical stability, a master copy of weights is maintained in FP32, and dynamic loss scaling is often used to prevent underflow in gradients. Libraries such as NVIDIA's Apex or native support in PyTorch and TensorFlow enable automatic mixed-precision training. This method is especially effective on modern hardware such as NVIDIA's Tensor Cores or Google's TPUs, which are optimized for low-precision computation.

Figure 19.1 summarizes these strategies:

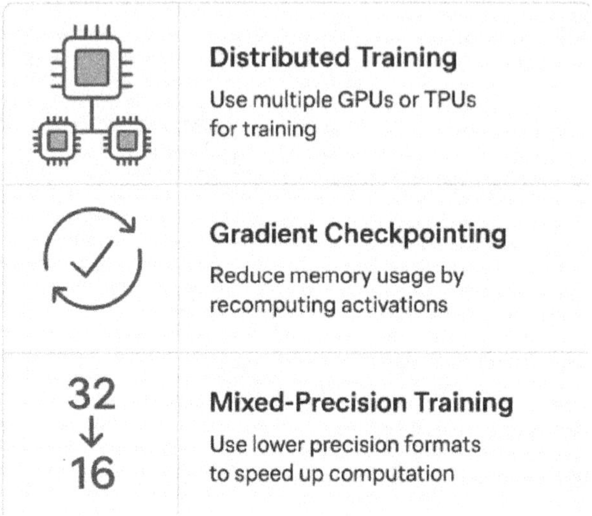

Distributed Training
Use multiple GPUs or TPUs
for training

Gradient Checkpointing
Reduce memory usage by
recomputing activations

Mixed-Precision Training
Use lower precision formats
to speed up computation

Figure 19.1 – Strategies for scaling RLHF

Here's an example of how to implement gradient checkpointing:

```
from transformers import GPT2LMHeadModel

def enable_gradient_checkpointing(model):
    if hasattr(model, "gradient_checkpointing_enable"):
        model.gradient_checkpointing_enable()
    else:
        model.base_model.gradient_checkpointing_enable()
    return model

base_model = GPT2LMHeadModel.from_pretrained("gpt2-large")
base_model = enable_gradient_checkpointing(base_model)
```

This function enables gradient checkpointing for the model, which can significantly reduce memory usage during training, allowing for larger batch sizes or model sizes.

Limitations of RLHF in language modeling

While RLHF is powerful, it faces several challenges:

- **Reward hacking**: Models may exploit loopholes in the reward function
- **Limited feedback**: Human feedback may not cover all possible scenarios

- **Suboptimal local optima**: The optimization process may get stuck in suboptimal solutions

- **Scaling issues**: Obtaining high-quality human feedback at scale is challenging

To address reward hacking, consider implementing a constrained optimization approach:

```
def constrained_ppo_step(
    base_model, reward_model, constraint_model,
    optimizer, prompt, constraint_threshold=0.5
):
    outputs = base_model.generate(prompt, max_length=100,
        return_dict_in_generate=True, output_scores=True
    )
    generated_text = tokenizer.decode(
        outputs.sequences[0], skip_special_tokens=True
    )

    reward = reward_model(generated_text)
    constraint_value = constraint_model(generated_text)

    if constraint_value > constraint_threshold:
        return base_model  # Skip update if constraint is violated

    # Compute and apply policy update (similar to previous ppo_step)
    # ...

    return base_model
```

This function adds a constraint check before updating the model, helping to prevent reward hacking by ensuring the generated text meets certain criteria.

This method modifies the standard training flow by evaluating a generated output not just for reward alignment but also for compliance with an external constraint model. The process begins with a response being generated from the base model using a given prompt. The resulting text is passed through both a reward model and a constraint model. The reward model assigns a scalar reward value based on its alignment with desired behaviors or objectives. In parallel, the constraint model evaluates whether the output satisfies specified limitations, such as avoiding harmful content, staying within factual bounds, or respecting legal or ethical filters.

The constraint model returns a scalar value that quantifies the degree of constraint violation. This value is compared against a predefined threshold. If the value exceeds the threshold, indicating that the output violates the constraint, the training step is aborted for this sample. No gradient is calculated, and the model parameters remain unchanged. This selective update mechanism ensures that only outputs that both align with human preferences and satisfy safety or policy constraints contribute to learning. This design decouples the constraint signal from the reward function, maintaining clear boundaries between learning objectives and constraint enforcement. As a result, it preserves the integrity of both components and makes the system more interpretable and modular.

Applications of RLHF

RLHF can be applied to various LLM tasks, including the following:

- Open-ended text generation
- Dialogue systems
- Content moderation
- Summarization
- Code generation

Here's an example of applying RLHF to a summarization task:

```
def rlhf_summarization(
    base_model, reward_model, text, num_iterations=5
):
    prompt = f"Summarize the following text:\n{text}\n\nSummary:"

    for _ in range(num_iterations):
        summary = base_model.generate(prompt, max_length=100)
        reward = reward_model(summary)

        # Update base_model using PPO or another RL algorithm
        # ...

    return summary

# Example usage
long_text = "..."  # Long text to summarize
summary = rlhf_summarization(base_model, reward_model, long_text)
print(summary)
```

This function applies RLHF to the task of text summarization, iteratively improving the summary based on rewards from the reward model.

The key steps involve generating a summary using a base model, receiving feedback from a reward model, and updating the base model iteratively to improve the summarization over time.

Here's a breakdown of how summarization works in this code:

1. **Prompt construction**: The function takes text as input and creates a prompt that asks the model to summarize that text. This is done by formatting the input text into a string that includes a directive to summarize the content. An example of such a prompt is `Summarize the following text:\n{text}\n\nSummary:`. This prompt is sent to the base model so that a summary can be generated.

2. **Base model summary generation**: The `base_model.generate` function is used to generate a summary from the prompt. The generated summary is limited to a maximum length of 100 tokens (`max_length=100`). The summary is based on the input text and is the first attempt at summarization.

3. **Reward model feedback**: After the base model generates a summary, the reward model evaluates the quality of the summary. The reward model is a separate model that measures how well the generated summary aligns with desired qualities (such as being accurate, concise, or coherent). The reward function assigns a score to the summary, which reflects its quality based on the model's internal criteria.

4. **Iterative process**: This process of generating a summary and receiving feedback is repeated for `num_iterations` times (in this case, five times by default). Each iteration involves generating a new summary, receiving feedback from the reward model, and potentially updating the base model to improve the summary in future iterations.

5. **Model update (placeholder)**: The placeholder comment, `# Update base_model using PPO or another RL algorithm`, indicates that after each iteration, the base model should be updated using a reinforcement learning algorithm, such as PPO. This update will adjust the parameters of the base model to generate better summaries based on feedback from the reward model. However, the actual code for model updating isn't provided here and would typically involve reinforcement learning techniques to fine-tune the base model based on the rewards it receives.

6. **Final output**: After completing the specified number of iterations, the function returns the final summary generated by the base model. This summary is expected to be the result of multiple improvements made based on the feedback that's received from the reward model during the iterative process.

Summary

RLHF is a powerful technique used by many frontier model providers, such as OpenAI and Anthropic, in fine-tuning pre-trained models. This chapter discussed some basic ideas behind this pattern. RLHF still has its limitations since humans are involved in the process of training a reward model, and as such, it doesn't scale well. Recently, some more generic reinforcement learning without human feedback has been tested by companies such as DeepSeek. However, this is beyond the scope of this book. You can refer to the following research paper by DeepSeek for more information: `https://arxiv.org/pdf/2501.12948`.

As we move forward, we'll explore advanced prompt engineering techniques for LLMs. In the next chapter, we'll delve into sophisticated methods for guiding LLM behavior and outputs through carefully crafted prompts, building on the alignment techniques we've discussed here. These advanced prompting strategies will enable you to leverage the full potential of your LLMs while maintaining fine-grained control over their outputs.

Get This Book's PDF Version and Exclusive Extras

UNLOCK NOW

Scan the QR code (or go to `packtpub.com/unlock`). Search for this book by name, confirm the edition, and then follow the steps on the page.

Note: Keep your invoice handly. Purchase made directly from packt don't require one.

Part 4:
Advanced Prompt
Engineering Techniques

In this part, we explore advanced techniques that enhance the capabilities of LLMs through innovative prompting strategies and reasoning methods. You will learn how to use chain-of-thought and tree-of-thoughts prompting to guide models through complex reasoning processes. We also cover techniques for reasoning without direct observation, enabling LLMs to tackle hypothetical scenarios and abstract problems. Reflection techniques will show you how to prompt LLMs for iterative self-improvement, while methods for automatic multi-step reasoning and tool use will teach you how to extend LLMs into sophisticated, multi-functional systems. By mastering these advanced approaches, you will gain the ability to unlock the full potential of LLMs, allowing them to address even the most challenging problems.

This part has the following chapters:

- *Chapter 20, Chain-of-Thought Prompting*
- *Chapter 21, Tree-of-Thoughts Prompting*
- *Chapter 22, Reasoning and Acting*
- *Chapter 23, Reasoning WithOut Observation*
- *Chapter 24, Reflection Techniques*
- *Chapter 25, Automatic Multi-Step Reasoning and Tool Use*

20
Chain-of-Thought Prompting

Chain-of-thought (CoT) prompting originated from a research paper titled *Chain-of-Thought Prompting Elicits Reasoning in Large Language Models*, published by Google researchers Jason Wei, Xuezhi Wang, Dale Schuurmans, Maarten Bosma, Brian Ichter, Fei Xia, Ed Chi, Quoc Le, and Denny Zhou in 2022.

The key innovation of CoT prompting was encouraging language models to break down complex reasoning problems into intermediate steps before arriving at a final answer. This was done by including demonstrations where the model is shown examples of step-by-step reasoning.

The researchers demonstrated that by prompting LLMs with a few examples of reasoning chains (such as "Let's think step by step"), the models could significantly improve their performance on complex tasks requiring multi-step reasoning, such as arithmetic, commonsense, and symbolic reasoning problems.

Before CoT, most prompting techniques focused on getting direct answers. CoT showed that explicitly encouraging models to demonstrate their reasoning process led to more accurate results, especially for problems requiring several logical steps. CoT is beneficial in promoting transparency and ensuring accuracy by guiding the model through logical steps, whereas direct answering, while quicker, can miss intermediate steps that could clarify or validate the reasoning behind the answer.

This research was particularly significant because it showed that reasoning abilities could emerge primarily through scale and prompting rather than requiring architectural changes to the models.

In this chapter, you'll learn to leverage CoT prompting to improve your LLM's performance on complex reasoning tasks.

In this chapter, we'll be covering the following topics:

- Designing effective CoT prompts
- Using CoT prompting for problem solving
- Combining CoT prompting with other techniques
- Evaluating CoT prompting outputs
- Limitations of CoT prompting
- Future directions

Designing effective CoT prompts

The process of creating effective CoT prompts helps in fostering clarity, logical progression, and structured reasoning, which in turn ensures more accurate and coherent outputs. By providing a well-defined problem statement, breaking the task into smaller steps, using explicit markers to guide the reasoning, and including a sample CoT response, the model is better equipped to follow a systematic approach that aligns with human problem-solving methods, leading to clear and rational conclusions:

1. **Provide a clear problem statement**: A precise problem statement directs the reasoning toward a specific goal, eliminating ambiguity and ensuring that the model understands exactly what is being asked. This helps prevent misinterpretations and guides the entire reasoning process in the right direction.

2. **Break down the problem into logical steps**: Dividing a complex task into smaller, manageable steps helps in organizing the reasoning and makes the overall problem easier to tackle. This breakdown aids in focusing on one aspect at a time, promoting clarity and reducing the risk of missing important details.

3. **Use explicit reasoning markers**: Markers such as "First," "Next," and "Finally" act as signposts for the logical flow of the reasoning process. They help structure the thought process in a clear sequence, ensuring that each part of the problem is addressed in the right order, which increases the overall coherence of the response.

4. **Include a sample CoT response in the prompt**: Providing an example helps establish a standard for the reasoning format and sets clear expectations for the process. It also serves as a reference point, guiding the model in how to structure its response and making it easier to generate consistent and logically sound outputs.

Here's an example of implementing a CoT prompt:

```
def cot_prompt(question):
    return f"""Solve the following problem step by step:

Problem: {question}
```

```
Let's approach this step by step:
1) First, we need to...
2) Next, we should...
3) Then, we can...
4) Finally, we...

Therefore, the answer is...

Now, solve this new problem using the same step-by-step approach:

Problem: If a train travels 120 km in 2 hours, what is its average
speed in km/h?

Let's solve this step by step:
"""

# Example usage
problem = "If a train travels 120 km in 2 hours, what is its average
speed in km/h?"
prompt = cot_prompt(problem)
print(prompt)
```

This function generates a CoT prompt for a given problem (If a train travels 120 km in 2 hours, what is its average speed in km/h?), providing a structure for step-by-step reasoning. Here are the sample steps using CoT:

```
Solve the following problem step by step:
Problem: If a train travels 120 km in 2 hours, what is its average
speed in km/h?
Let's approach this step by step:
1) First, we need to recall the formula for average speed, which is:
   Average Speed = Total Distance / Total Time.
2) Next, we should identify the total distance traveled, which is 120
km.
3) Then, we can identify the total time taken, which is 2 hours.
4) Now, we will apply the formula:
   Average Speed = 120 km / 2 hours.
5) Finally, we calculate the result:
   Average Speed = 60 km/h.
```

Therefore, the answer is 60 km/h.

CoT prompting can be applied to various problem-solving scenarios. Let's see one such scenario next.

Using CoT prompting for problem solving

Let's implement a function that uses CoT for mathematical word problems:

```python
from transformers import AutoModelForCausalLM, AutoTokenizer

def solve_math_problem(model, tokenizer, problem):
    prompt = cot_prompt(problem)
    inputs = tokenizer(prompt, return_tensors="pt")
    outputs = model.generate(
        inputs, max_length=500, num_return_sequences=1
    )
    solution = tokenizer.decode(
        outputs[0], skip_special_tokens=True
    )
    return solution

# Example usage
model_name = "gpt2-large"  # Replace with your preferred model
model = AutoModelForCausalLM.from_pretrained(model_name)
tokenizer = AutoTokenizer.from_pretrained(model_name)

problem = "If a recipe calls for 2 cups of flour for 8 servings, how
many cups of flour are needed for 12 servings?"
solution = solve_math_problem(model, tokenizer, problem)
print(solution)
```

This function applies CoT prompting to solve a mathematical word problem (for example, `If a recipe calls for 2 cups of flour for 8 servings, how many cups of flour are needed for 12 servings?`), guiding the LLM through a step-by-step reasoning process.

In addition to using CoT prompting for problem solving, we can also combine it with other techniques to improve LLM performance.

Combining CoT prompting with other techniques

CoT can be combined with other prompting techniques to further enhance LLM performance. Let's implement a function that combines CoT with **few-shot learning** (**FSL**):

```python
def few_shot_cot_prompt(question, examples):
    prompt = "Solve the following problems step by step:\n\n"
    for example in examples:
        prompt += f"Problem: {example['question']}\n\n"
        prompt += f"Solution: {example['solution']}\n\n"
```

```
    prompt += f"Problem: {question}\n\nSolution:"
    return prompt

def solve_with_few_shot_cot(model, tokenizer, problem, examples):
    prompt = few_shot_cot_prompt(problem, examples)
    inputs = tokenizer(prompt, return_tensors="pt")

    outputs = model.generate(inputs, max_length=500,
        num_return_sequences=1)
    solution = tokenizer.decode(outputs[0], skip_special_tokens=True)

    return solution

# Example usage
examples = [
    {
        "question": "If a car travels 60 miles in 2 hours, what is its
average speed?",
        "solution": "1) First, we identify the given
information:\n    - Distance traveled = 60 miles\n    - Time taken =
2 hours\n\n2) We know that average speed is calculated by dividing
distance by time:\n    Average Speed = Distance / Time\n\n3) Let's plug
in the values:\n    Average Speed = 60 miles / 2 hours\n\n4) Perform
the division:\n    Average Speed = 30 miles per hour\n\nTherefore, the
car's average speed is 30 miles per hour."
    }
]

problem = "If a train travels 180 km in 3 hours, what is its average
speed in km/h?"
solution = solve_with_few_shot_cot(model, tokenizer, problem,
    examples)
print(solution)
```

This function combines FSL with CoT prompting, providing examples of step-by-step solutions to guide the LLM in solving a new problem (see the code example for If a train travels 180 km in 3 hours, what is its average speed in km/h?). Combining methods such as CoT + FSL has been shown to improve performance in recent benchmarks (https://aclanthology.org/2023.emnlp-main.782.pdf).

Next, let's see how we can evaluate the quality of CoT prompts.

Evaluating CoT prompting outputs

Evaluating the outputs of CoT prompts involves assessing both the final answer and the reasoning process. Let's implement a simple evaluation function:

```python
def evaluate_cot_output(output, correct_answer):
    # Extract the final answer from the CoT output
    final_answer = extract_final_answer(output)

    # Check if the final answer is correct
    answer_correct = final_answer == correct_answer

    # Evaluate the reasoning steps
    reasoning_score = evaluate_reasoning_steps(output)

    return {
        "answer_correct": answer_correct,
        "reasoning_score": reasoning_score
    }

def extract_final_answer(output):
    # Implement logic to extract the final answer from the CoT output
    # This could involve parsing the last line or looking for specific
phrases
    pass

def evaluate_reasoning_steps(output):
    # Implement logic to evaluate the quality of the reasoning steps
    # This could involve checking for logical consistency,
completeness, etc.
    pass

# Example usage
problem = "If a train travels 180 km in 3 hours, what is its average
speed in km/h?"
correct_answer = 60
cot_output = solve_math_problem(model, tokenizer, problem)
evaluation = evaluate_cot_output(cot_output, correct_answer)
print(evaluation)
```

This evaluation function assesses both the correctness of the final answer and the quality of the reasoning steps in the CoT output.

Limitations of CoT prompting

While CoT prompting is powerful, it has some limitations:

- High token usage and computation time

- Potential for error propagation in multi-step reasoning

- Dependence on the quality of the initial prompt

- May not be suitable for all types of problems

To address some of these limitations, consider implementing a dynamic CoT approach:

```python
def dynamic_cot(model, tokenizer, problem, max_steps=5):
    prompt = f"Problem: {problem}\n\nLet's solve this step by step:"
    for step in range(1, max_steps + 1):
        prompt += f"\n\nStep {step}:"
        inputs = tokenizer(prompt, return_tensors="pt")
        outputs = model.generate(
            inputs, max_length=len(prompt) + 100,
            num_return_sequences=1
        )
        new_step = tokenizer.decode(
            outputs[0][len(inputs['input_ids'][0]):],
            skip_special_tokens=True
        )
        prompt += new_step

        if "Therefore, the final answer is" in new_step:
            break

    return prompt

# Example usage
problem = "If a recipe calls for 2 cups of flour for 8 servings, how
many cups of flour are needed for 12 servings?"
solution = dynamic_cot(model, tokenizer, problem)
print(solution)
```

The `dynamic_cot` function implements a dynamic CoT approach to break down and solve a problem step by step using a language model. It starts by creating an initial prompt that introduces the problem and instructs the model to solve it incrementally. The function then enters a loop, iterating up to `max_steps` times (default is 5), where in each iteration, it feeds the model a growing prompt that includes all the steps generated so far. The model processes this prompt, generates the next step in the reasoning process, and appends it to the prompt. The new step is decoded from tokenized outputs and added to the prompt string. The function checks for the phrase `Therefore, the final answer is` in the generated step, signaling that the model has reached a conclusion and should stop. If this phrase is found, the loop breaks early; otherwise, it continues until the maximum steps are reached. Finally, the function returns the complete prompt, which includes all the reasoning steps leading to the solution. However, in real-world use, token limitations of the model may impact long multi-step prompts. As the prompt grows with each new step, it might exceed the model's maximum token limit, which could result in truncated inputs, loss of earlier context, or failure to generate accurate steps, especially in complex or lengthy problems. This is a significant consideration when dealing with problems requiring many steps or substantial context.

Future directions

As CoT prompting continues to evolve, several promising directions emerge:

- **Adaptive CoT**: Dynamically adjusting the reasoning process based on problem complexity

- **Multi-modal CoT**: Incorporating visual or auditory information in the reasoning process (https://arxiv.org/abs/2302.00923)

- **Collaborative CoT**: Combining insights from multiple LLMs or human-AI collaboration (https://arxiv.org/html/2409.07355v1)

- **Meta-learning for CoT**: Meta-learning and CoT approaches have emerged as powerful techniques for addressing the challenges of few-shot relation extraction (https://arxiv.org/abs/2311.05922)

Here's a conceptual implementation of adaptive CoT:

```
def adaptive_cot(
    model, tokenizer, problem, complexity_threshold=0.7
):
    # Assess problem complexity
    complexity = assess_problem_complexity(problem)

    if complexity > complexity_threshold:
        # Use detailed CoT for complex problems
        return detailed_cot(model, tokenizer, problem)
```

```
    else:
        # Use simple direct approach for simpler problems
        return simple_solve(model, tokenizer, problem)

def assess_problem_complexity(problem):
    # Implement logic to assess problem complexity
    # This could involve keyword analysis, sentence structure, etc.
    pass

def detailed_cot(model, tokenizer, problem):
    # Implement detailed Chain-of-Thought approach
    pass

def simple_solve(model, tokenizer, problem):
    # Implement simple direct solving approach
    pass

# Example usage
problem = "What is the result of 25 divided by 5?"
solution = adaptive_cot(model, tokenizer, problem)
print(solution)
```

This adaptive CoT approach assesses problem complexity and chooses an appropriate solving strategy, balancing efficiency and reasoning depth.

The `adaptive_cot` function adapts the CoT approach based on the complexity of the problem. It first assesses the problem's complexity by calling the `assess_problem_complexity` function, which could involve analyzing keywords, sentence structure, or other features to determine how complex the problem is (though the logic for this is yet to be implemented). If the complexity score exceeds a predefined threshold (`complexity_threshold`), the function uses a detailed CoT approach via the `detailed_cot` function, which would generate a more elaborate, step-by-step solution. For simpler problems, it uses a straightforward solving method via the `simple_solve` function, which provides a direct answer without breaking down the problem into multiple steps. The result is returned based on which approach is deemed appropriate for the given problem. This dynamic approach allows the model to choose the most efficient method of solving a problem based on its complexity.

Summary

In this chapter, you learned how to design effective CoT prompts that guide LLMs through step-by-step reasoning processes. We covered applications of this technique in various problem-solving scenarios and discussed how to combine it with other prompting strategies. You also learned how to evaluate the quality of CoT outputs and understood the limitations of this approach.

By implementing the strategies and considerations discussed in this chapter, you can significantly improve your LLM's performance on complex problem-solving tasks, while also gaining insights into the model's reasoning process.

In the next chapter, we will investigate **tree-of-thoughts** (**ToT**) prompting, an advanced technique that extends the concepts of CoT to create even more sophisticated reasoning structures.

Subscribe for a free eBook

New frameworks, evolving architectures, research drops, production breakdowns—AI_Distilled filters the noise into a weekly briefing for engineers and researchers working hands-on with LLMs and GenAI systems. Subscribe now and receive a free eBook, along with weekly insights that help you stay focused and informed. Subscribe at `https://packt.link/8Oz6Y` or scan the QR code below.

21

Tree-of-Thoughts Prompting

Tree-of-thoughts (ToT) prompting is a technique that was developed to enhance the problem-solving capabilities of LLMs by enabling more structured exploration of different reasoning paths.

The formal ToT approach was introduced in a 2023 research paper titled *Tree of Thoughts: Deliberate Problem Solving with Large Language Models* by Yao et al. (researchers from Princeton University, Google DeepMind, and Google Research). Also visit `https://arxiv.org/abs/2305.10601`.

The primary inspiration for ToT came from how humans approach complex problems—we often consider multiple possible solution paths, evaluate their promise, backtrack when necessary, and explore alternatives. Traditional prompting techniques such as CoT (see *Chapter 20*) allowed step-by-step reasoning but lacked the ability to explore multiple paths or reconsider earlier steps.

ToT builds on several techniques:

- CoT prompting, which enables step-by-step reasoning
- Self-consistency methods that generate multiple reasoning paths
- Human problem-solving approaches that involve exploration and backtracking

The key innovation of ToT is treating thinking as a tree search problem, where at each step, the model can generate and evaluate multiple "thoughts" (intermediate reasoning steps) and then select the most promising paths to continue exploring. This allows for more sophisticated problem-solving that includes exploration, evaluation, and backtracking capabilities.

In this chapter, you'll learn how to implement ToT prompting to tackle complex reasoning tasks with your LLMs.

In this chapter, we'll be covering the following topics:

- Designing ToT prompts

- Search strategies

- Pruning and evaluation

- Applying ToT to solve a multi-step problem

- Challenges in implementation

- Future directions

Designing ToT prompts

To create effective ToT prompts, you should do the following:

1. **Encourage branching thoughts**: This creates a non-linear exploration process where multiple possible solution paths can be considered simultaneously. By explicitly asking the model to generate several different initial approaches or perspectives, you prevent it from committing too early to a single line of reasoning that might lead to suboptimal results.

2. **Provide a clear problem statement**: A well-defined problem statement gives the model a concrete goal and constraints to work within. This clarity helps the model understand exactly what it needs to solve and provides the foundation for generating relevant thought branches. Without this, the branching process could become unfocused and inefficient.

3. **Guide the model to explore alternative paths**: This ensures the model doesn't prematurely converge on an apparently promising but ultimately suboptimal solution. By explicitly requesting the exploration of different approaches, you help the model overcome potential bias in its reasoning and discover novel solutions it might otherwise miss.

4. **Include evaluation mechanisms**: This component enables the model to assess the quality of different branches and make informed decisions about which paths to pursue further. Without evaluation criteria, the model would have no systematic way to determine which branches are most promising, potentially wasting computational resources on unpromising paths.

ToT is particularly powerful for complex reasoning tasks because it mimics human problem-solving approaches where we often mentally explore multiple possibilities before committing to a solution. The explicit branching and evaluation structure helps language models overcome limitations in their sequential reasoning abilities.

Here's an example of implementing a basic ToT prompt:

```
def tot_prompt(question, num_branches=3):
    prompt = f"""Solve the following problem using a Tree-of-Thoughts
approach:

Problem: {question}

Let's explore multiple reasoning paths:

Path 1:
1) First, we could...
2) Then, we might...
3) This leads us to...

Path 2:
1) Alternatively, we could start by...
2) Following this approach...
3) This results in...

Path 3:
1) Another perspective is...
2) If we consider this...
3) The outcome would be...

Now, let's evaluate these paths and determine the most promising
solution:

Evaluation:
1) Path 1: ...
2) Path 2: ...
3) Path 3: ...

Based on this evaluation, the most promising solution is...

Therefore, the final answer is...

Now, apply this Tree-of-Thoughts approach to solve the given problem:

{question}

Let's explore multiple reasoning paths:
"""
```

```
    return prompt

Let's look at an example usage:

problem = "What is the most efficient way to sort a list of a million
integers?"
prompt = tot_prompt(problem)
print(prompt)
```

This function generates a ToT prompt for a given problem (`"What is the most efficient way to sort a list of a million integers?"`), providing a structure for exploring and evaluating multiple reasoning paths.

This code creates a ToT prompt template by implementing four key principles: it encourages branching thoughts through explicit path structures with different starting phrases and numbered steps, ensuring the model explores multiple distinct solution approaches; it provides clarity by framing the problem twice to establish context and refocus attention before solution generation; it guides exploration of alternative approaches through contrasting language and separate reasoning paths; and it facilitates evaluation through a dedicated comparison section with prompts for selecting the most promising solution. The overall structure creates a cognitive scaffold that helps language models overcome linear thinking tendencies by forcing them to generate, develop, and critically compare multiple solution paths before reaching a conclusion—mimicking how humans tackle complex problems through divergent thinking followed by critical evaluation.

Implementing effective search strategies is crucial for navigating the ToT. Let's check out two of them in the following section.

Search strategies

We have two commonly used search strategies:

- **Depth-first search (DFS)**: This is a graph traversal algorithm that explores as far as possible along each branch before backtracking. In the context of a tree of thoughts, DFS systematically dives deep into one path, exploring each thought or branch completely before moving to the next. It works by starting at the root, pushing each node's children onto a stack, and then recursively exploring the deepest node first. This approach is particularly useful when you want to fully explore a line of reasoning or investigate the most profound or complex thoughts before branching out, making it valuable for problem-solving, decision-making, and understanding complex conceptual landscapes.

- **Breadth-first search (BFS):** In contrast to DFS, BFS explores the tree of thoughts by systematically examining all neighboring nodes at the present depth before moving to nodes at the next depth level. Using a queue data structure, BFS starts at the root and explores all immediate connections before going deeper. In the context of thought exploration, BFS is particularly effective when you want to get a broad, panoramic view of different ideas and their immediate interconnections. This strategy is ideal for understanding the width and diversity of thoughts, finding the shortest path between concepts, or when you need to explore multiple potential reasoning paths simultaneously before diving deep into any single branch (see *Figure 21.1*).

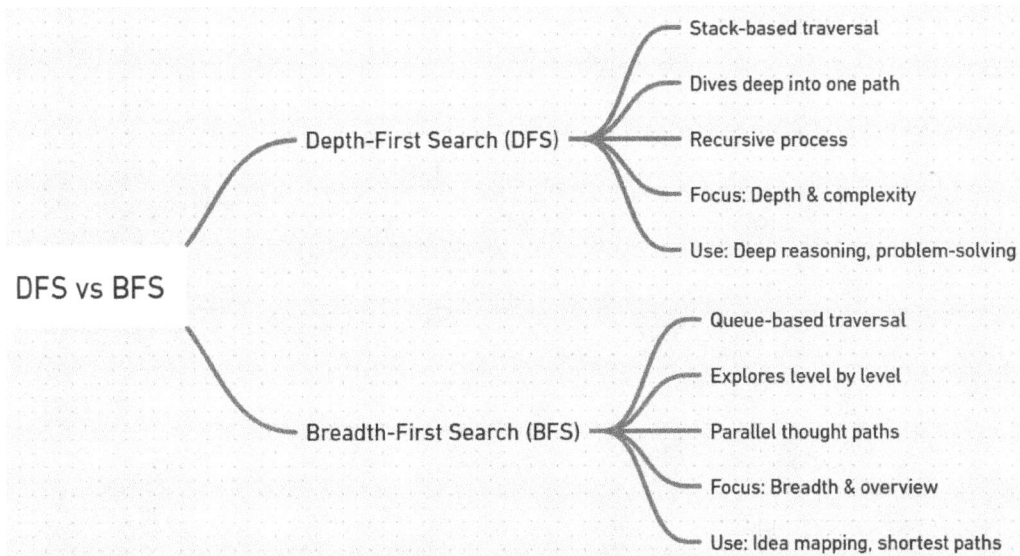

Figure 21.1 – DFS versus BFS

As an example, let's implement a simple DFS strategy:

```
from transformers import AutoModelForCausalLM, AutoTokenizer

def dfs_tot(model, tokenizer, problem, max_depth=3, max_branches=2):
    def explore_branch(current_thought, depth):
        if depth == max_depth:
            return current_thought

        prompt = f"{current_thought}\n\nLet's explore further:\n"
        inputs = tokenizer(prompt, return_tensors="pt")
        outputs = model.generate(
            inputs, max_length=len(prompt) + 100,
            num_return_sequences=max_branches
```

```
            )

        branches = [
            tokenizer.decode(
                output[len(inputs['input_ids'][0]):],
                skip_special_tokens=True
            ) for output in outputs
        ]

        results = []
        for branch in branches:
            results.append(
                explore_branch(
                    current_thought + branch, depth + 1
                )
            )

        return max(
            results, key=lambda x: evaluate_thought(x)
        )  # Select the best branch

    initial_prompt = tot_prompt(problem)
    return explore_branch(initial_prompt, 0)

def evaluate_thought(thought):
    # Implement logic to evaluate the quality of a thought
    # This could involve coherence, relevance, depth of reasoning,
etc.
    pass
```

This code implements a DFS algorithm to explore a ToT generated by a language model. It starts with an initial problem and then uses the model to generate multiple potential continuations (branches). The code recursively explores each branch, extending the "thought" until it reaches a maximum depth. At each step, generated text is turned into model inputs, and the model outputs are decoded back into text.

The evaluate_thought function, which is a key part of the selection process, is intended to score the quality of each generated thought. The code utilizes this scoring to decide which branches to explore further, effectively navigating the ToT toward a potentially optimal solution. The final result is the highest-scoring thought found during the DFS.

Here's an example usage of the preceding code snippet:

```
model_name = "gpt2-large"  # Replace with your preferred model
model = AutoModelForCausalLM.from_pretrained(model_name)
tokenizer = AutoTokenizer.from_pretrained(model_name)

problem = "What are the potential long-term effects of artificial
intelligence on employment?"
solution = dfs_tot(model, tokenizer, problem)
print(solution)
```

This code snippet demonstrates how to use a pre-trained GPT-2 LLM to generate a solution to a given problem using the previously described `dfs_tot` function. First, it specifies the model to be used (`"gpt2-large"`) and loads both the model and its associated tokenizer using `AutoModelForCausalLM` and `AutoTokenizer` from the `transformers` library. This ensures the text is correctly processed for the model.

Then, it defines the problem as a question about the long-term effects of AI on employment. The `dfs_tot` function is called with the loaded model, tokenizer, and the problem as input, initiating the depth-first search for a solution. The returned `solution`, which represents the model's generated response after exploring various "thoughts", is finally printed to the console.

Next, we will discuss pruning and evaluation within the ToT framework to improve efficiency and focus the search. Pruning is essential for managing the computational cost associated with exploring numerous thought branches, while evaluation provides the criteria for deciding which branches to discard.

Pruning and evaluation

Pruning in the ToT approach is an effective mechanism for managing cognitive complexity by systematically reducing the search space. The process involves selectively eliminating less promising thought branches through intelligent evaluation techniques, using heuristic scoring methods that assess each potential path's likelihood of leading to an optimal solution. By dynamically filtering out low-potential thoughts and focusing computational resources on the most promising reasoning trajectories, ToT pruning enables more efficient and targeted problem solving, balancing exploration breadth with reasoning depth.

1. Let's implement a basic pruning strategy by defining a simple pruning function:

    ```
    def pruning_tot(
        model, tokenizer, problem, max_depth=3,
        max_branches=3, prune_threshold=0.5
    ):
        def explore_and_prune(current_thought, depth):
            if depth == max_depth:
    ```

```
        return current_thought

    prompt = f"{current_thought}\n\nLet's explore
further:\n"
    inputs = tokenizer(prompt, return_tensors="pt")
    outputs = model.generate(
        inputs, max_length=len(prompt) + 100,
        num_return_sequences=max_branches
    )

    branches = [
        tokenizer.decode(
            output[len(inputs['input_ids'][0]):],
            skip_special_tokens=True
        ) for output in outputs
    ]
```

The core of the logic is in the `explore_and_prune` function, which handles the recursive search through the reasoning tree. The code works by generating multiple possible continuations (branches) from the current thought using LLM. The function is designed to explore the reasoning tree up to a specified maximum depth, with each level containing a controlled number of branches. When the maximum depth is reached, the code returns the current thought as the final result. The pruning mechanism is illustrative and should not be used for production.

2. Once we've defined our function, we evaluate and prune branches:

```
    evaluated_branches = [
        (branch, evaluate_thought(current_thought + branch))
        for branch in branches
    ]
    pruned_branches = [
        b for b, score in evaluated_branches
        if score > prune_threshold
    ]

    if not pruned_branches:
        return current_thought   # If all branches are
pruned, return current thought

    results = []
    for branch in pruned_branches:
        results.append(
            explore_and_prune(current_thought + branch,
                depth + 1)
```

```
            )

        return max(results, key=lambda x: evaluate_thought(x))

    initial_prompt = tot_prompt(problem)
    return explore_and_prune(initial_prompt, 0)
```

First, the code evaluates each generated branch by pairing it with a score from the `evaluate_thought` function, which assesses the quality of the reasoning path. It then filters out low-quality branches by keeping only those scoring above the defined threshold. If all branches are pruned (none meet the threshold), the algorithm returns the current thought without further exploration. For the remaining promising branches, the code recursively explores each one by calling the same function at an increased depth level. Finally, it selects the best overall reasoning path by returning the result with the highest evaluation score from all explored paths. The outer function initializes the search with a formatted prompt containing the original problem statement.

3. Define an `evaluate_thought` function. This function evaluates a given thought or branch of reasoning by scoring it based on its complexity (length) and linguistic diversity (the number of unique words used), returning a normalized score between 0 and 1:

```
def evaluate_thought(branch, threshold=0.5):
    """
    Simple evaluation function for ToT branch assessment

    Args:
        branch (str): The branch/thought to evaluate
        threshold (float): Minimum score for considering a
branch viable

    Returns:
        float: Evaluation score
    """
    # Basic heuristics for evaluation
    complexity_score = len(branch.split()) / 20  # Reward
moderate complexity
    uniqueness_score = len(
        set(branch.split())) / len(branch.split()
    )  # Reward unique words

    # Combined score, normalized
    score = (complexity_score + uniqueness_score) / 2

    return min(1.0, max(0.0, score))
```

4. Let's look at an example:

```
problem = "What are the ethical implications of genetic
engineering in humans?"
solution = pruning_tot(model, tokenizer, problem)
print(solution)
```

This implementation adds a pruning step to remove low-quality branches, focusing the search on the most promising paths.

Now, let's apply ToT to solve a multi-step problem.

Applying ToT to solve a multi-step problem

ToT can be particularly effective for complex reasoning tasks. Let's implement a ToT approach for multi-step problem solving:

```
def multi_step_tot(model, tokenizer, problem_steps):
    full_solution = ""
    for step, question in enumerate(problem_steps):
        prompt = f"""Step {step + 1} of the problem:
{question}

Previous steps solution:
{full_solution}

Let's use Tree-of-Thoughts to solve this step:
"""
        step_solution = pruning_tot(model, tokenizer, prompt)
        full_solution += (
            f"\n\nStep {step + 1} Solution:\n"
            f"{step_solution}"
        )

    return full_solution

# Example usage
problem_steps = [
    "What are the main factors contributing to climate change?",
    "How do these factors interact with each other?",
    "What are potential solutions to mitigate climate change?",
    "What are the challenges in implementing these solutions?"
]
```

```
solution = multi_step_tot(model, tokenizer, problem_steps)
print(solution)
```

This code implements a multi-step problem solver using the ToT reasoning approach. The `multi_step_tot` function breaks down complex problems into sequential steps and solves them one at a time, building upon previous solutions.

For each step in the provided problem sequence, the function creates a prompt that includes the current question, the accumulated solutions from previous steps, and instructions to use ToT reasoning. It then calls the previously defined `pruning_tot` function to generate a solution for that specific step. Each step's solution is appended to a growing `full_solution` string, creating a comprehensive answer that maintains continuity of thought across the entire problem. The example demonstrates how this approach could be applied to analyze climate change through a sequence of progressively deeper questions, from identifying causes to exploring implementation challenges of potential solutions.

Challenges in implementation

While powerful, ToT faces several challenges:

- **Computational complexity**: Exploring multiple paths can be computationally expensive
- **Evaluation difficulty**: Determining the quality of different thought paths can be challenging
- **Coherence across branches**: Ensuring consistency when combining insights from different branches
- **Prompt design complexity**: Creating effective ToT prompts requires careful consideration

To address the computational complexity, consider implementing a parallel processing approach. Parallel processing can improve the ToT reasoning approach by addressing its inherent computational bottlenecks. The following code implements concurrent exploration of multiple reasoning branches simultaneously rather than sequentially, which can dramatically reduce the total computation time for complex problems:

```
import concurrent.futures

def parallel_tot(model, tokenizer, problem, max_workers=3):
    def explore_branch(branch):
        return pruning_tot(model, tokenizer, branch)

    initial_branches = generate_initial_branches(problem, max_workers)

    with concurrent.futures.ThreadPoolExecutor(
        max_workers=max_workers
    ) as executor:
        futures = [
```

```
            executor.submit(explore_branch, branch)
            for branch in initial_branches
        ]
        results = [
            f.result()
            for f in concurrent.futures.as_completed(futures)
        ]

    return max(results, key=lambda x: evaluate_thought(x))

def generate_initial_branches(problem, num_branches):
    # Implement logic to generate initial branches for the problem
    pass

# Example usage
problem = "What are the potential implications of quantum computing on
cryptography?"
solution = parallel_tot(model, tokenizer, problem)
print(solution)
```

In the preceding code, the implementation uses Python's `concurrent.futures` module with a `ThreadPoolExecutor` to distribute the workload across multiple workers. Each worker independently explores a different initial branch of the reasoning tree, effectively searching multiple promising paths in parallel. This approach is particularly valuable for ToT reasoning since the branching nature of the algorithm creates numerous independent subproblems that can be solved concurrently without dependencies on each other's intermediate results. The final step consolidates these parallel explorations by selecting the highest-quality solution from all completed branches.

This implementation uses parallel processing to explore multiple branches simultaneously, potentially reducing computation time for complex ToT problems.

Future directions

As ToT continues to evolve, several promising directions emerge:

- **Dynamic tree structures**: Adapting the tree structure based on the problem complexity.
- **Hybrid ToT-CoT approaches**: Combining the strengths of both techniques (`https://arxiv.org/html/2409.17433v1`).
- **Meta-learning for ToT**: Training LLMs to generate effective ToT structures automatically. This approach has not been explored by anyone yet.
- **Incorporating external knowledge**: Integrating domain-specific knowledge into ToT reasoning (`https://arxiv.org/html/2407.00653v1`).

Here's a conceptual implementation of a dynamic ToT structure:

```python
def dynamic_tot(model, tokenizer, problem, max_depth=5):
    def adapt_structure(current_thought, depth):
        if depth == max_depth:
            return current_thought

        complexity = assess_complexity(current_thought)
        num_branches = determine_branches(complexity)

        branches = generate_branches(
            model, tokenizer, current_thought, num_branches
        )

        results = []
        for branch in branches:
            results.append(
                adapt_structure(
                    current_thought + branch, depth + 1
                )
            )

        return max(results, key=lambda x: evaluate_thought(x))

    def assess_complexity(thought):
        # Implement logic to assess the complexity of the current
thought
        pass

    def determine_branches(complexity):
        # Determine the number of branches based on complexity
        return max(2, min(5, int(complexity  10)))

    def generate_branches(model, tokenizer, thought, num_branches):
        # Generate branches using the model
        pass

    initial_prompt = tot_prompt(problem)
    return adapt_structure(initial_prompt, 0)
```

The preceding code implements a dynamic ToT approach that adapts its exploration strategy based on the complexity of the current reasoning path. The core function `adapt_structure` recursively builds a solution by examining the complexity of the current thought at each step and dynamically determining how many branches to explore. Unlike fixed branching strategies, this adaptive approach allocates more computational resources (more branches) to complex reasoning paths that might benefit from broader exploration, while using fewer branches for simpler concepts. The implementation includes helper functions to assess thought complexity, determine the appropriate number of branches, and generate new thought continuations using the language model. The algorithm terminates when reaching the maximum depth and returns the highest-scoring complete reasoning path.

Here's an example of how to use the preceding code to solve a problem such as "How might advancements in nanotechnology impact medicine in the next decade?":

```
problem = "How might advancements in nanotechnology impact medicine in
the next decade?"
solution = dynamic_tot(model, tokenizer, problem)
print(solution)
```

This dynamic ToT approach adapts the tree structure based on the assessed complexity of each thought, allowing the more flexible and efficient exploration of complex problem spaces.

Summary

In this chapter, you learned how to design and implement ToT prompts for LLMs, including strategies for managing the branching thought processes. We covered search techniques and methods for pruning and evaluating different reasoning paths. By implementing the strategies and considerations discussed here, you can significantly enhance your LLM's ability to handle ambiguous, multi-faceted problems and generate more robust and insightful solutions.

Revisiting *Chapter 20*, which focuses on CoT, let's compare CoT and ToT from a use case perspective. Use CoT prompting when the task involves linear, sequential reasoning that can be decomposed into intermediate steps with a single, dominant solution path. CoT is particularly effective in math word problems, deductive reasoning, basic logical puzzles, and step-by-step procedural tasks. It works well when the problem has low branching complexity and does not require exploration of multiple alternatives. CoT is computationally cheaper because it produces a single chain of reasoning in a forward, deterministic manner. This technique is most helpful when the LLM needs a scaffold to "think aloud" and make its intermediate steps explicit to prevent hallucinations or faulty leaps in logic.

Use ToT prompting when the task involves multi-step reasoning with branching decision points, especially where multiple solution paths are possible and need to be evaluated in parallel. ToT is suited for creative problem-solving, planning tasks, theorem proving, code synthesis, and decision-making under uncertainty. It becomes advantageous when the problem space can be structured as a search tree, where intermediate reasoning nodes can be revisited, evaluated, and compared. ToT often incorporates strategies such as self-consistency sampling, lookahead evaluation, and value-based selection among branches. It is computationally more intensive because it maintains and expands multiple reasoning paths in parallel, potentially involving rollouts, backtracking, or node scoring.

If the problem is constrained and well-formed (e.g., SAT-style questions or straightforward derivations), CoT is usually sufficient and more efficient. If the problem is open-ended, has multiple conflicting goals, or if optimal solutions require comparing alternative paths (as in planning routes, game moves, or formal proofs), ToT yields better performance by simulating exploration and deliberation.

In practice, CoT can serve as a base technique, while ToT builds on it by orchestrating multiple chains. For example, ToT nodes may each use CoT internally to generate coherent thoughts. Therefore, the two are not mutually exclusive but hierarchically related in terms of complexity and structure.

In the upcoming chapter, we will explore the **Reasoning and Acting** (**ReAct**) pattern, which is commonly used in many agentic AI applications.

22

Reasoning and Acting

Reasoning and Acting (**ReAct**) is a prompting technique developed by researchers from Princeton University and Google that enhances an LLM's ability to perform reasoning and acting in simulated environments (`https://arxiv.org/pdf/2210.03629`). It allows LLMs to mimic human-like operations in the real world, where we reason verbally and take actions to gain information. ReAct combines *reasoning* and *acting* to solve complex language reasoning and decision-making tasks.

While CoT prompting enables LLMs to generate reasoning traces, its lack of access to the external world can lead to issues such as fact hallucination. ReAct addresses this by allowing LLMs to generate both *verbal reasoning traces* and *text actions* for a task. These text actions enable the model to interact with its environment (for example, by querying an external knowledge source or using a tool), gather information, and adjust its reasoning accordingly.

The key characteristics of ReAct are as follows:

- **Reasoning traces**: LLMs generate text that explains their thought process step by step

- **Action generation**: LLMs produce text actions that represent interactions with external tools or environments

- **Observation incorporation**: The results of actions (observations) are fed back into the LLM's context, influencing subsequent reasoning and actions

- **Iterative process**: ReAct typically involves multiple *Thought/Action/Observation* steps, allowing for dynamic problem solving

ReAct excels in the following scenarios:

- When a task requires information beyond the LLM's pre-trained knowledge (for example, multi-hop question answering or fact verification)

- When an LLM needs to navigate and interact with a simulated environment (for example, online shopping or text-based games)

- When you need to combine the power of LLMs with the capabilities of external tools (for example, search engines, calculators, and APIs)
- When the task requires a problem to be broken down into smaller steps and decisions must be made based on intermediate results

In this chapter, we'll be covering the following topics:

- Implementing ReAct in LangChain
- Building ReAct agents with LangChain's Expression Language
- Completing tasks and solving problems
- Evaluating ReAct's performance
- Safety, control, and ethical considerations
- Limitations and future directions

Implementing ReAct in LangChain

The open source LLM framework LangChain (`https://www.langchain.com/`) provides a powerful and flexible implementation of the ReAct framework through its `Agent` class. Let's explore how to create and use ReAct agents in LangChain:

1. Install the necessary packages:

    ```
    # !pip install langchain openai duckduckgo-search youtube_search
    wikipedia langchainhub
    ```

    These packages enhance language model capabilities within the LangChain framework:

    - LangChain serves as a framework for developing applications powered by language models, enabling them to connect to external data sources and tools
    - OpenAI provides access to powerful language models through its API, forming the core of many LangChain applications
    - `duckduckgo-search` and `youtube_search` integrate search engine functionalities, allowing language models to retrieve real-time information from the web and YouTube, respectively
    - `wikipedia` enables language models to access and utilize information from Wikipedia, broadening their knowledge base
    - `langchainhub` is a central repository for sharing and discovering LangChain assets, such as prompts, chains, and agents

2. Initialize the language model and tools such as `wikipedia`, `ddg-search`, and `llm-math`. These are listed in the following code snippet:

```
import os
import getpass

os.environ["OPENAI_API_KEY"] = getpass.getpass("Enter Your
OpenAI API Key:")

from langchain.agents import load_tools
from langchain.chat_models import ChatOpenAI

# load the language model, you can use any model you like
llm = ChatOpenAI(model = "gpt-4o", temperature=0)

# load tools
tools = load_tools(['wikipedia', 'ddg-search','llm-math'],
    llm=llm)
```

Here, we import the necessary modules from `langchain`. Then, a language model (`ChatOpenAI`) is initialized with the specified model (`gpt-4-1106-preview` and `temperature`. Finally, we load some tools that our agent will use.

3. Initialize the ReAct agent. Here, the `initialize_agent` function creates and initializes an agent:

```
from langchain.agents import initialize_agent
from langchain.agents import AgentType

# initialize agent
agent = initialize_agent(
    tools,
    llm,
    agent=AgentType.ZERO_SHOT_REACT_ DESCRIPTION,
    verbose=True
)
```

In the preceding code, we list `tools` and `llm`, which refers to the language model, as well as specify the agent type as `AgentType.ZERO_SHOT_REACT_DESCRIPTION`. Here, `verbose=True` enables detailed logging of the agent's thought process.

4. Inspect the ReAct agent's prompt. The following line prints the prompt template used by the ReAct agent. This prompt provides instructions to the LLM on how to use the available tools and follow the ReAct format (*Thought*, *Action*, *Action Input*, and *Observation*):

```
print(agent.agent.llm_chain.prompt.template)
```

Inspecting the ReAct agent's prompt is important because it reveals the structure and logic that guide the behavior of the language model during tool-augmented reasoning and action. By printing the prompt template with `print(agent.agent.llm_chain.prompt.template)`, you're not just seeing arbitrary instructions – you're inspecting the behavioral scaffold that governs how the agent sequences its reasoning and tool use. This includes how it interprets a user query, chooses a tool from its available action set, constructs the input to the tool, and integrates the tool's output (Observation) into further reasoning. If the prompt is poorly constructed, the model may misinterpret the tools, take invalid actions, or fail to chain thoughts coherently. Additionally, the template often includes few-shot examples that demonstrate how to alternate between the ReAct components properly. These examples act as implicit instructions for formatting and logic, helping the model generalize to unseen tasks. Inspecting them can reveal whether the agent was trained or instructed using general patterns or highly specific use cases. It also helps developers debug unexpected behavior or hallucinations since modifying the template directly influences the agent's action selection, reasoning fidelity, and overall alignment with the intended ReAct cycle.

5. The following code block demonstrates how to customize the prompt template. You can modify the instructions, examples, and formatting to better suit your specific use case:

```
prompt = """
You are an intelligent agent designed to solve complex queries
by breaking them down systematically and using available tools
strategically. Follow the ReAct (Reasoning and Acting) framework
to approach each task.

ReAct Principles:
1. Reasoning: Always start by carefully analyzing the question
and developing a clear, step-by-step thought process.
2. Tool Selection: Critically evaluate which tools will be most
effective for addressing the specific query.
3. Iterative Interaction: Be prepared to cycle between reasoning
and action multiple times, refining your approach as you gather
more information.
4. Comprehensive Understanding: Aim to not just find an answer,
but to truly comprehend the underlying context and nuances of
the question.
5. Transparent Decision-Making: Clearly articulate your
reasoning, actions, and thought process at each step.


Available Tools:
- Wikipedia: Retrieve factual information about people, places,
historical events, and general knowledge topics.
- Google Search: Fetch current information, recent events, and
up-to-date context.
- Calculator: Perform mathematical calculations and numerical
analysis.
```

```
Interaction Format:
Question: The specific query to be solved
Thought: Detailed reasoning about the approach, breaking down
the problem
Action: Selected tool (Wikipedia/Google Search/Calculator)
Action Input: Precise query for the selected tool
Observation: Results obtained from the tool
... (Repeat reasoning, action, and observation as needed)
Thought: Final synthesized understanding
Final Answer: Comprehensive and well-reasoned response to the
original question

Important Guidelines:
- Be methodical and explicit in your reasoning
- Use tools judiciously and avoid unnecessary actions
- Integrate information from multiple sources when appropriate
- Provide a clear, concise, and informative final answer

Begin!
Question: {input}
Thought:{agent_scratchpad}
"""
```

Here, `agent.agent.llm_chain.prompt.template = prompt` updates the agent's prompt with the custom template.

6. Next, you can modify the descriptions of the tools to provide more specific guidance to the LLM on when and how to use each tool:

```
tools[1].description = "A date retrieval tool that provides the
current date and time, useful for temporal queries, scheduling,
age calculations, or understanding time-sensitive contexts."

tools[2].description = "A powerful computational tool capable of
performing various mathematical operations, including arithmetic
calculations, algebraic computations, percentage calculations,
unit conversions, and advanced mathematical functions."
```

7. The following line executes the agent with a sample query. The agent will use the ReAct framework to perform reasoning, select tools, execute actions, and generate a final answer:

```
agent.run("What is the population of the largest city in Canada?
How many days would it take for that city's population to count
to 1 billion if each person counts one number per second without
breaks? Then, compare this time to the average lifespan of a
human in years, and explain which is longer.")
```

Next, we'll look at an example of using ReAct for document processing that leverages LangChain.

ReAct Document Store

LangChain also provides a `DocstoreExplorer` class for implementing ReAct logic with document stores such as Wikipedia. We'll demonstrate an example by using `DocstoreExplorer` with Wikipedia for document-based ReAct:

```python
from langchain import Wikipedia
from langchain.agents import initialize_agent, Tool
from langchain.agents import AgentType
from langchain.agents.react.base import DocstoreExplorer

docstore = DocstoreExplorer(Wikipedia())

search_tool = Tool(name="Search",
                   func=docstore.search,
                   description="Search for latest information about
any topic"
                   )

lookup_tool = Tool(name="Lookup",
                   func=docstore.lookup,
                   description="Lookup tool for get information from a
keyword"
                   )

tools = [search_tool, lookup_tool]

llm = OpenAI(temperature=0)

react = initialize_agent(tools,
                         llm,
                         agent=AgentType.REACT_DOCSTORE,
                         verbose=True)

question = "Who is the current governor of Texas and when was he born
?"
react.run(question)
```

This code sets up a LangChain agent designed to answer questions by interacting with Wikipedia. Here's a breakdown:

1. **Wikipedia access**: First, it initializes a connection to Wikipedia, allowing the agent to retrieve information from it.

2. **Tool creation**: Next, it defines two tools: `Search` and `Lookup`. The `Search` tool enables the agent to find relevant Wikipedia pages, whereas the `Lookup` tool lets it extract specific information from those pages.

3. **Agent initialization**: Then, it creates a ReAct agent. This agent is configured to use the previously defined tools and an OpenAI language model. In the preceding code, `AgentType.REACT_DOCSTORE` explicitly configures the agent for document store interactions – in this case, those for Wikipedia.

4. **Question execution**: Finally, it runs the agent with a question that requires accessing and processing information from Wikipedia. The agent will use the `Search` tool to find relevant pages and the `Lookup` tool to extract the answer.

Building ReAct agents with LangChain's Expression Language

LangChain Expression Language (**LCEL**) offers a declarative approach to constructing ReAct agents. Instead of manually orchestrating the steps, LCEL allows you to define a processing graph that handles user input, reasoning, action selection, and final response generation. This section demonstrates how to implement a ReAct agent using this powerful framework.

The core idea is to establish a data pipeline that takes a user's query, uses an LLM to reason through a series of steps, potentially leveraging external tools, and ultimately arrives at an answer. This pipeline can be succinctly expressed using LCEL.

The following is a Python code example demonstrating this process:

```python
from langchain_core.prompts import ChatPromptTemplate
from langchain_core.runnables import chain
from langchain.agents.format_scratchpad import format_log_to_str
from langchain.agents.output_parsers import(
    ReActSingleInputOutputParser)
from langchain.tools import DuckDuckGoSearchRun
from langchain_openai import ChatOpenAI


# 1. Define Tools: In this simple example, we are using a search tool.
tools = [DuckDuckGoSearchRun()]

# 2. Construct the Prompt:  Instead of pulling from a hub, we'll
define a basic prompt template.
template = """Answer the following questions as best you can. You have
access to the following tools:

{tool_descriptions}
```

```
Use the following format:

Question: the input question you must answer
Thought: you should always think about what to do
Action: the action to take, should be one of [{tool_names}]
Action Input: the input to the action
Observation: the result of the action
... (this Thought/Action/Action Input/Observation can repeat N times)
Thought: I now know the final answer
Final Answer: the final answer to the original input question

Begin!

Question: {input}
{agent_scratchpad}"""

prompt = ChatPromptTemplate.from_template(template)

prompt = prompt.partial(
    tool_names=", ".join([t.name for t in tools]),
    tool_descriptions="\n".join(
        [f"{t.name}: {t.description}" for t in tools]
    ),
)

# 3. Instantiate the LLM:  We use ChatOpenAI, but any LLM can be used.
llm = ChatOpenAI(temperature=0)

#  We also configure it to stop when it sees '\nObservation:'
llm_with_stop = llm.bind(stop=["\nObservation:"])


# 4. Construct the Agent Pipeline using LCEL:
agent = (
    {
        "input": lambda x: x["input"],
        "agent_scratchpad": lambda x:
            format_log_to_str(x["intermediate_steps"]),
    }
    | prompt
    | llm_with_stop
    | ReActSingleInputOutputParser()
)
```

Let's take a closer look at this setup:

1. A custom prompt template is defined to guide the LLM's reasoning and action selection, instead of one being fetched from a hub. This template instructs the LLM on the expected format of the interaction (*Question, Thought, Action, Observation, Final Answer*).

2. ChatOpenAI serves as the LLM, configured to halt generation upon encountering the \ nObservation: string. This signal indicates that the agent has completed an action and is awaiting the result.

3. The agent pipeline is constructed via LCEL, which is the chaining operation (|). This pipeline orchestrates the flow of information:

    -   It formats the input and agent's scratchpad (previous reasoning steps)

    -   It feeds the formatted input to the prompt

    -   The LLM, with its configured stopping criteria, processes the prompt

    -   Finally, `ReActSingleInputOutputParser` parses the LLM's output, distinguishing between actions to be taken and the final answer

Explaining ReActSingleInputOutputParser

This component is key for interpreting the LLM's output and determining the next step in the ReAct loop:

-   **Instantiation**: You create an instance of the parser, ready to process LLM-generated text

-   **Functionality**: It examines the LLM's output for patterns that indicate either an `AgentAction` object (requesting the execution of a tool) or an `AgentFinish` object (providing the final answer)

    -   If it detects `AgentAction`, it extracts the tool's name and the input to be passed to the tool

    -   If it finds `AgentFinish`, it extracts the final answer

-   **Usage**: The parser receives the raw text output from the LLM and returns either `AgentAction` or `AgentFinish`

-   **Error handling**: If the LLM's output doesn't conform to the expected ReAct format (for example, it's missing `Action:` or `Final Answer:`), the parser raises an exception, indicating a problem with the LLM's reasoning or the prompt

Running the agent with AgentExecutor

In the following code, `AgentExecutor` is a component responsible for managing the execution of an agent's actions, which are chosen based on the agent's decision-making process. It acts as a driver for the agent, facilitating the interaction between the agent and external tools.

Here's an example:

```
from langchain.agents import AgentExecutor

agent_executor = AgentExecutor(agent=agent, tools=tools, verbose=True)

response = agent_executor.invoke(
    {
        "input": "Who is the current CEO of Microsoft and what is
their age squared?"
    }
)

print(response)
```

Here, the following occurs:

1. We create an AgentExecutor instance, providing it with the agent pipeline we defined earlier and the available tools, before setting verbose=True to see the agent's thought process.

2. The agent_executor.invoke method starts the process. It takes a dictionary containing the user's input ("input": "Who is the current CEO of Microsoft and what is their age squared?").

3. Then, AgentExecutor manages the ReAct loop:

    I.   It feeds the input to the agent pipeline.

    II.   The agent (LLM and parser) decides on an action (for example, using a search tool to find the CEO's name).

    III. The AgentExecutor executes the action (calls the search tool).

    IV.   It passes the result back to the agent as an "Observation."

    V.   This process repeats until the agent decides it has enough information to produce a final answer.

This example demonstrates the basic structure of a ReAct agent built with LCEL. It showcases how you can define a clear, modular pipeline for complex reasoning tasks by combining prompts, language models, parsers, and external tools. This approach promotes code readability, maintainability, and flexibility in designing intelligent agents. This particular example asks who the current CEO of Microsoft is and then what their age is squared, demonstrating simple multi-turn reasoning from name recall to arithmetic calculation.

Completing tasks and solving problems

The ReAct framework, with its ability to integrate reasoning and acting, is highly applicable in various task completion and problem-solving scenarios:

- **Question-Answering (QA) with external knowledge**: ReAct can be used to create QA systems that can access and reason about external knowledge sources, such as Wikipedia or a search engine, to provide more accurate and up-to-date answers

- **Web navigation and interaction**: ReAct agents can navigate websites, interact with web elements, and gather information, enabling tasks such as automated web research, data scraping, and online shopping assistance

- **Software application control**: By integrating with APIs and tools, ReAct agents can control software applications, automate workflows, and perform complex tasks that require interacting with multiple systems

- **Robotics and physical world interaction**: While LLMs primarily operate in the textual domain, ReAct principles can be extended to controlling robots or other physical systems, where actions involve physical movements or interactions with the real world

- **Multi-step problem solving**: ReAct is well-suited for tasks that require breaking down a complex problem into smaller steps, reasoning about each step, taking actions, and using the observations to inform subsequent steps

Evaluating ReAct's performance

Evaluating ReAct agents involves assessing both the quality of the reasoning and the effectiveness of the actions taken. The following metrics can be used:

- **Success rate**: The percentage of tasks successfully completed by the agent

- **Efficiency**: The number of steps or the amount of time taken to complete a task

- **Reasoning accuracy**: The correctness and relevance of the LLM's reasoning traces

- **Action relevance**: The appropriateness of the actions chosen by the agent

- **Observation utilization**: How effectively the agent incorporates observations into its subsequent reasoning and actions

- **Error analysis**: Identifying common failure modes or weaknesses in the agent's performance

Let's consider some evaluation techniques that can be used:

- **Human evaluation**: Having human experts evaluate the agent's reasoning, actions, and final outputs
- **Automated metrics**: Using automated scripts or LLMs to assess specific aspects of the agent's performance, such as the correctness of answers or the relevance of actions
- **Benchmarking**: Comparing the agent's performance against predefined benchmarks or other agents on standardized tasks
- **Ablation studies**: Systematically removing or modifying components of the ReAct framework (for example, removing the reasoning steps) to understand their contribution to overall performance

Safety, control, and ethical considerations

ReAct systems, especially when integrated with external tools, raise several safety, control, and ethical concerns:

- **Unpredictable behavior**: The combination of LLM reasoning and external tool use can lead to unpredictable or unintended behavior
- **Safety of actions**: Actions taken by the agent may have real-world consequences, especially if the agent is connected to systems that can affect the physical world
- **Bias and fairness**: ReAct agents may inherit and amplify biases present in the training data of the LLM or the external tools they use
- **Misuse potential**: Malicious actors could potentially use ReAct agents for harmful purposes, such as generating misinformation or automating attacks
- **Accountability**: Determining responsibility for the actions and decisions of a ReAct agent can be challenging due to the non-deterministic nature of the underlying LLM models

The following are some mitigation strategies for these issues:

- **Sandboxing**: Running ReAct agents in isolated environments to limit their potential impact
- **Human oversight**: Incorporating human review and approval into the ReAct process, especially for critical decisions or actions
- **Safety rules and constraints**: Implementing rules and constraints to prevent the agent from taking harmful or unethical actions
- **Monitoring and auditing**: Continuously monitoring the agent's behavior and maintaining logs for auditing purposes
- **Transparency and explainability**: Designing ReAct agents that can explain their reasoning and decision-making process to improve understanding and trust

Limitations and future directions

While ReAct is a powerful framework, it has certain limitations:

- **Dependency on external tools**: ReAct's effectiveness is partly dependent on the capabilities and reliability of the external tools it uses

- **Error propagation**: Errors in tool use or interpretation of observations can propagate through the reasoning process, leading to incorrect conclusions or actions

- **Token limitations**: The iterative nature of ReAct can lead to long sequences of text, potentially exceeding the token limits of some LLMs

- **Computational cost**: Multiple rounds of reasoning, action, and observation can be computationally expensive, especially when using LLMs or complex tools

- **Prompt engineering challenges**: Designing effective ReAct prompts that properly guide the LLM's reasoning and action selection can be challenging and may require experimentation

Figure 22.1 shows the limitations of ReAct pattern:

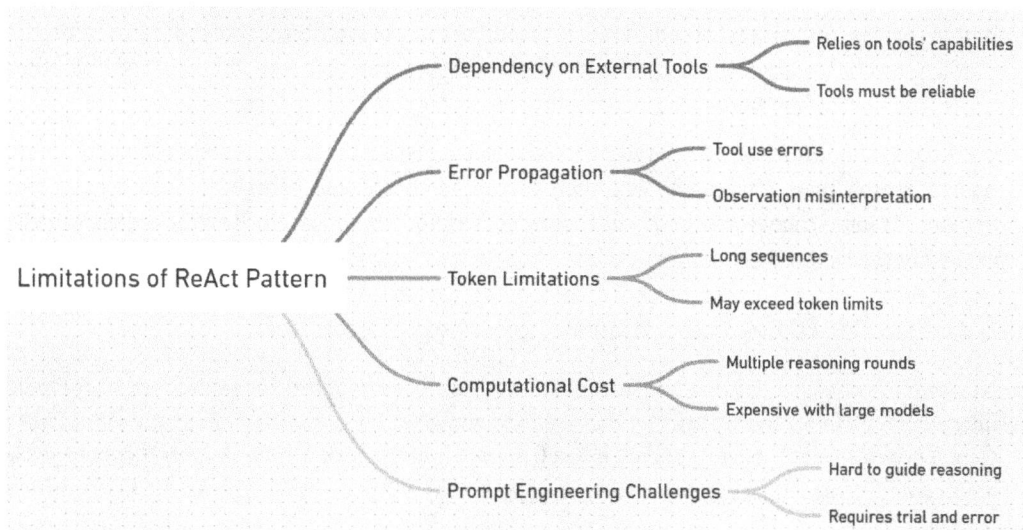

Figure 22.1 – Limitations of the ReAct pattern

However, by combining the power of LLMs with the ability to take actions and incorporate external information, ReAct provides new possibilities for creating more capable and versatile AI systems:

- **Improved tool integration**: Developing more seamless and robust methods for integrating LLMs with external tools

- **Enhanced reasoning capabilities**: Combining ReAct with other advanced reasoning techniques, such as ToT, to handle more complex scenarios

- **Learning from experience**: Enabling ReAct agents to learn from their past interactions and improve their performance over time

- **Multi-agent ReAct**: Exploring scenarios where multiple ReAct agents collaborate or compete to solve problems

- **Real-world deployment**: Moving beyond simulated environments and deploying ReAct agents in real-world applications with the appropriate safety and control mechanisms

Summary

In this chapter, you learned about the ReAct framework, a powerful technique for prompting your LLMs to not only reason through complex scenarios but also plan and simulate the execution of actions, similar to how humans operate in the real world.

The ReAct framework represents a significant advancement in the development of intelligent agents that can reason, plan, and interact with their environment. ReAct can also be considered a precursor to more advanced frameworks such as **Reasoning WithOut Observation** (**ReWOO**), something we'll explore in the next chapter.

Subscribe for a free eBook

New frameworks, evolving architectures, research drops, production breakdowns—AI_Distilled filters the noise into a weekly briefing for engineers and researchers working hands-on with LLMs and GenAI systems. Subscribe now and receive a free eBook, along with weekly insights that help you stay focused and informed. Subscribe at `https://packt.link/8Oz6Y` or scan the QR code below.

## 23

Reasoning WithOut Observation

Reasoning WithOut Observation (**ReWOO**), proposed by Xu et al. (`https://arxiv.org/abs/2305.18323`), is a framework that combines a multi-step planner and variable substitution for effective tool use. It aims to improve upon ReAct-style agents by reducing token consumption and execution time by generating the full chain of tool usage in a single pass, thus minimizing redundant LLM calls. It also aims to simplify the fine-tuning process by enabling fine-tuning without actually invoking tools as planning data doesn't depend on tool outputs (in theory).

ReAct operates through a cyclical "think-act-observe" pattern, where an AI engages in reasoning, performs an action, examines the resulting feedback, and then adjusts its subsequent actions accordingly, facilitating a dynamic and responsive problem-solving strategy. In contrast, ReWOO emphasizes comprehensive upfront planning, generating a complete sequence of actions before any execution occurs, thereby minimizing the necessity for continuous observation and feedback. This distinction allows ReWOO to pursue greater efficiency by reducing token consumption and computational costs, shifting from ReAct's iterative feedback loop to a more streamlined "plan-act" methodology.

So, ReWOO refers to an LLM's ability to make inferences, predictions, or decisions about scenarios it has not directly observed or been trained on. ReWOO enhances this by incorporating external tool use into the reasoning process.

ReWOO's ability to plan and reason without direct observation makes it suitable for complex planning and decision-making tasks:

- **Strategic planning**: As mentioned, ReWOO can generate strategic plans based on hypothetical situations, goals, and constraints

- **Scenario analysis**: ReWOO can explore multiple potential outcomes of a given scenario, considering various factors and uncertainties

- **Resource allocation**: By planning tool use and reasoning about their results, ReWOO can optimize resource allocation in complex environments

- **Risk assessment**: ReWOO can help assess potential risks and develop mitigation strategies by simulating different scenarios and their consequences

In this chapter, we'll be covering the following topics:

- Implementing ReWOO with LangGraph
- Advantages of ReWOO
- Evaluating quality and ethical considerations
- Future directions

Implementing ReWOO with LangGraph

LangGraph is an open source framework designed for building stateful, multi-agent applications using LLMs. It extends the capabilities of the LangChain ecosystem by introducing a directed graph model, where nodes represent functions (including LLM invocations) and edges represent transitions between states based on logic, conditions, or memory. Unlike traditional sequential chains, LangGraph allows complex workflows involving conditional branching, loops, memory passing, and asynchronous agent coordination. LangGraph is particularly useful for implementing systems where interactions are dynamic, iterative, and dependent on state changes. This includes multi-agent collaboration, decision trees, retrieval-augmented generation with control flow, and autonomous agents that need to revisit prior steps or loop through subtasks until certain goals are met.

LangGraph leverages concepts from graph theory and automata, representing execution flows as state machines or directed acyclic graphs (or cyclic graphs when loops are needed). Developers define a graph with nodes (functions or tools), edges (state transitions), and conditions (logic for routing). The runtime engine then executes the graph in response to inputs, updating the state at each step.

LangGraph supports both synchronous and asynchronous execution, and it integrates with LangChain's components, such as tools, memory, and agents. It also supports streaming responses, fine-grained control over state, and multi-modal inputs/outputs, making it suitable for production-level applications.

In practice, LangGraph is used to build agentic systems where different agents interact, coordinate, and share memory, while still following a well-defined computational graph. This makes it different from naive agent loops or unstructured LLM orchestration methods.

LangGraph is available at `https://github.com/langchain-ai/langgraph` and supports Python-based implementation, with core dependencies on LangChain and state machine execution frameworks.

The ReWOO architecture consists of three modules:

- **Planner**: Generates a high-level plan to solve the problem, including identifying which tools to use and their arguments, potentially using **variable substitution** to represent dependencies between steps. Variable substitution in AI planning, particularly within systems such as ReWOO, enables the creation of flexible and efficient plans by employing placeholders to represent values that are determined during execution. This technique allows the AI to define dependencies between steps, such as using the output of a search tool as the input for a price extraction tool, without needing to know the specific values in advance. By using variables such as `search_result` or `price`, the AI can construct a clear blueprint of the task, deferring the resolution of dynamic information until it becomes available, thereby streamlining the planning process and avoiding unnecessary computations.

- **Worker**: Executes the tool with the provided arguments, potentially using variable substitution from previous steps.

- **Solver**: Generates the final answer based on the tool observations and the plan.

This architecture may seem a little abstract initially. Let's implement ReWOO using LangGraph. We'll use a Tavily search engine as an example tool:

1. Install the necessary packages and set API keys:

    ```
    # %pip install -U langgraph langchain_community langchain_openai
    tavily-python
    ```

    Tavily is a search engine designed specifically for AI agents. It's built to provide accurate and reliable information retrieval, tailored to the needs of AI systems performing complex tasks (see `https://tavily.com/`).

    The following script sets environment variables for API keys if they haven't been defined yet:

    ```
    import getpass
    import os


    def _set_if_undefined(var: str):
        if not os.environ.get(var):
            os.environ[var] = getpass.getpass(f"{var}=")


    _set_if_undefined("TAVILY_API_KEY")
    _set_if_undefined("OPENAI_API_KEY")
    ```

2. Next, define the graph state. To do so, define the state dictionary so that it can hold the task, plan, steps, results, and final result:

```
from typing import List
from typing_extensions import TypedDict

class ReWOO(TypedDict):
    task: str
    plan_string: str
    steps: List
    results: dict
    result: str
```

3. Create the planner prompt and logic:

```
from langchain_openai import ChatOpenAI

model = ChatOpenAI(model="gpt-4o")

prompt = """For the following task, create a series of plans
that can solve the problem step-by-step. For each plan, specify
which external tool and its corresponding input should be used
to gather evidence. You can store the evidence in a variable #E
(e.g., #E1, #E2, #E3, etc.) that can be referenced by subsequent
tools. Note that all the variables are independent, so make sure
to include all necessary information in each tool input.

Tools can be one of the following:

Google[input]: A search engine worker that retrieves results
from Google. Use this when you need concise answers or
information about a specific topic. The input should be a search
query.

LLM[input]: A pretrained Large Language Model (like me). Use
this when you need to leverage general world knowledge, common
sense, or perform complex reasoning. Prioritize this tool
when you are confident in solving the problem without external
assistance. The input can be any instruction or question.

Calculator[input]: A tool that can perform mathematical
calculations. Use this when you need to perform arithmetic
operations. The input should be a valid mathematical expression.

WolframAlpha[input]: A computational knowledge engine. Use this
when you need to solve equations, perform symbolic calculations,
or get data-driven answers. The input should be a query in
Wolfram Language or natural language related to a math or
science problem.
```

For example,

Task: Alice, Bob, and Carol earned a total of $540 from their part-time jobs last week. Alice earned y dollars. Bob earned $20 more than three times what Alice earned, and Carol earned $15 more than Bob. How much money did Carol earn?

Plan: Given Alice earned y dollars, translate the problem into algebraic expressions and solve with Wolfram Alpha.
#E1 = WolframAlpha[Solve y + (3y + 20) + ((3y + 20) + 15) = 540]

Plan: Find out the amount of money Alice earned.
#E2 = LLM[What is y, given #E1]

Plan: Calculate the amount of money Carol earned.
#E3 = Calculator[((3 * #E2) + 20) + 15]

Begin!
Describe your plans with rich details. Each Plan should be followed by only one #E.

Task: {task}"""

4. Create a LangGraph node for the planner:

```python
import re
from langchain_core.prompts import ChatPromptTemplate

regex_pattern = (
    r"Plan:\s*(.+)\s*(#E\d+)\s*=\s*(\w+)\s*"
    r"\[(([^\]]+)\]"
)
prompt_template = ChatPromptTemplate.from_messages(
    [("user", prompt)]
)
planner = prompt_template | model

def get_plan(state: ReWOO):
    task = state["task"]
    result = planner.invoke({"task": task})
    matches = re.findall(regex_pattern, result.content)
    return {"steps": matches, "plan_string": result.content}
```

5. Instantiate the search engine and define the tool execution logic:

```
from langchain_community.tools.tavily_search import
TavilySearchResults

search = TavilySearchResults()

def _get_current_task(state: ReWOO):
    if "results" not in state or state["results"] is None:
        return 1
    if len(state["results"]) == len(state["steps"]):
        return None
    else:
        return len(state["results"]) + 1

def tool_execution(state: ReWOO):
    _step = _get_current_task(state)
    _, step_name, tool, tool_input = state["steps"][_step - 1]
    _results = (state["results"] or {}) if "results" in state
else {}
    for k, v in _results.items():
        tool_input = tool_input.replace(k, v)
    if tool == "Google":
        result = search.invoke(tool_input)
    elif tool == "LLM":
        result = model.invoke(tool_input)
    else:
        raise ValueError
    _results[step_name] = str(result)
    return {"results": _results}
```

6. Create the solver prompt and logic:

```
solve_prompt = """Solve the following task or problem. To solve
the problem, we have made step-by-step Plan and \
retrieved corresponding Evidence to each Plan. Use them with
caution since long evidence might \
contain irrelevant information.

{plan}

Now solve the question or task according to provided Evidence
above. Respond with the answer
directly with no extra words.

Task: {task}
Response:"""
```

```python
def solve(state: ReWOO):
    plan = ""
    for _plan, step_name, tool, tool_input in state["steps"]:
        _results = (
            (state["results"] or {}) if "results" in state else {}
        )
        for k, v in _results.items():
            tool_input = tool_input.replace(k, v)
            step_name = step_name.replace(k, v)
        plan += (
            f"Plan: {_plan}\n"
            f"{step_name} = {tool}[{tool_input}]\n"
        )

    prompt = solve_prompt.format(plan=plan, task=state["task"])
    result = model.invoke(prompt)
    return {"result": result.content}
```

7. Build the LangGraph workflow:

```python
def _route(state):
    _step = _get_current_task(state)
    if _step is None:
        return "solve"
    else:
        return "tool"

from langgraph.graph import END, StateGraph, START

graph = StateGraph(ReWOO)
graph.add_node("plan", get_plan)
graph.add_node("tool", tool_execution)
graph.add_node("solve", solve)
graph.add_edge("plan", "tool")
graph.add_edge("solve", END)
graph.add_conditional_edges("tool", _route)
graph.add_edge(START, "plan")

app = graph.compile()
```

The provided code establishes an AI workflow using StateGraph, a data structure for managing multi-step processes. The _route function acts as a conditional director, determining the next step based on the current state. It checks if further tool-based actions are required; if not, it routes the process to the "solve" node for final answer generation. Otherwise, it directs it to the "tool" node for tool execution.

Here, `StateGraph` defines the execution flow: starting with `"plan"` for strategy creation, proceeding to `"tool"` for external tool usage, and finally, to `"solve"` for result generation, culminating in the END state. The `_route` function's conditional logic within the `"tool"` node is key, allowing dynamic routing based on the task's progression.

`StateGraph` is crucial for structured workflow management, enabling conditional branching for adaptive AI behavior, especially in tool-dependent tasks. It ensures logical action sequencing, improving robustness and clarity, and facilitating ReWOO's planned execution. Compiling the graph into an `"app"` makes it executable.

8. Let's look at an example use case, and test the ReWOO agent:

```
task = "what is the exact hometown of the 2024 mens australian
open winner"

for s in app.stream({"task": task}):
    print(s)
    print("---")
```

The preceding code provides a simple implementation of the ReWOO framework using LangGraph. It defines the state, planner, executor, and solver modules, and connects them into a graph. This example usage demonstrates how to run the agent on a sample task.

Advantages of ReWOO

ReWOO offers several advantages over traditional ReAct-style agents:

- **Reduced token consumption and execution time**: By generating the entire plan in a single pass and using variable substitution, ReWOO minimizes redundant LLM calls and context passing
- **Simplified fine-tuning**: The independence of the planning data from tool outputs (in theory) allows for fine-tuning without the need to invoke the tools
- **Efficient LLM calls**: The LLM tool receives less of the prompt, making calls more token-efficient compared to the ReACT paradigm

Evaluating quality and ethical considerations

Evaluating the quality of ReWOO's reasoning can be challenging as it often deals with hypothetical scenarios. Possible approaches include the following:

- **Human evaluation**: Using human experts to assess the coherence, relevance, and completeness of the generated plans and reasoning

- **Comparison with ground truth**: For scenarios with known outcomes, ReWOO's predictions can be compared with actual results

- **Benchmarking**: Using standardized test sets designed to evaluate abstract reasoning and planning capabilities

It is also crucial to keep ethical considerations in mind while doing any evaluation:

- **Bias amplification**: ReWOO might inherit and amplify biases present in the training data of the underlying LLM

- **Misuse potential**: The ability to generate plans and reason about hypothetical scenarios could be misused for malicious purposes

- **Overreliance**: Users might place too much trust in ReWOO's outputs without considering their speculative nature

Future directions

As research progresses, ReWOO and related techniques will likely play an increasingly important role in the development of more capable and versatile AI systems. The following are some promising directions for ReWOO:

- **Human-in-the-loop systems**: Integrating human oversight and feedback into the ReWOO framework to improve accuracy and address ethical concerns

- **Improved planning algorithms**: Developing more sophisticated planning algorithms that can handle more complex scenarios and larger search spaces

- **Enhanced tool integration**: Seamlessly integrating a wider range of tools, including specialized APIs and knowledge bases

- **Multi-agent collaboration**: Enabling multiple ReWOO agents to collaborate on complex tasks, potentially leading to more robust and diverse solutions

- **Meta-learning**: Applying meta-learning techniques to improve the agent's ability to generalize and adapt to new scenarios over time

Summary

This chapter delved into ReWOO, a framework designed to empower LLMs with the ability to reason about hypothetical situations and leverage external tools effectively. ReWOO utilizes a multi-step planner coupled with variable substitution, enabling it to generate comprehensive action plans in a single pass, thereby minimizing token consumption and execution time compared to the iterative "think-act-observe" cycle of ReAct agents. This chapter demonstrated the implementation of ReWOO using LangGraph, highlighting its architecture, components (planner, worker, solver), and advantages, such as simplified fine-tuning and efficient LLM calls.

Beyond simply reiterating the framework's mechanics, this chapter emphasized ReWOO's potential for strategic planning, scenario analysis, resource allocation, and risk assessment. However, it also touched upon the critical ethical considerations surrounding ReWOO, including the potential for bias amplification, misuse, and overreliance on its outputs. This chapter concluded with a view toward the future, discussing the need for human-in-the-loop systems, improved planning algorithms, enhanced tool integration, multi-agent collaboration, and the application of meta-learning techniques to further refine ReWOO's capabilities and ensure responsible application in real-world scenarios.

In the next chapter, we will discuss techniques that enable LLMs to engage in self-reflection and iterative improvement.

24
Reflection Techniques

Reflection in LLMs refers to a model's ability to analyze, evaluate, and improve its own outputs. This meta-cognitive capability allows LLMs to engage in iterative refinement, potentially leading to higher-quality results and more robust performance.

There are several key aspects of reflection:

- Self-evaluation of outputs
- Identification of weaknesses or errors
- Generation of improvement strategies
- Iterative refinement of responses

Here, we'll explore techniques that enable LLMs to engage in self-reflection and iterative improvement.

In this chapter, we'll be covering the following topics:

- Designing prompts for self-reflection
- Implementing iterative refinement
- Correcting errors
- Evaluating the impact of reflection
- Challenges in implementing effective reflection
- Future directions

Designing prompts for self-reflection

To encourage reflection in LLMs, prompts should be designed to achieve the following:

1. Request an initial response.
2. Prompt for self-evaluation.

3.   Encourage identification of areas for improvement.

4.   Guide the model to generate refined outputs.

Here's an example of implementing a reflection prompt:

```
def Reflection_prompt(task, initial_response):
    prompt = f"""Task: {task}

Initial Response:
{initial_response}

Now, let's engage in self-reflection:

1. Evaluate the strengths and weaknesses of your initial response.
2. Identify any errors, inconsistencies, or areas for improvement.
3. Suggest specific ways to enhance the response.
4. Provide a revised and improved version of the response.

Your self-reflection and improved response:
"""
    return prompt

# Example usage
task = "Explain the concept of quantum entanglement to a high school
student."
initial_response = "Quantum entanglement is when two particles are
connected in a way that measuring one instantly affects the other, no
matter how far apart they are."

prompt = Reflection_prompt(task, initial_response)
print(prompt)
```

This code defines a function named `Reflection_prompt` that is used to generate a self-reflective prompt for improving an initial response to a task. It follows a structured meta-cognitive approach commonly used in prompt engineering to enhance the quality of outputs, especially for AI systems or human-in-the-loop workflows.

For example, given the task `"Explain the concept of quantum entanglement to a high school student"` and the initial response `"Quantum entanglement is when two particles are connected in a way that measuring one instantly affects the other, no matter how far apart they are"`, the generated prompt encourages self-reflection by asking for evaluation, identification of issues, improvement suggestions, and a revised version. The model might respond by acknowledging that while the original explanation is concise and intuitive, it lacks precision and may imply faster-than-light communication. It could then offer a revised explanation using a clearer analogy that emphasizes shared quantum states rather than causal influence.

To process such responses programmatically, a response handler can segment the text using a regular expression to extract numbered sections corresponding to evaluation, issues, suggestions, and the revised answer. This parsed structure allows downstream systems to log reflections, compare versions, or use the improved response in subsequent steps, supporting workflows in iterative refinement or supervised learning scenarios.

Implementing iterative refinement

Iterative refinement is a process where a model's response is progressively improved through repeated cycles of self-evaluation and revision. Each cycle uses a reflection prompt to guide the model in critiquing and enhancing its prior output, aiming to converge on a more accurate or well-articulated result.

To implement iterative refinement, we can create a loop that repeatedly applies the reflection process. Here's an example:

1. Define the `iterative_Reflection` function:

```
from transformers import AutoModelForCausalLM, AutoTokenizer

def iterative_Reflection(
    model, tokenizer, task, max_iterations=3
):
    response = generate_initial_response(model, tokenizer, task)

    for i in range(max_iterations):
        prompt = Reflection_prompt(task, response)
        inputs = tokenizer(prompt, return_tensors="pt")
        outputs = model.generate(
            inputs, max_length=1000, num_return_sequences=1
        )
        reflection = tokenizer.decode(outputs[0],
            skip_special_tokens=True)

        # Extract the improved response from the reflection
        response = extract_improved_response(reflection)

        if is_satisfactory(response):
            break

    return response
```

In the preceding code, the `iterative_Reflection` function initializes with a baseline response generated for the given task. It then enters a loop where each iteration feeds the current response into a structured self-reflection prompt. The model processes this prompt to generate a revised response, which is extracted and assessed for quality using `is_satisfactory()`. If the response meets the criteria, the loop exits early. Otherwise, it continues refining up to the defined iteration limit, returning the final improved response.

2. Define other functions to reflect on responses:

```python
def generate_initial_response(model, tokenizer, task):
    prompt = f"Task: {task}\n\nResponse:"
    inputs = tokenizer(prompt, return_tensors="pt")
    outputs = model.generate(inputs, max_length=500,
        num_return_sequences=1)
    return tokenizer.decode(outputs[0],
        skip_special_tokens=True)


def extract_improved_response(reflection):
    # Implement logic to extract the improved response from the
reflection
    # This could involve text parsing or using markers in the
generated text
    pass


def is_satisfactory(response):
    # Implement logic to determine if the response meets quality
criteria
    # This could involve length checks, keyword presence, or
more advanced metrics
    pass
```

The `generate_initial_response` function constructs a simple prompt from the task and passes it to a language model to generate a baseline answer, which is then decoded from token IDs into text. The `extract_improved_response` function is a placeholder meant to isolate the revised answer from the full reflection output, typically through parsing or predefined markers. Similarly, `is_satisfactory` serves as a customizable checkpoint to evaluate whether the current response meets specific quality thresholds, such as content accuracy, completeness, or coherence, allowing iterative refinement to terminate early if a sufficient answer is reached.

3. Here's an example usage of the defined code block:

```
model_name = "gpt2-large"  # Replace with your preferred model
model = AutoModelForCausalLM.from_pretrained(model_name)
tokenizer = AutoTokenizer.from_pretrained(model_name)

task = "Explain the process of photosynthesis in plants."
final_response = iterative_Reflection(model, tokenizer, task)
print(final_response)
```

This function implements an iterative reflection process, repeatedly refining the response until it meets satisfactory criteria or reaches a maximum number of iterations.

Next, let's take a look at how we can make use of reflection to correct errors in LLMs.

Correcting errors

Reflection techniques can be particularly useful for self-improvement and error correction in LLMs. Here's an example of how to implement error correction using reflection:

```
def error_correction_Reflection(
    model, tokenizer, task, initial_response, known_errors
):
    prompt = f"""Task: {task}

Initial Response:
{initial_response}

Known Errors:
{' '.join(f'- {error}' for error in known_errors)}

Please reflect on the initial response, focusing on correcting
the known errors. Provide an improved version of the response that
addresses these issues.

Corrected Response:
"""

    inputs = tokenizer(prompt, return_tensors="pt")
    outputs = model.generate(inputs, max_length=1000,
        num_return_sequences=1)
    corrected_response = tokenizer.decode(outputs[0],
        skip_special_tokens=True)
```

```
        return corrected_response

# Example usage
task = "Describe the structure of an atom."
initial_response = "An atom consists of a nucleus containing protons
and neutrons, with electrons orbiting around it in fixed circular
orbits."
known_errors = [
    "Electrons do not orbit in fixed circular paths",
    "The description doesn't mention electron shells or energy levels"
]

corrected_response = error_correction_Reflection(
    model, tokenizer, task, initial_response, known_errors
)
print(corrected_response)
```

The `error_correction_Reflection` function constructs a prompt that includes the task, an initial response, and a list of known errors, instructing the model to revise the response with a focus on correcting these issues. The prompt is tokenized and passed to the model, which generates a new version of the response intended to address the identified mistakes. The output is then decoded into text and returned as the corrected response. This approach allows for targeted self-correction by explicitly guiding the model's attention toward specific flaws, rather than relying solely on general reflection.

Keep in mind that token length could become an issue with large prompts, depending on the model used. If the combined length of the task, initial response, error list, and instructions exceeds the model's context window, it can lead to an error. To mitigate this, it's important to monitor token usage, simplify prompts where possible, or use models with extended context windows to ensure all critical information is retained during generation.

Evaluating the impact of reflection

To assess the effectiveness of reflection techniques, we need to compare the quality of responses before and after the reflection process. Here's a simple evaluation framework:

```
def evaluate_Reflection_impact(
    initial_response, Reflection_response, criteria
):
    initial_scores = evaluate_response(initial_response, criteria)
    Reflection_scores = evaluate_response(Reflection_response,
        criteria)

    impact = {
        criterion: Reflection_scores[criterion]
```

```
            - initial_scores[criterion]
        for criterion in criteria
    }

    return {
        "initial_scores": initial_scores,
        "Reflection_scores": Reflection_scores,
        "impact": impact
    }

def evaluate_response(response, criteria):
    scores = {}
    for criterion in criteria:
        # Implement criterion-specific evaluation logic
        scores[criterion] = evaluate_criterion(response, criterion)
    return scores

def evaluate_criterion(response, criterion):
    # Placeholder for criterion-specific evaluation
    # In practice, this could involve NLP techniques, rubric-based
scoring, or even another LLM
    return 0  # Placeholder return

# Example usage
criteria = ["Accuracy", "Clarity", "Completeness", "Conciseness"]

evaluation = evaluate_Reflection_impact(initial_response,
    corrected_response, criteria)
print("Evaluation Results:")
print(f"Initial Scores: {evaluation['initial_scores']}")
print(f"Reflection Scores: {evaluation['Reflection_scores']}")
print(f"Impact: {evaluation['impact']}")
```

This evaluation framework compares the initial and reflection-improved responses across multiple criteria, providing insights into the impact of the reflection process.

The code evaluates text quality using four criteria: **accuracy**, **clarity**, **completeness**, and **conciseness**. Accuracy assesses whether the response contains correct and factually valid information. Clarity checks if the content is expressed in an understandable manner. Completeness determines whether the response fully addresses all parts of the task, and conciseness evaluates the avoidance of unnecessary verbosity while preserving core content. These criteria align with common practices in evaluating written responses in educational and model assessment settings. The code's modular design allows for easy expansion by modifying the `criteria` list and implementing corresponding logic in `evaluate_criterion`.

Challenges in implementing effective reflection

While powerful, implementing effective reflection in LLMs faces several challenges:

- **Computational cost**: Iterative reflection can be computationally expensive
- **Potential for circular reasoning**: LLMs might reinforce their own biases or mistakes
- **Difficulty in true self-awareness**: LLMs lack a genuine understanding of their own limitations
- **Balancing improvement with originality**: Excessive reflection might lead to overly conservative outputs

To address some of these challenges, consider implementing a controlled reflection process. This controlled reflection process limits the number of iterations and stops when improvements become marginal, balancing the benefits of reflection with computational efficiency:

```python
def controlled_Reflection(
    model, tokenizer, task, max_iterations=3,
    improvement_threshold=0.1
):
    response = generate_initial_response(model, tokenizer, task)
    previous_score = evaluate_response(
        response, ["Overall_Quality"]
    )["Overall_Quality"]

    for i in range(max_iterations):
        improved_response = apply_Reflection(model, tokenizer,
        task, response)
        current_score = evaluate_response(improved_response,
            ["Overall_Quality"]
        )["Overall_Quality"]

        if current_score - previous_score < improvement_threshold:
            break

        response = improved_response
        previous_score = current_score

    return response

def apply_Reflection(model, tokenizer, task, response):
    # Implement a single step of Reflection
    pass
```

```
# Example usage
task = "Explain the theory of relativity."
final_response = controlled_Reflection(model, tokenizer, task)
print(final_response)
```

The controlled_Reflection function iteratively improves a model-generated response to a task. It starts by generating an initial response and then evaluates it using an "Overall_Quality" score. In each iteration, it applies apply_Reflection to revise the response, re-evaluates it, and checks if the improvement exceeds a defined threshold. If not, it stops early. This continues up to a maximum number of iterations, returning the best response. The apply_Reflection function, which must be implemented separately, represents one step of reflective improvement.

However, quality scoring can be subjective, especially when relying on a single metric like "Overall_Quality". Small revisions might not reflect meaningful improvements, or automated scorers might be inconsistent across different outputs. To mitigate this, it's better to use multiple evaluation dimensions, ensemble scoring, or confidence-weighted methods. If scoring remains unstable, adding human oversight or qualitative checks between iterations can improve the reliability of the refinement loop.

Future directions

As reflection techniques for LLMs continue to evolve, several promising directions emerge:

- **MetaReflection**: An offline reinforcement learning technique that enhances reflection by augmenting a semantic memory based on experiential learnings from past trials (https://arxiv.org/abs/2405.13009)

- **Incorporating external knowledge in reflection**: Using up-to-date information to guide the reflection process (https://arxiv.org/html/2411.15041)

- **Reflection-aware architecture**: Developing LLM architectures specifically designed for effective self-reflection (https://arxiv.org/abs/2303.11366)

Here's a conceptual implementation of a multi-agent reflection approach:

1. Define the function:

```
def multi_agent_Reflection(
    models, tokenizers, task, num_agents=3
):
    responses = [
        generate_initial_response(
        models[i], tokenizers[i], task
        )
        for i in range(num_agents)
    ]
```

```
        for _ in range(3):  # Number of reflection rounds
            Reflections = []
            for i in range(num_agents):
                other_responses = responses[:i] + responses[i+1:]
                reflection = generate_Reflection(
                    models[i], tokenizers[i], task,
                    responses[i], other_responses
                )
                Reflections.append(Reflection)

            responses = [extract_improved_response(Reflection)
                for reflection in Reflections]
```

2. Combine or select the best response from the final set:

```
        return select_best_response(responses)

    def generate_Reflection(
        model, tokenizer, task, own_response, other_responses
    ):
        prompt = f"""Task: {task}

Your Response:
{own_response}

Other Responses:
{' '.join(f'- {response}' for response in other_responses)}

Reflect on your response in light of the other responses.
Identify strengths and weaknesses in each approach and propose
an improved response that incorporates the best elements from
all perspectives.

Your reflection and improved response:
"""
        inputs = tokenizer(prompt, return_tensors="pt")
        outputs = model.generate(
            inputs, max_length=1500, num_return_sequences=1
        )
        return tokenizer.decode(outputs[0], skip_
            special_tokens=True)
```

```
def select_best_response(responses):
    # Implement logic to select or combine the best elements
from multiple responses
    pass
```

3. Consider an example usage:

```
task = "Propose a solution to reduce urban traffic congestion."
final_response = multi_agent_Reflection(models, tokenizers,
    task)
print(final_response)
```

This multi-agent reflection approach leverages multiple LLM instances to generate diverse perspectives and collaboratively improve the response through iterative reflection.

Summary

Reflection techniques offer powerful ways to enhance the performance and reliability of LLMs by enabling them to engage in self-improvement and error correction. In this chapter, you learned how to design prompts that encourage LLMs to evaluate and refine their own outputs. We covered methods for implementing iterative refinement through self-reflection and discussed applications in self-improvement and error correction. You also learned how to evaluate the impact of reflection on LLM performance.

By implementing the strategies and considerations discussed in this chapter, you can create more sophisticated LLM systems capable of producing higher-quality outputs through iterative refinement and self-reflection.

In the next chapter, we will take a look at automatic multi-step reasoning and tool use, which builds upon the reflexive capabilities we've discussed here to create even more autonomous and capable AI systems.

Subscribe for a free eBook

New frameworks, evolving architectures, research drops, production breakdowns—AI_Distilled filters the noise into a weekly briefing for engineers and researchers working hands-on with LLMs and GenAI systems. Subscribe now and receive a free eBook, along with weekly insights that help you stay focused and informed. Subscribe at `https://packt.link/8Oz6Y` or scan the QR code below.

25
Automatic Multi-Step Reasoning and Tool Use

Multi-step reasoning and tool use in LLMs involve the model's ability to break down complex tasks into manageable steps and leverage external resources or APIs to accomplish these tasks. This capability significantly extends the problem-solving potential of LLMs, allowing them to tackle more complex, real-world scenarios. Its key characteristics include the following:

- **Task decomposition:** This refers to the model's ability to take a complex input or goal and divide it into smaller, more manageable sub-tasks that can be solved sequentially or hierarchically. Instead of trying to solve an entire problem in one step, the model creates a structured plan or sequence of reasoning steps that progressively leads to a solution. This process mimics the way humans often approach complex problems by identifying dependencies, sequencing actions, and breaking large goals into intermediate objectives. Techniques such as chain-of-thought prompting explicitly encourage this behavior by prompting the model to articulate each reasoning step before arriving at an answer.

- **External tools**: The capabilities of LLMs can be enhanced by integrating additional resources, such as databases, APIs, or specialized services, that LLMs cannot access directly due to limitations in their training environment. These tools enable the LLMs to interact with real-time data, perform specific tasks beyond their built-in knowledge, or offer enhanced functionalities such as web browsing, file handling, or executing external scripts. For example, an LLM can use an external tool to query up-to-date weather data, retrieve specific information from a live API, or run computations that require specialized algorithms. This integration allows LLMs to offer more dynamic, relevant, and specialized responses, particularly for applications requiring real-time information or complex multi-step processes.

- **Reasoning about tool applicability**: This involves the model's judgment in recognizing when an external capability is required to solve a particular sub-task. The model must assess the nature of the sub-task and determine whether internal reasoning suffices or whether delegating part of the task to a tool would yield better or even necessary results.

- **Tool selection and invocation**: This refers to the model's ability to identify which tool is appropriate for a given sub-task and to formulate the correct input to trigger its use. This requires the model to understand the functionality and input requirements of each available tool and to match these against the demands of the current step in the reasoning process. For example, if the task requires accessing up-to-date weather information, the model must choose a weather API and generate a syntactically correct and semantically relevant query to that API. This phase includes formatting inputs, calling the tool, and ensuring that the request aligns with both the current problem context and the tool's capabilities.

- **Integration of tool outputs**: This describes the model's capability to interpret the results returned by the external tool and incorporate them into the ongoing reasoning process. After a tool is invoked and responds with data—such as a numerical value, a structured object, or a text snippet—the model must parse the result, extract relevant elements, and update its understanding or intermediate outputs accordingly. This step often involves interpreting heterogeneous output formats, managing type mismatches, and maintaining continuity in the reasoning chain. Effective integration ensures that tool use is not isolated but meaningfully contributes to solving the broader task.

- **Iterative problem solving**: This refers to the model's recursive application of the previous stages—decomposition, tool reasoning, selection, invocation, and integration—in a loop until the task is resolved or further steps become unproductive. The model continuously reassesses its progress, determines whether additional sub-tasks remain, and decides whether further tool use is necessary. This iterative behavior enables the model to handle tasks with dynamic structure, uncertainty, or errors from prior steps by adjusting the plan or refining previous actions. In agent-based architectures, this process may be explicitly managed by a planner or controller, while in prompt-based settings, it often emerges through recursive self-queries and prompt augmentation.

In this chapter, we'll delve into advanced techniques for enabling LLMs to perform complex multi-step reasoning and utilize external tools.

In this chapter, we'll be covering the following topics:

- Designing prompts for complex task decomposition

- Integrating external tools

- Implementing automatic tool selection and use

- Complex problem solving

- Evaluating multi-step reasoning and tool use

- Challenges and future directions

Designing prompts for complex task decomposition

To enable effective multi-step reasoning, prompts should guide the LLM to break down complex tasks into smaller, manageable steps. Here's an example of a task decomposition prompt:

```python
def task_decomposition_prompt(task, available_tools):
    prompt = f"""Given the following complex task:

{task}

And the following available tools:
{' '.join(f'- {tool}' for tool in available_tools)}

Please break down the task into smaller, logical steps. For each step,
indicate if a specific tool should be used. If no tool is needed,
explain the reasoning required.

Your task decomposition:

Step 1:
Step 2:
Step 3:
...

Ensure that the steps are in a logical order and cover all aspects of
the task.
"""

    return prompt

# Example usage
task = "Analyze the sentiment of tweets about a new product launch and
create a summary report with visualizations."
available_tools = ["Twitter API", "Sentiment Analysis Model",
    "Data Visualization Library"]

prompt = task_decomposition_prompt(task, available_tools)
print(prompt)
```

This function generates a prompt that guides the LLM to decompose a complex task into steps, considering the available tools.

Integrating external tools

To enable LLMs to use external tools such as search, calculations, API calls, and so on, we need to create an interface between the model and the tools. Here's a simple implementation:

1. Perform the necessary imports and define the `ToolKit` class:

```
import requests
from textblob import TextBlob
import matplotlib.pyplot as plt

class ToolKit:
    def __init__(self):
        self.tools = {
            "Twitter API": self.fetch_tweets,
            "Sentiment Analysis": self.analyze_sentiment,
            "Data Visualization": self.create_visualization
        }
```

The preceding code defines a `ToolKit` class that organizes and offers access to different functionalities through its methods. In the `__init__` method, a dictionary named `tools` is initialized with keys representing tool names such as `"Twitter API"`, `"Sentiment Analysis"`, and `"Data Visualization"`, and values that reference the corresponding methods for fetching tweets, performing sentiment analysis using the TextBlob library, and creating data visualizations using Matplotlib. The `requests` library is imported for making HTTP requests, while `TextBlob` is used for natural language processing tasks such as sentiment analysis, and `matplotlib.pyplot` is imported for generating visualizations. The code sets up the structure for these tools but is incomplete as the `fetch_tweets`, `analyze_sentiment`, and `create_visualization` methods are not defined, leaving room for further implementation of these functionalities.

2. Define three methods: `fetch_tweets` for generating mock tweets based on a query, `analyze_sentiment` for computing sentiment polarity scores for a list of texts using TextBlob, and `create_visualization` for creating and saving a histogram of the sentiment data with a specified title:

```
    def fetch_tweets(self, query, count=100):
        return [f"Tweet about {query}" for _ in range(count)]

    def analyze_sentiment(self, texts):
        sentiments = [TextBlob(text).sentiment.polarity
            for text in texts]
        return sentiments
```

```python
    def create_visualization(self, data, title):
        plt.figure(figsize=(10, 6))
        plt.hist(data, bins=20)
        plt.title(title)
        plt.xlabel("Sentiment")
        plt.ylabel("Frequency")
        plt.savefig("sentiment_visualization.png")
        return "sentiment_visualization.png"
```

3. Define the `use_tool` method to execute a specified tool with given arguments if it exists in the tools dictionary; otherwise, return an error message:

```python
    def use_tool(self, tool_name, *args, kwargs):
        if tool_name in self.tools:
            return self.tools[tool_name](*args, kwargs)
        else:
            return f"Error: Tool '{tool_name}' not found."
```

4. The following example demonstrates using a `ToolKit` class to fetch tweets about a product launch, analyze their sentiments, create a sentiment visualization, and print the path to the generated visualization file:

```python
toolkit = ToolKit()
tweets = toolkit.use_tool(
    "Twitter API", "new product launch", count=50
)
sentiments = toolkit.use_tool("Sentiment Analysis", tweets)
visualization = toolkit.use_tool(
    "Data Visualization", sentiments,
    "Sentiment Analysis of Product Launch Tweets"
)
print(f"Generated visualization: {visualization}")
```

This `ToolKit` class provides an interface for the LLM to interact with external tools, simulating API calls and data processing tasks.

Implementing automatic tool selection and use

To enable LLMs to automatically select and use tools, we can create a system that interprets the model's output and executes the appropriate tools. Here's an example:

1. First, we define a function, `auto_tool_use`, that uses a pre-trained language model and tokenizer from Hugging Face's Transformers library to decompose a task into executable steps using a prompt, parses the decomposition into steps, executes tools as needed using a toolkit, and collects the results:

```python
from transformers import AutoModelForCausalLM, AutoTokenizer

def auto_tool_use(model, tokenizer, task, toolkit):
    # Generate task decomposition
    decomposition_prompt = task_decomposition_prompt(
        task, toolkit.tools.keys()
    )
    inputs = tokenizer(decomposition_prompt,
        return_tensors="pt")
    outputs = model.generate(
        inputs, max_length=1000, num_return_sequences=1
    )
    decomposition = tokenizer.decode(outputs[0],
        skip_special_tokens=True)

    # Parse decomposition and execute tools
    steps = parse_steps(decomposition)
    results = []
    for step in steps:
        if step['tool']:
            result = toolkit.use_tool(step['tool'],
                *step['args'])
        else:
            result = f"Reasoning: {step['reasoning']}"
        results.append(result)
```

2. Then we generate a final report. The generated report contains the task description, a breakdown of each step along with its result, and a concluding summary. The model uses the provided steps and results to generate a more cohesive and comprehensive narrative of the task:

```python
report_prompt = f"Task: {task}\n\nSteps and Results:\n"
for i, (step, result) in enumerate(zip(steps, results), 1):
    report_prompt += (
        f"Step {i}: {step['description']}\n"
        f"Result: {result}\n\n"
```

```
        )
        report_prompt += "Please provide a comprehensive report
    summarizing the results and insights."

        inputs = tokenizer(report_prompt, return_tensors="pt")
        outputs = model.generate(
            inputs, max_length=1500, num_return_sequences=1
        )
        report = tokenizer.decode(outputs[0],
            skip_special_tokens=True)

        return report
```

3. Then, we implement logic to parse the decomposition into structured steps. This is a simplified placeholder implementation:

```
def parse_steps(decomposition):

    steps = []
    for line in decomposition.split('\n'):
        if line.startswith("Step"):
            tool = "Twitter API" if "Twitter" in line else \
                    "Sentiment Analysis" if "sentiment" in line
    else \
                    "Data Visualization" if "visualization" in
    line else None
            steps.append({
                'description': line,
                'tool': tool,
                'args': [],
                'reasoning': line if not tool else ""
            })
    return steps
```

4. The following example usage demonstrates loading a language model and tokenizer using `AutoModelForCausalLM` and `AutoTokenizer`, defining a task to analyze tweet sentiments and generate a summary report with visualizations, and using an `auto_tool_use` function to automate the task via `ToolKit`, with the final report being printed:

```
model_name = "llama3.3"  # Replace with your preferred model
model = AutoModelForCausalLM.from_pretrained(model_name)
tokenizer = AutoTokenizer.from_pretrained(model_name)

task = "Analyze the sentiment of tweets about a new product
launch and create a summary report with visualizations."
```

```
toolkit = ToolKit()

report = auto_tool_use(model, tokenizer, task, toolkit)
print(report)
```

This code snippet shows at a high level how to enable the LLM to automatically decompose tasks, select appropriate tools, and generate a final report based on the results.

The first three sections of this chapter laid the groundwork by covering prompt design, integrating external tools, and implementing automatic tool selection to enhance AI functionality. In the following section, we will explore how to design prompts for complex problem solving.

Complex problem solving

Multi-step reasoning and tool use can be applied to various complex problem-solving scenarios. Here's an example of how to use this approach for market analysis:

```
def market_analysis(model, tokenizer, toolkit, product_name):
    task = f"""Conduct a comprehensive market analysis for the
product: {product_name}.
    Include competitor analysis, sentiment analysis of customer
reviews, and market trends visualization."""

    analysis_report = auto_tool_use(model, tokenizer, task, toolkit)
    return analysis_report

# Example usage
product_name = "SmartHome AI Assistant"
market_report = market_analysis(model, tokenizer, toolkit,
        product_name)
print(market_report)
```

The market_analysis function automates the generation of a market research report for a given product by constructing a structured task prompt and passing it to an external utility, auto_tool_use, which is assumed to orchestrate tool-augmented responses from a language model. The prompt requests a multi-part analysis—covering competitors, sentiment analysis of customer feedback, and visualization of market trends—targeted to the specific product_name supplied. This design leverages the model and toolkit to produce a consolidated report without manual intervention, enabling a consistent and repeatable approach to product market research through prompt-driven execution.

Evaluating multi-step reasoning and tool use

To assess the effectiveness of multi-step reasoning and tool use, we need to evaluate both the process and the outcome. Here's a simple evaluation framework:

```
def evaluate_multistep_tooluse(
    task, generated_report, ground_truth, criteria
):
    scores = {}
    for criterion in criteria:
        scores[criterion] = evaluate_criterion(generated_report,
            ground_truth, criterion)

    # Evaluate tool use effectiveness
    tool_use_score = evaluate_tool_use(task, generated_report)
    scores['Tool Use Effectiveness'] = tool_use_score

    return scores

def evaluate_criterion(generated_report, ground_truth, criterion):
    # Implement criterion-specific evaluation logic
    # This is a placeholder implementation
    return 0.0  # Return a score between 0 and 1

def evaluate_tool_use(task, generated_report):
    # Implement logic to evaluate how effectively tools were used
    # This could involve checking for specific tool outputs or
insights
    # This is a placeholder implementation
    return 0.0  # Return a score between 0 and 1

# Example usage
criteria = ['Accuracy', 'Comprehensiveness', 'Insight Quality',
    'Logical Flow']
ground_truth = "Ideal market analysis report content..."  # This would
be a benchmark report

evaluation_scores = evaluate_multistep_tooluse(task, market_report,
    ground_truth, criteria)
print("Evaluation Scores:", evaluation_scores)
```

This evaluation framework assesses both the quality of the generated report and the effectiveness of tool use in the process.

Challenges and future directions

While powerful, multi-step reasoning and tool use in LLMs face several challenges:

- **Tool selection accuracy**: Ensure LLMs choose the most appropriate tools for each task

- **Error propagation**: Mitigate the impact of errors in the early steps of the reasoning process; keep in mind that error propagation across multiple steps can be a major risk in complex tool chains if not mitigated early

- **Scalability**: Manage the complexity of integrating a large number of diverse tools

- **Adaptability**: Enable LLMs to work with new, unseen tools without retraining

To address some of these challenges, consider implementing a self-correction mechanism:

```python
def self_correcting_tooluse(
    model, tokenizer, task, toolkit, max_attempts=3
):
    for attempt in range(max_attempts):
        report = auto_tool_use(model, tokenizer, task, toolkit)

        # Prompt the model to evaluate its own work
        evaluation_prompt = f"""Task: {task}

Generated Report:
{report}

Please evaluate the quality and completeness of this report. Identify
any errors, omissions, or areas for improvement. If necessary, suggest
specific steps to enhance the analysis.

Your evaluation:
"""
        inputs = tokenizer(evaluation_prompt, return_tensors="pt")
        outputs = model.generate(
            inputs, max_length=1000, num_return_sequences=1
        )
        evaluation = tokenizer.decode(outputs[0],
            skip_special_tokens=True)

        if "satisfactory" in evaluation.lower() and "no major issues"
in evaluation.lower():
            break

        # If issues were identified, use the evaluation to improve the
next attempt
```

```
        task += f"\n\nPrevious attempt evaluation: {evaluation}\
    nPlease address these issues in your next attempt."

    return report

# Example usage
final_report = self_correcting_tooluse(model, tokenizer, task,
    toolkit)
print(final_report)
```

Self-correcting in this context refers to a method where a language model iteratively refines its output by evaluating and improving its own previous responses without external feedback. In the `self_correcting_tooluse` function, this is implemented by first generating a report using `auto_tool_use` and then prompting the model to assess the quality of that report. If the model's self-evaluation does not include indicators of adequacy—such as "satisfactory" and "no major issues"—the evaluation is appended to the task description, effectively guiding the next iteration to address identified shortcomings. This loop continues for a set number of attempts (`max_attempts`) until the output meets the model's own acceptance criteria, allowing self-guided refinement across multiple passes.

We can identify the following three promising research areas for overcoming the challenges from some research conducted by AI/ML communities:

- **Enhanced tool learning and discovery**: Future LLMs will be able to dynamically learn about and integrate new tools without explicit programming. This involves mechanisms for understanding tool documentation and API specifications and even experimenting with tools to infer their functionality. This will allow LLMs to adapt to a constantly evolving landscape of software and services, expanding their capabilities beyond a fixed set of pre-defined tools. This will involve techniques such as meta-learning, reinforcement learning from tool interactions, and semantic understanding of tool descriptions (`https://arxiv.org/abs/2305.17126`).

- **Robust and adaptive reasoning with uncertainty**: Future LLMs will incorporate probabilistic models to handle uncertainty in multi-step tasks. This means assigning probabilities to different reasoning paths, outcomes, and tool effectiveness. Bayesian methods, Monte Carlo simulations, and other probabilistic techniques will be integrated into the reasoning process. This will enable LLMs to make more robust decisions in complex scenarios with incomplete or noisy information and to better manage the inherent uncertainty of real-world problems. LLMs will be better equipped to handle unexpected situations, recover from errors, and provide more reliable solutions when faced with ambiguity (`https://arxiv.org/abs/2310.04406`).

- **Human-in-the-loop multi-step reasoning with explainability**: Future systems will involve closer collaboration between humans and LLMs in multi-step problem solving. This means creating interfaces that allow humans to understand the LLM's reasoning process, provide guidance, correct errors, and work together on complex tasks. Explainability will be key, with LLMs able to articulate their reasoning steps, justify tool choices, and present alternative solution paths. This will foster trust and allow for more effective human-AI collaboration, especially in critical domains such as healthcare, finance, and scientific research. This could involve visualizations of reasoning graphs, natural language explanations, and interactive debugging tools: `https://www.microsoft.com/en-us/research/blog/guidance-for-developing-with-large-language-models-llms/`.

Summary

Automatic multi-step reasoning and tool use significantly expand the problem-solving capabilities of LLMs, enabling them to tackle complex, real-world tasks.

In this chapter, you learned how to design prompts for complex task decomposition and implement systems that allow LLMs to interact with external tools and APIs. We looked at strategies for automatic tool selection and use and explored applications in complex problem-solving scenarios. You also learned how to evaluate the effectiveness of multi-step reasoning and tool use in LLMs. By implementing the techniques and considerations discussed in this chapter, you can create sophisticated AI systems that can decompose problems, leverage external tools, and generate comprehensive solutions to multi-faceted challenges.

As we move forward, the next part of the book will focus on retrieval and knowledge integration. This will build upon the tool use capabilities we've discussed here, exploring how LLMs can be enhanced with external knowledge, improving their ability to access and utilize information effectively.

Part 5:
Retrieval and Knowledge Integration in Large Language Models

We conclude this book by examining techniques that enhance LLMs with external knowledge through retrieval-augmented generation (RAG) methods. You will learn how to design retrieval systems that efficiently access relevant information, integrate structured knowledge into model outputs, and leverage graph-based retrieval to enrich responses with contextual relationships. Advanced RAG patterns, such as iterative and adaptive retrieval, will be explored, helping you create models capable of dynamic knowledge integration. We also discuss evaluation methodologies to measure retrieval quality and effectiveness. The final chapter introduces agentic patterns, enabling you to build autonomous systems that combine reasoning, planning, and decision-making. By mastering these techniques, you will be able to create LLMs that are not only informed but also capable of goal-directed behavior.

This part has the following chapters:

26
Retrieval-Augmented Generation

Retrieval-augmented generation (**RAG**) is a technique that enhances the performance of AI models, particularly in tasks that require knowledge or data not contained within the model's pre-trained parameters. It combines the strengths of both retrieval-based models and generative models. The retrieval component fetches relevant information from external sources, such as databases, documents, or web content, and the generative component uses this information to produce more accurate, contextually enriched responses.

RAG is implemented by integrating a retrieval mechanism with a language model. The process begins by querying a knowledge base or external resource for relevant documents or snippets. These retrieved pieces of information are then fed into the language model, which generates a response by incorporating both the prompt and the retrieved data. This approach improves the model's ability to answer questions or solve problems with up-to-date or domain-specific information that it would otherwise lack.

In this chapter, we'll introduce you to RAG. You'll learn how to implement a simple RAG system that can enhance LLM outputs with relevant external information.

The key benefits of RAG include enhanced factual accuracy, access to current information, improved domain-specific knowledge, and reduced hallucination in LLM outputs.

In this chapter, we'll cover embedding and indexing techniques of vector databases for efficient retrieval, query formulation strategies, and methods for integrating retrieved information with LLM generation. By the end of this chapter, you'll be able to implement basic RAG systems to augment your LLMs with external knowledge.

In this chapter, we'll be covering the following topics:

- Building a simple RAG system for LLMs

- Embedding and indexing techniques for LLM retrieval

- Query formulation strategies in LLM-based RAG

- Integrating retrieved information with LLM generation

- Challenges and opportunities in RAG for LLMs

Building a simple RAG system for LLMs

This section provides a practical illustration of a simple RAG system, leveraging the robust search capabilities of **SerpApi**, the semantic understanding of sentence embeddings, and the generative prowess of OpenAI's GPT-4o model. SerpApi is a web scraping API that provides real-time access to search engine results, offering structured data for Google, Bing, and other platforms without the need for manual scraping.

Through this example, we will explore the fundamental components of a RAG system, including query-based web searching, snippet extraction and ranking, and, ultimately, the generation of a comprehensive answer using a state-of-the-art LLM, highlighting the interplay between these elements in a step-by-step manner.

The code for the simple RAG system we'll be building contains the following:

- **SerpApi**: To find relevant web pages based on the user's query.

- **Sentence embeddings**: To extract the most relevant snippets from the search results using sentence embeddings and cosine similarity. Sentence embeddings are dense numerical representations of text that capture semantic meaning by mapping words, phrases, or entire sentences into high-dimensional vector space, where similar meanings are positioned closer together. Cosine similarity measures the angle between these embedding vectors (ranging from -1 to 1), rather than their magnitude, making it an effective way to evaluate semantic similarity regardless of text length; when two embeddings have a cosine similarity close to 1, they're highly similar in meaning, while values closer to 0 indicate unrelated content and negative values suggest opposing meanings. This combination of techniques powers many modern **natural language processing** (**NLP**) applications, from search engines and recommendation systems to language translation and content clustering.

- **OpenAI's GPT-4o**: To generate a comprehensive and coherent answer based on the retrieved snippets (context) and the original query.

First, let's install the following dependencies:

```
pip install google-search-results sentence-transformers openai
```

In the preceding command, we install `serpapi` for searching, `sentence_transformers` for embedding, and `openai` for accessing GPT-4o.

Next, let us see how a complete RAG system is implemented using search APIs, embeddings, and an LLM:

1. We first import the installed libraries along with `torch` for tensor operations. The code snippet also sets up API keys for SerpApi and OpenAI. Remember to replace the placeholders with your actual API keys:

```
from serpapi import GoogleSearch
from sentence_transformers import SentenceTransformer, util
import torch
import openai

SERPAPI_KEY = "YOUR_SERPAPI_KEY"  # Replace with your SerpAPI
key
OPENAI_API_KEY = "YOUR_OPENAI_API_KEY"  # Replace with your
OpenAI key
openai.api_key = OPENAI_API_KEY
```

2. We then initialize the search engine and Sentence Transformer. The following code defines the search function to perform a Google search using SerpApi and initializes the Sentence Transformer model (`all-mpnet-base-v2`) for creating sentence embeddings:

```
def search(query):
params = {
    "q": query,
    "hl": "en",
    "gl": "us",
    "google_domain": "google.com",
    "api_key": SERPAPI_KEY,
}
search = GoogleSearch(params)
results = search.get_dict()
return results

model = SentenceTransformer('all-mpnet-base-v2')
```

3. Next, we retrieve relevant snippets. We define the `retrieve_snippets` function, which takes the search results, extracts snippets, computes their embeddings, and calculates the cosine similarity between the query embedding and each snippet embedding. It then returns the top *k* snippets that are most similar to the query:

```
def retrieve_snippets(query, results, top_k=3):
  snippets = [
```

```
            result.get("snippet", "")
            for result in results.get("organic_results", [])
    ]
    if not snippets:
        return []

    query_embedding = model.encode(query,
        convert_to_tensor=True)
    snippet_embeddings = model.encode(snippets,
        convert_to_tensor=True)

    cosine_scores = util.pytorch_cos_sim(
        query_embedding, snippet_embeddings
    )[0]
    top_results = torch.topk(cosine_scores, k=top_k)

    return [snippets[i] for i in top_results.indices]
```

4. We then define the `generate_answer` function to generate an answer using GPT-4o. This is the core of the generation part of our RAG system:

```
def generate_answer(query, context):
    messages = [
        {
            "role": "system",
            "content": "You are a knowledgeable expert. Answer
the user's query based only on the information provided in the
context. "
                        "If the answer is not in the context,
say 'I couldn't find an answer to your question in the provided
context.'",
        },
        {
            "role": "user",
            "content": f"Context: {context}\n\nQuery: {query}",
        },
    ]

    response = openai.chat.completions.create(
        model="gpt-4o",
        messages=messages,
        temperature=0.7,
        max_tokens=256
    )
    return response.choices[0].message.content
```

This function constructs a structured prompt for an LLM to generate an answer constrained strictly to a given context. It formats the conversation as a system-user message pair, instructing the model to act as a subject matter expert and restrict its answer to the supplied information, explicitly avoiding speculation. If the information isn't present, the system is directed to return a fallback message indicating that the answer couldn't be found. The query and context are embedded directly into the user message, and the LLM (in this case, gpt-4o) is queried with a moderate creativity level via temperature=0.7 and a response length cap of 256 tokens. This design makes the function reliable for context-grounded Q&A tasks, particularly in RAG pipelines or constrained-answering settings such as document QA or compliance tools.

5. Here's the main RAG function and example usage:

```
def rag_system(query):
  search_results = search(query)
  relevant_snippets = retrieve_snippets(query, search_results)
  if not relevant_snippets:
      return "Could not find any information related to your
query"
  context = " ".join(relevant_snippets)
  answer = generate_answer(query, context)
  return answer


# Example usage
query = "What are the latest advancements in quantum computing?"
answer = rag_system(query)
print(answer)
```

This code defines the rag_system function, which orchestrates the entire process: searching, retrieving snippets, and generating an answer. It then demonstrates how to use rag_system with an example query, printing the generated answer to the console

The rag_system function answers a query by first searching for relevant information using search(query) and then extracting relevant snippets through the API called retrieve_snippets(query, search_results). If no snippets are found, it returns a message indicating no information was found. If snippets are available, they are combined into a single context string and used to generate an answer through generate_answer(query, context). Finally, the function returns the generated answer based on the context. In the example usage, the function is called with the query "What are the latest advancements in quantum computing?" and will return a generated response based on the relevant search results. In real production systems, we should implement retries and error handling around retrieve_snippets API calls.

Before we move on to the next section, here are some things to remember:

- **API keys**: Make sure you have valid API keys for both SerpApi and OpenAI and have replaced the placeholders in the code.

- **OpenAI costs**: Be mindful of OpenAI API usage costs. GPT-4o can be more expensive than other models.

- **Prompt engineering**: The quality of the generated answer heavily depends on the prompt you provide to GPT-4o. You might need to experiment with different prompts to get the best results. Consider adding instructions about the desired answer format, length, or style.

- **Error handling**: For a production-ready system, add error handling (e.g., `try-except` blocks) to handle potential issues such as network problems, API errors, or invalid inputs.

- **Advanced techniques**: This is a basic RAG system. You can improve it further by doing the following:

  - **Better snippet selection**: Consider factors such as source diversity, factuality, and snippet length

  - **Iterative retrieval**: Retrieve more context if the initial answer is not satisfactory

  - **Fine-tuning**: Fine-tune a smaller, more specialized language model on your specific domain for potentially better performance and lower costs

We've successfully built a simple RAG system, covering the core components of retrieval and generation. Now that we have a functional RAG system, let's dive deeper into the crucial techniques that enable efficient retrieval from large datasets: embedding and indexing. We'll explore different methods for representing text semantically and organizing these representations for fast similarity search.

Embeddings and indexing for retrieval in LLM applications

Embedding and indexing techniques provide efficient and effective retrieval in RAG-based LLM applications. They allow LLMs to quickly find and utilize relevant information from vast amounts of data. The following subsections provide a breakdown of common techniques.

Embeddings

Embeddings are numerical vector representations of data, such as text, images, or audio, that map complex, high-dimensional data into a continuous vector space where similar items are positioned close to each other. These vectors capture the underlying patterns, relationships, and semantic properties of the data, making it easier for machine learning models to understand and process. For text, for example, word embeddings transform words or phrases into dense vectors that represent their meaning in a way that reflects semantic relationships, such as synonyms being closer together in the vector space. Embeddings are typically learned from large datasets through techniques such as neural networks, and they serve as a foundation for tasks such as information retrieval, classification, clustering, and recommendation systems. By reducing the dimensionality of data while preserving important features, embeddings enable models to generalize better and make sense of varied input data efficiently.

For LLMs, text embeddings are most relevant. They are generated by passing text through a neural network (like the Sentence Transformer models we used in the previous section).

Why do we need embeddings?

Embeddings are important for RAG applications for the following reasons:

- **Semantic search**: Embeddings enable semantic search, where you find information based on meaning rather than just keyword matching

- **Contextual understanding**: LLMs can use embeddings to understand the relationships between different pieces of information, improving their ability to reason and generate relevant responses

- **Efficient retrieval**: When combined with appropriate indexing, embeddings allow for the fast retrieval of relevant information from large datasets

Common embedding technologies

Several embedding technologies are commonly used in RAG systems, and these vary in their underlying models, methods, and suitability for different applications. Here are some prominent embedding technologies for RAG:

- **Pre-trained transformer-based embeddings (e.g., BERT, RoBERTa, and T5)**: Transformer models such as **Bidirectional Encoder Representations from Transformers** (BERT) and its variants, such as RoBERTa and T5, have been widely used to generate dense, contextual embeddings for text. These models are fine-tuned on large corpora and capture a rich understanding of language semantics. In a RAG system, these embeddings can be used to retrieve relevant passages from a document store based on semantic similarity. The embeddings are typically high-dimensional and are generated by feeding text through the transformer model to produce a fixed-size vector.

- **Sentence-BERT (SBERT)**: A variation of BERT designed for sentence-level embeddings, SBERT focuses on optimizing the model for tasks such as semantic textual similarity and clustering. It uses a Siamese network architecture to map sentences into a dense vector space where semantically similar sentences are closer together. This makes it particularly effective for tasks such as information retrieval in RAG, where retrieving semantically relevant passages from a large corpus is essential.

- **Facebook AI Similarity Search (Faiss)**: Faiss is a library developed by Facebook AI Research that provides efficient similarity search through **approximate nearest neighbor (ANN)** search. Faiss is not an embedding technology by itself but works in conjunction with various embedding models to index and search over large collections of vectors. When used in RAG, Faiss enables the fast retrieval of relevant documents or passages by comparing the similarity of their embeddings against a query embedding.

- **Dense retriever models (e.g., DPR and ColBERT)**: **Dense Passage Retrieval (DPR)** is an approach to information retrieval that uses two separate encoders (usually BERT-based models) to encode both queries and passages into dense vectors. DPR outperforms traditional sparse retrieval methods by leveraging the contextual knowledge encoded in dense embeddings. ColBERT, on the other hand, is another dense retrieval model that balances the efficiency of dense retrieval and the effectiveness of traditional methods. These models are especially useful for RAG when retrieving high-quality passages that are semantically related to a query.

- **Contrastive Language-Image Pre-Training (CLIP)**: While originally designed for multimodal applications (text and image), CLIP has been adapted for text-only tasks as well. It learns embeddings by aligning text and image data in a shared vector space. Although CLIP is primarily used for multimodal tasks, its ability to represent language in a common space with images provides a flexible embedding framework that can be used in RAG, especially when working with multimodal data.

- **Deep semantic similarity models (e.g., USE and InferSent)**: Models such as the **Universal Sentence Encoder (USE)** and InferSent generate sentence embeddings by capturing deeper semantic meaning, which can be used for various NLP tasks, including document retrieval. These models produce fixed-size vector representations that can be compared for similarity, making them useful for RAG when paired with retrieval systems.

- **Doc2Vec**: An extension of Word2Vec, Doc2Vec generates embeddings for entire documents rather than individual words. It maps variable-length text into a fixed-size vector, which can be used to retrieve semantically similar documents or passages. Though not as powerful as transformer-based models in terms of semantic richness, Doc2Vec is still an effective tool for more lightweight retrieval tasks in RAG applications.

- **Embedding-based search engines (e.g., Elasticsearch with dense vectors)**: Some modern search engines, such as Elasticsearch, have integrated support for dense vectors alongside traditional keyword-based indexing. Elasticsearch can store and retrieve text embeddings, allowing for more flexible and semantically aware searches. When used with RAG, these embeddings can be used to rank documents by their relevance to a query, improving retrieval performance.

- **OpenAI embeddings (e.g., GPT-based models)**: OpenAI's embeddings, derived from models such as GPT-3, are also used for RAG tasks. These embeddings are based on the language model's ability to generate high-quality text representations, which can be indexed and searched over large corpora. While they are not as specifically tuned for retrieval as some other models (such as DPR), they are highly flexible and can be used in general-purpose RAG applications.

These embedding technologies provide various advantages depending on the specific requirements of a RAG system, such as retrieval speed, model accuracy, and the scale of the data being processed. Each of them can be fine-tuned and optimized for specific use cases, and the choice of embedding technology will depend on factors such as the nature of the documents being retrieved, computational resources, and latency requirements.

Indexing

Indexing is the process of organizing embeddings in a data structure that allows for fast similarity search. Think of it like the index of a book, but for vectors instead of words.

Using a more detailed description using LLM terminology, vector indexing technologies optimize embedding storage and retrieval by creating specialized data structures that organize high-dimensional vectors according to their similarity relationships, rather than sequential order. These structures— whether graph-based (connecting similar vectors through navigable pathways), tree-based (recursively partitioning the vector space), or quantization-based (compressing vectors while preserving similarity)— all serve the fundamental purpose of transforming an otherwise prohibitively expensive exhaustive search into a manageable process by strategically limiting the search space, enabling vector databases to handle billions of embeddings with sub-second query times while maintaining an acceptable trade-off between speed, memory efficiency, and result accuracy.

Why is indexing important?

Indexing is important for LLMs for the following reasons:

- **Speed**: Without indexing, you would have to compare a query embedding to every single embedding in your dataset, which is computationally expensive and slow
- **Scalability**: Indexing allows LLM applications to scale to handle massive datasets containing millions or even billions of data points

Common indexing techniques

Let's look at some of the common indexing techniques for LLMs.

For a visual diagram of these index techniques, I recommend you check out the following website: `https://kdb.ai/learning-hub/articles/indexing-basics/`

- **Flat index (brute force)**:
  - **How it works**: Stores all embeddings in a simple list or array. During a search, it calculates the distance (e.g., cosine similarity) between the query embedding and every embedding in the index.
  - **Pros**: Simple to implement and perfect accuracy (finds the true nearest neighbors).

- **Cons**: Slow and computationally expensive for large datasets, as it requires an exhaustive search.

- **Suitable for**: Very small datasets or when perfect accuracy is an absolute requirement.

- **Inverted file index (IVF)**:

  - **How it works**:

    - **Clustering**: Divides the embedding space into clusters using algorithms such as k-means

    - **Inverted index**: Creates an inverted index that maps each cluster centroid to a list of the embeddings belonging to that cluster

    - **Search**:

    i.   Finds the nearest cluster centroid(s) to the query embedding

    ii.   Only searches within those clusters, significantly reducing the search space

  - **Pros**: Faster than a flat index; relatively simple to implement

  - **Cons**: Approximate (might not always find the true nearest neighbors); accuracy depends on the number of clusters

  - **Suitable for**: Medium-sized datasets where a good balance between speed and accuracy is needed

- **Hierarchical navigable small world (HNSW)**:

  - **How it works**:

    - **Graph-based**: Constructs a hierarchical graph where each node represents an embedding.

    - **Layers**: The graph has multiple layers, with the top layer having long-range connections (for faster traversal) and the bottom layer having short-range connections (for accurate search).

    - **Search**: Starts at a random node in the top layer and greedily moves towards the query embedding by exploring connections. The search progresses down the layers, refining the results.

  - **Pros**: Very fast and accurate; often considered the state of the art for ANN search

  - **Cons**: More complex to implement than IVF, and higher memory overhead due to the graph structure

  - **Suitable for**: Large datasets where both speed and accuracy are crucial

- **Product quantization (PQ)**:

  - **How it works**:

    - **Subvectors**: Divides each embedding into multiple subvectors.

    - **Codebooks**: Creates separate codebooks for each subvector using clustering. Each codebook contains a set of representative subvectors (centroids).

    - **Encoding**: Encodes each embedding by replacing its subvectors with the closest centroids from the corresponding codebooks. This creates a compressed representation of the embedding.

    - **Search**: Calculates the approximate distance between the query and the encoded embeddings using pre-computed distances between the query's subvectors and the codebook centroids.

  - **Pros**: Significantly reduces memory usage by compressing embeddings; fast search.

  - **Cons**: Approximate, and accuracy depends on the number of subvectors and the size of the codebooks.

  - **Suitable for**: Very large datasets where memory efficiency is a primary concern.

- **Locality sensitive hashing (LSH)**:

  - **How it works**: Uses hash functions to map similar embeddings to the same "bucket" with high probability

  - **Pros**: Relatively simple; can be distributed across multiple machines

  - **Cons**: Approximate, and performance depends on the choice of hash functions and the number of buckets

  - **Suitable for**: Very large, high-dimensional datasets

Now that we've covered different indexing methods, let's introduce some popular libraries and tools that implement these indexing techniques, making them easier to use in practice. This will provide a practical perspective on how to leverage these technologies in your RAG applications.

The following are some libraries and tools for implementing indexing:

- **Faiss**: A highly optimized library developed by Facebook AI for efficient similarity search and clustering of dense vectors. It implements many of the indexing techniques mentioned previously (flat, IVF, HNSW, and PQ).

- **Approximate Nearest Neighbors Oh Yeah (Annoy)**: Another popular library for ANN search, known for its ease of use and good performance. It uses a tree-based approach.

- **Scalable Nearest Neighbors (ScaNN)**: A library developed by Google, designed for large-scale, high-dimensional datasets.

- **Vespa.ai**: Provide tools to query, organize, and make inferences in vectors, tensors, text, and structured data. It is used by `https://www.perplexity.ai/`.

- **Pinecone, Weaviate, Milvus, Qdrant**: Vector databases designed specifically for storing and searching embeddings. They handle indexing, scaling, and other infrastructure concerns.

The best embedding and indexing techniques for your LLM application will depend on several factors:

- **Dataset size**: For small datasets, a flat index might be sufficient. For large datasets, consider HNSW, IVF, or PQ.

- **Speed requirements**: If low latency is critical, HNSW is generally the fastest option.

- **Accuracy requirements**: If perfect accuracy is required, a flat index is the only choice, but it's not scalable. HNSW often provides the best accuracy among approximate methods.

- **Memory constraints**: If memory is limited, PQ can significantly reduce storage requirements.

- **Development effort**: Faiss and Annoy offer a good balance between performance and ease of implementation. Vector databases simplify infrastructure management.

By carefully considering these factors and understanding the strengths and weaknesses of each technique and library, you can choose the most appropriate embedding and indexing methods to build efficient and effective LLM applications.

We'll now demonstrate an example involving embedding, indexing, and searching using Faiss, a powerful library for efficient similarity search. I'll use the `all-mpnet-base-v2` Sentence Transformer model to generate embeddings. Since the code will be more than 20 lines, I'll break it down into blocks with explanations preceding each block.

Example code demonstrating embedding, indexing, and searching

In this section, we'll be showing the code for a typical workflow for using embeddings and indexing to enable fast similarity search within a collection of text documents: Here's what it does:

1. **Loads a Sentence Transformer model**: Initializes a pre-trained model for generating sentence embeddings.

2. **Creates sample data**: Defines a list of example sentences (you would replace this with your actual data).

3. **Generates embeddings**: Uses `SentenceTransformer` to create embeddings for each sentence.

4. **Creates an index**: Builds a Faiss index (using `IndexFlatL2` for a flat L2 distance index in this example) to store the embeddings.

5. **Adds embeddings to the index**: Adds the generated embeddings to the Faiss index.

6. **Defines a search query**: Sets a sample query for which we want to find similar sentences.

7. **Encodes the query**: Creates an embedding for the search query using the same Sentence Transformer model.

8. **Performs a search**: Uses the Faiss index to search for the *k* most similar embeddings to the query embedding.

9. **Prints the results**: Displays the indices and distances of the *k* nearest neighbors found in the index.

Before we check out the code, let us install the following dependencies:

```
pip install faiss-cpu sentence-transformers
# Use faiss-gpu if you have a compatible GPU
```

Let us now see the code example:

1. First, we import the necessary libraries—`sentence_transformers` for creating embeddings and `faiss` for indexing and searching—and load the `all-mpnet-base-v2` Sentence Transformer model:

    ```
    from sentence_transformers import SentenceTransformer
    import faiss
    import numpy as np


    # Load the SentenceTransformer model
    model = SentenceTransformer('all-mpnet-base-v2')
    ```

2. We then prepare the data by defining some sample sentences (you can replace these with your actual data) and then use the Sentence Transformer model to generate embeddings for each sentence (the embeddings are converted to float32, which is required by Faiss):

    ```
    # Sample sentences
    text_data = [
        "A man is walking his dog in the park.",
        "Children are playing with toys indoors.",
        "An artist is painting a landscape on canvas.",
        "The sun sets behind the mountain ridge.",
        "Birds are singing outside the window."
    ]


    # Generate vector representations using a SentenceTransformer
    model
    import numpy as np
    from sentence_transformers import SentenceTransformer


    model = SentenceTransformer('all-MiniLM-L6-v2')   # Replace with
    your model if different
    ```

```
vectors = model.encode(text_data, convert_to_tensor=True)

# Ensure compatibility with Faiss by converting to 32-bit
floating point and moving to CPU
vectors = vectors.detach().cpu().numpy().astype(np.float32)
```

3. We then create a Faiss index and add the embeddings to it:

```
# Get the dimensionality of the embeddings
dimension = embeddings.shape[1]

# Create a Faiss index (flat L2 distance)
index = faiss.IndexFlatL2(dimension)

# Add the embeddings to the index
index.add(embeddings)
```

Here, we're using IndexFlatL2, which is a flat index that uses L2 distance (Euclidean distance) for similarity comparisons. This type of index provides accurate results but can be slow for very large datasets. The index is created with the correct dimensionality (768 for this Sentence Transformer model).

4. Next, we define a sample search query and encode it into an embedding using the same Sentence Transformer model. The query embedding is also converted to float32:

```
# Define a search query
query = "What is the dog doing?"

# Encode the query
query_embedding = model.encode(query, convert_to_tensor=True)
query_embedding = \
    query_embedding.cpu().numpy().astype('float32')
```

5. Finally, we perform similarity search using the index.search() method. We search for the two most similar sentences (k=2). The method returns the distances and the indices of the nearest neighbors. We then print the indices and distances of the nearest neighbors found:

```
# Search for the k nearest neighbors
k = 2
distances, indices = index.search(query_embedding, k)

# Print the results
print("Nearest neighbors:")
for i, idx in enumerate(indices[0]):
    print(f"  Index: {idx}, Distance: {distances[0][i]},
    Sentence: {sentences[idx]}")
```

The following is sample output you might get from running the preceding code blocks:

```
Nearest neighbors:
   Index: 0, Distance: 0.634912312, Sentence: A man is walking his dog
in the park.
   Index: 1, Distance: 1.237844944, Sentence: Children are playing with
toys indoors.
```

This demonstrates how semantic similarity search works using Sentence Transformers and Faiss. Note that actual numbers will vary depending on the hardware, model versions, and runtime conditions.

Here's what's happening.

The query `"What is the dog doing?"` is embedded and compared against all embedded sentences in the list. Faiss retrieves the two most semantically similar sentences based on Euclidean (L2) distance in the embedding space. The smallest distance indicates the highest similarity. In this example, the sentence about the man walking his dog is closest to the query, which makes sense semantically.

If you're running this on your machine, your values may look different due to the non-determinism in model initialization and floating-point precision, but the closest sentence should consistently be the one most semantically related to the query.

> **Important**
>
> **Index type**: For very large datasets, you would likely want to use a more advanced index type, such as `IndexIVFFlat` or `IndexHNSWFlat` from Faiss, to improve search speed.
>
> **GPU acceleration**: If you have a compatible GPU, you can install `faiss-gpu` to significantly speed up indexing and searching.
>
> **Data preprocessing**: For real-world applications, you might need to perform additional data preprocessing steps, such as lowercasing, removing punctuation, or stemming/lemmatization, depending on your specific needs and the nature of your data.
>
> **Distance metrics**: Faiss supports different distance metrics. We used L2 distance here, but you could also use the inner product (IndexFlatIP) or other metrics depending on how your embeddings are generated and what kind of similarity you want to measure.
>
> **Vector databases**: For production-level systems, consider using a dedicated vector database such as Pinecone, Weaviate, or Milvus to manage your embeddings and indexes more efficiently. They often provide features such as automatic indexing, scaling, and data management, which simplify the deployment of similarity search applications.

We've covered the fundamentals of embeddings, indexing, and searching with Faiss, along with important considerations for real-world implementation. Now, let's turn our attention to another crucial aspect of RAG: query formulation. We'll explore various strategies to refine and expand user queries, ultimately leading to more effective information retrieval from the knowledge base.

Query formulation strategies in LLM-based RAG

Query formulation strategies in LLM-based RAG systems aim to enhance retrieval by improving the expressiveness and coverage of user queries. Common expansion strategies include the following:

- **Synonym and paraphrase expansion**: This involves generating semantically equivalent alternatives using LLMs or lexical resources. For example, expanding "climate change impact" to include "effects of global warming" or "environmental consequences of climate change" can help match a broader range of documents.

- **Contextual reformulation**: LLMs can reinterpret queries by inferring their intent based on conversational or document context. This helps in tailoring the query to better align with how the information might be expressed in the knowledge base.

- **Pseudo-relevance feedback**: Also known as blind relevance feedback, this strategy involves running an initial query, analyzing the top-ranked documents for salient terms, and using these terms to expand the query. While effective, it requires safeguards against topic drift.

- **Template-based augmentation**: Useful in structured domains, this method uses domain-specific templates or patterns to systematically generate variants. For example, a medical query about "treatment for hypertension" might also include "hypertension therapy" or "managing high blood pressure."

- **Entity and concept linking**: Named entities and domain concepts in the query are identified and replaced or augmented with their aliases, definitions, or hierarchical relations. This is often guided by ontologies or knowledge graphs.

- **Prompt-based query rewriting**: With LLMs, prompts can be crafted to explicitly instruct the model to generate reformulated queries. This is particularly useful in multilingual or multi-domain RAG systems, where queries need to be adapted to match the style and vocabulary of the target corpus.

Each strategy contributes differently to recall and precision. Choosing or combining them depends on the structure and variability of the underlying knowledge base.

In the following code, the `QueryExpansionRAG` implementation uses a prompt-based query rewriting strategy powered by a pre-trained sequence-to-sequence language model (specifically, T5-small). This approach instructs the model to generate alternative phrasings of the input query by prefixing the prompt with `"expand query:"`. The generated expansions reflect paraphrastic reformulation, where the model synthesizes semantically related variations to increase retrieval coverage:

```
from transformers import pipeline


class QueryExpansionRAG(AdvancedRAG):
    def __init__(
        self, model_name, knowledge_base,
```

```
        query_expansion_model="t5-small"
    ):
        super().__init__(model_name, knowledge_base)
        self.query_expander = pipeline(
            "text2text-generation", model=query_expansion_model
        )

    def expand_query(self, query):
        expanded = self.query_expander(
            f"expand query: {query}", max_length=50,
            num_return_sequences=3
        )
        return [query] + [e['generated_text'] for e in expanded]

    def retrieve(self, query, k=5):
        expanded_queries = self.expand_query(query)
        all_retrieved = []
        for q in expanded_queries:
            all_retrieved.extend(super().retrieve(q, k))

        # Remove duplicates and return top k
        unique_retrieved = list(dict.fromkeys(all_retrieved))
        return unique_retrieved[:k]

# Example usage
rag_system = QueryExpansionRAG(model_name, knowledge_base)
retrieved_docs = rag_system.retrieve(query)
print("Retrieved documents:", retrieved_docs)
```

This code defines a `QueryExpansionRAG` class that extends a RAG framework by incorporating query expansion using a pre-trained T5 model. When a user submits a query, the `expand_query` method uses the T5 model through a text-to-text generation pipeline to produce multiple alternative phrasings of the query, which are then combined with the original query. The `retrieve` method iterates over these expanded queries, retrieving documents for each one and aggregating the results while removing duplicates. This approach increases the chances of retrieving relevant content by broadening the lexical and semantic scope of the original query, making it especially effective when the knowledge base expresses information in varied ways.

Keep in mind that poorly expanded queries can introduce noise and reduce retrieval precision. In this implementation, expansions generated by the T5 model are combined with the original query, increasing coverage. However, to maintain a balance, consider reranking results using similarity scores or assigning lower weights to generated expansions during retrieval. This helps ensure that expansions improve recall without compromising the alignment with the original intent.

We've seen how query expansion can enhance retrieval in RAG systems, but it's essential to manage the trade-off between recall and precision. Now, let's shift our focus to the other side of the RAG pipeline: integrating the retrieved information with the LLM to generate the final answer. We'll explore how to craft prompts that effectively leverage the retrieved context.

Integrating retrieved information with LLM generation

To integrate retrieved information with LLM generation, we can create a prompt that incorporates the retrieved documents:

```python
from transformers import AutoModelForCausalLM

class GenerativeRAG(QueryExpansionRAG):
    def __init__(
        self, retriever_model, generator_model, knowledge_base
    ):
        super().__init__(retriever_model, knowledge_base)
        self.generator = \
            AutoModelForCausalLM.from_pretrained(generator_model)
        self.generator_tokenizer = \
            AutoTokenizer.from_pretrained(generator_model)

    def generate_response(self, query, max_length=100):
        retrieved_docs = self.retrieve(query)
        context = "\n".join(retrieved_docs)
        prompt = f"Context:\n{context}\n\nQuestion: {query}\nAnswer:"

        inputs = self.generator_tokenizer(prompt, return_tensors="pt")
        outputs = self.generator.generate(inputs,
            max_length=max_length)
        return self.generator_tokenizer.decode(
            outputs[0], skip_special_tokens=True)

# Example usage
retriever_model = "all-MiniLM-L6-v2"
generator_model = "gpt2-medium"
rag_system = GenerativeRAG(
    retriever_model, generator_model, knowledge_base
)
response = rag_system.generate_response(query)
print("Generated response:", response)
```

In the preceding code snippet, the `GenerativeRAG` class extends a RAG pipeline by integrating a causal language model for answer generation. It inherits from `QueryExpansionRAG`, which already provides retrieval functionality, and adds a generator component using Hugging Face's `AutoModelForCausalLM`. In the constructor, it initializes the generator model and tokenizer based on the given model name. The `generate_response` method first retrieves relevant documents for a given query, concatenates them into a single context string, and constructs a prompt that combines this context with the question. This prompt is then tokenized and passed into the language model, which generates a text continuation as the answer. The final output is obtained by decoding the generated tokens into a string. This modular structure separates the retrieval and generation steps, making it easy to scale or replace individual components depending on the task or model performance requirements.

Having covered the basics of RAG systems, we will now focus on real-world challenges, such as scalability, dynamic updates, and multilingual retrieval. Specifically, we will discuss how a sharded indexing architecture can improve retrieval efficiency at scale, highlighting its impact on performance in data-heavy environments.

Challenges and opportunities in RAG for LLMs

Some key challenges and opportunities in RAG include the following:

- **Scalability**: Efficiently handling very large knowledge bases.
- **Dynamic knowledge updating**: Keeping the knowledge base current.
- **Cross-lingual RAG**: Retrieving and generating in multiple languages.
- **Multi-modal RAG**: Incorporating non-text information in retrieval and generation.

  Keep in mind that cross-lingual and multi-modal RAG will need specialized retrieval pipelines or adapters because standard retrieval approaches often struggle with semantic matching across languages or modalities, requiring dedicated components that can properly encode, align, and retrieve relevant information regardless of the source language or format while maintaining contextual understanding and relevance.

- **Explainable RAG**: Providing transparency in the retrieval and generation process.

To keep this chapter from becoming too long, in this section, we will only show an example on how to address the scalability challenge by implementing a sharded index. A sharded index refers to a distributed data structure that partitions the index into multiple smaller, manageable segments called shards, each stored and maintained independently across different nodes or storage units. This approach enables parallel processing, reduces lookup time, and mitigates bottlenecks associated with centralized indexing, making it suitable for handling large-scale datasets or high query volumes commonly encountered in AI applications:

```
class ShardedRAG(GenerativeRAG):
    def __init__(
        self, retriever_model, generator_model,
```

```
        knowledge_base, num_shards=5
    ):
        super().__init__(retriever_model, generator_model,
            knowledge_base)
        self.num_shards = num_shards
        self.sharded_indexes = self.build_sharded_index()

    def build_sharded_index(self):
        embeddings = self.get_embeddings(self.knowledge_base)
        sharded_indexes = []
        shard_size = len(embeddings) // self.num_shards

        for i in range(self.num_shards):
            start = i * shard_size
            end = start + shard_size if i < self.num_shards - 1
                else len(embeddings)
            shard_index = faiss.IndexFlatL2(embeddings.shape[1])
            shard_index.add(embeddings[start:end])
            sharded_indexes.append(shard_index)

        return sharded_indexes

    def retrieve(self, query, k=5):
        query_embedding = self.get_embeddings([query])[0]
        all_retrieved = []

        for shard_index in self.sharded_indexes:
            _, indices = shard_index.search(
                np.array([query_embedding]), k)
            all_retrieved.extend([self.knowledge_base[i]
                for i in indices[0]])

        # Remove duplicates and return top k
        unique_retrieved = list(dict.fromkeys(all_retrieved))
        return unique_retrieved[:k]

# Example usage
sharded_rag = ShardedRAG(retriever_model, generator_model,
    knowledge_base)
response = sharded_rag.generate_response(query)
print("Generated response:", response)
```

In the preceding code, the scalability is handled by dividing the knowledge base into multiple smaller indexes, or shards, each containing a portion of the overall data. This approach reduces the computational and memory burden on any single index and allows retrieval operations to remain efficient even as the dataset grows. During a query, the system embeds the query once, searches across all shards independently, and then merges the results. This design avoids bottlenecks that would arise from searching a single large index and makes it feasible to scale to much larger knowledge bases. It also lays the groundwork for further optimizations, such as parallelizing shard queries or distributing them across multiple machines.

Summary

RAG is a powerful technique for enhancing LLMs with external knowledge. By implementing the strategies and techniques discussed in this chapter, you can create more informed and accurate language models capable of accessing and utilizing vast amounts of information.

As we move forward, the next chapter will explore graph-based RAG for LLMs, which extends the RAG concept to leverage structured knowledge representations. This will further enhance the ability of LLMs to reason over complex relationships and generate more contextually appropriate responses.

Subscribe for a free eBook

New frameworks, evolving architectures, research drops, production breakdowns—AI_Distilled filters the noise into a weekly briefing for engineers and researchers working hands-on with LLMs and GenAI systems. Subscribe now and receive a free eBook, along with weekly insights that help you stay focused and informed. Subscribe at `https://packt.link/8Oz6Y` or scan the QR code below.

27
Graph-Based RAG

In this chapter, we'll learn how to leverage graph-structured knowledge in RAG for LLMs. You'll learn about graph-based knowledge representation and how to design RAG architectures that can utilize this structured information.

A graph-based knowledge representation structures information as nodes and edges in a graph, where nodes represent concepts or facts and edges capture their relationships. When used with RAG, this approach enables richer information retrieval by leveraging both the individual pieces of information and their interconnections, allowing for more contextual and relationship-aware responses.

We'll cover graph embedding techniques for retrieval, query expansion using graph structures, and methods for integrating graph information into LLM generation. You'll also explore various applications and use cases of graph RAG in LLMs.

By the end of this chapter, you'll be able to implement advanced RAG systems that can leverage the rich relationships in graph-structured data.

 In this chapter, we'll be covering the following topics:

- Introduction to graph-based knowledge representation for LLMs
- Designing graph RAG architectures for LLMs
- Graph embedding techniques for LLM retrieval
- Query expansion using graph structures in LLMs
- Integrating graph information into LLM generation
- Applications and use cases of graph RAG in LLMs
- Challenges and future directions in graph-based RAG

Introduction to graph-based knowledge representation for LLMs

Graph-based knowledge representation allows complex relationships to be encoded between concepts and facts, which can significantly enhance the contextual understanding of LLMs. In a graph, nodes represent entities, and edges represent relationships between them.

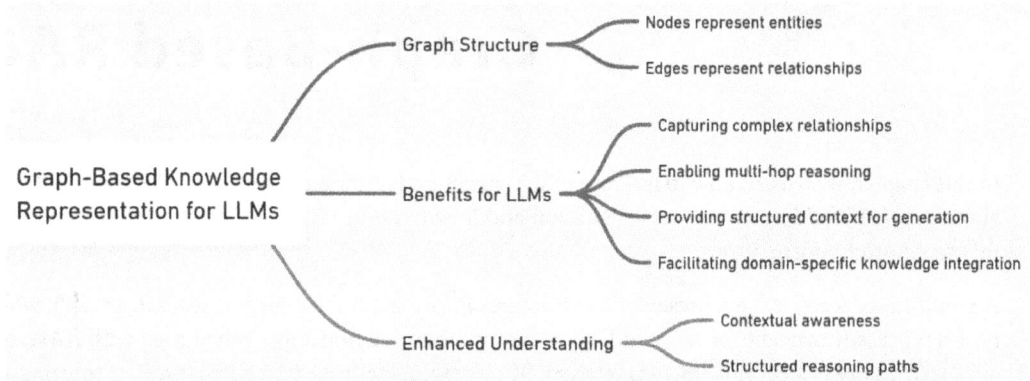

Figure 27.1 – Graph-based knowledge representation for LLMs

The following are the key benefits of graph-based knowledge for LLMs:

- Captures complex relationships
- Enables multi-hop reasoning
- Provides structured context for generation
- Facilitates domain-specific knowledge integration

Let's start by implementing a simple graph structure:

```python
from typing import Dict, List, Tuple

class KnowledgeGraph:
    def __init__(self):
        self.nodes: Dict[str, Dict] = {}
        self.edges: Dict[str, List[Tuple[str, str]]] = {}

    def add_node(self, node_id: str, properties: Dict):
        self.nodes[node_id] = properties
```

```
    def add_edge(self, source: str, target: str, relation: str):
        if source not in self.edges:
            self.edges[source] = []
        self.edges[source].append((target, relation))

    def get_neighbors(
        self, node_id: str) -> List[Tuple[str, str]
    ]:
        return self.edges.get(node_id, [])

# Example usage
kg = KnowledgeGraph()
kg.add_node("Paris", {"type": "City", "country": "France"})
kg.add_node("France", {"type": "Country", "continent": "Europe"})
kg.add_edge("Paris", "France", "capital_of")

print(kg.get_neighbors("Paris"))
```

This code implements a foundational `KnowledgeGraph` class in Python, allowing knowledge to be represented as a network of interconnected entities. The class uses dictionaries to store nodes and edges, where nodes are identified by unique IDs and hold associated properties, and edges define relationships between nodes through source, target, and relation labels. The `add_node` method populates the `nodes` dictionary, while `add_edge` establishes connections within the `edges` dictionary. The `get_neighbors` method allows nodes directly connected to a given node to be retrieved, along with the corresponding relationship types.

This example demonstrates how to create a graph, add nodes representing `Paris` and `France`, define the `capital_of` relationship between them, and then query the graph to find neighbors of `Paris`. This structure provides a basis for encoding complex relationships and facilitating knowledge-aware applications.

Next, we'll discuss how to design graph RAG architecture.

Designing graph RAG architectures for LLMs

To design a graph RAG system, we need to integrate our knowledge graph with the retrieval and generation components:

```
import networkx as nx
from sentence_transformers import SentenceTransformer
import torch
```

```python
class GraphRAG:
    def __init__(self, kg: KnowledgeGraph, model_name: str):
        self.kg = kg
        self.model = SentenceTransformer(model_name)
        self.graph = self.build_networkx_graph()
        self.node_embeddings = self.compute_node_embeddings()

    def build_networkx_graph(self):
        G = nx.DiGraph()
        for node_id, properties in self.kg.nodes.items():
            G.add_node(node_id, properties)
        for source, edges in self.kg.edges.items():
            for target, relation in edges:
                G.add_edge(source, target, relation=relation)
        return G

    def compute_node_embeddings(self):
        embeddings = {}
        for node_id, properties in self.kg.nodes.items():
            text = f"{node_id} {' '.join(properties.values())}"
            embedding = self.model.encode(text)
            embeddings[node_id] = embedding
        return embeddings

    def retrieve(self, query: str, k: int = 5) -> List[str]:
        query_embedding = self.model.encode(query)
        similarities = {
            node_id: torch.cosine_similarity(
                torch.tensor(query_embedding),
                torch.tensor(emb), dim=0
            )
            for node_id, emb in self.node_embeddings.items()}
        return sorted(
            similarities, key=similarities.get, reverse=True
        )[:k]

# Example usage
kg = KnowledgeGraph()
# Add more nodes and edges to the knowledge graph
graph_rag = GraphRAG(kg, "all-MiniLM-L6-v2")
retrieved_nodes = graph_rag.retrieve("What is the capital of France?")
print("Retrieved nodes:", retrieved_nodes)
```

In the preceding code, we used the NetworkX Python package. The NetworkX package is designed for creating, manipulating, and studying the structure, dynamics, and functions of complex networks. It provides tools for working with graphs, which are collections of nodes (vertices) and edges (connections between nodes), and offers a wide range of algorithms for analyzing network properties, making it invaluable for fields such as social network analysis, biology, and infrastructure studies.

This code defines a `GraphRAG` class that combines a `KnowledgeGraph` object with a Sentence Transformer model to enable context-aware information retrieval. The class initializes with a `KnowledgeGraph` object and a Sentence Transformer model name, which it uses to build a `networkx` graph representation of the knowledge graph and compute embeddings for each node based on its ID and properties. The `build_networkx_graph` method converts the custom `KnowledgeGraph` object into a `networkx` directed graph, preserving node properties and edge relationships. The `compute_node_embeddings` method generates embeddings for each node by concatenating its ID and properties into a text string and encoding it using the Sentence Transformer model.

The `retrieve` method takes a query, encodes it using the same Sentence Transformer, calculates the cosine similarity between the query embedding and each node embedding, and returns the top *k* most similar node IDs. This architecture leverages graph structure and semantic embeddings to retrieve relevant knowledge based on query context, bridging the gap between symbolic knowledge representation and neural information retrieval.

Now, let's explore more advanced techniques for representing our graph data to further enhance the performance of our LLM retrieval system. Specifically, we'll delve into graph embedding techniques for LLM retrieval.

Graph embedding techniques for LLM retrieval

Graph embedding techniques aim to represent the nodes of a graph in a low-dimensional vector space, capturing the graph's structural properties and relationships. Several methods exist, each with its own approach – for instance, **Node2Vec** explores neighborhoods through biased random walks, balancing breadth-first and depth-first exploration. **DeepWalk** is another random-walk-based approach but performs walks uniformly. **Graph convolutional networks** (**GCNs**) aggregate information from a node's neighbors using convolutional operations, learning node embeddings based on the graph's structure and node features. **Graph attention networks** (**GATs**) extend GCNs by incorporating an attention mechanism to weigh the importance of different neighbors when aggregating information. **Translating Embeddings for Knowledge Graphs** (**TransE**) is specifically designed for knowledge graphs, representing entities and relations as vectors such that if (h, r, t) holds (head, relation, tail), then $h + r \approx t$.

Let's focus on **Node2Vec** as an example. Node2Vec aims to create embeddings that preserve network neighborhoods. It achieves this by employing biased random walks that balance **breadth-first search (BFS)** and **depth-first search (DFS)**. BFS prioritizes exploring immediate neighbors and capturing local structural information, while DFS explores distant nodes, thereby capturing higher-order dependencies and community structures. The bias is controlled by two parameters, p (return parameter) and q (in-out parameter), which influence the likelihood of revisiting the previous node or exploring distant nodes, respectively. By learning embeddings that reflect these biased random walks, Node2Vec captures both local and global network structures, allowing for effective node classification, link prediction, and community detection:

```python
from node2vec import Node2Vec

class AdvancedGraphRAG(GraphRAG):
    def __init__(self, kg: KnowledgeGraph, model_name: str):
        super().__init__(kg, model_name)
        self.node2vec_embeddings = self.compute_node2vec_embeddings()

    def compute_node2vec_embeddings(self):
        node2vec = Node2Vec(
            self.graph, dimensions=64, walk_length=30,
            num_walks=200, workers=4
        )
        model = node2vec.fit(window=10, min_count=1)
        return {node: model.wv[node]
            for node in self.graph.nodes()
        }

    def retrieve(self, query: str, k: int = 5) -> List[str]:
        query_embedding = self.model.encode(query)
        combined_similarities = {}
        for node_id in self.graph.nodes():
            text_sim = torch.cosine_similarity(
                torch.tensor(query_embedding),
                torch.tensor(self.node_embeddings[node_id]),
                dim=0
            )
            graph_sim = torch.cosine_similarity(
                torch.tensor(query_embedding),
                torch.tensor(self.node2vec_embeddings[node_id]),
                dim=0
            )
            combined_similarities[node_id] = \
                0.5 * text_sim + 0.5 * graph_sim
```

```
        return sorted(
            combined_similarities,
            key=combined_similarities.get,
            reverse=True
        )[:k]

# Example usage
advanced_graph_rag = AdvancedGraphRAG(kg, "all-MiniLM-L6-v2")
retrieved_nodes = advanced_graph_rag.retrieve("What is the capital of
France?")
print("Retrieved nodes:", retrieved_nodes)
```

This code builds upon the GraphRAG class by incorporating Node2Vec embeddings for enhanced retrieval performance. It introduces an AdvancedGraphRAG class that inherits from GraphRAG and computes Node2Vec embeddings during initialization. The compute_node2vec_embeddings method utilizes the node2vec library to generate these embeddings, creating a Node2Vec object with specified dimensions, walk length, number of walks, and worker threads; it then trains the Node2Vec model by using random walks on the graph structure and extracts the learned node embeddings. The retrieve method is overridden to combine both the original text-based embeddings and the Node2Vec embeddings for similarity calculation. For each node, it computes the cosine similarity between the query embedding and both the text-based embedding and the Node2Vec embedding, then averages these two similarity scores with equal weights to produce a combined similarity score. Finally, it returns the top k nodes with the highest combined similarity scores, leveraging both semantic and structural information for more effective retrieval.

Now, let's explore how we can further improve retrieval by leveraging the graph structure to refine our queries. In the next section, we'll implement a simple yet effective technique to broaden the scope of our search.

Query expansion using graph structures in LLMs

We can leverage graph structures to expand queries and improve retrieval. Let's implement a simple query expansion technique:

```
import random

class QueryExpansionGraphRAG(AdvancedGraphRAG):
    def expand_query(
        self, query: str, num_expansions: int = 2
    ) -> List[str]:
        initial_nodes = super().retrieve(query, k=3)
        expanded_queries = [query]
        for node in initial_nodes:
            neighbors = list(self.graph.neighbors(node))
```

```
            if neighbors:
                random_neighbor = random.choice(neighbors)
                expanded_query = (
                    f"{query}"
                    f"{self.graph.nodes[random_neighbor].
                        get('type', '')}"
                    f"{random_neighbor}"
                )
                expanded_queries.append(expanded_query)
                if len(expanded_queries) >= num_expansions + 1:
                    break
        return expanded_queries

    def retrieve(self, query: str, k: int = 5) -> List[str]:
        expanded_queries = self.expand_query(query)
        all_retrieved = []
        for q in expanded_queries:
            all_retrieved.extend(super().retrieve(q, k))
        return list(dict.fromkeys(all_retrieved))[:k]

# Example usage
query_expansion_rag = QueryExpansionGraphRAG(kg, "all-MiniLM-L6-v2")
retrieved_nodes = query_expansion_rag.retrieve("What is the capital of
France?")
print("Retrieved nodes:", retrieved_nodes)
```

This code implements query expansion within a graph-based RAG system to enhance retrieval performance. The `QueryExpansionGraphRAG` class inherits from `AdvancedGraphRAG` and introduces an `expand_query` method that takes a query and the desired number of expansions as input. First, this method retrieves the top three most relevant nodes based on the initial query using the base class's `retrieve` method. It then iterates through these initial nodes, selecting a random neighbor for each and constructing an expanded query by appending the neighbor's type (if available) and the neighbor's ID to the original query. The `retrieve` method is overridden to first expand the input query using the `expand_query` method. It then retrieves results for each expanded query using the base class's `retrieve` method, concatenates the results, removes duplicates while preserving order, and returns the top k unique nodes. This approach leverages the graph structure to explore related concepts and broaden the search scope, potentially capturing more relevant information than a direct query alone.

Query expansion is particularly useful when the initial query is too narrow or underspecified, resulting in low recall. In graph-based retrieval settings, this often occurs when the query does not explicitly mention related entities or concepts that are semantically or structurally linked in the graph. By incorporating neighboring nodes into the query formulation, the system can uncover relevant content that would otherwise be overlooked, making query expansion especially beneficial in exploratory search scenarios or domains with sparse or highly interconnected data.

Now that we've explored techniques to enhance retrieval, let's shift our focus to improving the generation phase. We'll now delve into the process of integrating graph information into LLM generation, examining how we can incorporate graph knowledge directly into the generation process to create more informed and coherent responses.Integrating graph information into LLM generation

To integrate graph information into LLM generation, we can create a prompt that incorporates the retrieved graph context:

```python
from transformers import AutoModelForCausalLM, AutoTokenizer

class GenerativeGraphRAG(QueryExpansionGraphRAG):
    def __init__(
        self, kg: KnowledgeGraph, retriever_model:
        str, generator_model: str
    ):
        super().__init__(kg, retriever_model)
        self.generator = \
            AutoModelForCausalLM.from_pretrained(generator_model)
        self.generator_tokenizer = \
            AutoTokenizer.from_pretrained(generator_model)

    def generate_response(
        self, query: str, max_length: int = 100
    ) -> str:
        retrieved_nodes = self.retrieve(query)
        context = self.build_graph_context(retrieved_nodes)
        prompt = f"Graph Context:\n{context}\n\nQuestion: {query}\
nAnswer:"

        inputs = self.generator_tokenizer(
            prompt, return_tensors="pt"
        )
        outputs = self.generator.generate(
            inputs, max_length=max_length
        )
        return self.generator_tokenizer.decode(
            outputs[0], skip_special_tokens=True
        )

    def build_graph_context(self, nodes: List[str]) -> str:
        context = []
        for node in nodes:
            context.append(f"Node: {node}")
            context.append(f"Properties: {self.graph.nodes[node]}")
```

```
            for neighbor, edge_data in self.graph[node].items():
                context.append(
                    f"  Related to {neighbor} by
                    {edge_data['relation']}")
        return "\n".join(context)


# Example usage
generative_graph_rag = GenerativeGraphRAG(
    kg, "all-MiniLM-L6-v2", "gpt2-medium"
)
response = generative_graph_rag.generate_response("What is the capital
of France?")
print("Generated response:", response)
```

This code integrates an LLM for response generation within the graph-based RAG framework. The GenerativeGraphRAG class inherits from QueryExpansionGraphRAG and initializes with KnowledgeGraph, a retriever model name, and a generator model name. It loads a pre-trained causal language model and its corresponding tokenizer using transformers. The generate_response method orchestrates the entire process: first, it retrieves relevant nodes from the knowledge graph using the retrieve method inherited from the parent class. Then, it constructs a context string by calling build_graph_context, which formats the retrieved nodes, their properties, and their relationships to other nodes into a readable text. This context is then incorporated into a prompt alongside the original query, which is fed into the pre-trained language model. The language model generates a response based on the prompt, and the generated tokens are decoded back into a human-readable string, effectively leveraging the graph structure to inform the language model's response generation. The build_graph_context method formats retrieved graph information into the prompt, including node IDs, properties, and relationships to neighbors, providing a structured representation of the relevant knowledge to the LLM.

Now that we've explored how to integrate graph information into the generation process, let's consider the broader applications and potential uses of this approach.

Applications and use cases of graph RAG in LLMs

Graph-based RAG can be particularly effective in various applications:

- Question-answering over knowledge graphs
- Personalized recommendation systems
- Scientific literature analysis
- Drug discovery and biomedical research
- Social network analysis

Here's an example of how graph RAG could be used for a recommendation system:

```
class RecommendationGraphRAG(GenerativeGraphRAG):
    def get_recommendations(
        self, user_id: str, num_recommendations: int = 5
    ) -> List[str]:
        user_node = self.retrieve(f"User {user_id}", k=1)[0]
        user_interests = self.graph.nodes[user_node].
            get('interests', [])

        potential_recommendations = set()
        for interest in user_interests:
            related_items = self.retrieve(interest, k=3)
            potential_recommendations.update(related_items)

        recommendations = list(
            potential_recommendations - set(user_interests)
        )[:num_recommendations]
        return recommendations

    def explain_recommendation(
        self, user_id: str, item_id: str
    ) -> str:
        query = f"Why would User {user_id} be interested in {item_
id}?"
        return self.generate_response(query)


# Example usage
recommendation_rag = RecommendationGraphRAG(
    kg, "all-MiniLM-L6-v2", "gpt2-medium"
)
user_id = "12345"
recommendations = recommendation_rag.get_recommendations(user_id)
print(f"Recommendations for User {user_id}:", recommendations)

for item in recommendations[:2]:
    explanation = recommendation_rag.explain_recommendation(user_id,
        item)
    print(f"Explanation for recommending {item}:", explanation)
```

This example demonstrates how graph RAG can be used to generate personalized recommendations and explain those recommendations using the graph structure.

Challenges and future directions in graph-based RAG

Let's consider some key challenges and future research directions in graph-based RAG:

- Scalability to very large graphs

- Handling dynamic and evolving graph structures

- Incorporating uncertainty and probabilistic relationships

- Improving the interpretability of graph-based retrievals and generations

- Developing more sophisticated graph-aware language models

These are fascinating and complex research topics. In this chapter, we'll focus on the scalability aspect of graph-based RAG. You are encouraged to read the research paper titled *Graph Retrieval-Augmented Generation: A Survey* at `https://arxiv.org/abs/2408.08921` for more information on other challenges and research directions.

Real-world knowledge graphs can contain millions or even billions of nodes and edges. Querying and traversing such massive graphs can be computationally expensive, especially when incorporated into a real-time RAG pipeline. Furthermore, providing a huge subgraph as context to the LLM can exceed its context window limit and dilute the relevant information with noise.

Several factors contribute to this scalability bottleneck:

- **Graph traversal complexity**: Finding relevant nodes and their connections within a large graph can be time consuming. Standard graph algorithms such as BFS or DFS can become inefficient as the graph grows.

- **Embedding storage and retrieval**: Storing and retrieving node embeddings for a massive graph requires significant memory and computational resources. Computing similarity scores between the query embedding and all node embeddings becomes a bottleneck.

- **Context window limitations**: LLMs have a limited context window, meaning they can only process a fixed amount of text at a time. A large graph context can easily exceed this limit, forcing truncation and potentially resulting in the loss of important information.

- **Noise in context**: Including too much irrelevant information from the graph as context can confuse the LLM and degrade the quality of the generated response.

To address these scalability challenges, several strategies can be employed. One such strategy, which we will implement, is **subgraph sampling**. This involves extracting a smaller, more manageable subgraph from the overall knowledge graph that is most relevant to the user's query. This reduces the computational cost of graph traversal and embedding retrieval, while also ensuring that the LLM receives a focused and informative context. Other techniques for improving scalability include the following:

- **Graph databases**: Using specialized graph databases such as Neo4j or Amazon Neptune can significantly improve query performance and scalability compared to general-purpose databases

- **Approximate nearest neighbor (ANN) search**: Using ANN algorithms for embedding retrieval can significantly speed up the search process by sacrificing some accuracy

- **Knowledge graph summarization**: Condensing the knowledge graph into a smaller, more manageable representation while preserving its essential information

- **Hardware acceleration**: Utilizing GPUs or specialized hardware accelerators can speed up graph computations and embedding operations

- **Context distillation**: Techniques such as selective context injection or hierarchical retrieval can filter and prioritize the most relevant information for the LLM

Now, let's proceed with implementing subgraph sampling to see how it helps address scalability concerns:

```python
import networkx as nx


class ScalableGraphRAG(GenerativeGraphRAG):
    def __init__(
        self, kg: KnowledgeGraph, retriever_model: str,
        generator_model: str, max_subgraph_size: int = 1000
    ):
        super().__init__(kg, retriever_model, generator_model)
        self.max_subgraph_size = max_subgraph_size

    def retrieve(self, query: str, k: int = 5) -> List[str]:
        initial_nodes = super().retrieve(query, k=k)
        subgraph = self.sample_subgraph(initial_nodes)
        return self.rank_nodes_in_subgraph(subgraph, query)[:k]

    def sample_subgraph(self, seed_nodes: List[str]) -> nx.Graph:
        subgraph = nx.Graph()
        frontier = set(seed_nodes)
        while len(subgraph) < self.max_subgraph_size and frontier:
            node = frontier.pop()
            if node not in subgraph:
                subgraph.add_node(node, self.graph.nodes[node])
                neighbors = list(self.graph.neighbors(node))
                for neighbor in neighbors:
                    if len(subgraph) < self.max_subgraph_size:
                        subgraph.add_edge(
                            node, neighbor,
                            self.graph[node][neighbor]
                        )
                        frontier.add(neighbor)
```

```
                        else:
                            break
            return subgraph

        def rank_nodes_in_subgraph(
            self, subgraph: nx.Graph, query: str
        ) -> List[str]:
            query_embedding = self.model.encode(query)
            node_scores = {}
            for node in subgraph.nodes():
                node_embedding = self.node_embeddings[node]
                score = torch.cosine_similarity(
                    torch.tensor(query_embedding),
                    torch.tensor(node_embedding), dim=0
                )
                node_scores[node] = score
            return sorted(node_scores, key=node_scores.get, reverse=True)

    # Example usage
    scalable_graph_rag = ScalableGraphRAG(
        kg, "all-MiniLM-L6-v2", "gpt2-medium"
    )
    retrieved_nodes = scalable_graph_rag.retrieve("What is the capital of
    France?")
    print("Retrieved nodes:", retrieved_nodes)
```

This code introduces a `ScalableGraphRAG` class, which is designed to address the scalability challenges of graph-based RAG systems by implementing a subgraph sampling technique. Inheriting from `GenerativeGraphRAG`, it incorporates a `max_subgraph_size` parameter to limit the size of the extracted subgraph.

The overridden retrieve method first identifies an initial set of relevant nodes using the base class's retrieval mechanism. It then calls the `sample_subgraph` method to construct a subgraph centered around these initial nodes, limiting its growth to the specified `max_subgraph_size`.

The `sample_subgraph` method performs a breadth-first expansion from the seed nodes, adding nodes and edges to the subgraph until the size limit is reached, prioritizing nodes closer to the seed.

Subgraph sampling can be tuned by adjusting the `max_subgraph_size` parameter so that it balances context richness and computational efficiency. A smaller size results in faster processing but potentially misses crucial contextual information, while a larger size captures more context but increases computational cost. Additionally, the algorithm's node selection criteria during subgraph expansion can be tuned – for example, prioritizing nodes with higher semantic similarity to the query or nodes with stronger connectivity to the seed nodes. Experimenting with these parameters is useful for optimizing the RAG system's performance for specific applications and graph structures.

Finally, the `rank_nodes_in_subgraph` method calculates the relevance of each node within the subgraph to the query by computing the cosine similarity between the query embedding and the node's pre-computed embedding. Then, it returns a ranked list of nodes based on their similarity scores, ensuring that only the most relevant nodes within the sampled subgraph are considered for context augmentation.

Summary

Graph-based RAG extends the capabilities of traditional RAG systems by leveraging the rich structure of knowledge graphs. By implementing the techniques and approaches discussed in this chapter, you can create more sophisticated LLM systems capable of reasoning over complex relationships and generating more contextually appropriate responses. In the next chapter, we will explore advanced RAG patterns for LLMs. This will build upon the graph-based techniques we've discussed here so that you can create even more powerful and flexible RAG systems.

28
Advanced RAG

In *Chapter 26*, we covered the basics of the RAG pattern, a simple process where a user's query triggers a search in an external knowledge base. The information that's retrieved is then directly appended to the query, and this augmented prompt is passed to the LLM to generate a response, allowing it to access external data without complex processing.

Now, in this chapter, we'll move beyond these basic RAG methods and explore more sophisticated techniques designed to significantly enhance LLM performance across a wide range of tasks.

By the end of this chapter, you'll be equipped with the knowledge to implement these advanced RAG strategies, enabling your LLM applications to achieve greater accuracy and efficiency.

In this chapter, we'll be covering the following topics:

- Multi-step and iterative retrieval techniques for LLMs
- Adaptive retrieval based on context and task in LLMs
- Meta-learning for improved retrieval in LLMs
- Combining RAG with other LLM prompting techniques
- Handling ambiguity and uncertainty in LLM-based RAG
- Scaling RAG to very large knowledge bases
- Future directions in RAG research for LLMs

Multi-step and iterative retrieval techniques for LLMs

Using multi-step and iterative retrieval techniques for LLMs is a dynamic, recursive approach to information gathering where the model progressively refines its search strategy. The code provided in this section illustrates a multi-step RAG framework that expands context iteratively, retrieves additional documents, and generates responses through multiple steps, allowing for increasingly comprehensive and nuanced information retrieval by dynamically adjusting queries and integrating retrieved knowledge.

Here are some of its key characteristics:

- Iterative context expansion
- Multiple retrieval steps (configurable up to `max_steps`)
- Dynamic query refinement
- Contextual document retrieval
- Adaptive response generation

Multi-step and iterative retrieval techniques for LLMs, with their dynamic and recursive approaches, benefit use cases that require the following aspects:

- **Complex question-answering**: When questions require information to be synthesized from multiple sources or involve intricate logical reasoning, iterative retrieval allows the LLM to gather the necessary context progressively. Examples include legal document analysis, scientific research, and in-depth financial analysis.

- **Knowledge-intensive conversations**: In conversational AI scenarios where the dialogue involves exploring a topic in depth, iterative RAG enables the LLM to maintain context and refine its understanding over multiple turns. This is valuable for educational chatbots, technical support, and interactive tutorials.

- **Research and exploration**: For tasks such as literature reviews, market research, or investigative journalism, the ability to dynamically refine queries and explore related information is crucial. Iterative retrieval allows the LLM to act as a research assistant, uncovering connections and insights that would be difficult to find with a single query.

- **Technical documentation and troubleshooting**: When dealing with complex technical issues, iterative RAG can help the LLM navigate extensive documentation, progressively narrowing down the search to pinpoint relevant information. This improves the efficiency of troubleshooting and technical support.

- **Dynamic information gathering**: This includes any situation where the information that is needed isn't able to be gathered in a single pass. For example, if a user wants to find out all the news articles related to a specific court case and then wants to know what people are saying about those news articles on social media, multiple steps of information gathering would be required.

- **Dealing with ambiguous queries**: When a user's query is ambiguous, the LLM can ask clarifying questions and then use the user's response to refine the search.

In essence, any use case that demands a deep, nuanced understanding of information, and where a single retrieval step is insufficient, stands to gain significantly from multi-step and iterative RAG.

Let's take a look at the following code example:

```python
from typing import List, Dict
import torch
from transformers import AutoModelForCausalLM, AutoTokenizer

class MultiStepRAG:
    def __init__(self, retriever, generator, max_steps=3):
        self.retriever = retriever
        self.generator = generator
        self.tokenizer = AutoTokenizer.from_pretrained(generator)
        self.max_steps = max_steps

    def retrieve_and_generate(self, query: str) -> str:
        context = ""
        for step in range(self.max_steps):
            retrieved_docs = self.retriever.retrieve(
                query + " " + context, k=3
            )
            context += " ".join(retrieved_docs) + " "

            prompt = f"Context: {context}\nQuery: {query}\nResponse:"
            inputs = self.tokenizer(
                prompt, return_tensors="pt"
            )
            outputs = self.generator.generate(inputs, max_length=200)
            response = self.tokenizer.decode(
                outputs[0], skip_special_tokens=True
            )
            if self.is_response_complete(response):
                break
            query = self.generate_follow_up_query(query, response)
        return response
    def is_response_complete(self, response: str) -> bool:
        # Implement logic to determine if the response is complete
        return "I don't have enough information" not in response

    def generate_follow_up_query(
        self, original_query: str, current_response: str
    ) -> str:
        prompt = f"Original question: {original_query}\nCurrent answer: {current_response}\nGenerate a follow-up question to gather more information:"
        inputs = self.tokenizer(prompt, return_tensors="pt")
```

```
        outputs = self.generator.generate(inputs, max_length=50)
        return self.tokenizer.decode(outputs[0],
            skip_special_tokens=True)

# Example usage
retriever = SomeRetrieverClass()  # Replace with your actual retriever
generator = AutoModelForCausalLM.from_pretrained("gpt2-medium")
multi_step_rag = MultiStepRAG(retriever, generator)
response = multi_step_rag.retrieve_and_generate("What are the effects
of climate change on biodiversity?")
print(response)
```

In this pseudocode example, the `MultiStepRAG` class implements multistep retrieval through three critical methods:

- `retrieve_and_generate()`: This method iteratively expands context by retrieving documents, generating responses, and dynamically updating the search context across multiple steps. It manages the retrieval process, limiting iterations to a configurable maximum.

- `is_response_complete()`: This method evaluates response quality by detecting whether the generated answer addresses the query sufficiently, typically checking for indicators of incomplete information.

- `generate_follow_up_query()`: This method creates refined follow-up queries by using the language model to generate new questions based on the original query and current response, enabling intelligent context exploration.

This implementation allows for progressive information gathering, where each retrieval step dynamically refines the context and generates more comprehensive responses by recursively expanding the knowledge base.

Adaptive retrieval based on context and task in LLMs

Adaptive retrieval is a sophisticated approach to information retrieval that dynamically adjusts strategies based on specific task requirements.

The following code demonstrates this concept through an implementation that tailors retrieval and generation processes across different task types:

```
from enum import Enum

class TaskType(Enum):
    FACTUAL_QA = 1
    SUMMARIZATION = 2
    ANALYSIS = 3
```

```python
class AdaptiveRAG:
    def __init__(self, retriever, generator):
        self.retriever = retriever
        self.generator = generator
        self.tokenizer = AutoTokenizer.from_pretrained(generator)

    def retrieve_and_generate(self, query: str, task_type: TaskType
    ) -> str:
        if task_type == TaskType.FACTUAL_QA:
            k = 3
            prompt_template = "Context: {context}\nQuestion: {query}\
nAnswer:"
        elif task_type == TaskType.SUMMARIZATION:
            k = 10
            prompt_template = "Summarize the following information:\
n{context}\nSummary:"
        elif task_type == TaskType.ANALYSIS:
            k = 5
            prompt_template = "Analyze the following information:\
n{context}\nQuery: {query}\nAnalysis:"

        retrieved_docs = self.retriever.retrieve(query, k=k)
        context = " ".join(retrieved_docs)

        prompt = prompt_template.format(context=context, query=query)
        inputs = self.tokenizer(prompt, return_tensors="pt")
        outputs = self.generator.generate(inputs, max_length=300)
        response = self.tokenizer.decode(
            outputs[0], skip_special_tokens=True
        )

        return response

# Example usage
adaptive_rag = AdaptiveRAG(retriever, generator)
factual_response = adaptive_rag.retrieve_and_generate(
    "What is the capital of France?",
    TaskType.FACTUAL_QA
)
summary_response = adaptive_rag.retrieve_and_generate(
    "Summarize the causes of World War I",
    TaskType.SUMMARIZATION
)
```

```
analysis_response = adaptive_rag.retrieve_and_generate(
    "Analyze the impact of social media on mental health",
    TaskType.ANALYSIS
)
```

The preceding code introduces an `AdaptiveRAG` class that uses an `Enum` value called `TaskType` to define distinct retrieval strategies for different scenarios: factual question-answering, summarization, and analysis. Each task type receives customized treatment in terms of document retrieval volume and prompt formatting.

In the `retrieve_and_generate()` method, the system dynamically configures retrieval parameters:

- `Factual QA`: This retrieves three documents with a direct question-answer format
- `Summarization`: This retrieves ten documents with a summary-focused template
- `Analysis`: This retrieves five documents with an analytical prompt structure

The method retrieves relevant documents, constructs a context, generates a task-specific prompt, and produces a response tailored to the specific task type. This approach allows for more nuanced and contextually appropriate information retrieval and generation across different knowledge exploration scenarios.

This example usage demonstrates flexibility by generating responses for factual queries, summaries, and analytical tasks using the same adaptive framework.

Meta-learning for improved retrieval in LLMs

Meta-learning in retrieval systems is a dynamic approach where the model learns to improve its retrieval strategy by analyzing past performance and relevance feedback. In this implementation, meta-learning focuses on selecting and ranking documents adaptively based on learned relevance patterns.

Let's implement a simple meta-learning approach for RAG.

The following code demonstrates meta-learning by retrieving documents about dark matter theories and simulating relevance feedback to train the model, showcasing how the system can improve its information retrieval capabilities iteratively:

```
import numpy as np
from sklearn.linear_model import LogisticRegression

class MetaLearningRAG:
    def __init__(self, retriever, generator):
        self.retriever = retriever
        self.generator = generator
        self.tokenizer = AutoTokenizer.from_pretrained(generator)
```

```python
        self.meta_model = LogisticRegression()
        self.training_data = []

    def retrieve_and_generate(self, query: str) -> str:
        retrieved_docs = self.retriever.retrieve(query, k=10)

        if self.meta_model.coef_.size > 0:  # If the meta-model has
been trained
            relevance_scores = self.predict_relevance(
                query, retrieved_docs)
            top_docs = [
                doc for _, doc in sorted(
                    zip(relevance_scores, retrieved_docs),
                    reverse=True
                )
            ][:3]
        else:
            top_docs = retrieved_docs[:3]

        context = " ".join(top_docs)
        prompt = f"Context: {context}\nQuery: {query}\nResponse:"
        inputs = self.tokenizer(prompt, return_tensors="pt")
        outputs = self.generator.generate(inputs, max_length=200)
        response = self.tokenizer.decode(outputs[0],
            skip_special_tokens=True)

        return response

    def predict_relevance(self, query: str, docs: List[str]
    ) -> np.ndarray:
        features = self.compute_features(query, docs)
        return self.meta_model.predict_proba(features)[:, 1]   #
Probability of relevance

    def compute_features(self, query: str, docs: List[str]
    ) -> np.ndarray:
        # Compute features for the query-document pairs
        # This is a placeholder implementation
        return np.random.rand(len(docs), 5)  # 5 random features

    def update_meta_model(
        self, query: str, retrieved_docs: List[str],
        relevance_feedback: List[int]
    ):
```

```
        features = self.compute_features(query, retrieved_docs)
        self.training_data.extend(zip(features, relevance_feedback))

        if len(self.training_data) >= 100:  # Train the meta-model
periodically
            X, y = zip(*self.training_data)
            self.meta_model.fit(X, y)
            self.training_data = []  # Clear the training data after
updating the model

# Example usage
meta_learning_rag = MetaLearningRAG(retriever, generator)
response = meta_learning_rag.retrieve_and_generate(
    "What are the main theories of dark matter?"
)
print(response)

# Simulating relevance feedback
retrieved_docs = meta_learning_rag.retriever.retrieve(
    "What are the main theories of dark matter?",
    k=10
)
relevance_feedback = [1, 0, 1, 1, 0, 0, 1, 0, 0, 1]  # 1 for relevant,
0 for not relevant
meta_learning_rag.update_meta_model(
    "What are the main theories of dark matter?",
    retrieved_docs, relevance_feedback
)
```

The key meta-learning components in the preceding code include the following:

- **Relevance prediction:**

  - Uses logistic regression to predict document relevance

  - The predict_relevance() method estimates the probability of document usefulness

  - Dynamically adjusts document selection based on learned features

- **Feature computation:**

  - The compute_features() method generates document representation features

  - Currently, it uses randomly generated values as placeholder features for demonstration or testing purposes

  - In practice, it would include semantic similarity, keyword matching, and more.

- **Adaptive learning mechanism**:

  - Accumulates training data from relevance feedback

  - Retrains the meta-model when sufficient data is collected (100 samples)

  - Clears the training data after model updates to prevent overfitting

- **Retrieval strategy modification**:

  - Initially uses the top 10 retrieved documents

  - After meta-model training, it selects the top three documents based on learned relevance scores

  - Continuously refines the document selection process

The code implements a `MetaLearningRAG` class that dynamically enhances retrieval performance using machine learning techniques. The core innovation lies in its ability to learn from relevance feedback and adjust document selection strategies.

Let's look at the key methods:

- `retrieve_and_generate()`: Selects the top documents using a trained meta-model

- `predict_relevance()`: Estimates document relevance probabilities

- `compute_features()`: Generates feature representations for documents

- `update_meta_model()`: Periodically retrains the model based on relevance feedback

The implementation uses logistic regression to predict document relevance, progressively refining retrieval by learning from user interactions. When sufficient training data has been accumulated, the meta-model is retrained, allowing the system to adapt its document selection strategy based on historical performance and feedback.

In the context of meta-learning for retrieval systems, *relevance* refers to the contextual usefulness and information value of the documents that were retrieved for a specific query.

Let's look at the key *relevance* aspects shown in the preceding code:

- **Relevance scoring**:

  - Predicts the probability of the document being useful

  - Uses machine learning to learn relevance patterns

  - Allows dynamic document ranking

- **Feedback mechanism**:

  - Binary relevance labels (1 = relevant, 0 = not relevant)

- Enables the system to learn from user-provided quality signals

- Improves future document selection

- **Feature-based relevance:**

  - Computes document features representing potential usefulness

  - The preceding code uses random features

  - Captures semantic and contextual relationships

The core goal is to create an adaptive retrieval system that learns to select increasingly precise and valuable documents through iterative feedback and machine learning techniques.

Combining RAG with other LLM prompting techniques

We can enhance RAG by combining it with other prompting techniques, such as CoT (see *Chapter 20*) or few-shot learning. Here's an example that combines RAG with CoT:

```
class RAGWithCoT:
    def __init__(self, retriever, generator):
        self.retriever = retriever
        self.generator = generator
        self.tokenizer = AutoTokenizer.from_pretrained(generator)

    def retrieve_and_generate(self, query: str) -> str:
        retrieved_docs = self.retriever.retrieve(query, k=3)
        context = " ".join(retrieved_docs)

        cot_prompt = f"""Context: {context}

Question: {query}

Let's approach this step-by-step:
1) First, we should consider...
2) Next, we need to analyze...
3) Then, we can conclude...

Based on this reasoning, the final answer is:

Answer:"""

        inputs = self.tokenizer(cot_prompt, return_tensors="pt")
        outputs = self.generator.generate(inputs, max_length=500)
        response = self.tokenizer.decode(outputs[0],
            skip_special_tokens=True)
```

```
        return response

# Example usage
rag_with_cot = RAGWithCoT(retriever, generator)
response = rag_with_cot.retrieve_and_generate("What are the potential
long-term effects of artificial intelligence on employment?")
print(response)
```

The `RAGWithCoT` class implements a RAG approach enhanced with CoT reasoning. By retrieving relevant documents and constructing a prompt that encourages step-by-step problem solving, the method transforms standard query response generation into a more structured, analytical process.

The implementation guides the language model through an explicit reasoning framework, breaking complex queries into logical steps. This approach prompts the model to demonstrate intermediate reasoning, creating a more transparent and potentially more accurate response generation process.

The method combines contextual document retrieval with a carefully designed prompt template that explicitly structures the model's reasoning. By requiring the model to outline its thinking process before presenting a final answer, the implementation seeks to improve the depth and quality of generated responses.

As we explore advanced RAG techniques, the next critical challenge emerges: handling ambiguity and uncertainty in language-model-based information retrieval. The following section will delve into sophisticated strategies for managing complex, nuanced, and potentially conflicting information sources, highlighting approaches that enable more robust and reliable knowledge extraction and generation.

Handling ambiguity and uncertainty in LLM-based RAG

Ambiguity and uncertainty directly compromise the accuracy and reliability of generated responses. Ambiguous queries, for instance, can trigger the process of retrieving irrelevant or conflicting information, leading the LLM to produce incoherent or incorrect outputs. Consider the query, "What about apples?" This could refer to Apple Inc., the fruit, or specific apple varieties. A naive RAG system might pull data from all contexts, resulting in a confused response.

Furthermore, uncertainty in retrieved information – due to conflicting or outdated data in the knowledge base – exacerbates the problem. Without mechanisms to assess data reliability, the LLM may propagate inaccuracies. LLMs themselves operate on probabilities, adding another layer of uncertainty. For example, when addressing a niche topic, an LLM might generate a "best guess" that, without proper uncertainty estimation, could be presented as fact. Combining multiple pieces of uncertain information further compounds this issue, potentially leading to misleading and unreliable responses, ultimately undermining user trust and limiting the practical applications of RAG systems.

To handle ambiguity and uncertainty, we can implement a system that generates multiple hypotheses and ranks them based on confidence:

```python
class UncertaintyAwareRAG:
    def __init__(self, retriever, generator, n_hypotheses=3):
        self.retriever = retriever
        self.generator = generator
        self.tokenizer = AutoTokenizer.from_pretrained(generator)
        self.n_hypotheses = n_hypotheses

    def retrieve_and_generate(self, query: str) -> Dict[str, float]:
        retrieved_docs = self.retriever.retrieve(query, k=5)
        context = " ".join(retrieved_docs)

        prompt = (
            f"Context: {context}\n"
            "Question: {query}\n"
            f"Generate {self.n_hypotheses} possible answers "
            f"with confidence scores:\n"
        )

        inputs = self.tokenizer(prompt, return_tensors="pt")
        outputs = self.generator.generate(
            inputs, max_length=500,
            num_return_sequences=self.n_hypotheses
        )
        hypotheses = []
        for output in outputs:
            hypothesis = self.tokenizer.decode(
                output, skip_special_tokens=True
            )
            hypotheses.append(self.parse_hypothesis(hypothesis))

        return dict(
            sorted(
                hypotheses, key=lambda x: x[1], reverse=True
            )
        )

    def parse_hypothesis(self, hypothesis: str) -> Tuple[str, float]:
        # This is a simple parser, assuming the format "Answer
(Confidence: X%): ..."
        parts = hypothesis.split(":")
        confidence = float(
            parts[0].split("(Confidence: ")[1].strip("%)"))/100
        answer = ":".join(parts[1:]).strip()
        return (answer, confidence)
```

```
# Example usage
uncertainty_aware_rag = UncertaintyAwareRAG(retriever, generator)
hypotheses = uncertainty_aware_rag.retrieve_and_generate(
    "What will be the dominant form of energy in 2050?"
)
for answer, confidence in hypotheses.items():
    print(f"Hypothesis (Confidence: {confidence:.2f}): {answer}")
```

The preceding code implements an `UncertaintyAwareRAG` class that intelligently handles ambiguous queries by generating multiple possible answers with confidence scores. It works by initializing with a retriever component (for fetching relevant documents), a generator (language model), and a parameter for the number of hypotheses to generate. When `retrieve_and_generate` is called with a query, it retrieves relevant documents and combines them into a context, then constructs a specialized prompt asking for multiple possible answers with confidence scores. The generator produces multiple hypotheses using the `num_return_sequences` parameter, each including a confidence score. These hypotheses are parsed using the `parse_hypothesis` method, which extracts both the answer text and its confidence score from a standardized format of `"Answer (Confidence: X%): ..."`. The results are then sorted by confidence score and returned as a dictionary that maps answers to their confidence values. This approach is particularly valuable for questions that may not have a single definitive answer (such as future predictions or complex scenarios) as it explicitly acknowledges uncertainty and provides multiple plausible responses with their associated confidence levels, allowing users to make more informed decisions based on the range of possibilities and their relative likelihoods.

After implementing uncertainty handling in our RAG system, the next crucial challenge is dealing with massive document collections. As knowledge bases grow to millions or even billions of documents, traditional retrieval methods become impractical, requiring more sophisticated approaches. Let's explore how we can scale RAG so that it can handle very large knowledge bases efficiently through hierarchical indexing.

Scaling RAG to very large knowledge bases

We can scale RAG using a hierarchical system. A hierarchical RAG system is an advanced architecture that organizes document retrieval in a tree-like structure with multiple levels. Instead of searching through all documents linearly, it first clusters similar documents together and creates a hierarchy of these clusters. When a query comes in, the system identifies the most relevant cluster(s) at the top level, drills down to find the most relevant sub-clusters, and finally retrieves the most similar documents from within those targeted sub-clusters. Think of it like a library where books are first organized by broad categories (science, history, fiction), then by sub-categories (physics, biology, chemistry), and finally by specific topics – this makes finding a particular book much faster than searching through every single book.

The hierarchical approach to RAG offers significant advantages because it dramatically improves both the efficiency and scalability of document retrieval while maintaining high accuracy. By organizing documents into clusters and sub-clusters, the system can quickly narrow down the search space from potentially millions of documents to a much smaller, relevant subset, which not only speeds up retrieval but also reduces computational resources and memory requirements. This makes it possible to handle massive document collections that would be impractical with traditional flat retrieval approaches. The hierarchical structure also enables better parallelization of search operations and can even improve result quality by considering document relationships within the hierarchy.

The following code snippet defines a class for hierarchical RAG, leveraging Facebook's AI Similarity Search (Faiss) library for efficient similarity search and generation capabilities:

```python
import faiss

class HierarchicalRAG:
    def __init__(
        self, generator, embeddings, texts, n_clusters=1000
    ):
        self.generator = generator
        self.tokenizer = AutoTokenizer.from_pretrained(generator)
        self.embeddings = embeddings
        self.texts = texts

        # Create a hierarchical index
        self.quantizer = faiss.IndexFlatL2(embeddings.shape[1])
        self.index = faiss.IndexIVFFlat(
            self.quantizer, embeddings.shape[1], n_clusters
        )
        self.index.train(embeddings)
        self.index.add(embeddings)

    def retrieve(self, query: str, k: int = 5) -> List[str]:
        query_embedding = self.compute_embedding(query)
        _, indices = self.index.search(
            query_embedding.reshape(1, -1), k
        )
        return [self.texts[i] for i in indices[0]]

    def compute_embedding(self, text: str) -> np.ndarray:
        # Compute embedding for the given text
        # This is a placeholder implementation
        return np.random.rand(1, self.embeddings.shape[1])

    def retrieve_and_generate(self, query: str) -> str:
        retrieved_docs = self.retrieve(query)
        context = " ".join(retrieved_docs)
```

```
        prompt = f"Context: {context}\nQuery: {query}\nResponse:"
        inputs = self.tokenizer(prompt, return_tensors="pt")
        outputs = self.generator.generate(inputs, max_length=200)
        response = self.tokenizer.decode(outputs[0],
            skip_special_tokens=True)


        return response

# Example usage
embeddings = np.random.rand(1000000, 128)   # 1 million documents,
128-dimensional embeddings
texts = ["Document " + str(i) for i in range(1000000)]
hierarchical_rag = HierarchicalRAG(generator, embeddings, texts)
response = hierarchical_rag.retrieve_and_generate(
    "What are the latest advancements in quantum computing?"
)
print(response)
```

The preceding code implements a `HierarchicalRAG` class that creates an efficient retrieval system using **Facebook AI Similarity Search (Faiss)** to handle large-scale document collections. The class is initialized with a language model generator, document embeddings, and the actual texts, along with a parameter for the number of clusters (defaulting to `1000`) – it uses FAISS's `IVFFlat` index, which is a hierarchical index that first clusters the vectors and then performs an exact search within relevant clusters, where the quantizer (`IndexFlatL2`) is used to assign vectors to clusters during training. The `retrieve` method takes a query and returns k similar documents by first computing the query's embedding and then searching the hierarchical index. The `compute_embedding` method is a placeholder that would typically implement actual embedding computation. The `retrieve_and_generate` method ties everything together by retrieving relevant documents, concatenating them into a context, creating a prompt that combines the context and query, and then using the language model to generate a response. The example usage shows how to initialize the system with 1 million documents (using random embeddings for demonstration purposes) and perform a query about quantum computing. First, the `IVFFlat` index groups similar documents together during training (`index.train()`) and then uses these clusters to speed up search operations by only searching in the most relevant clusters instead of the entire dataset, making it much more efficient than a brute-force approach when dealing with large document collections.

Now that we've explored how to scale RAG systems to handle massive knowledge bases through hierarchical indexing, let's look ahead to some exciting future directions in RAG research for LLMs.

Future directions in RAG research for LLMs

As RAG continues to evolve, several promising research directions have begun to emerge:

- **Multi-modal RAG**: Incorporating image, audio, and video data in retrieval and generation

- **Temporal RAG**: Handling time-sensitive information and updates
- **Personalized RAG**: Adapting retrieval and generation to individual user preferences and knowledge
- **Explainable RAG**: Providing transparency in the retrieval and generation process
- **Continual learning in RAG**: Updating knowledge bases and retrieval mechanisms in real time

Here's a conceptual implementation of a multi-modal RAG system:

```python
from PIL import Image
import torch
from torchvision.transforms import Resize, ToTensor

class MultiModalRAG:
    def __init__(self, text_retriever, image_retriever, generator):
        self.text_retriever = text_retriever
        self.image_retriever = image_retriever
        self.generator = generator
        self.tokenizer = AutoTokenizer.from_pretrained(generator)
        self.image_transform = transforms.Compose([
            Resize((224, 224)),
            ToTensor(),
        ])

    def retrieve_and_generate(
        self, query: str, image_query: Image.Image = None
    ) -> str:
        text_docs = self.text_retriever.retrieve(query, k=3)
        text_context = " ".join(text_docs)

        if image_query:
            image_tensor = \
                self.image_transform(image_query).unsqueeze(0)
            image_docs = self.image_retriever.retrieve(
                image_tensor, k=2)
            image_context = self.describe_images(image_docs)
        else:
            image_context = ""

        prompt = f"""Text Context: {text_context}

Image Context: {image_context}

Query: {query}
```

```
Based on both the textual and visual information provided, please
respond to the query:

Response:"""

        inputs = self.tokenizer(prompt, return_tensors="pt")
        outputs = self.generator.generate(inputs, max_length=300)
        response = self.tokenizer.decode(outputs[0],
            skip_special_tokens=True)

        return response

    def describe_images(self, image_docs: List[Image.Image]) -> str:
        # This method would use an image captioning model to describe
the retrieved images
        # For simplicity, we'll use placeholder descriptions
        descriptions = [f"Image {i+1}: A relevant visual
representation" for i in range(len(image_docs))]
        return " ".join(descriptions)


# Example usage
text_retriever = SomeTextRetrieverClass()  # Replace with your actual
text retriever
image_retriever = SomeImageRetrieverClass()  # Replace with your
actual image retriever
multi_modal_rag = MultiModalRAG(
    text_retriever, image_retriever, generator
)

query = "Explain the process of photosynthesis in plants"
image_query = Image.open("plant_image.jpg")  # Load an image of a
plant

response = multi_modal_rag.retrieve_and_generate(query, image_query)
print(response)
```

Let's understand how this code implements a multi-modal RAG system that combines both text and image processing capabilities.

The `MultiModalRAG` class represents an advanced RAG system that can process both textual and visual information simultaneously to provide more comprehensive responses. It's initialized with three key components: a text retriever (for handling textual documents), an image retriever (for processing visual content), and a generator (language model for response generation), along with an image transformer that standardizes images to a consistent size (224 x 224). The core method, `retrieve_and_generate`, takes both a text query and an optional image query, first retrieving relevant text documents using the text retriever. Then, if an image is provided, it processes it through the image transformer and retrieves relevant images using the image retriever. These retrieved images are then converted into textual descriptions using the `describe_images` method (which, in a real implementation, would use an image captioning model). All this information is combined into a structured prompt that includes both text and image context, allowing the generator to create responses that incorporate both textual and visual information. This multi-modal approach is particularly powerful for queries that benefit from visual contexts, such as explaining scientific processes, describing physical objects, or analyzing visual patterns. This is demonstrated in the preceding example, where it's used to explain photosynthesis with both textual information and a plant image.

The preceding code represents an important step forward in RAG systems by doing the following:

- Breaking down the traditional text-only barrier

- Enabling richer, more contextual responses

- Creating a flexible framework that could be extended to other modalities

- Demonstrating how different types of information can be unified in a single system

Summary

This chapter elevated RAG from a basic data retrieval method to a dynamic framework for building truly adaptive LLM-powered systems. It explored techniques such as iterative and adaptive retrieval, meta-learning, and synergistic prompting, transforming RAG into a context-aware problem solver capable of complex analysis and nuanced understanding, mirroring expert-level research. Addressing ambiguity, uncertainty, and scalability isn't just about overcoming hurdles, but about building trust and enabling real-world deployment.

In the next chapter, we'll explore various evaluation techniques for RAG systems.

Subscribe for a free eBook

New frameworks, evolving architectures, research drops, production breakdowns—AI_Distilled filters the noise into a weekly briefing for engineers and researchers working hands-on with LLMs and GenAI systems. Subscribe now and receive a free eBook, along with weekly insights that help you stay focused and informed. Subscribe at `https://packt.link/8Oz6Y` or scan the QR code below.

29

Evaluating RAG Systems

RAG systems strive to produce more accurate, relevant, and factually grounded responses. However, evaluating the performance of these systems presents unique challenges. Unlike traditional information retrieval or **question-answering** (**QA**) systems, RAG evaluation must consider both the quality of the retrieved information and the effectiveness of the LLM in utilizing that information to generate a high-quality response.

In this chapter, we'll explore the intricacies of evaluating RAG systems. We'll examine the challenges inherent in this task, dissect the key metrics used to assess retrieval quality and generation performance, and discuss various strategies for conducting comprehensive evaluations.

This chapter aims to provide you with a thorough understanding of the principles and practices of RAG evaluation, equipping you with the knowledge you'll need to assess and improve these powerful systems.

In this chapter, we will be covering the following topics:

- Challenges in evaluating RAG systems for LLMs
- Metrics for assessing retrieval quality in LLM-based RAG
- Considerations for retrieval metrics in RAG
- Evaluating the relevance of retrieved information for LLMs
- Measuring the impact of retrieval on LLM generation
- End-to-end evaluation of RAG systems in LLMs
- Human evaluation techniques for LLM-based RAG
- Benchmarks and datasets for RAG evaluation

Challenges in evaluating RAG systems for LLMs

Evaluating RAG systems presents a unique set of challenges that distinguish it from evaluating traditional information retrieval or QA systems. These challenges stem from the interplay between the retrieval and generation components and the need to assess both the factual accuracy and the quality of the generated text.

The following sections will detail the specific challenges that are encountered when evaluating RAG systems for LLMs.

The interplay between retrieval and generation

The performance of a RAG system is a product of both its retrieval component and its generation component. Strong retrieval can provide the LLM with relevant and accurate information, leading to a better-generated response. Conversely, poor retrieval can mislead the LLM, resulting in an inaccurate or irrelevant answer, even if the generator itself is highly capable. Therefore, evaluating a RAG system requires assessing not only the quality of the retrieved information but also how effectively the LLM utilizes that information in its generation process.

Context-sensitive evaluation

Unlike traditional information retrieval, where relevance is often assessed based on the query alone, RAG evaluation must consider the context in which the retrieved information is used. A document might be relevant to the query in isolation but not provide the specific information needed to answer the question accurately in the context of the generated response. This necessitates context-sensitive evaluation metrics that consider both the query and the generated text when assessing the relevance of retrieved documents.

Beyond factual accuracy

While factual accuracy is a primary concern in RAG evaluation, it is not the only factor that determines the quality of a generated response. The response must also be fluent, coherent, and relevant to the user's query. These aspects of text quality are typically assessed through human evaluation, which can be expensive and time-consuming. Developing automated metrics that correlate well with human judgments of these qualitative aspects remains an open research challenge.

Limitations of automated metrics

Automated metrics, such as those borrowed from information retrieval (e.g., precision, recall) or machine translation (e.g., BLEU, ROUGE), can provide useful insights into RAG system performance. However, they often fall short of capturing the full picture. Retrieval metrics might not fully reflect the usefulness of a document for generation, while generation metrics might not adequately assess the factual grounding of the generated text in the retrieved context.

Difficulty in error analysis

When a RAG system produces an incorrect or low-quality response, it can be challenging to pinpoint the root cause. Was the retrieval component unable to find relevant documents? Did the LLM fail to utilize the retrieved information properly? Did the LLM hallucinate or generate a response that is not grounded in the provided context? Disentangling these factors requires careful error analysis and potentially the development of new diagnostic tools.

The need for diverse evaluation scenarios

RAG systems can be deployed in a wide range of applications, from open-domain QA to domain-specific chatbots. The specific challenges and evaluation criteria may vary, depending on the use case. Evaluating a RAG system's performance across diverse scenarios and domains is crucial for understanding its strengths and weaknesses.

Dynamic knowledge and evolving information

In many real-world applications, the underlying knowledge base is constantly evolving. New information is added, and existing information is updated or becomes outdated. Evaluating how well a RAG system adapts to these changes and maintains the accuracy of its responses over time is a significant challenge.

Computational cost

Evaluating RAG systems, especially those that use bigger LLMs, can be computationally expensive. Running inference with large models and performing human evaluations on a large scale can require significant resources. Finding ways to balance evaluation thoroughness with computational cost is an important consideration.

Let's take a look at some key metrics for evaluating the retrieval component in LLM-based RAG systems while focusing on relevance and utility for response generation.

Metrics for assessing retrieval quality in LLM-based RAG

The retrieval component plays a crucial role in the overall performance of a RAG system. It is responsible for providing the LLM with relevant and accurate information that serves as the basis for generating a response. Therefore, assessing the quality of the retrieval component is a vital aspect of RAG evaluation. We can adapt traditional information retrieval metrics to the RAG setting, focusing on the ability of the retriever to find documents that are not only relevant to the query but also useful for the LLM to generate a high-quality answer.

Recall@k

Recall@k measures the proportion of relevant documents that are successfully retrieved within the top *k* results. In the context of RAG, we can define a relevant document as one that contains the necessary information to answer the query accurately:

- **Formula**: *Recall@k = (Number of relevant documents retrieved in top k) / (Total number of relevant documents)*

- **Interpretation**: A higher Recall@k indicates that the retrieval component can find a larger proportion of the relevant documents

- **Example**: If five documents in the entire corpus contain information needed to answer a specific query, and the RAG system retrieves three of them within the top 10 results, then Recall@10 for that query would be 3/5 = 0.6

Precision@k

Precision@k measures the proportion of retrieved documents within the top *k* results that are relevant:

- **Formula**: *Precision@k = (Number of relevant documents retrieved in top k) / (k)*

- **Interpretation**: A higher Precision@k indicates that a larger proportion of the retrieved documents are relevant

- **Example**: If a RAG system retrieves 10 documents for a query, and four of them are relevant, then Precision@10 would be 4/10 = 0.4

Mean Reciprocal Rank (MRR)

MRR considers the rank of the first relevant document retrieved. It emphasizes the importance of retrieving relevant documents early in the ranking:

- **Formula**: *MRR = (1 / |Q|) * Σ (1 / rank_i) for i = 1 to |Q|*, where *|Q|* is the number of queries and *rank_i* is the rank of the first relevant document for query *i*.

- **Interpretation**: A higher MRR indicates that relevant documents are retrieved at higher ranks (closer to the top).

- **Example**: If the first relevant document for a query is retrieved at rank three, the reciprocal rank is 1/3. MRR averages these reciprocal ranks across multiple queries.

Normalized Discounted Cumulative Gain (NDCG@k)

NDCG@k is a more sophisticated metric that considers both the relevance of retrieved documents and their position in the ranking. It uses a graded relevance scale (e.g., 0, 1, 2, where 2 is highly relevant) and assigns higher scores to relevant documents retrieved at higher ranks:

- **Formula**: NDCG@k involves calculating the **Discounted Cumulative Gain** (**DCG**) of the retrieved list and normalizing it by the **Ideal Discounted Cumulative Gain** (**IDCG**), which is the DCG of the perfectly ranked list. The formula is complex but can be easily computed using libraries such as sklearn.

- **Interpretation**: A higher NDCG@k indicates that highly relevant documents are retrieved at higher ranks.

Next, let's discuss how to decide which retrieval metrics to use.

Considerations for retrieval metrics in RAG

In the context of RAG, we need to define relevance carefully. A document might be relevant to the query but not contain the specific information needed to answer it accurately. We might need to use a stricter definition of relevance, such as "contains the answer to the query." As mentioned earlier, relevance in RAG is often context-sensitive. A document might be relevant to the query in isolation but not be the most helpful document for generating a specific answer given the other retrieved documents.

While metrics such as Recall@k and Precision@k focus on the top *k* retrieved documents, it's also important to consider the overall quality of the retrieval across a wider range of results. Metrics such as **Average Precision** (**AP**) can provide a more holistic view.

Let's illustrate how to calculate Recall@k, Precision@k, MRR, and NDCG@k in Python using the sklearn library:

1. We first import the necessary libraries and define sample data representing a set of queries, the ground truth relevant documents for each query, and the documents that are retrieved by a RAG system for each query:

```
import numpy as np
from sklearn.metrics import ndcg_score

# Sample data
queries = [
    "What is the capital of France?",
    "Who painted the Mona Lisa?",
    "What is the highest mountain in the world?"
]
ground_truth = [
```

```
        [0, 1, 2],   # Indices of relevant documents for query 1
        [3, 4],      # Indices of relevant documents for query 2
        [5, 6, 7]    # Indices of relevant documents for query 3
    ]
    retrieved = [
        [1, 5, 0, 2, 8, 9, 3, 4, 6, 7],   # Ranked list of retrieved
    document indices for query 1
        [4, 3, 0, 1, 2, 5, 6, 7, 8, 9],   # Ranked list of retrieved
    document indices for query 2
        [6, 5, 7, 0, 1, 2, 3, 4, 8, 9]    # Ranked list of retrieved
    document indices for query 3
    ]
```

2. We then define a function, `calculate_recall_at_k`, to calculate Recall@k for a given set of queries, ground truth relevant documents, and retrieved document lists:

```python
def calculate_recall_at_k(ground_truth, retrieved, k):
    """Calculates Recall@k for a set of queries."""
    recall_scores = []
    for gt, ret in zip(ground_truth, retrieved):
        num_relevant = len(gt)
        retrieved_k = ret[:k]
        num_relevant_retrieved = len(
            set(gt).intersection(set(retrieved_k))
        )
        recall = (
            num_relevant_retrieved / num_relevant
            if num_relevant > 0 else 0
        )
        recall_scores.append(recall)
    return np.mean(recall_scores)
```

3. We next define a function, `calculate_precision_at_k`, to calculate Precision@k for a given set of queries, ground truth, and retrieved lists:

```python
def calculate_precision_at_k(ground_truth, retrieved, k):
    """Calculates Precision@k for a set of queries."""
    precision_scores = []
    for gt, ret in zip(ground_truth, retrieved):
        retrieved_k = ret[:k]
        num_relevant_retrieved = len(
            set(gt).intersection(set(retrieved_k))
        )
        precision = num_relevant_retrieved / k if k > 0 else 0
        precision_scores.append(precision)
    return np.mean(precision_scores)
```

4. We define a function, `calculate_mrr`, to calculate the MRR for a given set of queries, ground truth, and retrieved lists. A higher MRR indicates that the system consistently retrieves relevant documents at higher ranks:

```
def calculate_mrr(ground_truth, retrieved):
    """Calculates Mean Reciprocal Rank (MRR) for a set of
queries."""
    mrr_scores = []
    for gt, ret in zip(ground_truth, retrieved):
        for i, doc_id in enumerate(ret):
            if doc_id in gt:
                mrr_scores.append(1 / (i + 1))
                break
        else:
            mrr_scores.append(0)  # No relevant document found
    return np.mean(mrr_scores)
```

5. We also define a function, `calculate_ndcg_at_k`, to calculate NDCG@k. We'll use a simplified version here where relevance scores are binary (0 or 1):

```
def calculate_ndcg_at_k(ground_truth, retrieved, k):
    """Calculates NDCG@k for a set of queries."""
    ndcg_scores = []
    for gt, ret in zip(ground_truth, retrieved):
        relevance_scores = np.zeros(len(ret))
        for i, doc_id in enumerate(ret):
            if doc_id in gt:
                relevance_scores[i] = 1

        # sklearn.metrics.ndcg_score requires 2D array
        true_relevance = np.array([relevance_scores])
        retrieved_relevance = np.array([relevance_scores])

        ndcg = ndcg_score(
            true_relevance, retrieved_relevance, k=k
        )
        ndcg_scores.append(ndcg)
    return np.mean(ndcg_scores)
```

6. Finally, we calculate and print the retrieval metrics for different values of *k*:

```
k_values = [1, 3, 5, 10]
for k in k_values:
    recall_at_k = calculate_recall_at_k(ground_truth,
        retrieved, k)
```

```
        precision_at_k = calculate_precision_at_k(
            ground_truth, retrieved, k
        )
        ndcg_at_k = calculate_ndcg_at_k(ground_truth, retrieved, k)
        print(f"Recall@{k}: {recall_at_k:.3f}")
        print(f"Precision@{k}: {precision_at_k:.3f}")
        print(f"NDCG@{k}: {ndcg_at_k:.3f}")

    mrr = calculate_mrr(ground_truth, retrieved)
    print(f"MRR: {mrr:.3f}")
```

Evaluating the relevance of retrieved information for LLMs

While the retrieval metrics discussed in the previous section provide a general assessment of retrieval quality, they do not fully capture the nuances of relevance in the context of RAG. In RAG, the retrieved information is not the end product but rather an intermediate step that serves as input to an LLM. Therefore, we need to evaluate the relevance of the retrieved information not just to the query but also to the specific task of generating a high-quality response via the LLM.

Traditional information retrieval often focuses on finding documents that are topically relevant to the query. However, in RAG, we need a more nuanced notion of relevance that considers the following aspects:

- **Answerability**: Does the retrieved information contain the specific information needed to answer the query accurately? A document might be generally relevant to the query but not contain the precise answer.

- **Contextual utility**: Is the retrieved information useful in the context of the other retrieved documents? A document might be relevant in isolation but redundant or even contradictory when combined with other retrieved information.

- **LLM compatibility**: Is the retrieved information in a format that the LLM can easily understand and utilize? For example, a long and complex document might be relevant but difficult for the LLM to process effectively.

- **Faithfulness support**: Does the retrieved information provide sufficient evidence to support the claims made in the generated answer? This is crucial for ensuring that the LLM's response is grounded in the retrieved context.

Methods for evaluating the relevance of retrieved information

Here are some methods for evaluating the relevance of retrieved information that involve moving beyond traditional query relevance:

- **Human evaluation**:

  - **Direct assessment**: Human annotators can directly assess the relevance of retrieved documents to the query and the generated response. They can be asked to rate the relevance on a Likert scale (e.g., 1 to 5) or to provide binary judgments (relevant/not relevant).

  - **Comparative evaluation**: Annotators can be presented with multiple sets of retrieved documents and asked to rank them based on their usefulness for answering the query or to choose the best set.

  - **Task-based evaluation**: Annotators can be asked to use the retrieved documents to answer the query themselves. The accuracy and quality of their answers can serve as an indirect measure of the relevance and utility of the retrieved information.

- **Automated metrics**: Let's consider some commonly used automated metrics. Keep in mind that while automated metrics provide a quantitative measure of performance, human evaluation offers valuable qualitative insights into the relevance, coherence, and usefulness of the generated responses:

  - **Answer overlap**: We can automatically measure the overlap between the generated answer and the retrieved documents using metrics such as ROUGE or BLEU. Higher overlap suggests that the LLM is utilizing the retrieved information.

  - **QA metrics**: If we have ground truth answers, we can treat the retrieved context as the input to a QA system and evaluate its performance using standard QA metrics such as **Exact Match (EM)** and F1 score.

  - **Faithfulness metrics**: We can use techniques such as **Natural Language Inference (NLI)** to assess whether the generated answer is entailed by the retrieved context. We'll discuss NLI models in detail in later sections of this chapter.

  - **Perplexity**: We can measure the perplexity of the LLM when it's conditioned on the retrieved context. Lower perplexity suggests that the LLM finds the context informative and useful for generation.

As an example, let's illustrate how to implement simple answer overlap metrics using the `rouge-score` library in Python:

1. First, we run the following command to install the `rouge-score` library, which provides implementations of ROUGE metrics, and import the necessary modules:

    ```
    pip install rouge-score
    from rouge_score import rouge_scorer
    ```

2. Then, we define sample data representing a query, a generated answer, and a list of retrieved documents:

    ```
    query = "What is the capital of France?"
    answer = "The capital of France is Paris."
    retrieved_documents = [
        "Paris is the capital city of France.",
        "France is a country in Europe.",
        "The Eiffel Tower is a famous landmark in Paris.",
        "London is the capital of the United Kingdom."
    ]
    ```

3. We next define a function, `calculate_rouge_scores`, to calculate ROUGE scores between the generated answer and each retrieved document:

    ```
    def calculate_rouge_scores(answer, documents):
        """Calculates ROUGE scores between the answer and each
    document."""
        scorer = rouge_scorer.RougeScorer(
            ['rouge1', 'rouge2', 'rougeL'],
            use_stemmer=True
        )
        scores = []
        for doc in documents:
            score = scorer.score(answer, doc)
            scores.append(score)
        return scores
    ```

4. We then calculate and print the ROUGE scores for each document:

    ```
    rouge_scores = calculate_rouge_scores(answer,
        retrieved_documents)
    for i, score in enumerate(rouge_scores):
        print(f"Document {i+1}:")
        print(f"  ROUGE-1: {score['rouge1'].fmeasure:.3f}")
        print(f"  ROUGE-2: {score['rouge2'].fmeasure:.3f}")
        print(f"  ROUGE-L: {score['rougeL'].fmeasure:.3f}")
    ```

5. Finally, we calculate and print the average ROUGE scores across all documents:

```
avg_rouge1 = sum([score['rouge1'].fmeasure
    for score in rouge_scores]) / len(rouge_scores)
avg_rouge2 = sum([score['rouge2'].fmeasure
    for score in rouge_scores]) / len(rouge_scores)
avg_rougeL = sum([score['rougeL'].fmeasure
    for score in rouge_scores]) / len(rouge_scores)

print(f"\nAverage ROUGE Scores:")
print(f"  Average ROUGE-1: {avg_rouge1:.3f}")
print(f"  Average ROUGE-2: {avg_rouge2:.3f}")
print(f"  Average ROUGE-L: {avg_rougeL:.3f}")
```

Challenges in evaluating RAG-specific relevance

Having explored several methods for evaluating the relevance of retrieved information, we now turn to outlining some of the key challenges involved in this evaluation process:

- **Subjectivity**: Relevance judgments can be subjective, especially when considering factors such as contextual utility and LLM compatibility

- **Annotation cost**: Human evaluation can be expensive and time-consuming, especially for large-scale evaluations

- **Metric limitations**: Automated metrics might not fully capture the nuances of RAG-specific relevance and might not always correlate well with human judgments

- **Dynamic contexts**: The relevance of a document can change depending on the other documents that are retrieved and the specific generation strategy used by the LLM

Next, let's learn how to measure the impact of retrieval on LLM generation.

Measuring the impact of retrieval on LLM generation

In RAG systems, the quality of the generated response is heavily influenced by the information that's retrieved. Good retrieval provides the necessary context and facts, while poor retrieval can lead to irrelevant or incorrect responses. Enhancing retrieval through better models and filtering improves overall performance, which is measured by precision, faithfulness, and user satisfaction.

Therefore, a crucial aspect of evaluation involves measuring the impact of retrieval on LLM generation. Let's check out some of the key metrics and techniques.

Key metrics for evaluating retrieval impact

As mentioned, the quality of a response generated by an LLM is closely tied to the information it retrieves. Therefore, evaluating the impact of retrieval on the final response is crucial. This involves assessing how effectively the LLM leverages the retrieved context to generate answers that are accurate, relevant, and well-grounded. Let's now examine some of the key metrics used in this evaluation:

- **Groundedness/faithfulness**:

  Groundedness, also known as faithfulness, measures the extent to which the generated response is factually supported by the retrieved context. A grounded response should only contain information that can be inferred from the provided documents.

  Some of the techniques for evaluating this metric are as follows:

  - **Human evaluation**: Human annotators can directly assess the groundedness of each statement in the generated response by verifying whether it is supported by the retrieved context. This can involve binary judgments (grounded/not grounded) or more fine-grained ratings.

  - **Automated metrics**:

    - **NLI**: NLI models can be used to determine whether each sentence in the generated response is entailed by the retrieved context. We treat the concatenation of retrieved documents as the premise and each sentence in the response as the hypothesis. A high entailment score suggests that the sentence is grounded in the context.

    - **QA-based**: We can formulate questions based on the generated response and check whether a QA model can answer them correctly using the retrieved context as the source of information. A high answerability score indicates that the response is grounded.

    - **Fact verification models**: These models can be used to check whether each fact stated in the generated response is supported by the retrieved documents or external knowledge sources.

- **Answer relevance**:

  Answer relevance measures how well the generated response addresses the user's query, given the retrieved context. Even if the retrieved context is imperfect, a good RAG system should still strive to provide a relevant and helpful answer.

  Some of the techniques for evaluating this metric are as follows:

  - **Human evaluation**: Human judges can assess the relevance of the generated response to the query while taking into account the limitations of the retrieved context. They can rate relevance on a Likert scale or provide comparative judgments (e.g., ranking multiple responses).

  - **Automated metrics**:

    - **Query-answer similarity**: We can measure the semantic similarity between the query and the generated response using embedding-based techniques (e.g., cosine similarity) or other similarity metrics.

- **Task-specific metrics**: Depending on the specific application, we can use task-specific metrics. For example, in a QA scenario, we can measure the overlap between the generated answer and a gold-standard answer using metrics such as EM or F1 score.

- **Information retrieval metrics**: We can treat the generated response as a retrieved document and evaluate its relevance to the query using traditional IR metrics such as precision, recall, or NDCG, assuming we have relevance judgments for query-answer pairs.

- **Context utilization**:

  This aspect focuses on how effectively the LLM utilizes the retrieved context when generating the response. It goes beyond just measuring groundedness and assesses whether the LLM is integrating and synthesizing information from the context appropriately.

  Some of the techniques for evaluating this metric are as follows:

  - **Human evaluation**: Human annotators can assess the extent to which the LLM is using the retrieved context, identifying instances where the model is underutilizing or over-relying on the context

  - **Automated metrics**:

    - **Attribution analysis**: We can use techniques such as attention visualization or gradient-based attribution to identify which parts of the retrieved context the LLM is paying the most attention to during generation.

    - **Context ablation**: We can measure the change in the generated response when portions of the context are removed or modified. This can help with determining which parts of the context are most influential.

As an example, let's carry out a groundedness evaluation using an NLI model. For this example, we'll use the Transformers library:

1. We first run the following command, which installs the `transformers` library. This library provides tools for working with pre-trained transformer models such as NLI. We also import the necessary modules:

```
pip install transformers torch
from transformers import (
    AutoTokenizer, AutoModelForSequenceClassification
)
import torch
```

2. We then define sample data representing a query, a generated answer, and the retrieved context:

```
query = "What is the capital of France?"
answer = "The capital of France is Paris. It is a global center
for art, fashion, gastronomy, and culture."
context = """
```

```
Paris is the capital city of France. It is situated on the River
Seine, in northern France.
Paris has an area of 105 square kilometers and a population of
over 2 million people.
France is a country located in Western Europe.
"""
```

3. We load a pre-trained NLI model and its corresponding tokenizer. Here, we're using the `roberta-large-mnli` model, which is a RoBERTa model that's been fine-tuned on the MultiNLI dataset:

```
model_name = "roberta-large-mnli"
tokenizer = AutoTokenizer.from_pretrained(model_name)
model = \
    AutoModelForSequenceClassification.from_
pretrained(
    model_name
)
```

4. We then define a function, `calculate_claim_groundedness`, that calculates the entailment score for a single claim (a sentence from the generated answer) given the context:

```
def calculate_claim_groundedness(context, claim):
    """Calculates the entailment score for a single claim given
the context."""
    inputs = tokenizer(context, claim, truncation=True,
        return_tensors="pt")
    outputs = model(**inputs)
    probs = torch.softmax(outputs.logits, dim=1)
    entailment_prob = probs[0][2].item()  # Assuming label 2
corresponds to entailment
    return entailment_prob
```

5. We also define a function, `calculate_groundedness`, to calculate the overall groundedness score for the entire generated answer. It splits the answer into sentences, calculates the entailment score for each sentence, and then averages the scores:

```
def calculate_groundedness(context, answer):
    """Calculates the overall groundedness score for the
generated answer."""
    claims = answer.split(". ")  # Simple sentence splitting
    if not claims:
        return 0
    claim_scores = []
    for claim in claims:
        if claim:
```

```
            score = calculate_claim_groundedness(context, claim)
            claim_scores.append(score)
    return (
        sum(claim_scores) / len(claim_scores)
        if claim_scores
        else 0
    )
```

6.   Finally, we calculate and print the overall groundedness score for the sample data:

```
groundedness_score = calculate_groundedness(context, answer)
print(f"Groundedness Score: {groundedness_score:.3f}")
```

Challenges in measuring the impact of retrieval

Now that we've seen an example, let's take a look at some of the key challenges that are encountered in the evaluation process of RAG systems:

- **Defining the ground truth**: Determining the ground truth for groundedness and answer relevance can be challenging and subjective, especially when dealing with complex or nuanced queries

- **Attributing errors**: It can be difficult to determine whether an error in the generated response is due to poor retrieval, limitations of the LLM, or a combination of both

- **Computational cost**: Evaluating the impact of retrieval on generation can be computationally expensive, especially when using bigger LLMs or performing human evaluations

- **Inter-annotator agreement**: When using human evaluation, ensuring high inter-annotator agreement on subjective judgments such as groundedness and relevance can be difficult

While evaluating the individual components of a RAG system (retrieval and generation) is important, it is also crucial to assess the system's overall performance in an end-to-end manner. Let's see that next.

End-to-end evaluation of RAG systems in LLMs

While evaluating the individual components of a RAG system (retrieval and generation) is important, it is also crucial to assess the system's overall performance in an end-to-end manner. End-to-end evaluation considers the entire RAG pipeline, from the initial user query to the final generated response, providing a holistic view of the system's effectiveness.

Let's take a look at some holistic metrics:

- **Task success**: For task-oriented RAG systems (e.g., QA, dialogue), we can measure the overall task success rate. This involves determining whether the generated response completes the intended task successfully.

Here are some techniques for evaluating this metric:

- **Automated evaluation**: For some tasks, we can automatically evaluate task success. For example, in QA, we can check whether the generated answer matches the gold-standard answer.

- **Human evaluation**: For more complex tasks, human evaluation might be necessary to judge whether the RAG system successfully achieved the task's goal.

- **Answer quality**: This metric assesses the overall quality of the generated response while considering factors such as accuracy, relevance, fluency, coherence, and groundedness.

Here are some techniques for evaluating this metric:

- **Human evaluation**: Human judges can rate the overall quality of the generated response on a Likert scale or by using more detailed rubrics that consider multiple quality dimensions

- **Automated metrics**: While answer quality can be challenging to fully automate, some aspects of answer quality can be approximated using metrics such as the following:

  - **ROUGE/BLEU**: Measures the overlap between the generated response and a reference answer (if available)

  - **Perplexity**: Measures how well the LLM predicts the generated response (lower perplexity is generally better)

  - **Groundedness metrics (NLI, QA-based)**: Assesses the factual consistency of the response with the retrieved context

  - **Relevance metrics**: Measures the similarity between the query and the generated response

Now, let's look at some ways we can evaluate RAG systems.

Evaluation strategies

Evaluation strategies for RAG systems can be broadly categorized into black-box evaluation, glass-box evaluation, component-wise evaluation, and ablation studies, each offering distinct insights into system performance.

In black-box evaluation, the entire RAG system is treated as a single unit. Evaluators provide input queries and assess only the final generated responses without analyzing the intermediate retrieval or generation steps. This approach is particularly useful for measuring overall system performance and comparing different RAG implementations without having to delve into their internal mechanisms.

Glass-box evaluation, in contrast, involves a detailed examination of the internal workings of the RAG system. This method analyzes the retrieved context, the LLM's attention patterns, and the intermediate generation steps. By dissecting these elements, glass-box evaluation helps identify system strengths and weaknesses, pinpoint error sources, and provide insights for targeted improvements.

A more granular approach is component-wise evaluation, which assesses the retrieval and generation components separately. Retrieval performance is typically measured using metrics such as Recall@k and NDCG, while the quality of the generated text is evaluated using metrics such as BLEU and ROUGE or through human judgment based on a fixed set of retrieved documents. This method is particularly effective in isolating and diagnosing performance issues within individual components.

Finally, ablation studies offer a systematic way to measure the impact of different components on overall system effectiveness. By removing or modifying specific parts of the RAG system – such as testing performance with and without retrieval or swapping different retrieval and generation models – researchers can better understand how each component contributes to the system's functionality and overall success.

Challenges in end-to-end evaluation

Evaluating RAG systems holistically presents several challenges, particularly when assessing complex interactions between retrieval and generation components. Some of these challenges are as follows:

- **Defining the ground truth**: For open-ended tasks or tasks that involve generating complex responses, defining the ground truth can be difficult or even impossible

- **Attributing errors**: When the system generates an incorrect or low-quality response, it can be challenging to determine whether the error originated in the retrieval or generation component

- **Computational cost**: End-to-end evaluation can be computationally expensive, especially when using bigger LLMs or performing human evaluations on a large scale

- **Reproducibility**: Ensuring reproducibility can be difficult due to the complex interactions between the retrieval and generation components and the potential use of non-deterministic retrieval mechanisms or stochastic decoding strategies during generation, which may lead to variations in outputs across runs even with the same inputs.

Next, let's shift focus to the role of human evaluation in assessing LLM-based RAG systems, which complements automated metrics by capturing nuanced aspects such as relevance, coherence, and factual accuracy.

Human evaluation techniques for LLM-based RAG

While automated metrics provide valuable insights, human evaluation remains the gold standard for assessing the overall quality and effectiveness of RAG systems. Human judgment is particularly crucial for evaluating aspects that are difficult to capture with automated metrics, such as the nuanced relevance of retrieved information, the coherence and fluency of generated text, and the overall helpfulness of the response in addressing the user's need.

Human evaluators can assess various aspects of RAG system performance:

- **Relevance**: How relevant is the generated response to the user's query? Does it address the specific information needed expressed in the query?

- **Groundedness/faithfulness**: Is the generated response factually supported by the retrieved context? Does it avoid hallucinating or contradicting the provided information?

- **Coherence and fluency**: Is the generated response well-structured, easy to understand, and written in grammatically correct and natural-sounding language?

- **Helpfulness**: Does the response provide a useful and satisfactory answer to the user's query, considering the limitations of the retrieved context?

- **Context utilization**: How effectively does the system utilize the retrieved context in generating the response? Does it integrate and synthesize information from multiple sources appropriately?

- **Attribution**: Does the system provide clear citations or links to the sources in the retrieved context that support the generated claims?

Several methods can be used for the human evaluation of RAG systems:

- **Rating scales (Likert scales)**: Annotators rate different aspects of the generated response (e.g., relevance, groundedness, fluency) on a numerical scale, such as 1 to 5, where 1 represents poor quality and 5 represents excellent quality:

  - **Advantages**: Simple to implement and easy to collect and aggregate data

  - **Disadvantages**: Can be subjective, susceptible to annotator bias, and may not capture nuanced differences

- **Comparative evaluation (ranking/best–worst scaling)**: Annotators are presented with multiple RAG system outputs for the same query and asked to rank them based on their overall quality or specific criteria.

- **Best–worst scaling**: A specific form of comparative evaluation where annotators choose the best and worst options from a set of outputs:

  - **Advantages**: More reliable than absolute ratings and captures relative differences between systems effectively

  - **Disadvantages**: More complex to implement than rating scales and requires more effort from annotators

- **Task-based evaluation**: Annotators are asked to complete a specific task using the RAG system, such as finding an answer to a question, writing a summary, or engaging in a conversation. The quality of the RAG system is assessed based on the annotators' ability to complete the task successfully and their satisfaction with the system's performance:

  - **Advantages**: More realistic and user-centered and provides a direct measure of the system's utility

- **Disadvantages**: More complex to design and implement and can be time-consuming and expensive

- **Free-form feedback**: Annotators provide open-ended feedback on the strengths and weaknesses of the RAG system's output:

  - **Advantages**: Captures detailed insights and suggestions for improvement and can uncover unexpected issues

  - **Disadvantages**: More difficult to analyze and quantify and can be subjective and inconsistent

Best practices for human evaluation

To ensure the reliability and fairness of human evaluation, consider the following best practices:

- **Clear guidelines**: Provide annotators with clear and detailed guidelines that define the evaluation criteria and annotation procedures

- **Training and calibration**: Train annotators on the task and calibrate their judgments using example annotations

- **Inter-annotator agreement**: Measure inter-annotator agreement (e.g., using Cohen's Kappa or Fleiss' Kappa) to ensure the reliability of the annotations

- **Pilot studies**: Conduct pilot studies to refine the evaluation protocol and identify potential issues before launching a large-scale evaluation

- **Multiple annotators**: Use multiple annotators for each item to mitigate individual biases and improve the robustness of the evaluation

- **Diverse annotator pool**: Recruit a diverse pool of annotators to capture a wider range of perspectives and reduce potential biases

- **Quality control**: Implement mechanisms for identifying and correcting errors or inconsistencies in the annotations

Challenges in human evaluation

Evaluating the performance of RAG systems built on LLMs poses a unique set of challenges. Here, we outline the key obstacles encountered in conducting reliable, consistent, and meaningful human evaluations of such systems:

- **Cost and time**: Human evaluation can be expensive and time-consuming, especially for large-scale evaluations

- **Subjectivity**: Human judgments can be subjective and influenced by individual preferences and biases

- **Annotator training and expertise**: Ensuring that annotators are properly trained and have the necessary expertise to assess RAG system performance can be challenging

- **Reproducibility**: Replicating human evaluations can be difficult due to the inherent variability in human judgments

In the next section, we'll explore the role of standardized benchmarks and datasets in evaluating RAG systems, highlighting key benchmarks, evaluation criteria, and challenges.

Benchmarks and datasets for RAG evaluation

Standardized benchmarks and datasets play a crucial role in driving progress in RAG research and development. They provide a common ground for evaluating and comparing different RAG systems, facilitating the process of identifying best practices and tracking advancements over time.

Let's look at some key benchmarks and datasets:

- **Knowledge Intensive Language Tasks (KILT)**: A comprehensive benchmark for evaluating knowledge-intensive language tasks, including QA, fact-checking, dialogue, and entity linking:

  - **Data source**: Based on Wikipedia, with a unified format for all tasks

  - **Strengths**: Provides a diverse set of tasks, allows both retrieval and generation to be evaluated, and includes a standardized evaluation framework

  - **Limitations**: Primarily based on Wikipedia, which might not reflect the diversity of real-world knowledge sources

- **Natural Questions (NQ)**: A large-scale QA dataset collected from real user queries that is sent to the Google search engine:

  - **Data source**: Contains pairs of questions and Wikipedia pages that contain the answer

  - **Strengths**: Realistic queries, large scale, and includes both short and long answer annotations

  - **Limitations**: Since it primarily focuses on factoid questions, it might not be suitable for evaluating more complex reasoning or generation tasks

- **TriviaQA**: A challenging QA dataset containing question-answer-evidence triples:

  - **Data source**: Collected from trivia enthusiasts, it includes both web and Wikipedia evidence documents

  - **Strengths**: More difficult than NQ; it requires reading and understanding multiple evidence documents

  - **Limitations**: Primarily focused on factoid questions, the writing style of trivia questions might not be representative of real-world user queries

- **Explain Like I'm Five (ELI5)**: A dataset of questions and answers from the Reddit forum *Explain Like I'm Five*, where users ask for simplified explanations of complex topics:

  - **Data source**: Collected from Reddit, it includes questions and answers on a wide range of topics

  - **Strengths**: Focuses on long-form, explanatory answers, making it suitable for evaluating the generation capabilities of RAG systems

  - **Limitations**: The quality and accuracy of answers can vary and might require careful filtering or annotation

- **ASQA**: The first long-form QA dataset that unifies ambiguous questions:

  - **Data source**: The dataset is built from scratch by combining multiple ambiguous questions

  - **Strengths**: Can help evaluate long-form QA tasks

  - **Limitations**: Building a high-quality dataset from scratch can be challenging

- **Microsoft Machine Reading Comprehension (MS MARCO)**: A large-scale dataset for machine reading comprehension and QA:

  - **Data source**: Contains real anonymized user queries that are sent to the Bing search engine, along with human-generated answers and relevant passages.

  - **Strengths**: It provides a large-scale, diverse set of queries and answers that includes both passage-level and full-document annotations

  - **Limitations**: Primarily focused on extractive QA, it might not be ideal for evaluating the generation capabilities of RAG systems

- **Stanford Question Answering Dataset (SQuAD)**: A widely used dataset for reading comprehension consisting of questions posed by crowdworkers on a set of Wikipedia articles:

  - **Data source**: Contains question-paragraph-answer triples, where the answer is a span of text in the paragraph

  - **Strengths**: A large-scale, well-established benchmark for reading comprehension

  - **Limitations**: Primarily focused on extractive QA, it might not be suitable for evaluating the generation capabilities of RAG systems

As an example, let's illustrate how to use the KILT dataset to evaluate a RAG system. We'll use the KILT library in Python to do so:

1. Run the following code to install the kilt library and import the necessary modules:

```
pip install kilt==0.5.5
from kilt import kilt_utils as utils
from kilt import retrieval
from kilt.eval import answer_evaluation, provenance_evaluation
```

2. Next, download a specific KILT task, such as the Wizard of Wikipedia (WoW) dataset:

```
# Download the WoW dataset
utils.download_dataset("wow")
```

3. Then, load the downloaded dataset into memory:

```
# Load the dataset
wow_data = utils.load_dataset("wow", split="test")
```

4. Define a dummy RAG function that simulates the behavior of a RAG retrieval component. For demonstration purposes, it simply returns a fixed set of Wikipedia pages for each query. In a real-world scenario, you would replace this with your actual RAG retrieval implementation:

```
class DummyRetriever(retrieval.base.Retriever):
    def __init__(self, k=1):
        super().__init__(num_return_docs=k)
        self.k = k
    # retrieve some Wikipedia pages (or the entire dataset)
    # based on the query
    def retrieve(self, query, start_paragraph_id=None):
        # Dummy retrieval: return the same set of pages for each
query
        dummy_pages = [
            {
                "wikipedia_id": "534366",
                "start_paragraph_id": 1,
                "score": self.k,
                "text": "Paris is the capital of France."
            },
            {
                "wikipedia_id": "21854",
                "start_paragraph_id": 1,
                "score": self.k-1,
                "text": "The Mona Lisa was painted by Leonardo
da Vinci."
```

```
        },
        {
            "wikipedia_id": "37267",
            "start_paragraph_id": 1,
            "score": self.k-2,
            "text": "Mount Everest is the highest mountain
in the world."
        }
    ]
    return dummy_pages[:self.k]
# Example usage
retriever = DummyRetriever(k=2)
```

5. Define a dummy RAG generation function that simulates the behavior of a RAG generation component. For demonstration purposes, it simply returns a fixed answer for each query. In a real-world scenario, you would replace this with your actual LLM-based generation implementation:

```
def dummy_generate(query, retrieved_pages):
    """Simulates RAG generation by returning
    a fixed answer for each query."""
    if "capital of France" in query:
        return "Paris"
    elif "Mona Lisa" in query:
        return "Leonardo da Vinci"
    elif "highest mountain" in query:
        return "Mount Everest"
    else:
        return "I don't know."
```

6. Run the dummy RAG pipeline on the dataset, using the dummy retrieval and generation functions, and collect the generated predictions:

```
predictions = []
for element in wow_data[:10]:
    query = element["input"]
    retrieved_pages = retriever.retrieve(query)

    # Add provenance information to the element
    element["output"] = [{"provenance": retrieved_pages}]

    generated_answer = dummy_generate(query, retrieved_pages)

    # Add the generated answer to the element
    element["output"][0]["answer"] = generated_answer

    predictions.append(element)
```

7. Finally, evaluate the generated predictions using the KILT evaluation functions. Both the retrieval performance (using `provenance_evaluation`) and the answer quality (using `answer_evaluation`) are assessed:

```
kilt_scores = {}
kilt_scores["provenance_MAP@k"] = \
    provenance_evaluation.get_map_at_k(
    predictions, verbose=False
)
kilt_scores["answer_EM"] = answer_evaluation.get_exact_match(
    predictions, verbose=False
)
kilt_scores["answer_F1"] = answer_evaluation.get_f1(
    predictions, verbose=False
)
kilt_scores["answer_ROUGE-L"] = answer_evaluation.get_rouge_l(
    predictions, verbose=False
)
print(kilt_scores)
```

This code provides a basic example of how to use the KILT framework to evaluate a RAG system. In a real-world scenario, you would replace the dummy retrieval and generation functions with your actual RAG implementation and use a larger portion of the dataset for evaluation. You can adapt this example to other KILT tasks by downloading and loading the corresponding datasets.

Here are a few things to consider when choosing benchmarks and datasets:

- **Task alignment**: Select benchmarks and datasets that align with the specific task you are evaluating (e.g., QA, dialogue, summarization)

- **Knowledge domain**: Consider the knowledge domain covered by the benchmark. Some benchmarks are based on general knowledge (e.g., Wikipedia), while others focus on specific domains (e.g., scientific literature, medical records)

- **Retrieval setting**: Choose benchmarks that are appropriate for the retrieval setting you are using (e.g., open-domain retrieval, closed-domain retrieval, passage retrieval, document retrieval)

- **Generation requirements**: Consider the type of generation required by the task (e.g., extractive versus abstractive, short versus long answers)

- **Dataset size and quality**: Ensure that the dataset is large enough to provide statistically significant results and that the data is of high quality (e.g., accurate annotations and well-formed questions)

- **Evaluation metrics**: Check what evaluation metrics are used by the benchmark and whether they are appropriate for your specific evaluation goals

Summary

In this chapter, we discussed a wide range of metrics for evaluating both retrieval quality and generation performance, including traditional information retrieval metrics such as Recall@k, Precision@k, MRR, and NDCG, as well as more RAG-specific metrics such as groundedness, faithfulness, and answer relevance. We explored various techniques for measuring these metrics, including automated methods based on NLI and QA models, and human evaluation approaches using rating scales, comparative judgments, and task-based assessments.

We emphasized the crucial role of human evaluation in capturing the nuanced aspects of RAG performance that are difficult to assess with automated metrics alone. We also discussed best practices for designing and conducting human evaluations, such as providing clear guidelines, training annotators, measuring inter-annotator agreement, and conducting pilot studies. We need to keep in mind that tradeoffs between automated and human evaluation will be important in real-world deployments.

Furthermore, we explored widely used benchmarks and datasets for RAG evaluation, including KILT, NQ, TriviaQA, ELI5, ASQA, MS MARCO, and SQuAD, highlighting their strengths and limitations and providing guidance on selecting appropriate benchmarks for different tasks and domains.

As we conclude, it is clear that evaluating RAG systems is a complex and evolving field. The development of more sophisticated evaluation metrics, the creation of more diverse and challenging benchmarks, and the refinement of human evaluation methodologies will continue to be crucial for driving progress in RAG research and development.

In the next chapter, we'll explore agentic patterns in LLMs, focusing on how LLMs can perform tasks involving reasoning, planning, and decision-making autonomously using advanced retrieval and generation techniques.

30

Agentic Patterns

In this final chapter, we'll explore patterns for creating more autonomous and goal-directed AI agents using LLMs. You'll learn about goal-setting and planning in LLM-based agents, implementing memory and state management, and strategies for decision-making and action selection. We'll cover techniques for learning and adaptation in agentic LLM systems and discuss the ethical considerations and safety measures necessary when developing such systems.

By the end of this chapter, you'll be able to design and implement sophisticated AI agents powered by LLMs, opening up new possibilities for autonomous AI systems.

In this chapter, we will be covering the following topics:

- Introduction to agentic AI systems based on LLMs
- Goal-setting and planning in LLM-based agents
- Implementing memory and state management for LLM agents
- Decision-making and action selection in LLM-based agents
- Learning and adaptation in agentic LLM systems
- Ethical considerations and safety in LLM-based agentic AI
- Future prospects of agentic AI using LLMs

Introduction to agentic AI systems based on LLMs

Agentic AI systems using LLMs are designed to operate autonomously, make decisions, and take actions to achieve specified goals. These systems combine the powerful language understanding and generation capabilities of LLMs with goal-oriented behavior and environmental interaction.

Let's start by implementing a basic structure for an LLM-based agent:

```python
from typing import List, Dict, Any
import random

class LLMAgent:
    def __init__(self, llm, action_space: List[str]):
        self.llm = llm
        self.action_space = action_space
        self.memory = []
        self.current_goal = None
```

Here, the LLMAgent class is initialized with an LLM (llm) and a list of possible actions (action_space). It also maintains a memory of observations and a current_goal, which will be used to guide the agent's actions.

```python
    def set_goal(self, goal: str):
        self.current_goal = goal

    def perceive(self, observation: str):
        self.memory.append(observation)
```

Here, we define two methods: set_goal, which allows the agent to set its goal, and perceive, which enables the agent to take in observations from the environment and store them in its memory.

Next, we use the think method to generate a thorough process based on the agent's goal and recent observations:

```python
    def think(self) -> str:
        context = f"Goal: {self.current_goal}\n"
        context += "Recent observations:\n"
        context += "\n".join(self.memory[-5:])   # Last 5 observations
        context += "\nThink about the current situation and the goal.
  What should be done next?"

        return self.llm.generate(context)
```

The agent asks the language model for advice on the next step by providing a context string, which includes the current goal and the last five observations.

Once the agent has a thought, it must decide on the next action. The decide method uses the thought to generate a context, asking the LLM to pick the best action from the available options:

```python
    def decide(self, thought: str) -> str:
        context = f"Thought: {thought}\n"
        context += "Based on this thought, choose the most appropriate
```

```
action from the following:\n"
        context += ", ".join(self.action_space)
        context += "\nChosen action:"

        return self.llm.generate(context)
```

Then, the `act` method simulates taking an action by randomly selecting an outcome (success, failure, or an unexpected result). In real scenarios, this would involve interacting with the environment:

```
def act(self, action: str) -> str:
    outcomes = [
        f"Action '{action}' was successful.",
        f"Action '{action}' failed.",
        f"Action '{action}' had an unexpected outcome."
    ]
    return random.choice(outcomes)
```

Finally, the `run_step` method orchestrates the entire process of thinking, deciding, acting, and perceiving the outcome, completing one cycle of interaction with the environment:

```
def run_step(self):
    thought = self.think()
    action = self.decide(thought)
    outcome = self.act(action)
    self.perceive(outcome)
    return thought, action, outcome
```

Now that we understand the fundamental principles, let's translate these concepts into code.

Let's implement a basic LLM-based agent, establishing the core structure for autonomous operation. The agent is initialized with a hypothetical language model (`llm`) and a set of actions. It sets a goal and perceives the environment to begin interacting with it:

```
# Example usage
llm = SomeLLMModel()  # Replace with your actual LLM
action_space = ["move", "grab", "drop", "use", "talk"]
agent = LLMAgent(llm, action_space)

agent.set_goal("Find the key and unlock the door")
agent.perceive("You are in a room with a table and a chair. There's a
drawer in the table.")
```

In the following `for` loop, the agent runs for five steps, and each thought, action, and outcome is printed to show how the agent interacts with its environment over time:

```
for _ in range(5):  # Run for 5 steps
    thought, action, outcome = agent.run_step()
    print(f"Thought: {thought}")
    print(f"Action: {action}")
    print(f"Outcome: {outcome}")
    print()
```

Having established the fundamentals of agent behavior, let's explore more advanced capabilities. The following section focuses on goal-setting and planning, enabling the agent to proactively work toward complex objectives.

Goal-setting and planning in LLM-based agents

To enhance our agent with more sophisticated goal-setting and planning capabilities, let's implement a hierarchical goal structure and a planning mechanism.

First, we define a `HierarchicalGoal` class; this class allows the agent to break down large tasks into smaller subgoals:

```
class HierarchicalGoal:
    def __init__(
        self, description: str,
        subgoals: List['HierarchicalGoal'] = None
    ):
        self.description = description
        self.subgoals = subgoals or []
        self.completed = False

    def add_subgoal(self, subgoal: 'HierarchicalGoal'):
        self.subgoals.append(subgoal)

    def mark_completed(self):
        self.completed = True
```

The agent can complete these subgoals step by step, marking each as completed when done.

Next, we have a `PlanningAgent` class, which inherits from `LLMAgent` but adds the ability to handle hierarchical goals. It stores goals in a stack, working through subgoals as they are completed:

```
class PlanningAgent(LLMAgent):
    def __init__(self, llm, action_space: List[str]):
        super().__init__(llm, action_space)
```

```
        self.goal_stack = []
        self.current_plan = []

    def set_hierarchical_goal(self, goal: HierarchicalGoal):
        self.goal_stack = [goal]
```

The think method now also includes planning. If no current plan exists, it asks the LLM to generate a step-by-step plan to achieve the current goal:

```
    def think(self) -> str:
        if not self.current_plan:
            self.create_plan()

        context = f"Current goal: {self.goal_stack[-1].description}\n"
        context += "Current plan:\n"
        context += "\n".join(self.current_plan)
        context += "\nRecent observations:\n"
        context += "\n".join(self.memory[-5:])
        context += "\nThink about the current situation, goal, and
plan. What should be done next?"

        return self.llm.generate(context)
```

Then, the create_plan method generates a plan by prompting the LLM with the current goal and the list of actions. The generated plan is split into individual steps:

```
    def create_plan(self):
        context = f"Goal: {self.goal_stack[-1].description}\n"
        context += "Create a step-by-step plan to achieve this goal.
Each step should be an action from the following list:\n"
        context += ", ".join(self.action_space)
        context += "\nPlan:"

        plan_text = self.llm.generate(context)
        self.current_plan = [
            step.strip() for step in plan_text.split("\n")
            if step.strip()
        ]
```

The update_goals method checks whether the current goal is complete. If it is, it moves on to the next goal or subgoal and resets the plan accordingly:

```
    def update_goals(self):
        current_goal = self.goal_stack[-1]
        if current_goal.completed:
```

```
            self.goal_stack.pop()
            if self.goal_stack:
                self.current_plan = []   # Reset plan for the next goal
        elif current_goal.subgoals:
            next_subgoal = next(
                (
                    sg for sg in current_goal.subgoals
                    if not sg.completed
                ),
                None
            )
            if next_subgoal:
                self.goal_stack.append(next_subgoal)
                self.current_plan = []   # Reset plan for the new
    subgoal
```

The `run_step` method orchestrates the goal-setting and planning process, updating the goals as necessary:

```
def run_step(self):
    thought, action, outcome = super().run_step()
    self.update_goals()
    return thought, action, outcome
```

Let's take a look at an example.

In the following code snippet, the agent operates with a hierarchical goal to "escape the room." As the agent runs through multiple steps, it works through its subgoals, such as finding the key and unlocking the door, with each step updating the agent's internal goal stack and plan:

```
planning_agent = PlanningAgent(llm, action_space)

main_goal = HierarchicalGoal("Escape the room")
main_goal.add_subgoal(HierarchicalGoal("Find the key"))
main_goal.add_subgoal(HierarchicalGoal("Unlock the door"))

planning_agent.set_hierarchical_goal(main_goal)
planning_agent.perceive("You are in a room with a table and

a chair. There's a drawer in the table.")

for _ in range(10):   # Run for 10 steps
    thought, action, outcome = planning_agent.run_step()
    print(f"Thought: {thought}")
    print(f"Action: {action}")
```

```
    print(f"Outcome: {outcome}")
    print(f"Current goal: {planning_agent.goal_stack[-1].
description}")
    print()
```

In real-world applications, AI agent planning outputs from LLMs require constraints and validation due to the LLM's potential to generate impractical, unsafe, or constraint-violating plans; therefore, techniques such as rule-based systems, simulations, human-in-the-loop review, formal verification, and API/type validations are essential to ensure that generated plans adhere to physical, legal, ethical, and operational limitations, ultimately enhancing safety, reliability, and effectiveness.

Having demonstrated the agent's ability to pursue hierarchical goals, the next step is to enhance its capacity to learn from past experiences. The next section introduces a sophisticated memory system, enabling the agent to retain context and recall relevant information when making decisions.

Implementing memory and state management for LLM agents

To improve our agent's ability to maintain context and learn from past experiences, let's implement a more sophisticated memory system. This will enable the agent to recall relevant past observations when deciding on actions.

First, we define the `MemoryEntry` class, which represents an entry in the agent's memory. Each entry contains the text of the observation and its corresponding embedding vector, which helps with similarity searches:

```
from collections import deque
import numpy as np
from sklearn.metrics.pairwise import cosine_similarity


class MemoryEntry:
    def __init__(self, text: str, embedding: np.ndarray):
        self.text = text
        self.embedding = embedding
```

Then, we define the `EpisodicMemory` class; this handles the agent's memory, storing a fixed number of observations (`capacity`). This memory can grow up to the specified limit, at which point older entries are removed:

```
class EpisodicMemory:
    def __init__(self, capacity: int, embedding_model):
        self.capacity = capacity
        self.embedding_model = embedding_model
        self.memory = deque(maxlen=capacity)
```

The following code uses content-based episodic memory, which leverages semantic similarity search. The memory stores past observations (episodes) as text along with their vector embeddings, and retrieves relevant memories based on the semantic similarity (using cosine similarity) between a query embedding and the stored embeddings:

```python
def add(self, text: str):
    embedding = self.embedding_model.encode(text)
    self.memory.append(MemoryEntry(text, embedding))

def retrieve_relevant(self, query: str, k: int = 5) -> List[str]:
    query_embedding = self.embedding_model.encode(query)
    similarities = [
        cosine_similarity(
            [query_embedding],
            [entry.embedding]
        )[0][0] for entry in self.memory
    ]
    top_indices = np.argsort(similarities)[-k:][::-1]
    return [self.memory[i].text for i in top_indices]
```

The `retrieve_relevant` method searches for the most relevant past observations based on cosine similarity, returning the top *k* matching entries.

Then, we define the `MemoryAwareAgent` class; this class extends `PlanningAgent` by integrating an episodic memory system. This allows the agent to store and retrieve relevant past experiences during decision-making:

```python
class MemoryAwareAgent(PlanningAgent):
    def __init__(
        self, llm, action_space: List[str], embedding_model
    ):
        super().__init__(llm, action_space)
        self.episodic_memory = EpisodicMemory(
            capacity=1000, embedding_model=embedding_model
        )

    def perceive(self, observation: str):
        super().perceive(observation)
        self.episodic_memory.add(observation)
```

The think function defined in the following code incorporates relevant past experiences. The agent retrieves memories similar to its current goal and uses these in the context provided to the LLM when deciding what to do next:

```
def think(self) -> str:
    relevant_memories = self.episodic_memory.retrieve_relevant(
        self.current_goal, k=3
    )

    context = f"Current goal: {self.goal_stack[-1].description}\n"
    context += "Current plan:\n"
    context += "\n".join(self.current_plan)
    context += "\nRecent observations:\n"
    context += "\n".join(self.memory[-5:])
    context += "\nRelevant past experiences:\n"
    context += "\n".join(relevant_memories)
    context += "\nThink about the current situation, goal, plan,
and past experiences. What should be done next?"

    return self.llm.generate(context)
```

The preceding code snippet orchestrates an AI agent's decision-making process by first retrieving relevant memories based on the current goal, then constructing a comprehensive context for the LLM that includes the goal, current plan, recent observations, and retrieved memories, and finally utilizing the LLM to generate a response that determines the agent's next action or thought based on the provided contextual information.

Let's check out an example usage of the memory-aware agent. In this example, the agent is enhanced with memory capabilities. It now uses its past experiences to inform its decisions and actions:

```
embedding_model = SomeEmbeddingModel()  # Replace with your actual
embedding model
memory_agent = MemoryAwareAgent(llm, action_space, embedding_model)

main_goal = HierarchicalGoal("Solve the puzzle")
memory_agent.set_hierarchical_goal(main_goal)
memory_agent.perceive("You are in a room with a complex puzzle on the
wall.")
The agent continues to interact with its environment over 10 steps,
utilizing its memory system to make better decisions based on both
current observations and past experiences:
for _ in range(10):  # Run for 10 steps
    thought, action, outcome = memory_agent.run_step()
    print(f"Thought: {thought}")
    print(f"Action: {action}")
```

```
        print(f"Outcome: {outcome}")
        print()
```

Now that our agent can remember and recall past experiences, we'll focus on making better decisions. The next section introduces a structured approach to action selection, allowing the agent to choose the most effective action using an LLM. Keep in mind that memory retrieval is similarity-based, which works best when embedding quality is high.

Decision-making and action selection in LLM-based agents

To improve the agent's decision-making capabilities, we can introduce a more structured approach to action selection, evaluating potential actions based on multiple factors.

We first define the `ActionEvaluator` class, which uses the LLM to evaluate actions based on three key criteria: relevance to the current goal, probability of success, and potential impact. These evaluations help the agent choose the best possible action:

```
import numpy as np

class ActionEvaluator:
    def __init__(self, llm):
        self.llm = llm

    def evaluate_action(
        self, action: str, context: str
    ) -> Dict[str, float]:
        prompt = f"""
        Context: {context}
        Action: {action}
```

We then evaluate `"action"` that is passed into the `evaluate_action` function as a parameter based on the following criteria:

- Relevance to the current goal (0-1)

- Estimated success probability (0-1)

- Potential impact on overall progress (0-1)

```
        Provide your evaluation as three numbers separated by commas:
        """

        response = self.llm.generate(prompt)
        relevance, success_prob, impact = map(
```

```
            float, response.split(',')
        )
        return {
            'relevance': relevance,
            'success_probability': success_prob,
            'impact': impact
        }
```

Lastly, we have the `StrategicDecisionAgent` class, which extends `MemoryAwareAgent` to include a more strategic approach to decision-making. It evaluates all possible actions, scoring them based on their relevance, success probability, and impact, and selects the action with the highest score:

```
class StrategicDecisionAgent(MemoryAwareAgent):
    def __init__(
        self, llm, action_space: List[str], embedding_model
    ):
        super().__init__(llm, action_space, embedding_model)
        self.action_evaluator = ActionEvaluator(llm)

    def decide(self, thought: str) -> str:
        context = f"Thought: {thought}\n"
        context += f"Current goal: {self.goal_stack[-1].
description}\n"
        context += "Recent observations:\n"
        context += "\n".join(self.memory[-5:])

        action_scores = {}
        for action in self.action_space:
            evaluation = self.action_evaluator.evaluate_action(
                action, context
            )
            score = np.mean(list(evaluation.values()))
            action_scores[action] = score

        best_action = max(action_scores, key=action_scores.get)
        return best_action
```

Let's check out an example usage of `StrategicDecisionAgent`. In this example, the agent uses more sophisticated decision-making strategies by evaluating actions based on various factors before selecting the optimal one:

```
strategic_agent = StrategicDecisionAgent(
    llm, action_space, embedding_model
)
```

```
main_goal = HierarchicalGoal("Navigate the maze and find the
treasure")
strategic_agent.set_hierarchical_goal(main_goal)
strategic_agent.perceive("You are at the entrance of a complex maze.
There are multiple paths ahead.")
```

Over several steps, the agent strategically navigates a maze by continually evaluating the best actions to take based on its goal and environment:

```
for _ in range(10):   # Run for 10 steps
    thought, action, outcome = strategic_agent.run_step()
    print(f"Thought: {thought}")
    print(f"Chosen action: {action}")
    print(f"Outcome: {outcome}")
    print()
```

We will now conclude the chapter by discussing further enhancements for learning, ethical considerations, and future prospects for LLM-based agents.

Learning and adaptation in agentic LLM systems

To enable our agent to learn and adapt from its experiences, let's implement a simple reinforcement learning mechanism. This will allow the agent to improve its performance over time by learning from the outcomes of its actions.

We define the AdaptiveLearningAgent class, which extends StrategicDecisionAgent by introducing a simple Q-learning mechanism. It keeps track of q_values, which represents the expected rewards for taking specific actions in given states. The agent uses a learning rate to update these values based on new experiences:

```
import random
from collections import defaultdict

class AdaptiveLearningAgent(StrategicDecisionAgent):
    def __init__(self, llm, action_space: List[str], embedding_model):
        super().__init__(llm, action_space, embedding_model)
        self.q_values = defaultdict(lambda: defaultdict(float))
        self.learning_rate = 0.1
        self.discount_factor = 0.9
        self.epsilon = 0.1  # For exploration-exploitation tradeoff
```

Next, the agent decides its action based on a balance between exploration (trying random actions) and exploitation (using actions it has learned to be effective). The agent uses its Q-values to select the most rewarding action:

```
def decide(self, thought: str) -> str:
    if random.random() < self.epsilon:
        return random.choice(self.action_space)  # Exploration:
randomly pick an action

    state = self.get_state_representation()
    q_values = {action: self.q_values[state][action]
    for action in self.action_space}
    return max(q_values, key=q_values.get)  # Exploitation: pick
action with highest Q-value
```

We write the `get_state_representation` method to create a simplified representation of the current state, including the goal and the most recent observation. This state is used to look up and update Q-values:

```
def get_state_representation(self) -> str:
    return f"Goal: {self.goal_stack[-1].description},
        Last observation: {self.memory[-1]}"
```

The `update_q_values` method updates the Q-values based on the outcome of the agent's actions. It adjusts the expected reward for a state-action pair, factoring in both the immediate reward and the potential future rewards (via `next_max_q`):

```
def update_q_values(
    self, state: str, action: str, reward: float,
    next_state: str
):
    current_q = self.q_values[state][action]
    next_max_q = max(
        self.q_values[next_state].values()
    ) if self.q_values[next_state] else 0
    new_q = current_q + self.learning_rate * (
        reward + self.discount_factor * next_max_q - current_q
    )
    self.q_values[state][action] = new_q
```

The `run_step` method now not only performs the standard sequence of thinking, deciding, acting, and perceiving but also updates the agent's Q-values based on the outcome. The `compute_reward` method assigns a numeric reward depending on whether the outcome was successful, failed, or neutral:

```python
def run_step(self):
    state = self.get_state_representation()
    thought, action, outcome = super().run_step()
    next_state = self.get_state_representation()
    reward = self.compute_reward(outcome)
    self.update_q_values(state, action, reward, next_state)
    return thought, action, outcome

def compute_reward(self, outcome: str) -> float:
    if "successful" in outcome.lower():
        return 1.0
    elif "failed" in outcome.lower():
        return -0.5
    else:
        return 0.0
```

Let's see an example usage of `AdaptiveLearningAgent`. In this example, the agent is designed to explore and learn from a new environment. It uses reinforcement learning to gradually improve its ability to make effective decisions:

```python
adaptive_agent = AdaptiveLearningAgent(llm, action_space,
    embedding_model)

main_goal = HierarchicalGoal("Explore and map the unknown planet")
adaptive_agent.set_hierarchical_goal(main_goal)
adaptive_agent.perceive("You have landed on an alien planet. The
environment is strange and unfamiliar.")
```

The agent operates for 20 steps, learning from each action it takes. It prints out its thoughts, actions, and Q-values, showing how it updates its understanding of the environment over time:

```python
for _ in range(20):   # Run for 20 steps
    thought, action, outcome = adaptive_agent.run_step()
    print(f"Thought: {thought}")
    print(f"Chosen action: {action}")
    print(f"Outcome: {outcome}")
    print(
        f"Current Q-values: {dict(
            adaptive_agent.q_values[
                adaptive_agent.get_state_representation()
            ]
```

```
            )}"
    )
        print()
```

Now that we have equipped our agent with a basic reinforcement learning mechanism, allowing it to adapt and improve its decision-making over time, we also need to address the ethical implications of such autonomous systems. In the following section, we will explore how to integrate ethical safeguards into our agentic LLM system to ensure responsible and aligned behavior.

Ethical considerations and safety in LLM-based agentic AI

When developing agentic AI systems based on LLMs, it's crucial to consider ethical implications and implement safety measures. To ensure that the agent acts within ethical boundaries, we can add an ethical constraint system:

```
class EthicalConstraint:
    def __init__(self, description: str, check_function):
        self.description = description
        self.check_function = check_function
```

The `EthicalConstraint` class defines ethical rules the agent must follow. Each rule is described and enforced by a check function (`check_function`), which evaluates whether an action violates the ethical constraints.

The `EthicalAgent` class extends `AdaptiveLearningAgent` by integrating ethical constraints. If the agent selects an action that violates one of its ethical rules, it chooses a different action that complies with the rules:

```
class EthicalAgent(AdaptiveLearningAgent):
    def __init__(
        self, llm, action_space: List[str],
        embedding_model,
        ethical_constraints: List[EthicalConstraint]
    ):
        super().__init__(llm, action_space, embedding_model)
        self.ethical_constraints = ethical_constraints
    def decide(self, thought: str) -> str:
        action = super().decide(thought)
        if not self.is_action_ethical(action, thought):
            print(f"Warning: Action '{action}' violated ethical
constraints. Choosing a different action.")
            alternative_actions = [
                a for a in self.action_space if a != action]
            return (
                random.choice(alternative_actions)
```

```
                      if alternative_actions
                      else "do_nothing"
                )
            return action

      def is_action_ethical(self, action: str, context: str) -> bool:
          for constraint in self.ethical_constraints:
              if not constraint.check_function(action, context):
                  print(f"Ethical constraint violated: {constraint.
description}")
                  return False
          return True
```

The following ethical constraints prevent the agent from causing harm or violating privacy. They can be passed to `EthicalAgent` as part of its initialization:

```
def no_harm(action: str, context: str) -> bool:
    harmful_actions = ["attack", "destroy", "damage"]
    return not any(ha in action.lower() for ha in harmful_actions)

def respect_privacy(action: str, context: str) -> bool:
    privacy_violating_actions = ["spy", "eavesdrop", "hack"]
    return not any(
        pva in action.lower()
        for pva in privacy_violating_actions
    )
```

This code defines two Python functions, `no_harm` and `respect_privacy`, which serve as ethical constraints for an AI agent. The `no_harm` function checks whether a given action contains any keywords related to causing harm (such as "attack" or "destroy"), returning `True` if the action is deemed safe and `False` if it contains harmful keywords. Similarly, the `respect_privacy` function checks whether an action contains keywords related to privacy violations (such as "spy" or "hack"), also returning `True` for safe actions and `False` for actions violating privacy. These functions are designed to be used by an `EthicalAgent` to ensure its actions align with ethical guidelines by preventing it from performing harmful or privacy-violating actions.

Let's check out an example usage of `EthicalAgent`. In this example, the agent is tasked with gathering information about an alien civilization while following ethical guidelines to avoid harm and respect privacy:

```
ethical_constraints = [
    EthicalConstraint("Do no harm", no_harm),
    EthicalConstraint("Respect privacy", respect_privacy)
]
```

```
ethical_agent = EthicalAgent(
    llm, action_space + ["attack", "spy"],
    embedding_model, ethical_constraints
)

main_goal = HierarchicalGoal("Gather information about the alien
civilization")
ethical_agent.set_hierarchical_goal(main_goal)
ethical_agent.perceive("You've encountered an alien settlement. The
inhabitants seem peaceful but wary.")
```

The agent operates within the constraints, ensuring that its actions do not violate ethical rules. It prints out its thoughts, actions, and outcomes as it interacts with its environment:

```
for _ in range(15):  # Run for 15 steps
    thought, action, outcome = ethical_agent.run_step()
    print(f"Thought: {thought}")
    print(f"Chosen action: {action}")
    print(f"Outcome: {outcome}")
    print()
```

Future prospects of agentic AI using LLMs

Looking to the future, several exciting possibilities for agentic AI using LLMs come to the forefront:

- **Multi-agent collaboration**: Agents working together in a shared environment can exchange information, strategize, and coordinate their actions for more complex tasks.

- **Long-term memory and continual learning**: Agents could maintain a lifelong memory and continue learning from their interactions, becoming more intelligent over time.

- **Integration with robotics and physical world interaction**: As LLM-based agents evolve, they may integrate with physical systems, enabling autonomous robots to perform tasks in the real world.

- **Meta-learning and self-improvement**: Future agents could learn to optimize their learning processes, becoming better at learning from experiences.

- **Explainable AI and transparent decision-making**: Ensuring that LLM-based agents can explain their decisions is crucial for building trust and ensuring accountability in AI systems.

- **Agent sandboxing and simulation environments**: Creating restricted "walled gardens" limits an agent's access to resources, preventing unintended system impacts, while simulation environments, such as those offered by E2B, allow developers to replicate real-world scenarios, including interactions with tools, files, and simulated web browsers, enabling the identification and mitigation of potential issues and risks, including adversarial prompts, thereby enhancing agent reliability and safety.

Summary

Agentic patterns for LLMs open up exciting possibilities for creating autonomous, goal-directed AI systems. By implementing sophisticated planning, memory management, decision-making, and learning mechanisms, we can create agents that can operate effectively.

Future directions in LLM patterns and their development

Several promising LLM design patterns are emerging, with innovations coming from open source communities as well as frontier model developers, thus shaping the design patterns of future models. This section highlights some of these key innovations, including **Mixture of Experts (MoE)** architectures, **Group Relative Policy Optimization** (GRPO), **Self-Principled Critique Tuning** (SPCT), and emerging patterns documented in the publication *OpenAI GPT-4.5 System Card* (`https://openai.com/index/gpt-4-5-system-card/`).

MoE architectures are a type of neural network architecture where, instead of a single large network, there are multiple smaller "expert" networks. During inference, a "routing network" dynamically selects and activates only a specific subset of these expert networks based on the input, optimizing computational efficiency. Unlike dense models, which engage all parameters for every task, MoE models route computations through sparsely activated sub-networks. This method reduces redundancy and tailors computational resources to the demands of specific tasks, allowing for efficient scaling to trillion-parameter models without a proportional increase in computational cost. DeepSeek's implementation exemplifies this approach.

Streamlined reinforcement learning with GRPO streamlines the reinforcement learning process. GRPO is a reinforcement learning technique that generates multiple responses to each prompt, calculates their average reward, and uses this baseline to evaluate relative performance. This method was introduced by DeepSeek, an open source AI company from China. GRPO replaces traditional value networks with group-based reward averaging, reducing memory overhead and maintaining stable policy updates. By fostering internal self-assessment through comparing multiple reasoning paths, GRPO enables adaptive problem solving.

GRPO enhances safety by incorporating **Kullback–Leibler (KL) divergence penalties**, which constrain policy updates. KL divergence measures how one probability distribution diverges from a second, expected probability distribution. In this context, it measures the difference between the model's updated behavior (policy) and its previous, baseline behavior. KL divergence penalties are a term that's added to the reward function that penalizes the model if its updated behavior deviates too much from that baseline, helping to ensure stability and prevent the model from shifting to undesirable behaviors.

The **SPCT framework** integrates self-critique mechanisms directly into the model's reward system, enabling autonomous alignment with ethical guidelines. SPCT involves the model generating its own responses, as well as generating internal critiques of those responses against predefined principles (e.g., safety guidelines and ethical considerations). By generating internal critiques, the model refines outputs without relying on external classifiers or human feedback, promoting autonomous learning and alignment.

We can also implement **scalable alignment techniques**, which utilize data derived from smaller, more easily controlled models to train larger, more capable ones, allowing for scalable alignment without requiring a proportional increase in human oversight. This technique focuses on improving the model's steerability, its understanding of nuance, and its ability to engage in natural and productive conversations, going beyond traditional methods such as **supervised fine-tuning** and RLHF to foster safer and more collaborative AI systems. While GPT-4.5 development emphasized new, scalable methods to align the model better with human needs and intent using data derived from smaller models, future models are expected to incorporate more advanced techniques such as GRPO and SPCT to further enhance alignment and safety. This focus will continue to ensure steerability, understanding nuance, and facilitating more natural conversation.

OpenAI has also paved the way for comprehensive safety evaluation via its **Preparedness Framework** (*Preparedness Framework (Beta)*, `https://cdn.openai.com/openai-preparedness-framework-beta.pdf`). This framework represents a core design pattern for responsible AI development that involves applying a rigorous evaluation process systematically before model deployment. This proactive framework encompasses a wide range of internal and external tests, including assessments for disallowed content generation, jailbreak robustness, hallucinations, bias, and specific catastrophic risks such as chemical/biological weapons, persuasion, cybersecurity threats, and model autonomy. The framework also utilizes red teaming exercises and third-party audits to provide comprehensive risk assessments, culminating in a classification of the model's risk level across different categories. By thoroughly evaluating potential risks before release, OpenAI aims to ensure the safe and responsible deployment of its LLMs.

Finally, let's talk about GPT-4.5's **instruction hierarchy enforcement**. To improve robustness against prompt injection and ensure predictable behavior, models are trained to prioritize instructions given in the system message over potentially conflicting instructions within the user message, which is evaluated explicitly using targeted tests. Future advancements could enhance this pattern by incorporating more dynamic and context-aware methods for managing instruction conflicts.

This concludes our book on LLM design patterns. In this book, we covered the core design patterns. We plan to publish another book on more advanced design patterns in the near future, to cover security, safety, governance, and various other topics.

Subscribe for a free eBook

New frameworks, evolving architectures, research drops, production breakdowns—AI_Distilled filters the noise into a weekly briefing for engineers and researchers working hands-on with LLMs and GenAI systems. Subscribe now and receive a free eBook, along with weekly insights that help you stay focused and informed. Subscribe at `https://packt.link/8Oz6Y` or scan the QR code below.

## 31

Unlock Your Exclusive Benefits

Your copy of this book includes the following exclusive benefit:

- ☁ Next-gen Packt Reader
- 📄 DRM-free PDF/ePub downloads

Follow the guide below to unlock them. The process takes only a few minutes and needs to be completed once.

Unlock this Book's Free Benefits in 3 Easy Steps

Step 1

Keep your purchase invoice ready for *Step 3*. If you have a physical copy, scan it using your phone and save it as a PDF, JPG, or PNG.

For more help on finding your invoice, visit `https://www.packtpub.com/unlock-benefits/help`.

> **Note**
>
> If you bought this book directly from Packt, no invoice is required. After *Step 2*, you can access your exclusive content right away.

Step 2

Scan the QR code or go to `packtpub.com/unlock`.

On the page that opens (similar to *Figure 31.1* on desktop), search for this book by name and select the correct edition.

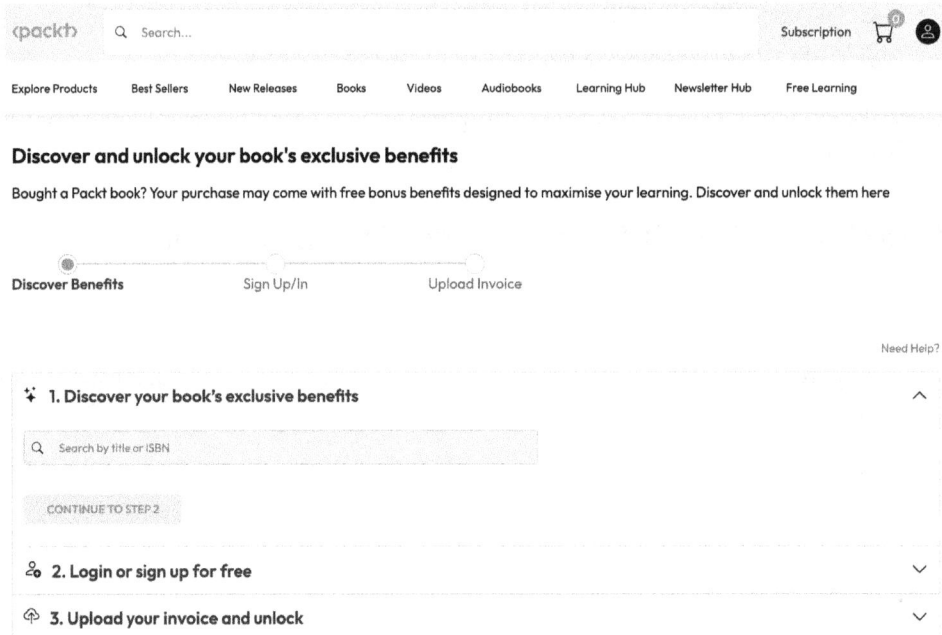

Figure 31.1 – Packt unlock landing page on desktop

Step 3

After selecting your book, sign in to your Packt account or create one for free. Then upload your invoice (PDF, PNG, or JPG, up to 10 MB). Follow the on-screen instructions to finish the process.

Need help?

If you get stuck and need help, visit `https://www.packtpub.com/unlock-benefits/help` for a detailed FAQ on how to find your invoices and more. This QR code will take you to the help page.

> **Note**
>
> If you are still facing issues, reach out to `customercare@packt.com`.

Index

A

N

named entity recognition (NER) 86-89
Natural Language Inference (NLI) 451
natural language processing
    (NLP) 56, 86, 388
natural language understanding (NLU) 221
    benchmarks 221
natural language understanding
    (NLU), benchmarks
    MMLU 222
    SuperGLUE 222, 224
    TruthfulQA 224-226
Natural Questions (NQ) 462
neural networks 4
Node2Vec 413, 414
noise injection 153
    activation noise 154
    implementing 154, 155
    input noise 153
    weight noise 153
Non-Volatile Memory Express (NVMe) 122
Normalized Discounted Cumulative
    Gain (NDCG@k) 447

O

OpenAI API 43
optimization hyperparameters 124
Optuna 134
    used, for implementing
        multi-objective optimization 141-143
oversampling techniques 243

P

parallelization strategies 62-64
parallel processing 28

Pareto front 143
parts of speech (POS) 22
perplexity 19
    clean text perplexity 20
    noisy text perplexity 20
personally identifiable information (PII) 21
pipeline parallelism 122
population-based training (PBT) 136-140
post-training quantization (PTQ) 210, 211
power-law function 6
Precision@k measures 446
preprocess_function 57
pre-trained models
    leveraging 146
pre-training data
    stratified sampling 242, 243
probing method 259, 260
Prodigy 90
product quantization (PQ) 397
proximal policy optimization (PPO) 297
pruned model performance 203
prune.remove method 199
pruning 215-330
    combining, with quantization 215, 216
pruning during training approach 201
    versus post-training pruning
        approach 201, 202
pruning_tot function 331
pruning, with compression techniques 203
    knowledge distillation 204, 205
    quantization 204
publish-subscribe (pub-sub) model 67
PySpark 95
PyTorch 102

Z

‹packt›

Packtpub.com

Subscribe to our online digital library for full access to over 7,000 books and videos, as well as industry leading tools to help you plan your personal development and advance your career. For more information, please visit our website.

Why subscribe?

- Spend less time learning and more time coding with practical eBooks and Videos from over 4,000 industry professionals

- Improve your learning with Skill Plans built especially for you

- Get a free eBook or video every month

- Fully searchable for easy access to vital information

- Copy and paste, print, and bookmark content

At www.packt.com, you can also read a collection of free technical articles, sign up for a range of free newsletters, and receive exclusive discounts and offers on Packt books and eBooks.

Other Books You May Enjoy

If you enjoyed this book, you may be interested in these other books by Packt:

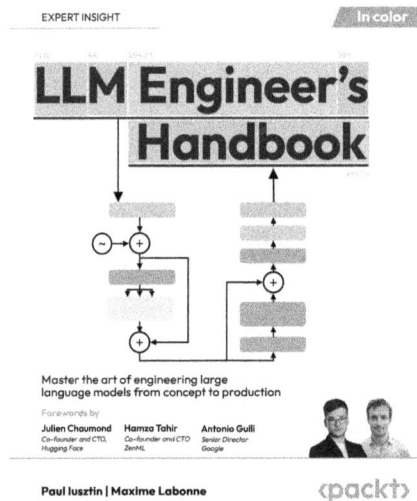

LLM Engineer's Handbook

Paul Iusztin, Maxime Labonne

ISBN: 978-1-83620-007-9

- Implement robust data pipelines and manage LLM training cycles
- Create your own LLM and refine it with the help of hands-on examples
- Get started with LLMOps by diving into core MLOps principles such as orchestrators and prompt monitoring
- Perform supervised fine-tuning and LLM evaluation
- Deploy end-to-end LLM solutions using AWS and other tools
- Design scalable and modularLLM systems
- Learn about RAG applications by building a feature and inference pipeline

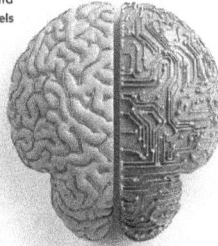

Unlocking Data with Generative AI and RAG

Keith Bourne

ISBN: 978-1-83588-790-5

- Understand RAG principles and their significance in generative AI
- Integrate LLMs with internal data for enhanced operations
- Master vectorization, vector databases, and vector search techniques
- Develop skills in prompt engineering specific to RAG and design for precise AI responses
- Familiarize yourself with AI agents' roles in facilitating sophisticated RAG applications
- Overcome scalability, data quality, and integration issues
- Discover strategies for optimizing data retrieval and AI interpretability

Packt is searching for authors like you

If you're interested in becoming an author for Packt, please visit `authors.packtpub.com` and apply today. We have worked with thousands of developers and tech professionals, just like you, to help them share their insight with the global tech community. You can make a general application, apply for a specific hot topic that we are recruiting an author for, or submit your own idea.

Share Your Thoughts

Now you've finished *LLM Design Patterns*, we'd love to hear your thoughts! Scan the QR code below to go straight to the Amazon review page for this book and share your feedback or leave a review on the site that you purchased it from.

`https://packt.link/r/1-836-20703-4`

Your review is important to us and the tech community and will help us make sure we're delivering excellent quality content.